TELEVISION PRODUCTION
disciplines and techniques

TELEVISION PRODUCTION second edition
disciplines and techniques

Thomas D. Burrows
Donald N. Wood
California State University, Northridge

ωcb
Wm. C. Brown Company Publishers
Dubuque, Iowa

wcb
group

Wm. C. Brown   *Chairman of the Board*
Mark C. Falb   *Executive Vice-President*

wcb

Wm. C. Brown Company Publishers, College Division

Lawrence E. Cremer   *President*
David Wm. Smith   *Vice-President, Marketing*
E. F. Jogerst   *Vice-President, Cost Analyst*
David A. Corona   *Assistant Vice-President, Production Development and Design*
James L. Romig   *Executive Editor*
Marcia H. Stout   *Marketing Manager*
William A. Moss   *Production Editorial Manager*
Marilyn A. Phelps   *Manager of Design*
Mary M. Heller   *Visual Research Manager*

Cover photo by Ted Streshinsky, courtesy of The Image Bank

Printed in the United States of America
10   9   8

To our many students who have helped make teaching the most rewarding of all professions.

about the authors

Thomas D. Burrows is an associate professor in the Radio-TV-Film Department at California State University, Northridge, in Los Angeles. He entered the teaching profession after a considerable career in the broadcast industry. Starting as a disc jockey in his hometown of Tucson, he worked his way to a position with ABC, Los Angeles, serving as the director of the KABC-TV evening news program and of the nationally syndicated rock music show, "Shivaree." Subsequently, Mr. Burrows was with KCET-TV in Los Angeles where he received the Christopher, Emmy, and Peabody awards as producer of the PBS series "The Advocates." He holds a Master of Arts degree from the School of Journalism at the University of Southern California.

Donald N. Wood, professor of Radio-TV-Film, has been teaching at California State University, Northridge, since 1970. He has also taught at San Diego State University, The University of Michigan, and Westminster College (Pennsylvania). Dr. Wood's professional background has been largely in educational broadcasting. He was program coordinator for National Educational Television, area coordinator for the Midwest Program on Airborne Television Instruction, and director of ETV for the Hawaii State Department of Education, during which time he was executive producer of more than eight hundred television productions. Dr. Wood is the coauthor of the textbook *Educational Telecommunications*. He has his M.A. and Ph.D. degrees from The University of Michigan.

contents

preface

This edition of *Television Production: Disciplines and Techniques* is designed as a basic introductory text for a college course in television production. It covers almost everything that would as a rule be included in such a course.

As the dedication implies, we have deliberately written this text with our students in mind. It is designed as a teaching text—not as a reference book, not as a theoretical discussion, not as a catalog. We have included the technical information that we feel is essential for the beginning student to know, but we have not tried to produce a basic engineering manual. We have centered our discussions and examples around the kinds of equipment that we feel most training institutions would be using—not always the latest state of the art and not always the sophisticated hardware found at network production centers. In fact, we have tried to emphasize the *process* and the *thinking* that go into TV production, not just equipment manipulation. We have touched upon the basic elements of directing, but without undue emphasis that would detract from the basic production material.

In short, this text is designed to teach the first-year student what he or she needs to know about audio, lighting, cameras and lenses, the switcher, recording and editing, single-camera production, pictorial elements, on-camera talent, other crew positions, and directing.

We are concerned not only with the *techniques* of TV production (operating equipment and performing basic crew assignments) but also with the *disciplines* of TV production—those intangible professional attitudes and behaviors involving responsibility, self-control, initiative, respect, and similar attributes. We hope that the reader will bear with us if we continue to return to this theme—but it is true that success in any aspect of the broadcasting field is going to depend more upon one's internalized set of attitudes than upon specific learned skills and techniques.

The text places essential information relating to equipment function and production crew organization within a sequence that is most suitable for broadcast laboratory instruction. We feel strongly that production proficiency (both the techniques and disciplines) can ultimately be gained only through continued involvement in a production operation. Students must have the opportunity to understand the creative process by working at all of the various positions within the crew structure. They must, however, be allowed to come to grips with the complexity of the ongoing production sequence by means of a series of planned gradual steps, each building upon previously mastered concepts and skills.

The two chapters on audio have been placed at the beginning of the book in order to present the student with an early model of the concepts of equipment function and crew organization. It is felt that this sequence of information—with an emphasis upon the audio signal flow—will facilitate a better understanding of comparable elements when they are later presented within the entire combined audio and video operation.

Since the writing of the first edition of the text the techniques of single-camera production have evolved rapidly. The realities of ENG (electronic news gathering) and EFP (electronic field production) are playing an increasingly important role in commercial, educational, and corporate telecommunications. Therefore, the second edition includes a separate chapter (chapter 9) on this development.

We realize that many instructors will wish to structure their course units in a manner different from our suggested order. Some may wish to get into cameras before audio—or place lighting considerations after basic camera structure and lens design. Others may want to discuss crew positions or basic directing skills earlier than our text does. To this end, we have tried to make each chapter as independent as possible—using appropriate cross-referencing of material.

At the end of each chapter we have included one or more suggested training exercises or class projects. It is strongly recommended that these exercises and projects be carried out—to the extent possible in various facilities—in order to reinforce and adapt the material presented in each chapter. These exercises have been designed to resemble, as nearly as possible, the production realities of the primary types of programming and are structured to permit individualized input by both student and instructor. Production project scripts and materials are provided in appendix D on perforated pages so they can be revised and used apart from the text in studio exercises.

We have had the advice and help of many colleagues and students in pulling this text together. Although we cannot hope to single out everybody who has assisted or influenced us in the writing of the text, we should like to thank specifically the following for their particular talents and definite contributions: Martha Alexander, Evert Anderson, Amanda Blanco, Mike Geller, Natalie Gould, Mollie Robbins, Dick Studebaker, Steve Wyskocil, Barton L. Griffith, Wayne Munson, Aaron

Bor, Thomas Ditzel, Robert Anderson, Howard Kleiman, Chris McClure, and Thomas Dolan. In addition, the many students who have served as our inspiration, our guinea pigs, and our evaluators—working with portions of the manuscript as it was being developed—deserve our deepest appreciation.

Despite the support and assistance from our colleagues and students, there undoubtedly are errors to be found. For these, we assume full responsibility.

Except for those otherwise credited, all photographs used in the text were taken by the authors.

TELEVISION PRODUCTION
disciplines and techniques

introduction to tv production 1

Electronic camera television production is a fascinating, demanding, and rewarding enterprise—whether done in a studio or on a remote location. There is not only the obvious intoxication of glamour and activity but also the quiet exhilaration of being part of a very captivating and important process of modern communications technology.

1.1 Techniques and Disciplines

Successful television is dependent upon the premise that every member of the production unit has, over a period of time, developed a set of individual *techniques* and *disciplines* in order to cope with the complexities of various types of programs. Although these two terms do not necessarily refer to mutually exclusive categories, they do describe somewhat differing aspects of the total production sequence.

For their use within the broadcast context, the following definitions of these terms will be utilized.

Techniques refer to specific skills unique to the performance of any single position within the television crew structure. A technique reflects a degree of formal (or possibly informal) training related to production equipment, electronic or otherwise. An audio engineer's ability to select and position microphones for correct balance would be considered a technique. Such a definition, however, does not preclude the possibility of interaction with other crew members. A director's method of using cameras is thought of as a matter of individual initiative and specialized talent—founded upon a few basic techniques and principles of television communication.

At the beginning, it may be easiest for students of TV production to think of techniques as being those particular skills used in operating various pieces of equipment—knowledge of which buttons to push, how far certain knobs should be twisted, and where to connect a given plug, for example.

Disciplines comprise a complete series of procedures that are shared by and relate to the entire production unit. The use of proper voice procedure on the intercom network is a specific example. The interaction of the stage manager, the stage crew, camera operators, and performers in a studio would involve a whole range of disciplines for efficient operation. Disciplines imply a consistency of individual action as well as a consideration for others in the same team effort.

One of the most crucial elements of TV-production discipline is that of *responsibility*. Dependability. A conscientious effort always to do one's best. In the complex chain of the television crew there can be no weak link. In any given production situation, the efforts of dozens of persons may be coordinated in an intricate pattern. If one person fails to carry out his or her specific function at the right moment, many precious minutes—or hours—of costly production time can be wasted.

Production discipline also implies many other intangible values and skills. An attitude of *respect* must be acquired—respect for equipment as well as for other members of the production crew. A balanced sense of *initiative* and *self-control* must be concurrently developed—knowing when to jump in with a suggestion or action and when to remain quiet and stick to your own job. Learning how to deal with your own anxiety—how to remain *calm* when the production elements start to fall apart—is another important aspect of developing a sense of television discipline.

As a television-production student you therefore must be concerned not only with the *techniques* of knowing precisely how to use all of the equipment but also with the development of your own sense of production *discipline* so that others will be able to depend upon you with confidence. In fact, one of the most revealing tests of your production capabilities is the answer to this simple question: Do other people want you on their production team? Unless you can answer *yes* to that query, you probably will want to rethink your studio attitudes, your sense of professional discipline and dedication, and your academic and professional goals.

1.2 Development of a Professional Attitude

In talking about abstract concepts such as *discipline* and the development of something called *professional attitude,* it may be helpful to think about them from two different perspectives—first, personal goals and self-image, and second, attitudes toward others.

Attitude and Self-Image

To begin with, you need to ask yourself something about your personal goals. *What are your professional aims?* What do you hope to do in broadcasting or film? Do you have specific occupational goals? Are you broadly concerned with doing something socially constructive with media? In any case, what role will education or specific training play in attaining those goals? Then ask yourself *what your immediate learning goals are.* What do you hope to get out of this class? What are you doing to ensure that it will be a constructive experience?

In answering queries such as these, you can come closer to defining a personal value system and a sense of direction. These, in turn, lead to a sharpening of your own sense of professional development and the need for internal discipline. This should help you begin to see specific goal-oriented tasks that revolve around the educational system. You are better able to recognize the need to learn.

You should be able to think in terms of educational course work beyond your immediate TV-production class. What other related academic work do you need? Journalism?

Business communications? Political science? Public relations? Management? Communication history? Government regulations? Message design? English? And what academic course work is needed in the liberal arts that will help give you a perspective on mankind and your place in contemporary society—an understanding of the *role* of modern telecommunications? Philosophy? History? Foreign cultures? Psychology? The arts? Environmental sciences? You cannot be a successful communicator unless you know something of the content you have to communicate—and unless you understand the environment of the communication process.

When asked what kind of broadcasting student they would like to hire, many top television executives and network officers reply, "Give me students who are intelligent, sensitive, aware of social issues, alert, concerned with human relations, adaptable, and able to solve problems, and I'll teach them the tools and techniques of the business in a few weeks on the job."

In this specific production course, you should begin to realize the need to learn how to understand the telecommunications process, how to use the tools of the communication enterprise. You will start to develop a sense of studio discipline that grows out of an appreciation of the total process of TV production.

One specific discipline mentioned in section 1.1 is the *balance between initiative and self-control*. There are numerous times on any television production when some little thing appears to be wrong. The lighting director is not adding enough back light. The director is ready to take the wrong shot. The stage manager looks as if he or she were going to walk in front of a camera. What do you do in each of these situations? Do you speak up or remain silent? Do you know enough about the total situation to understand what is really happening? Only with enough studio experience and

a knowledge of all equipment and all positions can you determine when you should take the initiative to avert a problem and when you should remain in your place because others probably know what they are doing.

Another kind of production self-discipline concerns the problem of *dealing with your own anxieties*. In any television production, various crew members are going to experience differing degrees of anxiety. First, you must accept the fact that some anxiety—some amount of nervousness—is good; it is what keeps you on your toes. People would not be able to turn in a peak performance if they were not a little bit edgy and apprehensive. Second, you will derive some solace from the fact that you are not alone. Every topflight director has gone through the same process, and everyone in your class is experiencing the same sensation to some extent. Third, you realize that anxiety is born of insecurity—ignorance of specific equipment or procedures. If you are uneasy about a particular assignment or function, make certain you find out what you can about it. Face your shortcomings and fill in your gaps. For example, review the special-effects buss of the switcher, or ask your instructor to go over the master control room patching again. With knowledge and experience comes confidence.

Attitudes Toward Others

As you cultivate more confidence and build a positive self-attitude, you will also be able to develop more of a sense of production discipline and an affirmative attitude toward the entire crew effort.

You must recognize the fact that studio television production is emphatically a *team effort*. There is no room in the production process for the lazy and the goldbricker (if you eventually want to succeed in the field). Neither is there room for the braggart and the ego-tripper (unless your uncle owns the station).

A strong sense of discipline and a professional attitude will result in a concern about the success of the program itself. If you are truly interested in the field, then you are, by definition, a *communicator*. In addition, if you are concerned with the communication process, then you want to see the communicative act—the creation of the television message—succeed. You *care* about contributing to a successful communication experience. If the communicative act, the television production, should not succeed, then you care—as a student of the process—to learn why it did not work. You analyze the problems and dissect the mistakes so that you can be part of a successful effort on the next production. If you do not deeply care about seeing the communication process work, then perhaps you should not pursue studies in this field.

As you deepen your sense of professional concern, you will also increase your professional responsibility toward others and toward the production. You will want to make certain that your dependability cannot be questioned. When you are assigned a job, it will be done. When you are supposed to be somewhere (including the start of a lab production), you will be there on time—or earlier.

Another important attribute of studio discipline is *respect*—respect for equipment and respect for other individuals, both **talent** and crew. As explained in the following chapters of this text, by gaining an understanding of the way most equipment works, you will begin to develop some appreciation and sense of *respect for the equipment*. The tools you are working with are not toys; they are not to be mistreated and played with. No professional handles a piece of equipment just to play with it. The tool is there to do a specific job, and that is what it is used for. Remember that the purchase and maintenance and repair of all equipment is limited by a very strict budget—whether in a plush network, a small studio, a

noncommercial station, or a university training facility. Once a piece of equipment is broken, two things happen: (1) the studio, or some small part of the studio operation, is out of commission for some period of time; (2) someone, somehow, must pay for the repair of the equipment.

You also show your respect for the equipment and studio by adhering to the established studio policies and regulations. Most studios will have certain operating policies concerning safety rules; supervision of use of facilities; prohibition of eating, drinking, and smoking in certain areas; storage of materials; and so forth. Make certain that you are aware of the specific regulations in the studio where you are working—and follow them.

Respect for individuals is manifest in several ways. Most of the people you are working with in a training situation are learners—as you are. They deserve the same respect and patient treatment to which you are entitled. Unless you feel that you are so superior to your colleagues that you are above evaluation, you have no right to treat others with disrespect. You show your respect—to crew members and performers alike—by being patient and understanding, by offering assistance, when appropriate, and by being genuinely appreciative and congratulatory when a good job is done.

There are several occasions when assistance is appropriate. Two specific instances are in setting up a production and in **striking**—or cleaning up—after a program is recorded. While a show is being set up, some crew members may have relatively little to do—camera operators, recording engineers, projectionists, technical directors, and the like. (Some of these crew members may have specific jobs assigned to them.) People who are free during the early stages of studio preparation should make themselves available to the lighting and staging director or directors to assist in the initial setup.

The same thing is true after the production is completed. Everyone has his or her own area to strike (camera operators coiling cables, audio engineer putting away microphones and cables), but some positions (for example, those of technical director, recording engineers) may be free sooner than others. Whenever these crew members have finished cleaning up their positions, they should assist in the general strike. It is everyone's job to see that the studio and all equipment are restored to their original condition—ready for the next production crew or class. (In unionized shops, of course, one should not cross union jurisdictions to assist someone else. Camera engineers do not handle stage props, and so forth.)

Whether and when to offer assistance often becomes a gray area. Do you move to "save" a fellow student if he or she is about to commit some obvious blunder? (This is related to finding a balance between initiative and self-control.) Do you, as technical director, follow the director's command when he or she tells you to punch up the wrong camera? Do you, as a floor assistant, obey the stage manager when he or she tells you to move an easel stand while the camera is on the air? In a professional, real-world situation you would probably be correct to hold off on executing the given instruction; you would try to save the person giving the instruction by quickly and considerately pointing out the apparent error. In a learning situation, however, you may not be doing the person a favor by saving him or her too frequently. If a director repeatedly makes the same kind of mistake by giving the wrong command and crew members repeatedly save the director by not following the command, are they really helping the director to learn? Or are they just helping reinforce a bad habit? The lab production is, after all, the place to learn by making mistakes—and seeing the results of those mistakes.

There are many similar gray areas where there is no fast and simple correct response. It is the challenge and excitement of these uncertainties that make television production the stimulating field it is. It is the quick-thinking professional who, because of his or her training and experience and sense of personal discipline, is able to make the right decisions.

1.3 Production Operations

At the outset it will be realized, of course, that there are several different levels of television production. Some TV productions are staged in mammoth studios with millions of dollars worth of equipment and crews consisting of dozens of people. On the other hand, many worthwhile productions are undertaken in tiny, makeshift quarters with a few hundred dollars' worth of equipment and a crew of two or three—or even one. In between these two extremes are most of the typical situations that you are likely to encounter.

Broadcast Categories

The most complex kind of studio productions are likely to be found at *network levels*—both commercial and noncommercial. Figure 1-1 shows a typical network production. (It should be stressed that noncommercial public television operations can—and often do—surpass commercial television productions in terms of program complexities, size of crews, glamour and excitement, and vital production challenges.) Productions at a network level usually will be well budgeted, housed in a large modern facility (although many network productions are still being turned out in older, but handsomely equipped, centers), and have large crews (some productions that originate from several different locations may have hundreds of crew members working in various engineering and production capacities).

At the *station level* of production there is a wide variety of origination complexities. Some commercial network-owned-and-operated stations and some of the major public TV stations will have production facilities that rival the network operations. At the other end of the station spectrum, many smaller stations will have woefully inadequate facilities—cramped studio or studios, small production crews, and older equipment patched together to meet minimal Federal Communications Commission (FCC) broadcast standards. (See fig. 1-2.)

Another level of professional operations includes *independent production centers.* There are many different kinds of facilities that are not directly connected with a broadcast outlet. Some are major studios producing commercials or independent programs for network-level distribution. Some are smaller outfits that produce a wide variety of commercial and noncommercial programing. Many independent companies turn out programming without any studio facilities or production crews of their own; they pull a package together and then go out and rent a studio and hire a crew to do the actual production. Most of the major network entertainment series, for example, are produced by independent production centers—ranging from large Hollywood film studios (Universal, Columbia, Paramount) to major independent television producers (Norman Lear, Garry Marshall, MTM) to specialized packagers (Goodson-Todman, Proctor & Gamble, Children's Television Workshop).

Nonbroadcast Telecommunications

A growing and increasingly important area of production operations is found in nonbroadcast areas. These afford many professional opportunities—with some fields outlined in the following discussion expanding at a rate of 30 to 40 percent a year. For example, over one billion dollars is spent annually on noncommercial programing for industry, government, schools, and religious groups.

The term *corporate video* (or *industrial TV* or *private video*) encompasses all types of telecommunications used for various business and industrial applications—sales training, corporate public relations, employee staff development, administrative and management communication, consumer relations, and so forth. When integrated with computers, laser distribution systems, and satellites, these uses result in some of the most advanced applications of the television medium.

One of the biggest fields of all is *government media.* Local, state, and federal agencies are involved in a myriad of telecommunications projects. The federal government, for example, is probably the world's largest television and film producer. Military applications, including the Armed Services Radio and Television Network, account for worldwide operations—as does the State Department's Voice of America.

Possibly the most rapidly expanding area is in the field of *medical and health services.* More than 80 percent of the 7,000 hospitals in the country use television and related media for patient education, in-service training (staff development), and/or public and community relations.

Another burgeoning field is in *religious productions.* Although many of the established denominations have long made use of free public-service time offered by commercial broadcasters ("Directions," "It Is Written," "Christophers"), the greatest use is with the evangelical or charismatic groups. At least three such church bodies operate their own satellite networks. The Christian Broadcasting Network in Norfolk, Virginia, claims to have the most advanced TV studios in the world.

School-level productions are another category to be considered. Thousands of schools, ranging from preschools to medical schools at universities, have television production facilities for various instructional and demonstration purposes. A typical media-center studio is illustrated in figure 1-3. Again, the quality of production facilities ranges from converted broom closets to massive **closed-circuit**

Figure 1-1 Major network studio productions can involve a crew of several dozen engineers, technicians, and production positions.
(Photo courtesy of KCET, Los Angeles.)

Figure 1-2 Even a small-station production will involve a crew of a dozen or so audio, camera, lighting, staging, and other production operators and technicians.

Figure 1-3 Many closed-circuit audiovisual television installations for schools and training centers will need a production crew of only two or three persons.

(CCTV) installations that rival anything seen at the network level. Most college and university facilities used for teaching TV production are probably equipped on a level comparable to that of a local station—barely adequate to do the job, never extensive enough to do everything desired. In the training situation, however, facilities are more likely to be monochrome, using older and smaller vidicon cameras and older helical-scan (nonbroadcast) video recorders.

A final major area to be considered is *cable TV production*. Although closely related to broadcast distribution in terms of quality and audience, cable TV represents another whole ancillary field. There are approximately 30,000 persons employed in the cable industry—mainly in sales, management, and distribution. However, another completely new field is mushrooming around the cable production companies—outfits such as Home Box Office, Showtime, Cable News Network, Black Entertainment Television, the Entertainment and Sports Programing Network

(ESPN), and dozens of others. Supplying programing to the cable systems via satellites, these companies—none of which existed prior to 1975—account for a rapidly expanding production market.

An idea of the significance and magnitude of all of these various nonbroadcast production operations can be gleaned by simply looking at respective employment figures. According to United States Department of Labor statistics, in 1980 there were approximately 195,000 people employed in broadcast operations, including both stations and networks. By contrast, it is estimated that about 230,000 people were employed in all of the nonbroadcast areas just discussed (cable, corporate, government and military, medical, religious, and school projects).

Small-Format Television

Although most of us tend to think of television in terms of the professional levels we have discussed above—and, indeed, most production courses and textbooks are geared toward this

Figure 1-4 One person
serves as audio-
engineer-camera
operator, while the other
half of the two-person,
small-format team is the
on-camera interviewer.

type of production—we should also be aware of an increasingly important phenomenon known as **small-format television** (often referred to as **video**). This term generally refers to nonbroadcast television designed for limited circulation. Many of the topics in this book—such as principles of audio, lighting, theory of camera operation, VTR recording and editing, and pictorial design—apply to small-format television as well as to professional uses.

During the past several years, we have seen a communications evolution (the term *communications revolution* is too much overworked) in the development of smaller, inexpensive television gear. For a few hundred dollars it is now possible to obtain a small, nonbroadcast standard, lightweight, handheld camera with a built-in microphone and a relatively lightweight portable videorecorder combination (often called a **portapak**). With this basic equipment, a two- or three-person crew—or even a one-person operation—is in the small-format television business. (See fig. 1-4.)

Small-format television operations are undertaken for a variety of reasons. Most of them could probably be divided into three basic areas: personal recording, community communicators, and video art. *Personal recording* includes several approaches and purposes. Basically, it is concerned with those video uses that are never intended to be seen by a large number of viewers. It may be thought of in part as an extension of home movies—recording family reunions, the baby's first steps, birthday parties, and so forth. It also may include more serious purposes, such as self-evaluation improvement programs, recording marriage counseling sessions, psychiatric training programs, or recording and analyzing an individual's golf backswing. What all of these personal recording applications have in common is that the product is never intended for distribution or viewing beyond a very small handful of participants.

The area of *community communicators,* however, gets into a little more ambitious use of the small-format medium. In this area we

Figure 1-5 Many types of video-art techniques can be achieved with the simplest kind of monochrome facilities.

have concerned individuals using what is sometimes called "guerrilla television" or "underground video" in order to try to tell a story or get a message across. Equipped with portable cameras and portapak, they will go out and record an event, a social happening, a neighborhood problem. Often dealing with consumer affairs, ethnic problems, or environmental concerns, the community communicators offer an alternative to establishment-type channels dominated by government bureaucracy and conventional economic enterprises. Using school closed-circuit systems, community cable TV systems in which large systems have public access channels, and portable video players at community meetings, they try to reach as large an audience as they can.[1]

Another whole category of video usage might be labeled *video art*. This is the intriguing use of video equipment to create artistic images and sounds perhaps entirely unrelated to actual reality. In video art the artist-producer is concerned solely with the artistic elements of composition—balance, mood, tone, intensity, shading, color, harmony, texture, and so forth. The artist may be concerned solely with the creation for its own aesthetic sake, or he or she may want to try to reach as large an audience as possible through any of the community channels. This usage of television may, of course, also be carried into the studio, as illustrated in figure 1-5. Using the variety of professional equipment available for

1. For an extended discussion of small-format television see, for example, Michael Murray, *The Videotape Book* (New York: Bantam Books, 1975); H. Allan Frederickson, *Community Access Video* (Santa Cruz, Calif.: Johnny Videotape, 1972); and Michael Shamberg and Raindance Corporation, *Guerrilla Television* (New York: Holt, Rinehart & Winston, 1971).

electronic controls, video manipulation, special effects, and signal distortion, the creator has moved far beyond small-format television.

1.4 Production Approaches

One other distinction should be made at this point. This is a distinction that somewhat parallels our discussion of professional and small-format television, although it applies primarily to major professional situations. Students of television production today should be acutely aware of the contrast between *multicamera production* and *single-camera production*.

Multicamera Production

Until a few years ago, any discussion of television production dealt almost entirely with multicamera production, which category was concerned primarily with multicamera *studio* production. All TV production was presumed to occur in a "real-time" situation—in which a thirty-minute program actually took thirty consecutive minutes of production time—with two or more cameras covering the action, and all editing decisions instantaneously executed as the director switched from one camera to another. Usually this took place in the TV studio, although location or *remote* productions such as political events or sporting contests could be covered wherever the action was taking place. The underlying principle of all multicamera productions remained the same, however: several cameras would cover the production from different angles and with different perspectives, with all **editing** (camera switching) being executed while the program was in progress.

During the first decade of popular television, up to the mid-1950s, this meant that all production was done *live*. It actually was happening while the viewers watched. Regardless of the rehearsal time involved, once the pro-

gram was on the air live—whether a drama, musical program, variety show, or wrestling match—the audience watched it at the exact time it was taking place. If the set fell down or the costumes ripped, the viewers saw it all. Although there are relatively few live productions on television today, those production personnel involved in live telecasts—whether a local parade, the news, the Olympics, or a national political event—would readily agree that this is still the most exciting, nerve-racking, and challenging area of television programing. The 1976 debate between Jimmy Carter and Gerald Ford when the audio line went dead for twenty-eight minutes is a good example.

In the mid-1950s, **videotape** recording came into existence. Now it was possible actually to record a program—in its entirety—on videotape and play it back at a later time. It was no longer necessary to present everything live as it happened. It was possible to schedule productions at more convenient times and to go back and rerecord a program that had a bad production problem. The era of **live-on-tape production** was born. Most programs—variety shows, talk shows, game shows—were still produced in their entirety, but were then recorded for later playback. Many multicamera productions, of course, are still produced in this manner today.

Next, in the late 1960s and early 1970s, **electronic editing** facilities became more and more sophisticated. It was now possible to record programs in segments and then piece them together in a **postproduction editing** process. Variety programs were one of the first genre to take advantage of this process. Segments with guest stars could be shot out of sequence; production numbers with costume and scenery changes could be interrupted while the changes were made; programs could be shot in different locations and edited together later. A sixty-minute variety-musical program might take all day to record. A ninety-minute extravaganza special might take days or even weeks to record and edit together. The principle, however, was still one of multicamera recording. Several cameras would be shooting each segment, with instantaneous editing decisions being made with the switcher; and the individual segments could be put together later. This process was carried into dramatic formats also with daytime serials (that always have been produced using video, nonfilm techniques) and some situation comedies (that started using multicamera video techniques and postproduction editing in the early 1970s).

Finally in the late 1970s, there evolved the ultimate adaptation of multiple-camera production—using separate videotape recorders to record each camera independently and simultaneously during the continuous performance. This *multiple-camera recording* process allows the director to concentrate on acting and camera work—without having to make instantaneous editing decisions. Then at some time well after the production recording, the director can sit down with his or her four or five videotapes of the program and use sophisticated computed-based postproduction editing equipment to put the program together—picking and choosing among the four or five camera angles available at any given moment in the action. Many major network-level productions now regularly use this technique. Although there are increased production costs incurred by the use of three or four extra video recorders and postproduction editing facilities, producers feel generally that the slicker paced and more polished final program is worth the slight increase in production price. (This multiple-camera recording process was pioneered in the 1950s, using multiple film cameras to record continuous action in the shooting of "I Love Lucy.")

Single-Camera Production

By the mid-1970s, however, it was evident that an entirely new television production process was evolving—**single-camera production.** With computer-based editing facilities, it was now possible to put together a very polished studio or location production using only a single electronic television camera. Actually, this evolution had two parallel movements.

On the one hand, single-camera production techniques came about as an attempt to emulate filmic techniques in recording *dramatic* programs. Motion picture films have almost always used a single-film camera in the making of dramatic pictures. This method represented the maximum control a director could have over the production elements. Each shot could be carefully staged; lighting could be arranged individually; microphone placement could be worked out for a single camera; actors could be positioned precisely; and so forth. This was an exactitude of control that was never attainable when shooting with multiple television cameras in a continuously running scene. The first experimentation with prime-time, full-length single-camera recording of television drama started in the early 1970s. As editing devices became more sophisticated, both commercial and noncommercial dramatic programs made more use of this production approach.

As a counterpart to the dramatic uses of single-camera production, *journalistic* applications evolved even faster. With the development of small, hand-held broadcast-quality video cameras in the 1970s, a new era of **electronic news gathering** (ENG) was ushered in. (Professsonal single-camera ENG techniques are not to be confused with small-format video, described in section 1.3.) Rapid coverage of news had always been hampered by film cameras because of the delay in processing the film. With the advent of small video cameras and portable recorders, however, news footage could be recorded on videotape, immediately edited as needed, and put on the air without delay. Thus, for both dramatic programs and journalistic purposes, the concept of single-camera video production came into its own in the mid-1970s.

By 1980, many other broadcast applications of single-camera *electronic field production* (EFP) were in common usage for local commercials, documentaries, location interviews, promos, talk-show segments, and so forth. And as the equipment became even lighter and less expensive, other nonbroadcast video programing turned to ENG/EFP techniques; corporate video, medical uses, training materials, government productions, schooling applications, and cable TV were all moving out of the studio and into the field. And the term *videography* was coined to refer to this new single-camera approach to TV production—adopting filmic techniques for video programs.

1.5   A Quick Survey of the Tools and Working Areas

Before getting into any of the specifics of television techniques and disciplines, it may be helpful to have a quick overview of the various elements of TV production. What are the tools we will be using? Where are they usually used? And, generally, how are they used?

Although this book is not to be concerned with the creative processes of writing and producing, it should nevertheless be stressed that the first tool used in any TV production is the *typewriter;* the first working area, the office or den. First and foremost, television is a medium of communication. The tools exist only so that people can attempt to communicate with one another, only so that they can send messages from one point to another. Without that message—without that attempt to communicate—the glamour of television is reduced to a meaningless pile of glittering gibberish.

Once the program is conceived, once the message is designed, we still are not ready to move into the arena of the television studio. Several other working areas come to our attention first. Are there sets to be built? Start in the *scene shop.* Are there props or furniture to be used? costumes to be obtained? Rummage through the *storage area.* Or visit commercial rental agencies where a Louis XIV chair or a coonskin cap can be rented. Are there graphics to be made? Get your order into the *artists' area.*

Many different kinds of TV productions will demand some type of simulated studio rehearsal before you can get into the actual facilities. If there are dramatic scenes to be rehearsed or complicated pieces of stage business that have to be worked out, reserve the *rehearsal hall,* find an empty studio, or use masking tape to mark off the area in the cafeteria.

The television **studio** (fig. 1-6) is, of course, the main center of activity that almost everyone associates with TV production. Whether a converted classroom, a remodeled warehouse, or a million-dollar facility, the studio is where everything is brought together and the action is frenzied. One of the first things you would notice upon entering a studio for the initial time would probably be the *permanent sets*—the news set over in that corner, the kitchen for the homemakers' program, the discussion set for the noontime talk show. There probably also is a cyclorama or other wall covering stretched out over two or three of the studio walls. Look overhead and you will see one of the key elements of any production—the tools of *television lighting.* The lighting instruments themselves—the spotlights and scoops—are probably hung on some sort of grid or catwalk suspended from the high ceiling of the studio. Many different types of lighting mounts are used in various studios. Possibly over in a corner will be the lighting

Figure 1-6 Typical medium-sized studio facility. Note the overhead lighting grid and the hanging cyclorama that can be stretched to cover two walls.

control center, a patching system, and a dimmer board; or these elements might be located in a control room.

Probably the most important tools in the production situation are those electronic pickup devices that can translate the pictures and sounds into electric impulses, which can then be handled electronically as separate elements of the television signal—the **camera** and the **microphone.** The cameras are the most obvious of these devices, stashed away in one corner of the studio. In a simple studio setup, there would probably be two or three small monochrome vidicon cameras mounted on basic tripods. In a large studio, there could be four or five professional color cameras mounted on pedestals, with at least one mounted atop a large crane or boom.

The microphones are more inconspicuous. Stored out of sight until time to set up for the production, they are then connected to cables and plugged into studio inputs located around the studio walls. Some of the microphones are mounted on stands for the announcer or newscasters. One might be attached to a **boom** or **giraffe** where it can be suspended above a performer's head and manipulated by an operator holding on to the other end of the boom arm. Many microphones are designed as **lavalieres** to be worn around the neck. Others will simply be carried in the hands of the performers.

Many productions, of course, do not take place in the studio. They may be **remote** recordings (or **live** broadcasts) from a concert hall, political convention, council chamber, sports arena, main street, or playing field. Once outside the studio, problems are considerably complicated. Extraneous noises cannot be controlled; lighting is inconsistent; background distractions cannot be eliminated. If indoors, the artificial lighting may have to be

Figure 1-7 The audio control room often overlooks the studio through a large, soundproof glass window. The audio operator also has a program monitor to see how the actual production looks on the air.

supplemented by portable television lighting. If outdoors, audio problems may be compounded by wind and crowd noises; lighting conditions may suddenly change; and so forth. The weather may be unpredictable; equipment may fail many miles from the repair shop; and local demonstrators may suddenly decide they want to be on television. Such is the fun and challenge of location productions.

Back in the production center, the next working area to examine would be the control rooms. There may be several different kinds of control areas associated with the TV studio. The first of these might be the **audio booth,** or **control room,** as shown in figure 1-7. This is where all of the sound elements are mixed and handled. The microphone inputs from the studio are terminated in the audio booth, usually in a **patch board.** Then the microphones can be mixed through a master audio board or console. Other audio elements can be added

here also—record turntables, audio recorders, sound from a film track, and so forth. The composite sound output can then be either recorded or sent to a master control room where it is mixed with the video signal and recorded onto videotape—or transmitted live.

In the **video control room,** or studio booth (fig. 1-8), we would find the comparable video mixing elements. Together with a bewildering array of television monitors of varying sizes and functions, the most important tool we would see would be the **TV switcher.** This is the piece of equipment that can select and mix television signals from various cameras and other sources in much the same way as the audio control board handles the sound sources and comes up with the final composite picture that is the visual half of the entire production. The studio control room also might contain the lighting controls and dimmer board if they were not located on the studio floor.

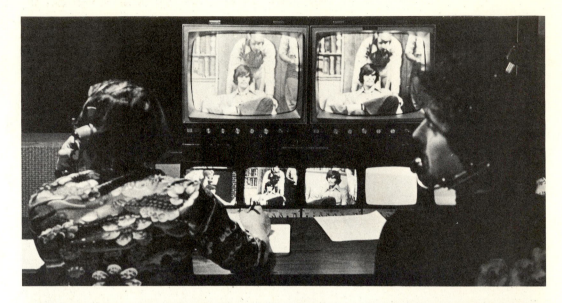

Figure 1-8   Two video control rooms. The director and assistant director, *top,* make shot selections from the smaller camera monitors; the large monitor on the left is the master program monitor, and the large monitor on the right is the preview monitor. The technical director, *bottom,* punches the buttons on the switcher to put the selected camera on the air. (Photo courtesy of KABC-TV, Los Angeles.)

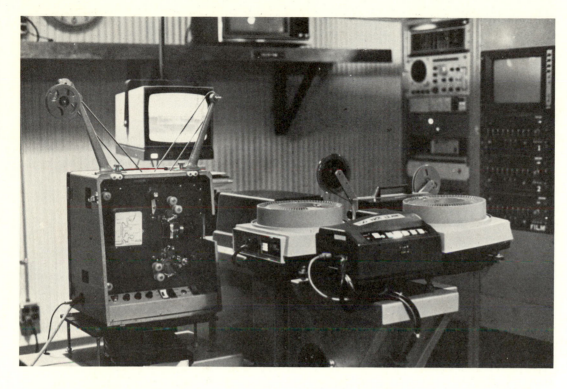

Figure 1-9 The master control room often houses the film chain, with its various film and slide projectors.

The next stop on our quick tour would probably be the **master control room.** (See fig. 1-9.) Located a little distance from the studio and control booths, the master control room is the hangout for the engineers. One of the most imposing items we would find here would be the **film chain** or **telecine.** This is a complex chain of equipment enabling the mixture of several different sources—such as 8mm and 16mm film and slides—into a multiplexer arrangement of mirrors and prisms that enable the selection of one input at a time to send into the television pickup camera on the film chain. The **videotape recorders** are also located here in master control. Depending upon the scope of the operation, this might be quite an imposing array of machines. Any electronic editing equipment ordinarily would be housed in the same area. Finally, and most important, the master control room usually would be the center for all camera-control functions—the generator for the synchronizing pulse that drives all cameras and the individual electronic controls for each camera.

If the production area is a remote location—outside of the studio—then the corresponding control rooms also have to be taken outside of the main production center. The audio control, video control, and master control functions would all be placed in some sort of van, truck, trailer, or motor home (as shown in fig. 1-10), which can be readily moved from one location to another. Depending upon the scope of the production, all of the control functions may be handled in one small van—or they may have to be housed (in the case of some major sporting events) in several portable buildings that are set up on location several days in advance of the production.

Figure 1-10 This remote unit, converted from a large motor home, contains complete control room and engineering facilities for a major production. (Photo courtesy of Learning Resources, California State University, Long Beach, Bob Freligh, photographer.)

If our quick tour of tools and working spaces was to include an actual station, then the final working area—but one with which we will not be concerned in this book—is the **transmitter** itself. Usually located on some high ground several miles from the studio operations and connected by a microwave link, the transmitter is the final engineering tool in the complex link that sends out the sounds and pictures of the television portion of the communication chain.

1.6   Producing and Directing

Although this book is concerned primarily with the technical aspects of television production—the techniques of operating the TV tools and the disciplines of functioning in a television team—it is necessary to introduce students to the concepts of producing and directing also. In most training situations, each member of the class undoubtedly will have to function as producer-writer-director as well as serve in the basic production positions.

In many television situations—especially in noncommercial TV—one person serves in a hyphenated producer-director capacity. The functions of these two positions can, however, still be differentiated.

The **producer** is the one key person who is responsible for pulling the total production together. He or she is ultimately in charge. From the communication standpoint, the producer is the person who determines the communication need, analyzes the potential audience, designs the television message, oversees the general construction and transmission of the message, and is the recipient (target) of viewer feedback and evaluation.

In practice, the producer is in charge of the entire program-making process: conceiving the program, hiring the script writers and other talent, setting up the budgets, dealing with all union and guild problems, taking care of all copyright and other clearance details, looking over the program director's shoulder during the actual production, worrying about legal problems such as libel and FCC fairness requirements, handling details of packaging, and selling the finished product.

In television, budgets and responsibilities are usually broken down into **above-the-line** and **below-the-line** costs. Above-the-line costs include creative and performing personnel such as the producer, associate producer(s), director, art director, writers, musicians, actors, and other performers. The producer is directly in charge of all these related functions, working closely with all personnel involved.

Below-the-line costs include all production and engineering standard costs such as those for associate director, stage manager, floor assistants, camera operators, technical director, lighting and staging crews, audio engineer, and other engineering positions. Although the producer is broadly in charge of the operation, it is the director who is in direct charge of the production positions, working with them on a close supervisory level.

One way of differentiating between the roles of the producer and the director is to think of the producer as the person who is in charge of pulling all of the elements of the program together prior to getting it into the studio. The director is in charge of everything once the production is at the studio stage— setting up the visual and graphic elements, deciding on the fine points of creative presentation, blocking all action, arranging for technical and production support positions, conducting rehearsals, handling the talent, directing the actual production, and following up on postproduction editing and other concerns.

The **director** generally will be the one most closely associated with the creative decisions involved in the final look and feel of the production—how the microphones are placed and used, how the action is blocked, how the cameras are placed, what actual shots get on the air, the overall artistic design of the visual elements, the timing and editing of the production, and so forth. It is sometimes helpful to think of the director in terms of three different competencies—as planner, as creative artist, and as executer.

As a *planner,* the director must be fully aware of all the demands and disciplines of the television medium. He or she must be dedicated to a meticulous preparation of myriad details prior to actual studio production. He or she must be concerned—in conjunction with the producer—with the ordering and reserving of all studio facilities and equipment needed, planning for graphics and special film, requisitioning props and scenery, arranging for crew and engineering personnel. The director must carefully lay out the basic scenic and graphic elements with the art director, lighting and staging personnel, and so forth. He or she must accurately prepare a marked working script and instructions for all other key crew positions—planning all shots and camera transitions well before production time. In short, the director must thoroughly prepare every aspect of the production during the time available before actually getting into the studio.

The director also must function as the *chief creative person* involved in the production. He or she must design the basic creative feel for the production—working with the art director, musicians, actors, lighting and staging designers, and so on. The director must plan the basic audio and visual impression of the program. How will cameras be used? What kind of shots will get on the air? What about the pacing and timing of the program? All of these creative decisions are up to the director.

Finally, the director must function as the actual *executer* of the program—sitting in the control chair and calling all shots during the program. He or she must be calm and cool, authoritative without being irritating, gentle without losing control, responsive without being excessively nervous. Possession of these qualities can be the final test of how well an individual can function under pressure.

Different directors will possess abilities— as planner, as creative artist, and as executer—in varying ratios. Some are excellent methodical planners without being creative; some are creative but tend to fall apart under pressure; some are outstanding at calling shots in the director's chair, but they hate to do the paperwork prior to production. Needless to say, the successful director is the person who can combine all three abilities to the fullest extent. In chapters 13 and 14, we will look more at the role of the director in greater detail.

Summary

Television production is a complex and confusing enterprise. Each individual member of the television team must master and demonstrate an exacting combination of *techniques* and *disciplines*—knowing technically how to use all of the TV equipment and being able to interact with all other team members and production elements to produce a successful television program.

This is true whether you are involved with *broadcast operations* (at the network, station, or independent producer level), *nonbroadcast telecommunications* (corporate video, government media, medical TV, religious productions, schooling applications, or cable TV), or with *small-format television* (personal recording, community communication, or creating video art).

Similar techniques and disciplines must be mastered whether you are involved with *multicamera* live productions (in the studio and on location) or if you are working with *single-camera* filmic procedures (for either dramatic or journalistic purposes).

In any kind of TV-production situation, you must be concerned with a wide variety of working areas and tools of the medium—the typewriter, studio facilities, sets, props and costumes, lighting instruments, cameras and microphones, audio and video mixing areas, the film chain, editing equipment, and various engineering and control facilities. Students in beginning TV production must also be familiar with the jobs of the producer and director. As a producer, you must assume ultimate responsibility for the entire program—from its initial conception to final audience feedback. As director, you are responsible for the specific elements of production—preproduction planning, creative use of the medium, and control room execution of the production. Each position entails its own set of techniques and disciplines.

In chapter 2, we will turn to the specific production elements that make up the sound and picture of the television message. It is often tempting to start first with the video process—the cameras and associated equipment. We prefer, however, to begin with the audio operation for two reasons. First, the audio part of the production is frequently slighted in the treatment of the larger and more complicated aspects of picture production; by beginning with audio we hope to give it the emphasis it deserves. Second, there are several functional similarities between audio and video signal production and manipulation; by studying the audio operation first it is easier to grasp the bigger and more complex picture of the video side of the program in subsequent chapters.

1.7 Training Exercise

Write a brief (500-word) essay setting forth your own personal professional goals in the broadcasting-film field. What do you hope to be able to accomplish in the area? What specifically do you feel that you will get from this course that will help you to achieve your goals? Can you get any more out of the course? How?

the audio system: signal flow and technical control

2

The task of understanding and ultimately operating television equipment becomes much easier if the individual components are seen in terms of the *functions* each piece of equipment is designed to perform. Each item has been developed to ensure that the crew and eventually the director will have the ability to control with split-second accuracy the flow of the numerous audio and video signals available during a production situation.

The **audio** system is an excellent place to start the process of comprehending the basics of television engineering structure. Once audio is understood, the same principles can easily be applied to video. Each audio component has a somewhat analogous counterpart in the video system.

2.1 Technical and Creative Functions of Audio

In many elements that comprise audio and video production, we will see that there coexists both a *technical function* and a *creative function*. It is necessary to meet certain requirements simply to get adequate sound and picture produced (technical function); it then is possible to manipulate these elements for certain aesthetic effects (creative function).

In the audio system, we will be initially concerned with the basic *technical requirements* to reproduce original sound faithfully. That is, we will be involved with controlling signal flow, understanding microphone construction and proper usage, mixing other prerecorded audio sources, and so forth. For the beginning audio director, the most important job is simply to be able to pick up and reproduce faithfully the actual sound that is being produced as the audio portion of the TV production. How do you control the tools and equipment to do this adequately?

The *creative side* of audio production involves such things as establishing a specific *mood* or *emotional setting* (often with background music or distortion of a normal audio signal), creating an atmosphere of *reality* (with sound effects or certain identifiable voice qualities, such as a telephone conversation), and *enhancing* or *emphasizing* particular sounds or frequencies (to accentuate low tones or high notes). Several of these elements are discussed in these next two chapters: **mixing** and **shaping** the audio signal (section 2.2); microphone selection and usage, including such considerations as acoustical differences, mike distance, sound balance, audio perspective (sections 3.2 and 3.3); and adding of other sources (section 3.4).

A more detailed discussion of the creative side of audio production, however, is beyond the scope of this book. It involves such specialized topics as musical balance and instrumental characteristics, performing and acting techniques, and advanced engineering concepts. The emphasis in these two chapters, therefore, will be primarily upon faithful technical reproduction of conventional television sound and basic elements of creative control.

2.2   The Seven Basic Control Functions

Each piece of equipment in the studio or control booth can perform one or more of seven basic control functions. If you look carefully at your own audio booth and adjoining studio, you will find that audio facilities are generally designed to move, modify, or otherwise control a signal in these seven ways: (1) *transducing,* or converting sound waves into electrical energy and back again; (2) *channeling,* or routing the sound, sending it wherever necessary; (3) *mixing* two or more sound sources; (4) *shaping* the sound, changing the quality of the tone; (5) *amplifying* the signal; (6) *recording* and/or *playing back;* and (7) *monitoring* the audio output, listening to and keeping track of the program audio.

In looking over this list, many examples of these functions will probably come to mind from your experience in operating a home stereo and audiotape recorder. In sorting them out, you will come to see that some pieces of equipment can perform more than one function. For example, the speaker that transduces a signal into listenable sound is also obviously a monitor.

Keep in mind that the terminology used to define the various components and their functions may vary somewhat with time and location. There is, however, a basic structure of functional design common to all audio control rooms. Understanding the essential elements of this structure in your own facility is the prerequisite that is necessary to successful operation of the equipment in a production situation.

2.2.1 Transducing

The entire process by which sound (voices, music) is converted into a broadcast signal (electrical information) is referred to as **transducing.** Figure 2-1 shows in simplified form how the transducing element—the microphone components that actually change sound waves into electrical energy—performs this function in a dynamic microphone.

The tone production of a human voice or musical instrument creates pressure waves in the molecules of the air. If these waves are produced at a constant rate of 440 cycles per second, the result is the musical tone of *A* above middle *C.*[1] These waves fall upon and

---

1. The term *cycles per second* (cps) is used as the basic unit of measure for sound pressure waves and, in the past, for electromagnetic waves. In recent years, engineering terminology has for the most part replaced the term *cycles per second* with the term *Hertz* (abbreviated Hz) in honor of Heinrich Hertz, who first demonstrated the existence of electromagnetic waves.

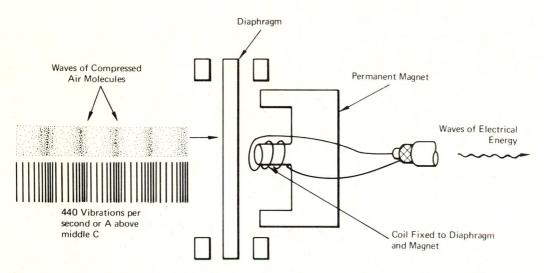

Diaphragm

Waves of Compressed
Air Molecules

Permanent Magnet

Waves of Electrical
Energy

440 Vibrations per
second or A above
middle C

Coil Fixed to Diaphragm
and Magnet

When sound waves, from a voice or musical instrument, strike the diaphragm of the microphone, the waves of compressed air molecules cause the attached coil to vibrate. As the coil moves back and forth within the magnetic field of the perma-nent magnet, a small fluctuating electric current is produced. This minute current, which will be amplified many times, carries the same information as the original sound waves.

Figure 2-1 Transducing element of a dynamic microphone.

vibrate the **diaphragm** of the microphone and cause the attached coil to vibrate around a part of the permanent magnet. When this coil moves within the resulting magnetic field, an electric current is produced. This signal is now in its new electronic form but retains the original **frequency** pattern of 440 oscillations per second.[2] (A more detailed explanation of wave theory is contained in appendix A.)

Thus far, we have been concerned only with those signal changes taking place within the studio and the audio control room. The

signal has been converted or transduced into an electronic pattern, amplified at several stages in its journey, and sent along to the transmitter. The signal is then **modulated** or superimposed within the assigned carrier frequency of the station and amplified more than a million times for transmission into the air. In figure 2-2, we see in simplified form how this modulation phase is but a part of the total broadcasting sequence.[3]

At the receiver, the whole procedure takes place once again. This time it is largely in reverse order and is called *demodulation*. The audio portion of a television set or radio separates the original signal from the carrier wave (demodulation), adds some necessary amplification, and sends the signal to the speaker.

2. Actually, the A 440 cps frequency in our example is only the fundamental tone. It is by far the most prominent of many tones that are simultaneously produced when a voice or instrument is sounded. The other tones, which are much softer in volume and occur at higher frequencies, are called "overtones" or "harmonics." Their presence and relative volume are what produce the distinctive quality of any individual voice or instrument. To reproduce any single complete tone accurately, all of these resultant frequencies must be picked up and simultaneously transduced into the electrical signal. A more complete explanation of the overtone series is presented in appendix B.

3. For a simplified explanation of how a carrier wave is theoretically modulated, both by amplitude modulation (AM) and by frequency modulation (FM), see appendix A. For a more detailed explanation see Sidney W. Head, *Broadcasting in America,* second edition (New York: Houghton Mifflin Company, 1972), chapters 1 and 2.

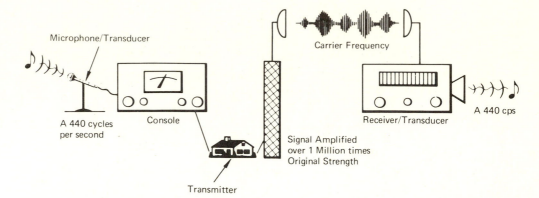

Microphone/Transducer

A 440 cycles
per second

Console

Transmitter

Carrier Frequency

Signal Amplified
over 1 Million times
Original Strength

Receiver/Transducer

A 440 cps

**Figure 2-2 Modulation
and demodulation in the
broadcasting sequence.**

The original sound waves (440 cps) are transduced into an electrical current which, at the transmitter, is modulated or superimposed over the assigned carrier frequency of the broadcasting station. This carrier wave is the specific broadcasting frequency assigned by the Federal Communications Commission—either part of the television channel or, in the case of radio, a separate part of the elec-

tromagnetic spectrum (see Appendix A), e.g., 690 kiloHertz ("six-ninety on your radio dial"). The TV or radio set then receives this carrier frequency, demodulates the superimposed program information, and the speaker transduces the electrical energy back into sound waves that the ear can perceive (440 cps).

The speaker, which is a transducer something like a microphone with the elements placed in reverse order, now vibrates against the molecules of the air to produce sound waves at a frequency of 440 cycles per second.

When one considers the continuous transducing process, an audio control booth speaker-monitor would be considered as a transducing component that provides this function of signal change. The cartridge in the pickup arm at the turntable also is a transducer that deserves to be included within this general category. In a way, it is a type of microphone that transforms the vibrations picked up by the needle into an electronic energy form.

2.2.2 Channeling

An audio system contains two main sets of channels or lines designed to allow us to route or send the signal from one point to another. There is the wiring system of the **console** itself, and there is a series of external lines that have been permanently installed to bring outside

signal sources, such as a microphone, into the console. The routing device that makes possible the connection of these two systems is the **patch bay.** (See fig. 2-3.)

The signal coming in on a line from a studio mike temporarily terminates its flow at the patch bay, where the round-holed receptacle is called an *output.* Any one of several lines designed to carry that mike signal from the patch bay into the console is labeled an *input* at its patch bay starting point. It is important that one gets the input and output concept clearly in mind. A patch cord placed into both receptacles completes the connection—linking the studio line output to the console line input—and the first part of the channeling has been established. The remainder of the journey of the signal through the audio board is largely a matter of clearing a pathway by means of opening a series of switches and **potentiometers (pots)**, or volume control faders. Figure 2-4 is a block diagram of a simplified one-mike, one-program channel audio system.

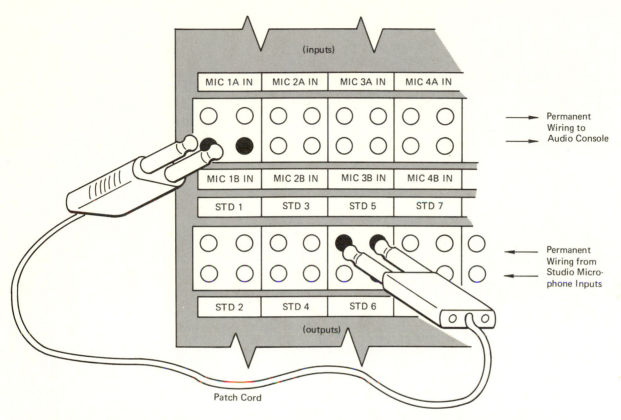

(inputs)

| MIC 1A IN | MIC 2A IN | MIC 3A IN | MIC 4A IN |

→ Permanent
Wiring to
→ Audio Console

| MIC 1B IN | MIC 2B IN | MIC 3B IN | MIC 4B IN |
| STD 1 | STD 3 | STD 5 | STD 7 |

← Permanent
Wiring from
Studio Micro-
phone Inputs

| STD 2 | STD 4 | STD 6 | |

(outputs)

Patch Cord

The lower two rows of receptacles are the terminals ("outputs") from studio microphone inputs. The next two higher rows ("inputs") are wired to microphone/potentiometer positions on the audio console. Thus, the pictured patch cord will connect the microphone plugged into studio input 5 with position 1B on the audio console.

Figure 2-3 Portion of a typical patch bay.

However complex an audio system's design may be, it is still only an extension of this basic structure.

2.2.3 Mixing

The primary function of the console board—such as those pictured in figure 2-5—is that of combining and blending the signals from different sources into a balanced whole. This, of course, gets into creative—as well as technical—considerations. Almost every element of the design of the audio board is in some way related to this mixing function. The process is of value from a production standpoint only when the volume level of each of the incoming signals can be separately controlled. The flow of the signal is so arranged that, after each potentiometer is adjusted to a desired level, they are all connected together on a single line called a mixing buss. This line is then connected to the final program or line output. Stereo and quad controls on the components in your home operate in much the same manner. The simplified block diagram in figure 2-6 of a three-input, one-program channel console shows the stage in the signal flow at which the mixing of the various signals takes place.

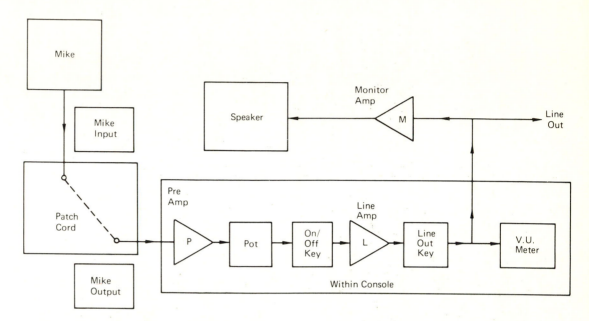

Figure 2-4 Simplified one-channel audio system.

A microphone is plugged into a mike input in the studio which is connected to the "studio output" on the patch bay. A patch cord connects this output with a microphone/pot position, through a preamplifier, with the corresponding potentiometer on the audio console. The pot is connected to a switch ("on/off key"), and (through a line amplifier) to the "line out key" which controls the output of the entire console. At this point, the audio signal is channeled in two directions— going into the "volume unit" meter so that a proper volume level can be maintained visually, and also going into the program line. This signal is again sent in two directions—to the control room speaker(s) for monitoring purposes (through a monitor amplifier), and the signal is also sent on the "line out" to its ultimate destination (master control room, videorecorder, transmitter).

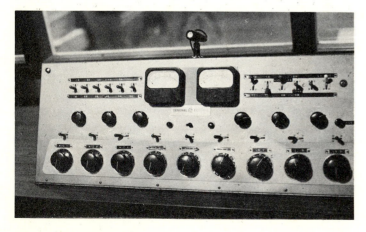

Figure 2-5 Two audio consoles. Older board with rotary knob-type pots, *left,* newer board with slide-faders, *right.*

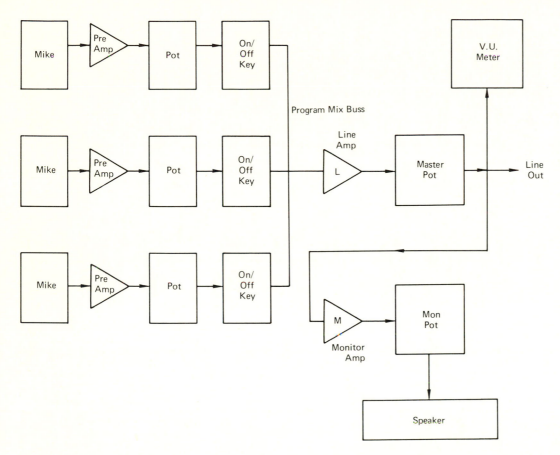

This three-input system is similar to the one-channel system diagrammed in figure 2-4, except that three different sources (microphones) are used. Note that after they are mixed at the "program mix buss," the volume of the combined (or mixed) audio is controlled by a master potentio- meter. This diagram also indicates the inclusion of a "monitor pot" that can control the volume of the control booth speaker(s) without affecting the level of the program audio being sent on the "line out."

Figure 2-6 Three-input audio system.

2.2.4 Shaping

The function of shaping—of altering the tonal qualities of the sound—is almost entirely a creative function. The use of the fader as just discussed is an example of one of the methods in which signal quality is altered or shaped. Volume control, however, is only one of many ways in which a sound signal can be changed to suit a specific purpose. Most turntables are equipped with one or more filtering devices to eliminate the high frequency scratch noise of older records. Microphone filters often are built into, or can be patched into, an audio console in order to filter out specified high frequency or low frequency tones or pitches and overtones in order to simulate desired audio situations (the effect of a telephone line conversation, for example).

In addition to filtering devices, well-equipped studios have sophisticated components that can shape audio in other ways—by emphasizing selected frequencies to produce a richer voice or musical quality, for example. An **equalizer** can be used to increase or decrease the levels of different frequencies, thus enriching high or low pitches. A **limiter** might be used to cut off levels when they reach a volume that is too strong. An **audio compressor** can be used to bring low levels up to a certain volume. Echo and other reverberation devices, often used for musical programs or certain dramatic effects, also fall into this shaping classification.

2.2.5 Amplifying

An electronic signal is an organized movement of negatively charged electrons within a wire. Amplification takes place by means of a component's ability to multiply the flow of electrons while retaining the same essential wave pattern. As we saw in figures 2-4 and 2-6, which portrayed the mixing and channeling functions, this process occurs more than once as the signal moves through the system. The signal from a microphone is relatively weak and must be strengthened before it can be mixed with other signals—such as an audio recorder—that have been amplified before reaching the audio console. Some special types of microphones need additional amplification even before their signals can be carried to the audio patch bay.

On most audio boards a distinction is made between pots that are designed to have microphones patched into them and pots that are to be used for sources such as audiotapes, records, feeds from videotape recorders, film projectors, and so forth. This is because the microphone positions have a **preamplifier** built in to boost the signal before it can be mixed with other sources. The other electronic sources of audio, such as recorders, already have their signals amplified and are ready for line amplification once the signals are mixed.

2.2.6 Recording and Playing Back

The basic functions of the control room record turntables—like audiotape recorders and cartridge machines—need little explanation. A person's own experience with similar equipment in the home serves as an excellent background. The ability to integrate their use in a production situation, however, does require considerable practice in the development of proper operational techniques. Section 3.4 details some specific techniques and applications of audio recorders and turntables.

The audio portion of most television programs is, of course, recorded directly onto the videotape recorder. There is little that the audio engineer has to do other than to make certain that the output of his or her audio console is connected to the videotape recorder (often by patching from the audio board to the master control room) and then to monitor the program audio (by watching the levels).

Playing back prerecorded material for program audio is a different matter. The audio operator has to be practiced in the techniques of cueing up various-sized records and different-speed audiotape recorders. Many audio booths will be equipped with audiotape **cartridge** systems. These playback units (some of which can hold up to ten different cartridges) can be very convenient in playing back sound effects, short announcements, brief musical selections, and the like. (Cartridges usually cannot hold more than four minutes worth of material.) Because each is a continuous tape loop that automatically cues itself, the cartridge is always ready at the push of a button.

2.2.7 Monitoring

For an operator to perform any of the functions necessary to signal flow and control, the audio engineer must have the benefit of some sort of simultaneous information **feedback** of that signal or combination of signals. It takes several components to perform that function adequately. The most obvious of such equipment is the **speaker** in the audio booth, which plays what is being fed out over the program line. In a broadcast situation, there usually is a separate air **monitor.** One must also have the ability to monitor separately any single sound source from among the several that are being mixed for transmission. This is done by means of a preview or *cue* channel.

The **volume unit (VU) meter** provides another essential informational feedback. In spite of the marvelous structure of the human ear, it is not able to register changes in volume to the same degree that electronic sound equipment can. From an engineering standpoint, this can cause some serious problems.

Within the interacting processes of mixing, shaping, and amplifying, there is a point of increase at which the electronic equipment ceases to function properly. At this point—which is theoretically 100 percent of the signal strength that can be handled by the equipment—the ability of the components to process the electronic wave patterns accurately begins to break down. The result is a distortion of the signal.

Most VU meters utilize two related scales of measurement to visualize the differing levels of volume on the program line. One of these scales shows signal strength in terms of proper signal modulation. It displays a range from zero to roughly 150 percent—with the area above 100 percent marked in red to indicate the possibility of signal distortion. (See fig. 2-7.) This scale is most useful during the ongoing production situation. (See section 3.3.)

During the preproduction setup period of any complicated program, audio inputs from many sources must be pretested and adjusted so that they provide a uniform level of sound volume. During this process the plus and minus **decibel** scale is of considerable impor-

Figure 2-7   Typical VU meter showing two scales: the upper scale indicates percentage of proper signal modulation (volume level); the lower scale is in decibels.

tance to the audio engineer. It allows the electronic strength of one signal to be compared with another in terms of a precise mathematical ratio. The VU meter has been designed to measure sound in its electromagnetic form within certain specifications of power and line resistance. This can be considerably different from the way in which one's ear and nervous system react to sound pressure waves coming from a studio monitor.

The trained engineer may put the VU meter to many uses in the process of setting up mikes and balancing various sound sources. For the student, however, it may be sufficient at first to acquire the ability to **ride gain** somewhere between 60 percent and 100 percent of modulation.

And there you have, in a very simplified form, an insider's guide to the audio control room. If this beginning knowledge makes you feel less of a stranger within the confines of the audio booth, it is probably because it is in reality only an expanded version of the tape recorders, cartridge machines, and stereo sets that have become so much a part of our lives.

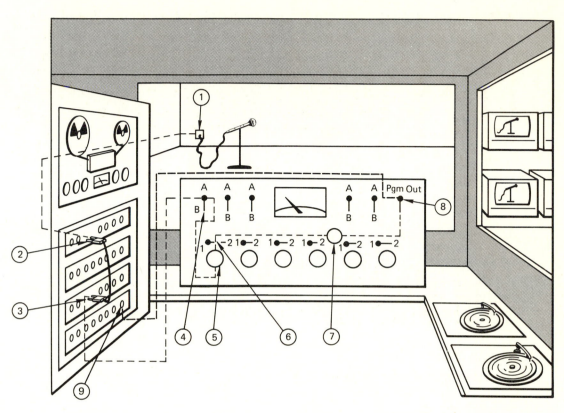

Figure 2-8   Audio signal flow model.

1. Studio microphone input. 2. Patch bay output. 3. Console input. 4. Input selector switch. 5. Potentiometer. 6. Channel selector or pot on/off key. 7. Master potentiometer. 8. Line out switch. 9. Program-out patch bay output.

2.3   Audio Signal Flow

The concept of signal flow is the first of several preliminary areas of knowledge you will need in order to master the techniques and disciplines of television production. This channeling procedure must be understood within a conceptual framework and not as a memorized list of patches made, switches moved, or pots opened. The only way to troubleshoot audio failure is to know each step of the sequence in its proper order.

Figure 2-8 is a typical model of audio facilities. It illustrates the basic steps in the flow of a signal from a studio mike, through a console or board, to a line output program monitor. Although equipment design and terminology could differ slightly, the basic sequence of functions should be easily projected into the equipment with which you will be working. Each numbered step is explained in some detail on subsequent pages. As a starting point, a quick review of the block diagrams in figures 2-4 and 2-6 may be helpful.

2.3.1   Studio Microphone Input

The microphone, connected to a mike cable, is plugged into a numbered studio receptacle. These inputs either may be gathered together at one junction box or may be spaced at intervals around the studio walls. In some studios, there may even be some input receptacles placed on the ceiling or on a lighting **catwalk** in order to facilitate hanging microphones.

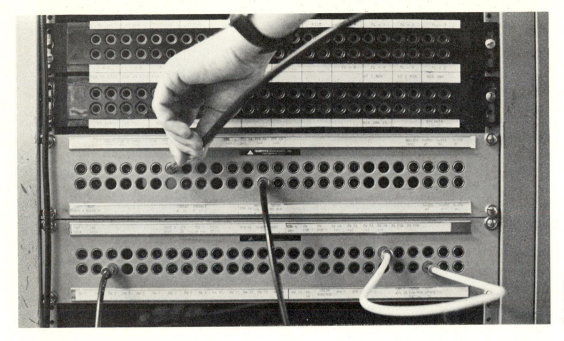

Figure 2-9 Typical
patch bay, incorporating
both audio and video
circuits.

2.3.2 Patch Bay Output

From the studio input point, the signal travels through a permanently constructed line to an output receptacle at the patch bay, such as the one illustrated in figure 2-9. The number of this output corresponds to the number of the studio input. A signal coming through Studio Input #2 is now labeled "studio 2" or "mike 2 out(put)."

Remember that all of the receptacles at the patch bay are either inputs or outputs. One group of these, not of our immediate concern, carries signals to and from the master control room where equipment such as VTR machines and projectors may be located. At this point in our signal flow model, however, we are dealing with those outputs that bring in signals from studio mikes or from turntables and cartridge machines and audiotape recorders right in the audio booth. Some of this equipment may be **normalled,** that is, it has its own permanent audio line directly wired into the console and needs no patching.

In some newer consoles such as those found in network studios and other modern production centers, steps 2 through 4 (patching and console input) have been replaced by an electronic switching unit. By means of this switcher, audio signals from a studio or from **telecine** (VTR and film sound) can be placed into any **buss** on the board simply by pressing a button.

2.3.3 Console Input

The next step in the audio signal flow deals with the group of inputs that carry those mike or other external signals into the mixing lines (microphone/potentiometer positions) of the console. With one end of a patch cord in the "mike 2 output," we now place the other end into an input that takes the signal into any one of several mixing lines within the audio board. Many consoles provide for two or even three optional lines from the patch bay leading to any single mixing line. From the patch bay, our "mike 2 out" example could be patched into line 1 (fader 1) by means of a 1A, 1B, or even 1C input.

2.3.4 Input Selector Switch

Whichever input line is patched, there must now be a corresponding connection at the **input selector switch** to bring the signal into our mixing "line 1 (pot 1)" example. Although all of these two or three lines could be connected back to microphones simultaneously, they can only be fed into our mixing line 1 one at a time. Your input selector switch may be a two- or three-position toggle switch or several push-button connectors.

On some consoles, optional inputs leading to a single pot and mixing buss can provide for different impedance level inputs (see section 3.1).

2.3.5 Potentiometer

The signal has now proceeded as far as the volume control (called the **attenuator, mixer, gain control, fader, potentiometer** or **pot**). When opened clockwise, the pot (fig. 2-10) acts much like a valve in allowing varying amounts of the amplified signal to pass through. The further the pot is opened, the greater the volume.

On modern electronic audio consoles, the rotary pot has been replaced by sliding faders. (See fig. 2-5.) With these slide-faders, you increase the volume by pushing the fader up, away from you; pulling the fader all the way down cuts out all signals. In addition to greater electronic reliability, there are two advantages to the slide-faders: (1) the audio operator can visually "see" the relative balance of sound or mixing pattern by noting the positions of the various faders; (2) it is possible for the audio operator to manipulate several audio lines simultaneously—one hand can control up to four different faders at the same time, whereas only one rotary pot can ordinarily be controlled single-handedly.

Figure 2-10 Rotary potentiometer, or volume control knob, with channel selector switch immediately above the pot.

2.3.6 Channel Selector or Pot On/Off Key

On many audio boards, the mixing busses are wired with two separate lines, creating *A* and *B* channels. Note the channel selector key above the pot in figure 2-10. All switches must be placed to the same channel position in order to mix any group of lines within the console. Dual-channel boards can be used to manage two completely separate program lines simultaneously. For instance, the audio engineer can be handling the primary program audio on the *A* channel (using one VU meter), sending the line-out audio up to the master control room to be recorded on the video recorder. At the same time the engineer can be using the *B* channel (and the second VU meter) to record an offstage announcer (who is in a separate booth) on audiotape—to be inserted at the end of the program for the closing credits.

Usually the alternate channel can also be utilized to submix several inputs, which are then fed as a group into the main channel. Whether toggle or push-button design, there is also usually an "off" position. In single-channel consoles there is still usually some type of on-and-off switch so that a signal from a preset level on a pot can be instantly sent into the mixing buss.

2.3.7 Master Potentiometer

All of the combined signals from the mixing buss must pass through the control of the master pot. This is the final volume adjustment point of the mixed signal that is amplified and sent out as the program line output. It generally is left open at a level calibrated by engineering personnel to fit with all other components in the system.

2.3.8 Line-Out Switch

The final point of control of a signal in its journey through the audio console is the line-out switch. As a safety factor, some consoles are designed so that the VU meter will not operate unless this line-out switch is activated. When this switch is closed, the audio signal is now ready to leave the control board. In most cases, the line-out position would be permanently connected to an input back on the patch bay (fig. 2-8). It is now available as the Program Line Output at a space on the patch panel.

2.3.9 Program-Out Patch

With the signal delivered back to the patch bay, it can now be physically routed from the audio booth anywhere desired. Typically, a patch connection will be made that will send the signal into the master control room where the audio is combined with video on the video recorder. However, the signal can also be patched into any of several other destinations: audiotape recorder, another studio, or directly to the transmitter for live transmission.

2.4   Sources of TV Audio

The previous discussion of audio signal flow represented a typical, somewhat simplified model, based upon the microphone as the audio source. Actually, the audio operator should think in terms of two different categories of audio sources—the *microphone* and other *prerecorded sources*. Each broad grouping has its own techniques and disciplines that must be mastered and practiced.

The signal produced by a microphone is relatively weak (section 2.2.5). It must be amplified as it comes into the console in order to bring it up to a suitable line level. Signals from other prerecorded sources of audio (audiotape, videotape, film, and turntables) are amplified at their points of origination and come to the board already at line strength. The audio operator must therefore be careful never to patch one of these already amplified signals into a console microphone input. The result would be an overloading of the system, indicated by a very loud hum or squeal.

Microphones

The microphone comes in a wide variety of types and sizes, designed for a multitude of specialized purposes. They vary as to *frequency response;* some will pick up low frequencies well, while others respond best to higher frequencies. Microphones differ as to *pickup pattern;* some will pick up everything around them (omnidirectional), while the performer has to stand directly in front of other microphones (unidirectional) to be heard well. Microphones will vary in the technical construction of their *transducing elements*—the way they actually transform sound waves into electrical energy. As a result, some are more rugged than others. Microphones vary in *physical design,* to be used in different ways; some are to be placed in mike stands, some are hand-held, others are worn around the neck or attached to special boom stands.

These different distinctions and differences are discussed in chapter 3. By becoming familiar with the different microphone classifications and characteristics, the audio operator will be able to select the most appropriate microphone for each application. Which microphones should be used for talk shows? drama? musical productions? What kinds of mikes are best suited for outdoor (location) productions? Which microphones are used for picking up sound from a great distance? What if you want a microphone that can be concealed or hidden? These are just some of the considerations that an audio operator has to be ready to think about.

Prerecorded Sound Sources

The basic audio signal flow concept also applies to sound from sources other than the microphone—although the path starts somewhere other than in the TV studio. The origination of the prerecorded sound may be in the master control or telecine room, or even in the audio booth itself; however, the same basic principles of signal flow apply.

Basically, the audio operator could probably think of prerecorded sound as coming from one of five broad sources: film, videotape, audiotape, cartridges, and records. Although other variations (such as audio **cassettes**) may occasionally be encountered, these five basic origination media represent the common non-microphone sources of television audio.

Film sound usually will be associated with 16mm film—although some stations and closed-circuit installations may use **sound-on-film (SOF)** for 8mm formats. Thirty-five mm film will seldom be encountered outside of major network operations. Usually the film and its associated sound track will originate in the master control or telecine room—as part of the film chain (see section 12.3). The audio operator ordinarily will not have to be concerned with loading and running the film projector—although several positions may be doubled up in smaller production situations. Once the film projector is properly threaded, the audio pickup will have to be connected to a source on the audio console. As a rule, this is accomplished through the patch bay—typically from the master control room to the audio control room. The primary jobs of the audio engineer are then correct operation of the board, riding gain, and so forth. (See section 3.6.)

Videotape audio tracks are handled—from the standpoint of the audio operator—in a manner similar to the film sound track. Many types of productions will have videotape inserts, in which a short, previously recorded videotape segment is incorporated into the body of another television production. The insert videotape recorder or recorders, like the film projector or projectors, usually will be located in master control or telecine or someplace other than the audio booth. Someone other than the audio operator will be responsible for threading up the videotape recorder and patching the audio line into the audio control room. Again, the primary concern of the audio person will simply be correct operation of the console, getting cues precisely, and so forth.

Audiotape playback, on the other hand, is usually completely in the hands of the audio engineer. The typical audio control room will have one or more audiotape recorders. (See fig. 2-11.) The audio engineer will be in com-

Figure 2-11 Production model audiotape recorder.

plete charge of making certain the tape is correctly threaded and patched or connected to the audio console. (Often the audiotape recorder will be normalled or permanently wired into the audio console. See section 2.3.2.) Audiotape frequently is the most convenient medium to use for prerecording longer segments of program inserts—background music or sound effects, announcements—and for premixing several sound sources. For example, if the production calls for an audio segment that has an off-camera announcer, background music, and a sound effect, it is easier—and much safer—to prerecord that segment rather than to try to mix those several elements during the actual television production.

In playing back audiotape, there are several factors that the audio operator has to watch for. First, the tape speed must be checked. Audiotape can be recorded at several different speeds: 3¾ inches per second (inches of tape travel per second) is the slowest commonly used speed for most recorders (some professional recorders do not have 3¾ ips capability); 7½ is a more common professional recording speed (the higher the tape speed, the better the fidelity of the recording); 15 ips is usually used only for high-quality, high-fidelity musical recordings. The audio operator must make certain that the booth audiotape recorder can play back at the correct speed. Second, the track configuration must be checked. Although most audiotape is ¼ inch, various recording configurations use the tape differently. It is possible to have full-track recording (rarely used today), half-track recording (wherein only half a track is used in each direction or both tracks are used for stereophonic recording in the same direction), and

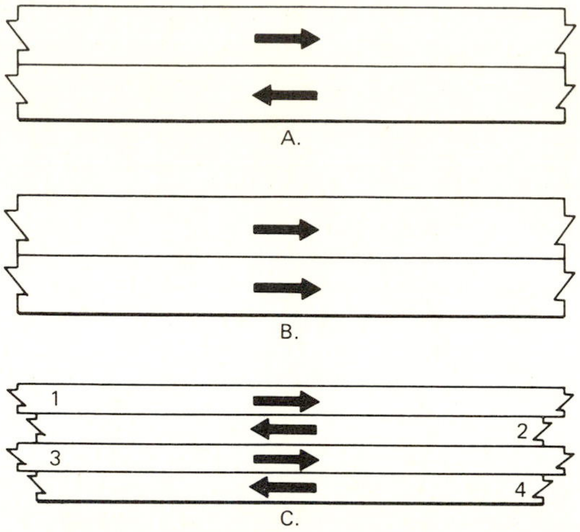

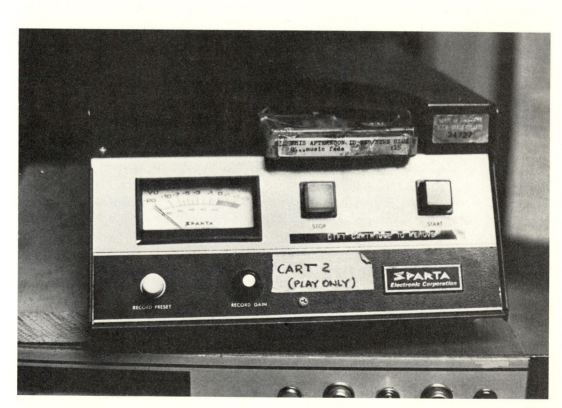

A. Half-track monaural. In monophonic recording, only half of the audiotape track is used for information as the tape is played in one direction. When the tape reels are reversed—the take-up reel is threaded up as the supply reel—and the tape is played in the other direction, the other half of the track is used.

B. Half-track stereo. Both tracks are used when the tape is played in one direction. One half contains the information for the left channel, and the other half-track is the right channel recording. In this configuration, the tape cannot be reversed and played back in the opposite direction.

C. Quarter-track (four-track stereo). In this more common stereo configuration, tracks 1 and 3 are used for left-channel and right-channel information when played in one direction. Tracks 2 and 4 are used for the stereo channels when the tape is reversed and played back in the opposite direction.

Figure 2-12   Audiotape track configurations.

Figure 2-13   Typical audio cartridge player.

quarter-track (or four-track) recording (most commonly used for stereo recording). (See fig. 2-12.) Finally, the audio operator must check to make certain that the supply reel (usually on the left side of the machine) and the take-up reel (which receives the audiotape, usually on the right side of the recorder) are the same size. Tape reels come in several diameters, and if the two reels are different sizes, there is a greater possibility of breaking the tape or spinning the tape off the reel when in either the fast-forward or rewind mode.

Audio cartridge playback was previously discussed (section 2.1.6). As a prerecorded source of sound in the audio signal flow model, cartridge playback would be handled in a manner similar to audiotape. The cartridge player would be located in the audio booth, convenient to the audio operator. Figure 2-13 shows a typical *cart* machine. Since there are no variations in tape speed, track configuration, and reel size, the use of the cartridge is uncomplicated. Also, because the cartridge automatically rewinds itself and is self-cueing, it is very simple to operate.

Records are still a very common source of prerecorded audio, primarily for musical selections and sound effects. Most audio control rooms will have one (ideally, two) record turntable (or turntables) capable of playing records at 78 rpm (revolutions per minute), 45 rpm, and 33⅓ rpm. As a source in the signal flow model, the turntables often are normalled into the audio console. The operator needs only to flip the right input selector switch, turn on the channel selector or off-on key, and the rec-

ord is on the air. In chapter 3 (section 3.4), we will discuss other aspects of operating these various audio sources—loading and threading audiotape, cueing up records and audiotape, special effects (such as echoes and cross-fading), riding gain, and using the television program monitor for audio cues.

Summary

As an introduction to the audio system, we have been concerned more with *technical* than with *creative* functions. The seven *basic control functions* are modulation (and demodulation), channeling, mixing, shaping, amplifiying, recording (and playback), and monitoring. These control functions were traced through the *audio signal flow* pattern: studio microphone input, through the patch bay, into the audio console, through an input selector switch, through the volume control or potentiometer/fader, into a specific channel, through the master potentiometer, out of the board through the line out, and back to the program-out position on the patch bay. This basic audio signal flow applies generally to any sound source—either a *microphone* or various *prerecorded sound sources* (film, videotape audio track, audiotape, audio cartridge, or record).

In the next chapter we will look more specifically at the microphone and consider some basic creative aspects of audio control.

2.5   Training Exercises

1. Make an outline of the equipment found in your own audio facility, using the seven control functions presented in this chapter.

2. Draw a sketch of both the audio patch panel and the audio console in your own facility. This will help you become familiar with the equipment, which will save considerable time as you later operate it.

3. Use the sketch along with the signal flow model in figure 2-8 to trace a signal flow sequence through the equipment of your own audio facility.

4. Compile a list of terms from this chapter that are somewhat unfamiliar. Write out an extended working definition relating to your own facilities. This is an excellent discipline to maintain with every chapter.

audio equipment and creative production techniques

3

As stated in chapter 2, the function of a microphone is that of translating the pressure waves that we can hear as music or voices (sound energy) into an electronic wave pattern (electrical energy). Most of what is broadcast, music or otherwise, is an incredible combination of fundamental and overtone frequencies. Imagine, if you will, a hundred-piece symphony orchestra, each instrument of which is producing at any given point in time a fundamental tone and ten or more related **overtone** frequencies—or **harmonics**—that fall within the range of the human ear. (See appendix B.) A relatively small number of well-placed microphones can do an amazing job of capturing sound. The problem faced in the design of a microphone is that of the accuracy or **fidelity** with which as many as possible of those frequencies are picked up and modulated.

3.1 The Microphone: Function and Construction

In order to be able to appreciate what kinds of microphones are best suited for specific jobs it is necessary to take a quick look at the phenomenon of audio **frequency range.**

Frequency Range

The optimum range of human hearing—from the lowest rumbles to the highest overtones—lies between 20 **hertz (Hz),** or **cycles per second,** and 20,000 cycles per second (Hz). Hearing ability, however, may vary greatly with the individual as a result of inherited characteristics or ear damage.

AM radio, FM stations, and television sound vary in ability to transmit a wide portion of the frequency range. AM transmission is somewhat limited in the broadcasting of music because of the fact that its upper frequency limit until recently was only 5,000 hertz. While an upper limit of 7,500 hertz has now been approved, most AM stations have not yet purchased the equipment necessary for this increased range. High fidelity sound is achieved on FM radio as a result of its ability to broadcast up to 15,000 hertz. The audio portion of the television signal is also received as FM sound with the same theoretical upper limit of 15,000 hertz. The average home TV set, however, is rarely equipped to take advantage of the higher frequencies, and as a result broadcasters do not utilize this potential.

One fundamental quality a person looks for in a microphone is the ability to capture the widest possible range of frequencies. Instruments become more expensive as the range of frequency response is expanded. A second important quality is that all of these frequencies should be picked up at the same proportion of volume at which they originally occur. Although some specialized mikes may reinforce high or low frequencies, it is the range and fidelity of frequency pickup that you pay for in a microphone.

Microphone Pickup Patterns

Another important criterion in selecting a microphone is its pickup pattern—the area within which the microphone can accurately pick up sound. Some microphones respond well to sound coming from only one direction; others can adequately pick up sound from all directions. In addition to information concerning the upper and lower limits of frequency response, most microphone manufacturers provide a pickup pattern for each model. It is an attempt to express pictorially the limits of a microphone's response pattern at stated decibel volume levels.

Such information has valuable applications for the trained audio engineer in determining its use. For the production student, the response pattern can be used more simply as an aid in determining the directional qualities of a mike. Such a two-dimensional visualization is called a *polar pattern* because it shows the limits of accurate mike response as they would be seen from above. The actual response pattern is in reality a three-dimensional sphere of varying shape.

Figure 3-1 shows an **omnidirectional** microphone (equal from all directions) response pattern. These microphones are also referred to as **nondirectional.** A mike with such a pattern would respond equally well to a sound source placed at any point on a circle (that is, sphere). The actual size of the circumference of the circle would vary with the volume level of the sound source. In other words, the effective range of a microphone can be expressed only in relation to a decibel volume level. (Obviously, the microphones in the illustrations have not been drawn to scale with the size of the response pattern.)

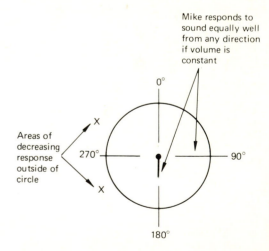

The omnidirectional microphone picks up sound equally well from all directions.

**Figure 3-1
Omnidirectional
microphone pickup
pattern.**

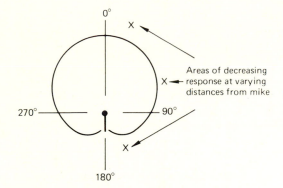

The cardioid or heart-shaped pattern represents a microphone which picks up sound primarily from one direction.

**Figure 3-2
Unidirectional
microphone pickup
pattern.**

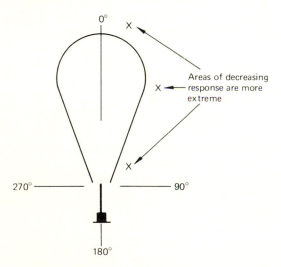

The highly directional microphone is designed to pick up sound, in a narrow response pattern, from relatively long distances.

**Figure 3-3   Highly
directional microphone
pickup pattern.**

Figure 3-2 illustrates a heart-shaped, or **cardioid** response pattern. Such a pattern is considered as being mainly from one direction, or **unidirectional.** Outside of the pattern area, some of the small **amplitudes** (lower volume) that constitute the sound source will not be picked up as well as others, if at all. The lesser amplitudes of overtone frequencies, for example, could be those that might be partly lost. The result is an **off-mike** distortion of the original sound.

Figure 3-3 illustrates a pear-shaped, *highly directional* pickup pattern. Specialized long distance, or **shotgun,** mikes operate with this sort of pattern structure. To further increase their sensitivity, they are sometimes used in conjunction with a parabolic dish, which can collect and concentrate a relatively distant audio source and reflect this focused audio beam directly into the microphone.

Standard radio production formats popularized the *bidirectional* microphone pickup pattern. These mikes picked up the sound equally well from either side of the instrument. This was a desired feature in radio drama and interviews because the speakers-actors could stand on either side of the microphone, facing each other while speaking. Obviously, there is little use for this feature in television production.

Microphone Construction: Transducing Elements

In addition to classification by pickup patterns, the audio operator should be familiar with the basic categories of microphone construction. Depending upon the purposes for which a microphone is to be used, there are several criteria that should determine selection of a mike for a particular job—*durability and ruggedness, frequency response, fidelity, physical use* (whether the mike is to be stationary or movable), *location* (to be used in a studio or outdoors), and *cost*. There are several ways that the actual transducing element of a microphone can be built; these different categories meet different criteria.

The **dynamic microphone** (see fig. 2-1) generally is the most rugged and dependable. It is sturdy and can stand more abuse than other commonly used microphones. It is especially useful for remote and outdoor locations. The diaphragm stands up well to moderate shocks and sudden variations in the intensity of sound, and they can be used close to the sound source, which is especially valuable in noisy locations where the announcer or singer must work very close to the mike. The frequency response is good, but not as sensitive as other types listed in the following discussion. The dynamic microphone, in its many variations and models, is probably the workhorse of the television industry today.

The **ribbon microphone** (also called velocity mike), by contrast, was the standard of radio production for many years. Its transducing element is a thin strip of metal foil. The mike is generally larger, less mobile, and considerably more delicate than the dynamic microphone. The quality and frequency response are very good, however, and it is an excellent mike for both voice and musical pickup, especially in the lower frequency range. Few new models have been developed in recent years, but the venerable standard still is in use in many television studios.

The **condenser microphone** (whose transducer is a variable capacitor activated by sound pressure waves) is also a high-quality, fragile instrument with a very wide frequency range. It requires a battery power source either within the mike itself or very near to it, which can be inconvenient at times. The excellent fidelity and wide frequency response, however, make this microphone popular for musical pickup wherever stationary mike placement is possible (for example, for an orchestral string section but not for a rock singer's hand mike). It is considered a superior microphone in professional recording studios.

Other types of transducing elements are used for specialized purposes, but none have the quality needed for broadcast usage. The less expensive *ceramic* and *crystal* elements, which translate vibrations from the diaphragm into electrical currents, have neither the fidelity nor the ruggedness needed for professional use. Granular *carbon* transducers are one of the earliest types of microphones. They are still used in telephones but have few other professional applications.

Impedance Levels

In our discussion of the audio console input selector switch (section 2.3.4), reference was made to differing impedance levels. **Impedance** refers to resistance to the flow of an electronic audio signal in the microphone cable. *High-impedance mikes* (those that have a high resistance) produce a stronger electrical signal than low-impedance mikes. They also tend, however, to lose the signal—especially the higher frequencies—if the cable length is much more than about fifteen feet. Microphones for home recorders are often high impedance.

The transducing element in a *low-impedance mike,* on the other hand, produces a lower output signal; but because there is low resistance to signal loss in the mike cable, the signal can be carried a greater distance to the audio console, where it is amplified. High-quality studio microphones are usually low impedance. Although the audio operator will seldom run into a high-impedance mike in a professional situation, it is important to be aware of this distinction. For example, many portable video recorders have provision for plugging in an external microphone. Although the patch connection may fit high-impedance mikes, the microphone input is probably low impedance; therefore, you cannot use your home microphone with the portapak.

3.2 Microphone Usage Categories

No single, all-purpose microphone has ever been designed. The most expensive microphone would have limitations in some situations. Instead, manufacturers provide a wide variety, each of which may combine a number of qualities suited to differing needs. A tremendous amount of time could be spent classifying the large variety of instruments available. However, it is not necessary for the television student to memorize a long list of microphones and their characteristics. It is of more immediate value if the student clearly understands some general usage classifications under which most mikes can be listed.

Some writers and practitioners have tried to classify microphones into the categories of *on-camera* and *off-camera*—those that are designed to be seen by the audience and those that are to be kept from view. Others have made the distinction between *stationary* and *mobile* microphones—depending upon whether or not the mikes are to be moved during the production. Rather than try to rely upon such clear-cut distinctions, which tend to overlap in practice, we would like to suggest the following three broad functional categories:

1. hand and/or stand mikes
2. limited-movement mikes
3. attached personal mikes

These categories are obviously artificial designations—devised for learning purposes only. (For instance, you will never find a section of a microphone cabinet labeled "attached personal mikes.") These classifications, however, should help you in thinking about the different ways in which microphones can be positioned and used—keeping in mind the positive qualities and limiting factors of each grouping. Also, these are not mutually exclusive categories; there is obvious overlap. Many mikes could fit into two of the groups.

Hand and/or Stand Mikes

Probably the most versatile group of mikes are those medium-sized, elongated instruments designed to work best at a range of six inches to three feet from a speaker or musical performer. Although a few require a fixed mount, most are structured to fit into a holder in a desk (for a news program or panel show) or a floor mike stand (for a performer). The same microphone is used as a hand-held mike for, say, an on-location news event or spontaneous interviews with members of an audience. This category overlaps both the stationary and mobile distinctions, for instance, in the case of a performer who begins a number by using a mike stand (stationary) and then removes the mike from the holder and concludes the number using it as a hand mike (mobile).

Resistance to the rugged handling of, say, a rock music performer is an important quality for such a mike. Most microphones in this category are *dynamic* mikes utilizing the coil and magnet transducer. Many such instruments have a **pop filter** that minimizes the plosive effect of *T*'s, *K*'s, and *P*'s. Such a mike is all the more useful if it is designed to function in the outdoor conditions of news and sports remotes. These mikes require a fairly wide angle of sound acceptance and are usually either omnidirectional or cardioid in their pickup pattern.

Limited-Movement Mikes

This category encompasses several different kinds of microphone applications from stationary, fixed position uses to a considerable amount of movement on large **perambulator booms.** Generally, microphones in this category would be larger than those that are intended to be hand held. Almost always, mikes in this grouping would not be intended for use on camera—they are seldom seen by the audience. As off-camera mikes, they are required to have good pickup qualities at relatively moderate to long distances. Some hand mikes, however, are designed to function adequately as omnidirectional boom mikes.

The label of boom mike can cover a wide variety of applications. The big boom, or *perambulator dolly* (see fig. 3-4), is a large, three-wheeled movable platform that holds the boom operator and has a long counterweighted boom arm that can be extended and tilted while the microphone itself can be rotated in almost a full circle. It is a large, cumbersome piece of equipment requiring two operators—one dolly pusher and one mike manipulator—and is effective only in spacious studios. They are used in pairs, for example, to cover the dramatic action in soap operas or to cover guests on a talk show such as "The Tonight Show."

A smaller boom, similar to that in figure 3-5, would be the *giraffe*—a counterweighted boom arm supported by a tripod on casters that can be operated by one person. Although not as flexible as the big boom, the giraffe can be moved easier and takes up much less floor space. Even though it is thought of as a movable boom, the giraffe is often stationed in a fixed position for an entire production.

Finally, we might consider the use of the **fishpole**—literally a small, lightweight pole to which the microphone is attached. The operator hand holds the pole in order to get the best audio position for any given scene. Although extremely flexible, the operation of this device can be quickly tiring, and it is prone to cause mistakes because of the inexactness in operation (causing boom shadows, dropping it into a picture, accidentally hitting scenery, and so forth).

There is today a group of larger and more versatile instruments, all of which have excellent omnidirectional frequency response for instrumental or voice pickup.

When sound must be picked up from unusually long distance (fifteen to twenty feet), there are several highly directional specialized instruments that are used. Older versions of the so-called shotgun mikes have a frequency range that is adequate for speech, or the related sound perspective of a sporting event, but not for instrumental music. Recent developments with the condenser shotgun, however, have resulted in a long-range microphone with excellent frequency response.

A special category of the fixed-position microphone would be the **hanging mike.** In certain situations (usually a drama) where it is impossible to mike a speaker in any other manner, it is possible to suspend an overhead microphone—hanging it from the catwalk or lighting grid. As a rule a dynamic microphone with a cardioid pattern would be used. Most audio directors would rely on a hanging mike only as a last resort because there are several disadvantages. The sound source is often fairly far from the microphone; the actor or speaker may be slightly out of position and no adjustment can be made to reposition the mike; the speaker is usually projecting—at best—at right angles to the microphone; and the mike is picking up the sound as reverberations off the studio floor, emphasizing any studio floor noises such as shoes and cables dragging. The result is most often a distant, off-mike quality with considerable ambient noise.

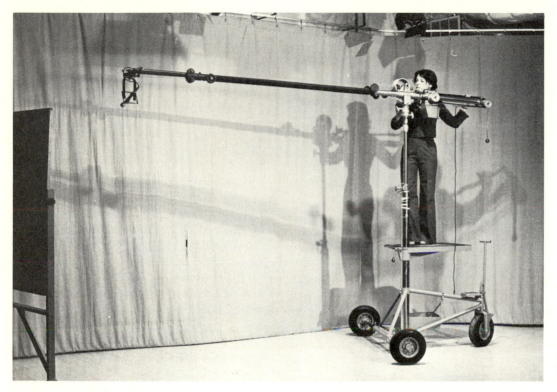

Figure 3-4 Medium-sized studio perambulator dolly microphone boom.

Figure 3-5 A giraffe or tripod microphone boom.

Attached Personal Mikes

Television created the necessity for an unobtrusive instrument that could move with the performer. The *lavaliere* microphone (worn around the neck) and the *lapel mike* are the result. Most of the earlier lavaliere models were effective omnidirectional mikes although they are limited to the frequency range of the human voice. Later models can filter out unwanted noise caused by clothing rubbing against the mike. The more recent lapel models have a frequency response more than adequate for instrumental pickup.

Since earlier models tended to be somewhat bulky and obvious, many performers tried to hide the lavaliere under a tie or inside a blouse with a resulting muffled audio quality. Later models are so compact (no larger than a small thimble) that they can be worn on top of clothing unobtrusively, with better audio pickup resulting.

The problems caused by mike cords have resulted in the development of the RF (radio frequency) **wireless microphone.** A miniature transmitter—either a part of the mike itself or in a concealed pack—sends an FM signal to a portable receiver that can be placed as far as several hundred feet from the performer. Although these systems have obvious advantages for television production, a propensity for dead spots in the transmission pattern and some limitations in frequency range have been the major limitations to their use. Recent progress with sophisticated receivers, however, has eliminated many of the problems.

3.3   Using the Microphone

The proper procedures for microphone utilization are largely a matter of common-sense application of a few simple principles. With this section, we begin to get specifically into the area of the creative functions of audio production. Most successful audio-microphone usage is just an extension of three basic considerations: selection of the correct microphone; microphone placement; and balance and perspective. To these add a considerable amount of experience.

Microphone Selection

In many small stations and university studios, the question of microphone selection may be purely academic. If you have nothing more than a few basic dynamic cardioid microphones, that is what you will use. In most larger situations, however, the audio engineer will have a choice of several different kinds of mikes for any particular production.

First define the audio job to be done. Let's take, for example, the task of picking up a well-tuned concert grand piano. Mikes should be selected on the basis of their known positive and negative qualities. Voice-frequency range lavalieres and older long-distance shotgun mikes are not going to pick up all of the true tonal quality of the piano. Any of several full-frequency ribbon or condenser stand mikes placed either inside or underneath the instrument can do this satisfactorily. These same mikes placed with the piano outside of the pickup pattern would be equally unsatisfactory.

If you are concerned with recording a pop vocal personality, you must take into consideration whether or not the singer is likely to want to use a microphone as part of the performance—as a hand prop. If the singer does, you would want to use a fairly rugged dynamic mike. If, however, the production calls for an off-camera boom mike, then a full-frequency condenser microphone might be used, especially if fidelity to the musical quality is uppermost.

When producing a news program or panel discussion, the full-frequency range of a condenser or ribbon mike is not necessary. Depending upon the "look" of the production, you may decide on either a dynamic desk mike (desk mikes are often subject to considerable table pounding and verbal abuse) or lavalieres.

Suppose you are to handle a remote assignment covering a parade or sporting event. You would probably want a rugged, relatively insensitive unidirectional dynamic mike for the narrator-announcer (to allow him or her to work closely to the mike, cutting out as much background as possible) coupled with a highly directional shotgun mike to pick up selected crowd or parade noise as desired. The first task, however, is always the same: define the job to be done in terms of frequency response needed, appropriate pickup pattern, physical abuse the microphone will likely be subjected to, and so forth.

Microphone Placement

Two factors dictate microphone placement. One is *aesthetic* and the other is *acoustical*. The aesthetic consideration is usually the desire of the director to avoid calling attention to the audio pickup device by trying to hide the microphone. In dramatic productions, the mike is camouflaged with the traditional vase in the center of the table or the boom mike is pulled far out of range in order to avoid boom shadow. On a newscast, the lavaliere is hidden under a shirt. It is attempted in a musical production to use boom mikes to pick up the sounds of a rock group instead of using stand mikes directly in front of the various instruments. In every case, audio quality is sacrificed for the sake of the picture. Be certain it is really worth the deterioration in audio reproduction before such aesthetic decisions are made.

Acoustical considerations for microphone placement can be thought of in terms of two areas: *audio direction* and *microphone distance*. Audio direction refers to having the source (voice or musical instrument) squarely in the path of the directional pickup of the

mike. (This applies, obviously only to unidirectional and highly directional mikes since omnidirectional microphones are, by definition, nondirectional.) If the audio source is not in the directional path of the microphone, or "on the beam," then the resulting pickup will be off-mike. This results in a hollow, distant effect similar to being too far away from the microphone.

The correct distance from source to microphone is at once a fairly simple and obvious matter and, at the same time, a highly complex study. As we discussed in section 3.1, the pickup pattern of any given microphone is relative to the volume of the sound source as measured in decibels (a standard unit of measurement of volume).

There is an important principle of physics that is of aid in figuring optimum microphone pickup distances and patterns. Although this textbook will not attempt to explain the mathematical complexities of the *inverse square law*, let us simply use the term as a way of identifying a concept that has important applications for microphone use. This law of physics states that as microphone-to-source distance is doubled, the loudness is reduced to one-fourth.

By looking at a VU meter, one can see that this is a considerable change in level. What this means in simple terms is that any change in source-to-mike distance is very critical when the sound source is working very close to a mike. The pickup level of a person speaking at a distance of one foot from a mike is considerably different from that of the same person standing two feet away. When that same person is either six or seven feet away, the difference of one foot is not as critical.

Depending upon the type of microphone and the audio quality desired, the optimum speaking distance may be anywhere from a few inches to several feet. A typical shotgun directional mike might give fairly good audio pickup as far away as ten or fifteen feet. Because of the pickup patterns, speakers should generally work closer to an omnidirectional mike than to a unidirectional mike. Under good studio conditions, with a normal speaking voice, the announcer or talent should work about a foot away from an omnidirectional mike and up to two feet away from a cardioid mike. These are only rough rules, of course, and much depends upon such factors as studio conditions, specific microphone characteristics, and vocal qualities.

Balance and Perspective

In establishing the overall sound quality, the audio director must also give consideration to the subjective factors of how various sources balance each other and sound in perspective to each other. No frequency response chart or VU meter can replace the human ear in determining the final sound of a program.

Getting the right proportion of volume levels from different sources is necessary. Are the musical instruments balanced? Is there too much piano for the vocal group? Are all of the panelists speaking at the same apparent level? Can a proper balance be achieved simply by adjusting volume levels with the faders, or should microphone placement be altered?

This last question gets into the area of audio **perspective**—an especially important concept in dramatic audio. Actors should appear to have an audio **presence**, or proximity that matches their video distance. The tighter a shot (the closer a character appears to camera), the closer a person should sound; as a character gets farther from camera, the more distant his or her voice should become. Thus, as two characters move in relation to each other on the screen, their audio perspective should change also. As a person walks out of a scene, his or her voice should appear to get

further off-mike; as a person looms larger on the screen, we should get the feeling of more presence. An extreme close-up shot often calls for an exaggerated audio intimacy—a stream-of-consciousness technique suggesting a stage whisper or aside to the audience.

This audio presence cannot be achieved simply by adjusting volume levels with the pots. Microphones have to move in relation to the actors. Either the actors walk further away from the microphones (to achieve audio distance) or the mikes, on booms or fishpoles, have to be moved away from the actors. Care must be taken to ensure that video distance and audio presence do not unintentionally contradict each other. Many an amateur dramatic effect has been ruined by using a hidden microphone concealed near a doorway in the rear of a set; the player then bids an emotional adieu only to have his or her audio presence increase as he or she walks away from the camera.

3.4 Adding Other Audio Sources

Up to this point we have been concerned entirely with the microphone as the source of television audio. We now turn our attention to other sources of prerecorded sound (as outlined in section 2.4).

Patching Audio Sources

All prerecorded audio sources generally come from one or two locations—either the audio control room or the telecine (the master control room). Those playback machines located in the audio booth (audiotape recorder, record turntables, cartridge player) either will be normalled (permanently wired) into the audio console or will be patched through the audio patch bay in the booth. Those audio sources coming from the telecine or master control (film projectors, videotape players) will probably be fed into the audio booth through some sort of external patching arrangement.

In many studio operations, the master control room has a patch bay similar to the one in the audio booth, except that the master control room patch bay has inputs not for microphones but for audio outputs from videotape recorders and film projectors. These audio outputs (and there often are two audio tracks per videotape recorder) can be fed to each other and to other terminals in master control and/or they can be connected to **tie lines.** The tie lines are used to connect the master control room with other key locations, such as a transmitter or the audio control room. It is these tie lines that are used for sending audio signals from the audio booth to master control (for example, the program audio from "line one out") where the audio can then be recorded on videotape recorders or sent out to the transmitter via further patching. Similar tie lines are used for sending various audio signals (for example, from film projectors and VTR machines) from master control to the studio audio booth for mixing into program audio.

Once the prerecorded audio sources are patched or normalled into the console, they then follow the signal flow as explained in section 2.3. The correct input selector switch for each source must be flipped on, the channel selector (pot on-off) key must be set, and the pot or fader is then used to control the volume. Like microphone levels, the volume level or gain of prerecorded audio should be adjusted to peak at close to 100 on the VU meter. Riding gain on prerecorded audio *should* be somewhat easier than riding gain on live microphones, because the prerecorded audio has already gone through a mixing and recording process and should be set at a fairly constant level.

Cueing Procedures

A crucial aspect of using prerecorded audio of any type is getting the sound **cued up** to exactly the right starting point so that the correct sound is available precisely when the director calls for it. Except for the audio cartridge, which cues itself automatically, this means that the audio operator is going to have to get the sound cued up at the correct spot.

For purposes of a detailed explanation, it would probably be most worthwhile to look at the specific procedures involved in cueing up a phonograph record. Although the layout of audio booths—the relationship of audio console and turntables—varies considerably, the following steps can be adapted to any situation.

1. Place the potentiometer in the **cue,** or **audition, position.** With a knob-type pot, this will be all the way to the left. With a slide-fader, this will be all the way to the bottom of the scale. This particular pot is now connected only to the cue audio system, which has its own speaker.

2. With the turntable power off, place the needle in the outside groove of the record. Lightly place your fingertips on the inside label of the record. Turn the record clockwise until the first tone is heard. (Most turntables are equipped with a felt pad that allows the record and the felt to move independently of the turntable surface.)

3. Stop the record at the first tone, now move it in a counterclockwise direction one-quarter of a revolution and stop. If the record is not backed up in this manner, it will **wow** as it comes up to speed when it is put on the air.

4. With your free hand, immediately take the fader (pot) out of the cue position, being careful to leave it at the "0" volume-level position. (More than one TV audio operator or beginning disk jockey has been blissfully unaware that the record he or she thinks is on the air is being heard only on the cue speaker.)

5. Just prior to playing, gently lay your fingers on the record. (With the slightest jolt, the needle will jump out of the groove.) Use your other hand to switch on the turntable power. This is called a *slip cue,* because the turntable is now up to playing speed while the record is being held in readiness.

6. At the proper command, the record is released and the pot is brought up to the desired level. The one-quarter turn now allows the felt to grip the turntable and bring the record up to playing speed. At this point, the timing of the operator is very critical. If the pot is already opened when the record is released, we will hear scratches prior to the first tone. If the operator is a fraction of a second late in opening the pot, the first tones will be **upcut.** This means that the beginning of the record either will not be heard at all or will be played at a very low level.

7. As soon as the record starts, you should immediately glance at the VU meter to see if any further adjustments in level are necessary. It is a good idea—prior to the actual production—to check the level of the opening section of any record to be used during a production situation. This *cannot* be done when cueing a record because the VU meter does not monitor any signal on the cue system.

If your turntable is equipped with a non-slip rubber mat, then the record must be started from a dead-stop position. In this case, a half revolution is suggested in order to bring the turntable up to playing speed to prevent a wow.

The practice of cueing up other audio sources is similar to the procedure involved in handling phonograph records, although the physical process of manipulating the medium is not as complex.

In fact, in working with videotape and film projection, the audio operator probably is not involved with loading the playback machine or concerned about the cueing process at all. This is usually handled by an engineer in master control or the projection-film chain area. The playback engineer will have the VTR machine or film projector threaded and cued up according to the film or videotape leader or footage counter, which indicates exactly how far before the desired sound and picture the machine is set. The primary job of the audio operator is simply to check his or her signal flow (input selector switch, channel selector key) and be ready to bring up the volume when directed to do so. In most studio situations, the audio booth will be equipped with a TV-line monitor. This enables the audio operator to see the actual TV program as it is being put together. Thus, the operator can get a visual cue for the videotape and film inserts—which reinforces the direct cue from the director—and time his or her audio starts accordingly.

In working with audiotape, however, the audio engineer has the responsibility for threading and cueing. Threading the audio-tape recorder is a simple process, as long as one carefully follows the threading diagram. Always check to be certain that the audiotape has not been incorrectly wound on the reel, that the magnetic side of the tape (usually dull) is threaded so that it comes in contact with the playback head of the recorder, and that the base (usually the shiny side) is facing away from the heads.[1] (The audio recorder has three or four heads arranged in a row— the erase head, the record head, and one or two playback heads. See fig. 3-6.)

In cueing up the audiotape, the principle is the same as for cueing records. Once the first tone is heard (with the pot set in the cue position), the supply and take-up reels should simultaneously be turned backwards by hand so that the first tone is about two inches from the playback head. (For tape recorded at 3¾ ips, it need only be about one inch; for 15 ips recordings, it should be closer to four inches.)

---

1. On most modern *video*tape, the oxide or magnetic side of the tape is the shiny side.

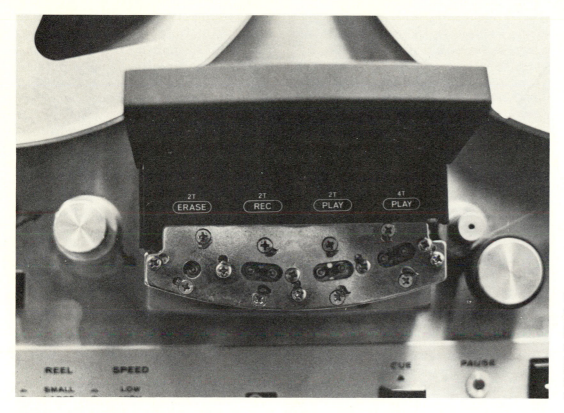

2T ERASE   2T REC   2T PLAY   4T PLAY

REEL   SPEED   CUE   PAUSE
SMALL   LOW

Figure 3-6 This stereophonic audiotape recorder has four heads—an erase head, record head, and two playback heads, depending upon the track configuration desired.

Mixing and Other Techniques

When two or more sound sources are mixed together—microphones and prerecorded sources or some of each—the audio operator must rely upon his or her ear to be sure that the balance is correct. Recorded music may vary considerably in volume within the space of twenty or thirty seconds of playing time. For this reason, the operator must be careful not to let a sudden increase in the volume of background music distract from what is being said. Unless otherwise occupied with cueing records or tapes, most audio engineers keep their hands right on the pots or faders in order to ride gain, constantly adjusting to even small changes in the input level.

Occasionally the audio mixing can be rather complex. Sometimes several microphones will have to be *potted down* (faded out)

simultaneously while a prerecorded announcer on audiotape is started. This can be accomplished on a dual-channel board if one of the channels has been converted (or can be switched) to a submaster; then the several microphones can be put on the submaster by means of the channel selector switch and controlled with one submaster pot.

At other times, there may be constant balancing and readjustment of several sound sources—say, background music on a tape, sound effects on a turntable, and two different microphones. Dramatic continuity may call for a **cross-fade** or **segue** between different musical selections. A cross-fade is a transition whereby one sound (musical record) is faded out while another is faded in, thereby effecting a temporary overlap of the two musical selections. A segue is similar except that the first sound is completely faded out before the second one is brought in. Both of these procedures call for the simultaneous control of two different turntables.

Continuous sound effects can be achieved with audiotape by **looping.** With a **reel-to-reel** player, a single tape loop can be spliced together and played continuously, which will give you several seconds of a background sound. With an audio cartridge player, by removing the stop-cue the entire cart loop will keep repeating.

Occasionally the audio operator may have to make some fast switching for special effects. Filters are often used to simulate a telephone conversation, for example. If the picture changes in the middle of one person's dialogue on the telephone (that is, if we are looking at John talking on the telephone and then the picture changes to Susan listening to John), we must instantaneously have a corresponding change in audio in order to maintain the proper sound perspective. Watching the TV-line monitor, the audio operator must make certain that we perceive the filter effect (to simulate the other end of the telephone conversation) when the picture changes from the speaker to a reaction shot of the listener.

Finally, mention should be made of echo effects. Even without fancy reverberation chambers and special devices, a simple echo effect can be achieved in most control booths with just one audiotape recorder. It is necessary only to patch and connect the tape recorder for simultaneous recording and playback. That is, the *line out* from the console must be patched into the *audiotape in* as well as the *audiotape out* being fed back into the console. Then by introducing an independent audio source, say a microphone from the studio, this source is recorded on the record head of the tape recorder and, as it passes over the playback head a split second later, fed back into the console. It can then be mixed—through the pot controlling the audiotape

playback—with the original sound coming directly from the studio microphone. The result is the original sound, followed a split second later by a recorded version of the same sound. Depending upon the level of the audiotape playback pot, this effect can range from a very slight echo suggestive of a large hall or cave to some very bizarre futuristic electronic distortions. When using this procedure, however, the operator must be careful to ride the gain on the master pot very closely; as the reverberation is increased, the feedback effect greatly amplifies the master level very rapidly.

3.5 Production Techniques

We are now approaching the point where you should be ready for your first production exercise. It may be helpful at this juncture to emphasize the difference between single-camera film techniques and the immediacy of a continuing process inherent in a multicamera TV production (see section 1.4). For this distinction generally shapes the nature of television production and determines the roles of the crew members.

Television and Film Production

Conventionally, live studio television seeks to achieve the nonstop production of entire programs or at least complete segments of programs. Film technique, especially as used in dramatic motion pictures, involves the shooting of multiple takes of short ten- to twenty-second segments. These are usually shot totally out of story sequence. Much of the art of filmmaking lies in the later painstaking editing process. In live television, the director is doing all of the editing as the program progresses. What you see (on the line monitor) is what you get.

With advances in technology, however, the two processes are gradually coming to resemble each other more and more. Various TV sports and public affairs programing borrows heavily from the film genre for its videotape editing techniques. The simultaneous use of three film cameras employed on several MTM productions is like live television, although there is a later editing process.

Television's primary virtue is that it is able to capture the reality of a continuing performance or event in real time, not a stop-and-go recreation of time. In the arts, this is an important ingredient of the creative process, especially for the performer. It is also essential to sports, news, and some public affairs programing.

Television's ability to function within the "real time" continuum, however, places considerable demands upon all of the crew members. Before beginning our initial class production exercise, we should mention the intercommunication network, the elements of vocal command procedures, and some audio setup procedures.

The Intercom Network

The system by which all production elements are brought together at the precise moment they are needed in a program is the intercommunication, or **intercom, network.** Also known as the **P.L.** (for *private line*), this is, in essence, a closed-circuit audio network that connects all primary production and engineering personnel by standard telephone **headsets** that have an earpiece and a small microphone or mouthpiece. Thus, the director can talk to the **stage manager** or **floor director**[2] without the conversation being picked up by any microphones; the technical director can talk to camera operators; the audio engineer can give

2. The terms *stage manager, floor manager,* and *floor director* are used interchangeably in this text. Used in different parts of the country, by different kinds of production centers, they all refer to the chief crew member on the floor—the director's surrogate for the studio stage.

commands to the boom operator; the associate director can check with the video recording engineer; and so forth.

Of course, with everyone trying to communicate with everyone else, the system would result in absolute and continual chaos—without a measure of discipline and self-restraint by all involved. Ordinarily the director predominates, and the system is at his or her disposal at all times; when the line is clear—or when the director specifically assigns the P.L. to some high priority function—the appropriate crew members have access to the system. In some large systems, separate P.L. networks may be set up for engineering and production personnel. Thus, the video engineer and technical director can carry on a conversation without interfering with the director and floor crew.

A double headset system also might be used by the audio personnel. This enables the audio director and boom operator(s) to hear the P.L. with one earpiece and to monitor the program audio with the other earpiece. This is invaluable for a boom operator who is following a fast-moving piece of dialogue among three people, for instance; he or she can directly monitor the balance and perspective being picked up while manipulating and adjusting the boom position.

The **studio address (S.A.),** or **studio talkback** system, is another link in the production crew intercommunication network. The S.A. talkback microphone in the control room (and there may be a parallel system out of the audio booth) enables the director to activate a special studio speaker so that he or she can talk to everybody in the studio, regardless of whether or not they are on P.L. headsets. (The S.A. speaker automatically cuts out the regular program microphone input to guard against any unintentional feedback, which could damage the audio system. Needless to say, the studio talkback should not be used

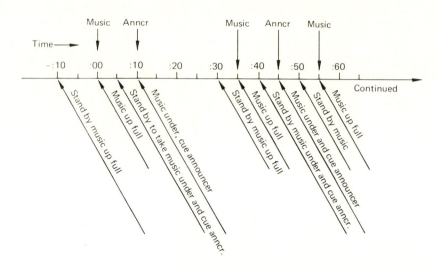

Figure 3-7   Time frame for a simple audio production.

This chart shows the commands to be given in a simple commercial announcement. The commercial starts at ":00" with music; the announcer reads the first copy starting at ":10"; music comes up full at ":35"; the second announcer starts at ":45"; music comes up full at ":55"; and so forth.

while microphones are activated during a program.) Part of the discipline of the television director is knowing when to use the S.A. (to communicate efficiently and quickly with the whole crew and all talent simultaneously) and when to rely on the floor manager (to interpret and carry out direct orders and implied threats).

The total intercommunication system is further extended—to the performing talent during the production—by the hand and arm signals of the floor manager. This is the pantomime system by which different directions can be given to persons while they are on camera without having to vocalize any commands and thereby possibly unintentionally getting these directions picked up as part of the program audio. (See appendix C for illustration of basic hand and arm signals.)

Vocal Command Procedures

At this stage, we also need to be aware of the vocal commands that are used to direct the entire production. Over the years, television production has evolved a system that separates commands into two phases—preparation and execution. The *commands of execution* are those cues that directly affect what goes out over the line monitor. "Take camera one" and "Cue the announcer" call for an immediate action at a precise point in time. For a crew member or performer to be able to respond with this immediate action, however, he or she must be given adequate preparation time to be mentally ready and/or physically prepared to perform some action or operate the equipment. For this reason, all commands of execution must be preceded at some point by a related *command of preparation*. Figure 3-7 shows how the commands fit into the time frame of the production sequence for a simple audio exercise. (The commands and timing indicated in fig. 3-7 are designed to be used with the commercial/production exercise in appendix D-1.)

The term *standby* (announcer, music, record, and so forth) is probably the most functional preparatory command for our present needs. *Cue* is quite often used to begin a command of execution. Sometimes just the term *music* or *announcer* can be used as the command of execution. Complete voice command procedure for a total television production is, of necessity, somewhat more complicated than what we have presented here; other commands will be discussed in conjunction with the explanation of video-switching procedures (section 7.5).

Audio Setup Procedures

Finally, prior to the initial class audio-production exercise, we should outline some basic steps in an audio setup. During any production setup, the audio assistants will follow the audio engineer's instructions as to which studio inputs to use and where to set up the mikes. This is an important introduction to the concept of position responsibility within the chain of command. By the same token, it is the director who has the ultimate responsibility for the operation.

The person in charge of audio should first go through the entire signal flow process mentally before giving any instructions. If a mike does not work, it is he or she who must initiate a step-by-step signal flow checkout. To gain the most from any training exercise, it is suggested that all patches and mike cords be unplugged and redone with new input numbers as each new director takes over.

Once the mikes are all working, the audio operator should get a **level** from each of the performers. Different person's voices vary considerably in strength. Using the VU meter, the audio operator can find an optimum position on the potentiometer for each voice. This is an average or middle position between the highest and lowest movements of the needle. The highest points or peaks should only occasionally exceed the 100 percent modulation position of the meter.

Summary

As part of the *technical* requirements for audio production, it is important to know something about *microphone construction*—frequency response, pickup patterns, construction of transducing elements (dynamic, ribbon, condenser, and other types), and impedance levels. These factors determine the way different microphones can be physically handled—as hand or stand mikes, limited-movement mikes, and attached personal mikes. Getting into *creative* considerations, the audio director must be concerned with the way microphones are utilized—*selection* and *placement* of the mikes, and *audio balance* and *perspective*. In adding other prerecorded sound sources, the audio operator must also be familiar with *patching* from different areas, *cueing* techniques for various media, and *mixing* procedures. In preparation for our first audio-production exercise, the audio operator must also understand basic television production procedures, the *intercom network, vocal commands,* and the *audio setup* operations.

In the next chapter, we turn from audio to video considerations as we look first at lighting requirements and techniques.

3.6   Training Exercises and Class Audio Project

Class Exercises

1. Prepare a list of all of the microphones that are available for use in your own facility. Using the manufacturer's specifications, if available, describe the specific design qualities for each, as well as any limitations that should be noted.

2. Go through a live demonstration for each mike, showing the pickup pattern and range of frequency response. Listen carefully for the distinctive differences in sound quality occurring in each of the basic types of instruments.

Class Audio Production Project (Appendix D-1)

This audio production exercise is in the form of a radio commercial. It is designed to develop the techniques and disciplines needed to set up microphones and mix two announcers with music. Although one mike could be adequate, it is suggested that two stand or desk mikes be used for the exercise. This use will provide more practice in setup, patching, and operational techniques. The mikes should be placed at least three feet apart and side by side so that both announcers can see the stage manager's signals. The announcers should work about twelve to eighteen inches from each mike.

First of all, let us consider the production elements that must fit together in a precise sequence for the initial portion of the commercial script. We will first establish the music, which is then faded under (that is, at low volume, below the announcer's voice but still audible) for the announcer who speaks for twenty-five seconds. The music is then brought up again for ten seconds, then under again as the second announcer speaks for twenty seconds. The music is brought up again, and we have completed the first part of the commercial. Figure 3-7 illustrated the production time frame.

It looks simple, and it really is, just as long as the two announcers and the audio engineer are able to coordinate their actions. For this we need some sort of director. In most smaller audio operations, the audio engineer would serve this function. As preparation for our later, more complicated television production exercises, it is suggested that a separate person act as director.

tv lighting equipment and techniques

4

Television production consists basically of two elements—audio and video. Chapters 2 and 3 dealt with audio. Chapters 5 through 10 deal specifically with different aspects of the television picture. (The rest of the book is concerned with putting it all together.) Before we can look at how cameras and lenses work, however, it is necessary to spend some time looking at that physical phenomenon that makes all vision possible—light! Without light there would be no video. And without good lighting there would be no good video.

4.1 Types of Light: Incident and Reflected

Light comes to us in two somewhat different forms. There is light that comes directly from a source such as the sun, a light bulb, or a candle. This is called **incident light** and, as important as it is, tells us little beyond the fact that we are looking at a light source.

We see as a result of a second kind of light, which has been reflected from and, as a result, altered by the surface of a material substance. It is this **reflected light** that transmits information to us regarding our environment. The brain has been conditioned to respond to this information as perceived by the eye.

As children, we had to touch things repeatedly to reinforce the realities of the input of other senses (sight, sound, taste, and smell). As we matured, we conditioned ourselves intellectually to "believe our eyes."

We can perceive the shape as well as other more subtle qualities of an object by the way in which light and shadow are reflected back to us from the object. Take as an example the instructor's desk in a classroom. The dimensions of the top of the desk are defined for us by the uniform intensity of the light reflected from all points of its surface.

The light reflected from the side of the desk is of a different intensity, possibly somewhat of a shadow; this tells us that these side surfaces are at a different angle from the top and indeed are the sides of the desk. Other features, such as drawer handles and the legs, are defined by the shadows the light molds around them. The metal parts of the desk will reflect light still differently.

Reflected light also tells us much about the texture of a surface. The even, shiny quality of light reflected from the desk top denotes a hard surface. Cloth would be much more light absorbent. We can perceive the texture of a heavy cloth material by the many shadows created by the design of the weave.

Although incident light is important as a way of measuring light intensity, we shall see that it is the way we shape and control reflected light that determines what the TV camera perceives as a picture.

4.2   Lighting Objectives: Basic Illumination

Broadly speaking, all television lighting is for one of two reasons: *basic illumination,* which refers to the minimum level of light needed to enable the TV camera to pick up an acceptable picture adequately; and *artistic* or *creative lighting,* which is the shaping and molding of light sources in order to achieve the desired aesthetic effect. These two categories correspond to the basic technical and creative functions as introduced in section 2.1.

In providing basic illumination, there are three different concepts that the lighting director must keep in mind: the minimum amount of light needed for adequate illumination, or the **base light;** the brightness contrast range, or **contrast ratio;** and the correct color quality of the light, or the **color temperature.**

Base Light

In establishing the base light the usual method is to light specific set areas and performers first—establishing the desired creative effects (see section 4.3) and then adding additional fill light as needed to bring all areas up to the requisite basic illumination levels. This method is especially important for productions where the creative lighting aspects play a key role in conveying the total message, for example, in dramatic productions, some documentary segments, and musical numbers.

The lighting director must be aware of the overall accumulation of both direct and reflected light that comprises the total base light. The light from the specific spotlights may reflect off the background and back onto the set. The portion of the back light (see section 4.5) that does not fall upon the head or shoulders can be reflected up from the floor or the top of a table. The lighting director should be aware of the amount of this accumulated light strength before setting the fill light, which contributes mainly to the basic illumination. In color television especially, it is important that the base light level be as consistent as possible throughout the entire set. When it is not, wide shots tend to show "muddy" areas of poor color quality.

In essence, the basic illumination requirements—or base light needs—are met once the proper levels of key, back, and fill lighting are established (see section 4.5). The base light is the sum total of the key, back, and fill lights.

Light Meter.   The human eye has a much greater tolerance for variations in the intensity of light than does the television camera. The relatively narrow range of what is acceptable as an adequate light level is difficult to judge with the unaided eye. For this reason, all lighting for television should be done with the aid of a **light meter.** Using the **footcandle** (ftc) as a unit of measurement, the meter shows the intensity of light coming from the direction in which the meter is pointed.[1] A camera's upper and lower limits, as stated in footcandles, are a known factor, in much the same way that a microphone manufacturer will list the upper and lower audio frequencies to which the microphone will respond. By using a light meter properly, the lighting director can take most of the guesswork out of a preproduction lighting session.

The strength of illumination for television purposes is measured in two different ways. We can find out how much light is falling upon a subject by holding the meter very near the subject and pointing it toward the light source.

1. One footcandle is the amount of light that would fall upon a surface placed at a distance of one foot from an established theoretical source approximating the light of one candle.

This incident light measure tells us only how much light arrives at a given point. The reading is helpful primarily in determining the correct amount of base light. Different kinds of television camera pickup tubes require different intensities for the base light. Generally, the newer cameras and more advanced tubes require lower light levels than the older image-orthicon and earlier vidicon tubes (see section 5.2).

Of even more importance to the television camera is the amount of light reflected from the various surfaces of the subject into the camera lens. For this reflected light reading, point the meter directly at the subject. The meter should be held close to the subject, but care must be taken to avoid blocking the light source. Obviously these two methods of measuring light (incident and reflected) will result in two greatly varying readings (see fig. 4-1).

Incident
Light
Reading

Reflected
Light
Reading

An incident light meter "reads" the actual amount of light, in footcandles, coming from the light source. A reflected light reading indicates the amount of light reflected back from the surface of the subject being lit.

Figure 4-1 Incident and reflected light readings.

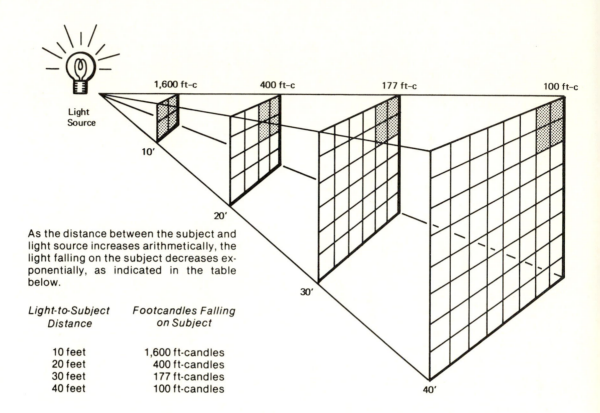

As the distance between the subject and light source increases arithmetically, the light falling on the subject decreases exponentially, as indicated in the table below.

Light-to-Subject Distance	Footcandles Falling on Subject
10 feet	1,600 ft-candles
20 feet	400 ft-candles
30 feet	177 ft-candles
40 feet	100 ft-candles

Figure 4-2 Inverse square law applied to television lighting.

These two different types of readings are used for different purposes.

Depending upon the texture and material of a surface, only a percentage of the original source light is reflected into the camera. A light green knitted dress could reflect 30 to 40 percent of the footcandles falling upon it. A black knitted dress might reflect less than 5 percent. A white vinyl jacket might reflect well over 90 percent.

Most lighting directors first set their base light levels by measuring incident footcandle power as it comes directly from the lighting instruments. Variations in skin tone and clothing are later checked as reflected readings when the performers are in place.

The same *inverse square law*, which determined for us that sound from a source drops off in ratio to the square of the distance from

that source as the distance is increased (see section 3.3), also applies to the rate at which light strength decreases with distance. Figure 4-2 gives an indication of how critical a move of even ten feet can be.

Note that, while stated in simple terms, the inverse square law of physics tells us that light diminishes in intensity at a constant rate. For television lighting, this drop-off rate is very critical when the distances to the source are relatively small. For this reason, most studio lighting (in larger studios) is done at a range of twenty to forty feet. We can use the example of a 2,000-watt lamp that projects a moderate amount of light when used as a key light at a distance of thirty feet. It becomes very powerful when used as a back light at a distance of less than fifteen feet (see section 4.5 for definitions of key light and back light.)

Contrast Ratio

Among the complexities of the television camera pickup tube is the way in which it reacts to differing degrees of brightness within a single picture. For example, in an evenly lit living room scene on a wide shot, the colors are correctly balanced and the detail of the picture is clear. Now, as we introduce into this shot a person wearing a white raincoat who fills one-quarter of the left-hand side of the frame, several rather drastic things happen.

Without any changes in either the lighting or the camera, the right-hand three-quarters of the picture will suddenly become much darker. The colors will have a somewhat muddy tone, with the details of the set obscured. The raincoat will be an out-of-focus blur and the person's face a dark spot. Stated in simple terms, the acceptable range of contrast between the brightest and the darkest elements of the picture has been greatly exceeded. The light level that was previously sufficient for a picture has been "compressed" by the introduction of an overpowering amount of light.

The human eye can accept a *contrast range* of up to one hundred to one. A somewhat conservative but safe figure for television would be nearer thirty to one—or even twenty to one. This means that the brightest elements within a picture should not be more than twenty or thirty times as bright as the darkest elements.

When elements reflect greatly varying amounts of light (such as the raincoat and the person's face in our example), the problem is even more critical. It is then referred to as a contrast ratio between the two elements. As a rule, lighting directors should try to avoid a contrast ratio more than about twenty to one. The picture generally will look better if an extreme ratio is avoided.

While the relative size and degree of brightness of the raincoat in our example is somewhat extreme, the basic principle of contrast range and contrast ratio is an important one to observe when lighting any set or, more important, the people within that set.

There is a very common error that often occurs as students are learning lighting techniques. The faces in the picture may seem too dark, so to solve the problem, more and more light is added to the set, which falls upon the face and on the background. The problem usually is that there is already too much light being reflected from a light-colored background in relation to the light reflected from the face. The problem is compounded if there is too much back light hitting the hair and shoulders (section 4.5).

In summary, it should be noted that the level of *basic illumination* can best be determined by a direct incident light meter reading. On the other hand, the contrast ratio can be determined only by a comparison of reflected light readings from the brightest and darkest elements in the picture.

Color Temperature

One other factor must be taken into consideration when working with base light for color television. This is the phenomenon of color temperature. You have probably noticed that different light sources may have slightly different color tints. A fluorescent bulb gives off more of a bluish light compared to a reddish incandescent tungsten bulb. When working with monochrome cameras, the color temperature of different light sources has no effect at all on the picture quality. In color television, however, the pickup tube is very sensitive to the color temperature of various kinds of light sources.

The color temperature of light is actually measured on a scale known as the Kelvin scale; different light sources are calibrated in degrees Kelvin (K). The redder a light source is, the lower the Kelvin temperature; the bluer a source, the higher the Kelvin temperature. A color temperature between 3,000 degrees K and 3,200 degrees K is considered to be the ideal white light for color television. Most color television lighting is designed to fall within the range of 3,000 degrees K to 3,400 degrees K.

If a light with an ideal Kelvin temperature (say 3,200 degrees K) is used on a dimmer, however, its color temperature will decrease as the lighting instrument is supplied with less and less voltage (see section 4.6). Thus, a light may give off a perfect white light when operated at full intensity; but when the light is brought down on the dimmer, the subject being lit gradually takes on a reddish tint. This color distortion is not readily perceived by the naked eye, but the color camera is very sensitive to any drop in color temperature over a couple of hundred degrees Kelvin. This is a common error that beginning lighting directors make. Once you have determined that a specific lighting instrument is the correct color temperature (most lighting sources designed for color television are rated at 3,200 degrees K), make certain that you do not lower the voltage of the light by using it on a dimmer.

4.3   Lighting Objectives: Creative Purposes

As a creative or artistic element, lighting can be said to have three main purposes: (1) to define the shape and texture of physical form; (2) to imitate the quality of light characteristic of a situation or setting in reality; and (3) to establish and enhance the psychological mood of a performance or setting. At first glance, it might seem that the last two of these purposes apply only to dramatic productions. This is not necessarily true. These principles apply to all types of programs from game shows to live news remote transmissions.

Shape and Texture

We view television on a flat surface. The illusion of depth is created, to a great extent, by an exaggerated use of the effects of light and shadow. (Careful attention to the rules of perspective is also an important lighting consideration but is more often thought of as a function of set design. See section 10.1.) It is through this artificially produced dimension of depth that the eye is able to reconstruct for the brain the real or intended shape and texture of an object.

The experienced lighting director knows that it is the manipulation of shadows, rather than bright spots, that can most effectively add form and texture to any object. Light coming from the side or rear of an object will throw shadows in certain shape-defining ways. Lighting from exactly the same direction as the camera can eliminate the shadows of a rough texture and make the surface look relatively smooth; whereas extreme side lighting (at right angles to the camera position) will emphasize textural quality by exaggerating shadows, making any object appear much rougher than it is.

Reality

Light operates on our conditioned responses in other equally important ways. We all have tuned in to the middle of a television play and watched a series of close-up shots. We usually, either consciously or unconsciously, are aware of being indoors or outdoors and of the time of day by the quality of light on the actor's face. It is probably outdoors and near noontime if the light is relatively bright and there are definite shadows under the eyebrows, nose, and chin of the actor. The scene may have been shot inside a studio, but the *imitation of reality* is a product of the lighting.

Other specific shadow and lighting effects suggest certain kinds of realistic situations. Shadows of venetian blinds or prison bars cast on the rear wall of a set help to suggest a particular locale. Other **off-camera** lighting effects help to pinpoint a setting: a low-angle flickering light indicates a campfire or fireplace; a continually flashing red light indicates the presence of an emergency vehicle. Other effects help to carry forth the dramatic narrative: a shaft of light coming from under a door of a room previously unoccupied indicates the presence of an intruder; a flashlight probing around a darkened room helps reveal evidence of a struggle.

Mood

Similarly, the psychological *mood* of a performance or production can be reinforced by the quality of light and its abundance or absence. Comedy is bright; **high-key lighting** is used, which gives an intense overall illumination with a fully lit background. Situation comedies, game shows, and big musical num-

bers in a variety program would rely on this kind of lighting to establish a light-hearted mood.

Conversely, tragedy or fear are communicated when the area surrounding an actor is dark or dimly lit. **Low-key lighting** refers to selective lighting that reveals only the necessary elements of a picture: usually the background is dark, extreme lighting angles may be used, and only part of the picture is disclosed. Again, specific dramatic moods may be reinforced by special effects: a flashing neon sign outside a sparsely furnished hotel room suggests a seedy part of town; lightning flashes create an eerie mood; lighting from a low angle tends to give a character a sinister, unnatural appearance.

Special low-key lighting effects are also used in nondramatic situations. **Cameo lighting**—where the performer is lit but the background is completely dark—may be used for a somber musical number (fig. 4-3). A **silhouette** effect—with the performers kept in darkness but outlined against a brightly lit

Figure 4-3 Typical cameo lighting: figure against a dark background.

Figure 4-4
Representative
silhouette lighting, dark
figures against a light
background.

background—may be desired for a dance routine (fig. 4-4). A single shaft of light may be used to accent a contestant in a suspenseful climax of a game show.

So, above and beyond the necessity of using enough light for basic illumination, the lighting director also must plan the lighting in order to add shape and texture, heighten the illusion of reality, or create and enhance a specific mood.

4.4 Types of Lighting Instruments

To understand the process whereby the basic illumination and creative purposes of lighting can be achieved—and before we turn to the fundamentals of lighting techniques—we should briefly examine the essential equipment that has been developed to achieve these various objectives. Allowing for some specialized variations, it can be said that all of the instruments used for studio and remote lighting are of two basic types: **spotlight** or **floodlight,** as illustrated in figure 4-5.

Although most of the illustrations used in this chapter are shown symbolically with an **incandescent** bulb, it should be noted that this type of bulb has largely been replaced by the smaller and more efficient quartz bulb, even though the incandescent bulb is still found in a wide variety of applications. Actually, the term **quartz light** is often loosely applied to a whole specialized variety of quartz-iodine, tungsten-halogen, and similar bulbs that have been developed in recent years.

The advantages of the quartz instruments are that they are much smaller than incandescent bulbs; they are much more efficient (often producing double the illumination of an incandescent bulb of the same wattage); they do not darken with carbon deposits as they age; and they do not vary in color temperature as they wear out, so they are especially valuable for color television. They do, however,

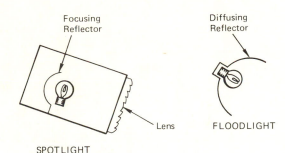

The distinguishing characteristics of the spotlight are the focusing reflector and the lens which combine to allow the light beam to be focused on a particular spot. The floodlight, on the other hand, throws a diffused or unfocused spread of light over a wide area.

Figure 4-5 Basic spotlight and floodlight.

have some disdavantages. Quartz bulbs wear out about twice as fast as incandescent bulbs; they operate at very hot temperatures, giving off quite a bit of heat; and the light beam cannot be focused and controlled as precisely as an incandescent bulb. For this last reason, in particular, many stations combine incandescent and quartz instruments, using quartz floodlights for a high intensity base light and incandescent spotlights for a more controllable specific lighting instrument.

Spotlights

The spotlight is used wherever a highly directional beam of light that can be shaped and focused is desired. Its chief characteristic is the ability to throw a spot of light on any particular area or performer. Probably the most versatile and widely used type of spotlight is the classic **Fresnel** (pronounced without the *s*).[2] Figure 4-6 shows the characteristic structure of the Fresnel lens.

2. The lens generally used in the instrument has a series of raised concentric rings on the outer face that help to dissipate the tremendous heat built up in the enclosed structure. Augustin Jean Fresnel was a nineteenth-century scientist who did important research into the nature of light.

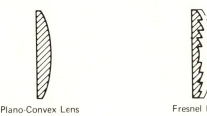

The plano-convex lens and the Fresnel lens have the same surface curvature, enabling them to share identical focusing characteristics. However, by using a succession of concentric ring-shaped steps—with the surface curvature of each concentric ring being congruent with the same relative spot on the corresponding surface of the plano-convex lens—the weight and bulk of the Fresnel lens is substantially reduced.

Many lighting personnel refer to any spotlight by the label of *Fresnel*—although the term specifically is a description of lens structure—regardless of the manufacturers' brand names. The focusing characteristics of the spotlight are shown in figure 4-7.

The most distinctive feature of a Fresnel spotlight is the movable bulb and reflector unit with its outside control spindle.[3] The beam, which is already focused by the action of the reflector and lens, can be further "pinned" to a small intense area or "spread" to cover a much wider area. Many models are designed to go from an intense spotlight with a beam angle of 10 degrees to a diffused floodlight effect with a beam angle of 60 degrees. The models most generally in use range from 500 watts to 10,000 watts. Fresnel spots are also classified by the diameter of the lenses. The most common studio sizes are the six-inch, eight-inch, ten-inch, and twelve-inch models.

The **ellipsoidal**, or **leko**, spotlight shown in figure 4-8 gains its name from its fixed reflecting mirror at the back of the unit. By

3. The focusing mechanism described here (and pictured in fig. 4-8) is moved forward or backward by turning a crank or focusing spindle. Other spotlights accomplish this by means of a focusing ring or ring focus, or (on smaller quartz instruments) by a horizontal focusing lever.

Figure 4-6 Design of the Fresnel lens.

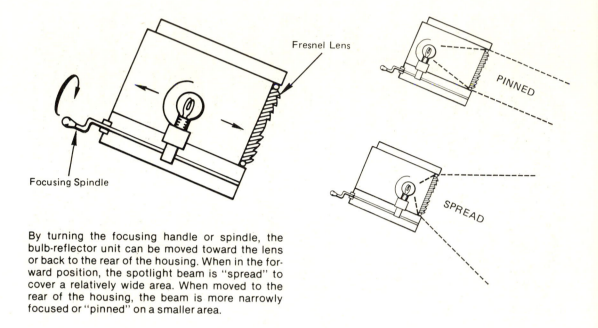

Fresnel Lens

PINNED

SPREAD

Focusing Spindle

By turning the focusing handle or spindle, the bulb-reflector unit can be moved toward the lens or back to the rear of the housing. When in the forward position, the spotlight beam is "spread" to cover a relatively wide area. When moved to the rear of the housing, the beam is more narrowly focused or "pinned" on a smaller area.

Figure 4-7 Focusing mechanism of the Fresnel spotlight.

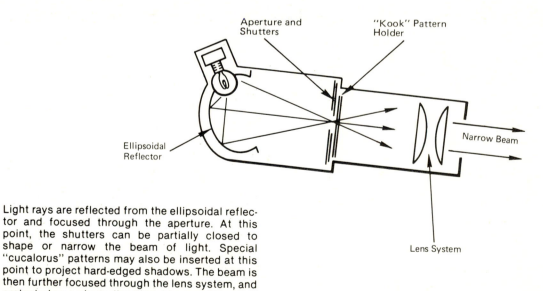

Aperture and Shutters

"Kook" Pattern Holder

Narrow Beam

Ellipsoidal Reflector

Lens System

Light rays are reflected from the ellipsoidal reflector and focused through the aperture. At this point, the shutters can be partially closed to shape or narrow the beam of light. Special "cucalorus" patterns may also be inserted at this point to project hard-edged shadows. The beam is then further focused through the lens system, and projected as a sharp directional beam with a well-defined edge.

Figure 4-8 Lens system of the ellipsoidal spotlight.

Figure 4-9 Example of a shadow pattern cast by a "cookie" inserted in a Leko (ellipsiodal) spotlight.

means of its tube shape and focused lens (either Fresnel or **plano-convex**), it projects an intense directional beam that is well defined at its edge point.

The beam can be further shaped by movable metal shutters located inside the lamp housing, behind the lens. At this point—where all the reflected rays of light are in sharp focus—there is also a place to insert a patterned metal design cutout. The shadow of this **cucalorus,** or **cookie**, or **kook** is then projected to add visual interest to large, plain background surfaces. Some common kook patterns include prison bars, arabesques and Moorish motifs (fig. 4-9), venetian blinds, crosses, squares and other geometric designs, cloud patterns, and so forth.

Because it throws a very harsh beam, the ellipsoidal spot is rarely used as the basic in-strument in lighting a person or object for tele-vision. It is to be used strictly as a special effects light.

There are several other varieties of fixed-beam spotlights. One popular type is much like an auto headlight with the lens, bulb, and reflector built together as a single unit. This *internal reflector* spotlight is common as a portable source of light, or—as a *clip light*—it often is used to fill in and highlight areas that are otherwise not adequately lighted.

Another type of portable spotlight is the *external reflector* model, which is a highly ef-ficient quartz lamp in a small housing with no lens. Although not as controllable and precise as a Fresnel spot, this model is lightweight, easily moved (often with a clip-on attachment or a lightweight tripod), and is more than ad-equate for most remote lighting assignments.

Floodlights

The job of the floodlight is to produce wide-spread diffused illumination from as undefined a source as can be achieved. Ideally, this means as little shadow as possible. This can best be accomplished by using a *large source area* rather than a pinpoint source such as a spotlight, with its harsh filament and focusing reflector.

To help achieve the shadowless effect of a large source area, the floodlight does not use a lens; it will probably have a diffusing reflector, which has the effect of spreading out the source; it may use a soft-light bulb with no exposed filament at all; and it may use a **scrim**—a soft, spun-glass filter or other translucent piece of material in a rigid frame, attached to the front of the instrument (see section 4.6).

The classic model for a floodlight is the one-half hollow globe structure known as a **scoop** (fig. 4-10). Scoop sizes vary, but the 1,000-watt and 2,000-watt bulbs generally are the most useful.

The development of the quartz lighting element has added to the popularity of a variety of square-shaped floodlights. (See fig. 4-11.)

Known variously as **pans** or **broads,** these instruments come in a wide variety of sizes, designed for both studio operation and remote locations. Their square shape makes possible the additional use of deflecting devices known as **barn doors** (see section 4.6).

When a series of pans are constructed in a continuous side-by-side row, they are called **strip lights.** (See fig. 4-12.)

Strip lights are most often used to project color—by means of colored **gels**—onto a background **cyclorama (cyc)** or other large set surface. In monochrome studios, strip lights are also used to help light the cyc; they are especially valuable in lighting the background cyc evenly from top to bottom for silhouette effects.

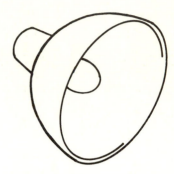

Scoops are designed both for incandescent bulbs and for quartz lighting. Popular sizes for most television studio applications are the 14-inch and 16-inch diameters.

Figure 4-10   The basic scoop.

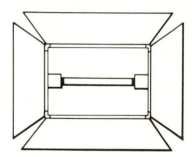

Pans and broads are popular quartz floodlights. Some have adjustable beams which enable them to be used from medium-flood to full-flood positions.

Figure 4-11   Pan with barn doors.

This brief review of lighting instruments barely suggests the number and variety of equipment that are available. In the past decade, leading manufacturers have developed a whole new generation of highly efficient, lightweight, and portable lighting systems. This section has been presented to provide a practical background for an understanding of the principles on which all stage, film, and television lighting is based.

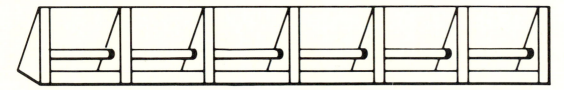

Designed either for incandescent or quartz lamps, the strip lights can be built in a number of different configurations—ranging from three to twelve bulbs in one strip.

Figure 4-12 Six-lamp strip light.

4.5 Fundamental Lighting Concepts

In lighting an individual performer or talent, there are three fundamental types of lighting that one needs to be concerned with. This basic lighting approach is sometimes referred to as **three-point lighting.**

Three-Point Lighting

The three primary sources of lighting for most nondramatic situations consist of the **key light,** the **fill light,** and the **back light.** They differ from each other in relative direction (or apparent source), intensity, and the degree to which they are either focused or diffused. Special effects and some kinds of dramatic circumstances might call for only one or two of the three to be used in a certain situation. Generally, in a well-balanced lighting setup, all three types are present. Figure 4-13 illustrates how the three are used in a typical situation. Taken together, this three-point lighting arrangement provides not only the *basic illumination* but also meets the *creative purposes* of form and texture, reality, and mood.

Key light is the primary, most important illumination in any lighting plan. It is the apparent source of the light hitting the talent. (See fig. 4-14.) Invariably, a spotlight is used for the key light; its strength and directional beam emphasize the contrast of light and shadow, bringing out the shape and texture of the subject. It is the use of the key that shapes the structure of the face and features, including the eye itself. The key should be placed off to one side of the talent, coming in at an angle between 30 and 45 degrees. (If the key light is placed directly in front of the talent, the result is a flat, washed out appearance with no shadows, no sculpting or molding of the face.) The height of the key will depend to a great extent upon the facial contours of the talent. It should be placed high enough to give some shadow under the chin and nose, yet it must be low enough to get the light directly in the eye socket itself. (If the talent has deep-set eyes and the key light is at too steep an angle, the result is simply two dark shadows under the eyebrows.)

Fill light is used to fill in on the dark side of the face or object being lit. It should come in at an angle on the side opposite from the key. Ordinarily a floodlight (such as a scoop or broad) would be used, although a spotlight in its *flooded* position often can be effective. In any case, a soft diffused light is desired. (See figs. 4-15 and 4-16.) It is used simply to soften the shadows and give some illumination to the otherwise dark side of the talent. Fill light should not be as strong or as directional as key light; it should not compete in creating shadows and countering the shaping qualities of the key.

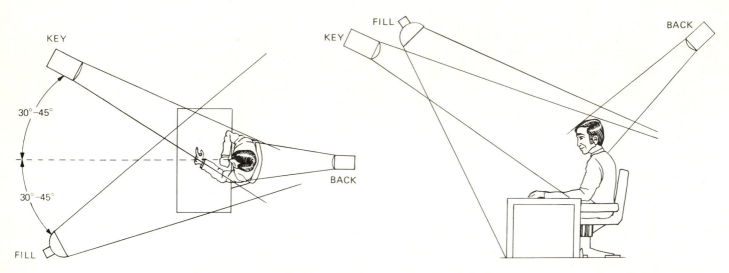

Figure 4-13   Three-point lighting.

The key light and the fill light should normally both be placed approximately thirty to forty-five degrees from a line drawn straight in front of the talent. The back light should theoretically be directly behind the talent, at a steeper angle than the two front lights.

Figure 4-14   Subject with key light only.

Figure 4-15 Subject
with fill light only. (Note
the spill on the
background cyc.)

Figure 4-16 Subject
with balanced key and
fill lighting.

Figure 4-17 Subject with back light only.

Figure 4-18 Subject with balanced three-point lighting (key, fill, and back).

In much color TV production, however, a great amount of fill light is used to achieve a consistently even *wash* of illumination over the entire set. In this application, the fill light comes close to serving the same purpose as base light (see section 4.2).

Back light, as the name implies, comes from behind and above the subject. A spotlight is virtually always used so that the light can be directed and focused like the key. The back light falls upon and, as a result, accentuates such features as hair, shoulders, and top surfaces of set elements. (see figs. 4-17 and 4-18.) This highlighting effect separates the talent from the background, adding to the illusion of depth within the total picture. Without adequate back light, the subject appears flat and tends to blend in with the background—as in figure 4-14. Back light requirements will vary with the color of the subject, the background, and the desired effect. For example, a brunette usually requires more back light than a blond.

Auxiliary Light Sources

There are several other terms that refer to more specialized types of lighting. They are really only variations of the three basic categories. A *side light* is an additional key, working roughly 90 degrees from the direction of the camera. A **kicker** is basically a back light that works usually at floor level and is placed more to the side than behind the subject.

One of the most important additional sources of illumination is the **background** or **set light** (not to be confused with the back light). This is the major source of lighting for the cyclorama or background set behind the performers. In addition to helping fill in the overall picture (basic illumination), background lighting can give form and texture to the setting, provide a sense of reality, or suggest mood (creative functions). Set lighting can tell the audience whether it is an indoor or outdoor locale, daytime or evening. Specific locations can be suggested by certain kinds of window effects or cookie patterns in the ellipsoidal spot (venetian blinds, prison bars). Mood can be reinforced with high-key or low-key lighting. Colored gels on a plain cyclorama can help to establish mood on a color production.

In one function or another, most types of lighting instruments can be appropriately used for background lighting. Floodlights (scoops or strip lights) are often used for general illumination of a cyclorama or flat space. Spotlights can be used to highlight certain areas or present dramatic lighting effects (for example, strong diagonal slashes of light or selected low-key elements). And, of course, the ellipsoidal spot can be used with a variety of cucalorus patterns for various shadow effects. (See figs. 4-9 and 10-14.)

Other special lighting effects depend upon careful background lighting. A good *silhouette* demands an evenly lit background, balanced from top to bottom as well as from side to side. A good *cameo* effect, on the other hand, requires a complete lack of any light hitting the background; front lighting must be carefully controlled to make certain that no spill is reflected onto the set behind the talent.

The background lighting must also be balanced with the three-point subject lighting to ensure that no undesired semi-silhouette effect is attained. As mentioned in section 4.2, if the background is too strongly lit, the faces of people in front of the background will tend to go dark by comparison.

Actually, in any moderately complicated lighting setup, the illumination is coming from many directions and angles. In addition, the subjects—the persons being lit—will be moving within the set. The concept of key, back, and fill lights should be used as a guide, not as a rigid set of rules. Auxiliary lighting and

Light	Footcandles	Relative Strength
Key	200 ftc	Reference point of 1
Back	200–300 ftc	1 to 1½ times the key
Fill	150 ftc	¾ of the key
Set	100–150 ftc	½ to ¾ of the key

Figure 4-19 Ratio of key, back, fill, and set lights.

These are rough guidelines that could serve as a starting point for lighting a basic setup for either color or monochrome vidicon cameras.

special effects will be added as needed for certain creative purposes. The important consideration is that the lighting director be totally in control of the *direction, intensity, quality* (harsh shadows or diffused), and *color* (if applicable) of light falling upon performers and set.

Balanced Lighting by Ratio

The first thing a lighting director must do in creating a three-point lighting pattern as shown in figure 4-13 is to decide on the relative strengths of each of the instruments. There are some basic guidelines that lighting directors use in their preliminary plans. Figure 4-19 shows the standard ratio of key, back, and fill lights that can be applied in most basic lighting situations. The footcandle figures represent incident meter readings that would be made at the point where light strikes the subject.

The key light, being the primary light source, is given the reference point of *one*. Other light sources are then adjusted in relation to the strength of the key. The back light is up to *one and one-half* the strength of the key. And the fill is about *three-fourths* of the strength of the key.

Such ratios are only guidelines, of course. Once the lights are turned on, the lighting director can then check the shot through the camera monitor and get a better picture of the reflective qualities of the subject and the rest of the set. The final lighting decisions have to be based upon many factors, such as color and shading of the object being lit, texture and shade of the background, the illusion of reality, and the desired mood. Particular care must be taken with skin tone and hair. Too much light on the hair and shoulders can cause the face to look relatively darker than it naturally would be. If any picture elements appear out of balance they should then be checked by reflected light meter readings.

Of the three fundamental light sources, the back light is the most difficult to measure and to work with. Achieving the desired effect of highlighting the hair, shoulders, and so forth, calls for considerable intensity. Because of the steep angle of the typical back light, much of this intensity does not reflect into the camera. The direct incident meter reading, therefore, will seem quite high in relation to the effect on the picture. Because it is usually much closer to the subject than the key light, the wattage needed in the back-light lamps will often be less than that used for the key lights.

The light falling upon the background, which usually has its own independent sources, also consists of some contribution (*spill*) by both the key and fill lights. For this reason, it is sometimes difficult to predict background light level accurately in the initial plan. The reflective quality of background materials varies considerably. The same amount of light falling upon a cyclorama and dark wood paneling will produce considerably different amounts of light reflected into the camera.

As we have stated, during the process of lighting setup, the basic lighting balance is achieved by means of incident light readings. When the performers are in place, there must be a final adjustment process that should utilize a more accurate set of reflected light readings. The footcandle readings will, of course, be on a much lower scale, but the same basic ratio will apply. Again, however, the final suitability of a picture should never rest with an arbitrary ratio and a light meter. Ultimately it comes down to how the picture looks on the monitor to the director and the lighting director.

Multiple Subject Lighting

The three-point lighting example shown in figure 4-13 is a simple illustration of the way motion pictures have been lit and shot for the past half century. With the single-camera film technique, every shot has its own lighting setup. When the subject and camera are moved, the lighting is changed. Enormous care is taken to sculpt the face and other features of the subject with the key light, thereby heightening the illusion of depth.

With television's multiple-camera technique, three-to-five-minute continuous segments of a soap opera or situation comedy are shot from three or four different camera angles. The basic three-point lighting system is still used, but it has to be somewhat compromised. As the subjects move from place to place in the set, they must be hit by key lights from all possible camera angles. This usually means that numerous key lights are set in a 180-degree arc around the set. Fill light floods the set from several different positions. The effect of this technique is called *wash,* or *flat,* lighting. The entire set is washed in light and the features of the subjects are, to some extent, flattened out.

Economy of Lighting

Frugality in the use of lighting instruments is an important consideration. Good lighting technique is often as much a matter of knowing when to take out or dim lights as it is of knowing how to add lights to a set. The modeling and texturing effects of a few well-placed key lights are easily wiped out by adding too many lights from too many directions. As newer cameras are developed that require less light for basic illumination, it is possible to be more artistic and creative in the use of selective lighting. Of course, for color television it is important to maintain a diffused, even base light or *wash* in order to guarantee equal intensity from all angles and a balanced color temperature throughout the set (see section 4.2). For this reason, it is easier to achieve many artistic lighting effects with black-and-white television than with color production.

Another important consideration is the manipulation and control of unwanted shadows. Remember that many facial and textural shadows are desired for modeling and dimension, but many kinds of shadows are undesirable and distracting. An obvious example is the shadow of a microphone boom on the set behind the performers. Other examples are the shadows often cast by other performers, by large props, or sometimes by the camera itself. Many a beginning lighting person has tried to counteract these unwanted shadows by adding more light to the shaded area—trying to "burn out" the shadow. In essence, what this does is to throw the overall lighting intensity out of balance, producing "hot spots" for the camera. The correct solution is to eliminate the shadow—either by moving or repositioning the object casting the shadow (such as raising the boom arm) or by moving or controlling the light source (for example, by lighting from another angle or by masking off part of the light with barn doors as outlined in section 4.6).

4.6 Studio Lighting Procedures

Having looked at some of the basic television lighting requirements and concepts, we are ready to consider the actual techniques and procedures involved in lighting a television setting. Several of these aspects also involve practice and discipline in the execution of specific lighting functions—for example, in the precise preparation and use of lighting plans and plots and in careful observance of all safety precautions.

Mounting Lighting Instruments

Our first concern should be with the way that the lights are actually mounted or supported. How are they to be positioned and held in place? Basically, there are two ways—by *hanging* them from above or by mounting them on a *floor stand.*

Hanging Mounts.   Most television studios are equipped with some **lighting grid** for mounting lights above the staging areas. This facility gets the lighting instruments up at about the right height for most applications and leaves the studio floor uncluttered for camera and talent movement, microphone placement, and various set elements. Most studios have some sort of pipe grid or batten system upon which the lights are actually suspended. The pipe grid is a rigid permanent arrangement of pipes a foot or two beneath the studio ceiling; the lights are fixed directly to the pipes by any one of several kinds of hanging devices. The counterweighted batten system, on the other hand, allows the battens to be raised or lowered by some sort of counterweight system so that lights can easily be worked on from the studio floor.

After lights are hung in the right position, final adjustments (**trimming**) have to be made at the operating height, even on a counter-weighted batten. Some of these might be accomplished with a *light pole*, which can be inserted into the ring-focus mechanism on some spotlights to adjust the spot-flood position of the bulb-reflector unit. Some larger studios will have a *catwalk,* which allows lighting operators to move around on a permanent scaffolding to reach most of the lights from above. In most studios, however, some sort of special movable *lighting ladder* is used that allows lighting personnel to climb up to any instrument for final adjustments and focusing. Two different types of studio ladders are pictured in figure 4-20.

Lighting instruments may actually be connected to the grid or batten with a variety of fastening devices. Many are simply placed into position with a **C-clamp,** which connects the light firmly to the grid but allows for no vertical adjustment of the instrument. (See fig. 4-21.) A *sliding rod* and a **telescope hanger** are two arrangements whereby a light can be attached to the bottom of a long rod that can be positioned at varying heights on the grid or batten. The **pantograph** is a scissors-like spring-counterbalanced hanger that allows lights to be pulled down or pushed up quickly and easily to any level. This is the most convenient arrangement for rapid adjustments and easy positioning of lighting instruments.

Floor Stands.   In many kinds of studio arrangements, the suspended lights often have to be supplemented by lights mounted on floor stands. Although too many floor stands would tend to clutter the studio floor and get in the way of other production elements, they do represent a certain degree of flexibility and simplicity of setup. Sometimes there are positions where it is simply impossible to get a light except on a floor stand.

Floor stands usually are mounted on tripods with casters that facilitate easy movement and quick repositioning. They come in

Figure 4-20 Two types of lighting ladders. One with four free-wheeling casters, *left*, must be steadied by an assistant on the floor. The one with a tricycle steering arrangement and a lockable wheel, *right*, can be operated by one person.

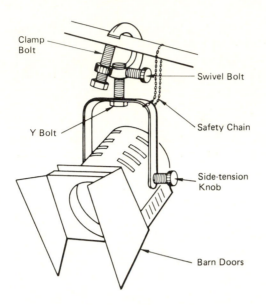

Clamp
Bolt

Swivel Bolt

Y Bolt

Safety Chain

Side-tension
Knob

Barn Doors

Figure 4-21 *C*-clamp.

The C-clamp holding this Fresnel spotlight to a pipe grid has four adjusting screws or bolts.

a variety of weights and sizes capable of handling many different kinds of lighting instruments. Of course, for location productions (wherever supplemental lighting is needed), the portable floor stand is indispensable.

Lighting Control

Television lighting can be controlled or altered in several different ways. It can be shaped, softened, routed, diminished, and colored. This can be done either mechanically at the instrument itself or electronically at some remote control point.

Instrument Controls. We have already mentioned a very obvious way in which the light from an instrument is shaped or otherwise altered—namely, by a lens. We have also discussed the focusing mechanism in a spotlight that enables us to move the bulb-reflector unit within the housing to produce either a widespread flood pattern or a more intense spot beam (see fig. 4-7). In addition, the need

often arises to trim the dimensions of a particular beam. No matter how carefully lights are hung from the grid, the beams tend to overlap, causing excess intensity in certain areas. For other situations, special mechanical focusing or diffusing effects may be needed. The most commonly used pieces of equipment for these purposes are either attached to the front of the instrument or mounted in front of it.

Barn doors are usually four movable shutters that attach to an instrument such as a Fresnel spot or a pan. By moving the shutters, both the length and width of the projected light can be limited (see fig. 4-21).

A *Snoot* is a stovepipelike attachment usually used with a Fresnel to reduce the beam to a smaller, clearly defined circle without increasing the intensity of the spot.

A *Flag* is a rectangular frame, covered with black cloth, that is hung or mounted separately from the instrument. It produces a precise edge on one side of the beam.

A *Scrim* is a clothlike opaque filter that greatly softens the quality of light. This filter is used with both spotlights and floodlights. Often made of fiberglass, the scrim cuts down the intensity of the light as well as diffusing it.

Color gels are thin, transparent, colored material or gelatin that when attached to the front of the light, project a specific color quality. This material is quite often used over strip lights to add color to a cyclorama.

The *Cucalorus*, the kook, or the cookie, as it is often called, is a cutout design that, when placed in front of a spot, projects a pattern upon a cyclorama or large set surface. Ellipsoidal spotlights are designed so that smaller metal kooks can be inserted into the lamp housing.

Intensity control can be achieved in several different ways. First, by selecting the right sized instrument to do the job; should you use a 2,000-watt spotlight instead of a 1,000-watt spot? Second, the distance from the lighting instrument to the subject will tremendously affect the lighting intensity (see fig. 4-2). Third, various scrims or other filters can be used to cut down the intensity of the light. And, finally, the light levels can be altered by the **dimmer board.** Keep in mind, however, that the dimmer board—by reducing the current being supplied to the filament—will change the color temperature of the lighting instrument (see section 4.2). Thus, the dimmer may be the least desirable method of altering lighting intensity for color production.

The Dimmer Board. Located at some distance from the actual lighting instruments—either in a corner of the studio or in some control room—is the patching and control equipment. In any kind of sizable studio operation, this is centered around the dimmer board. Although dimmers vary tremendously in construction and operation, they all function on the same general principle: by controlling the amount of power that flows to the lighting instrument, the lamp gives off more or less light. Two types of dimmer boards are shown in figure 4-22.

Patching and dimming equipment is, in many ways, analogous to the patch panel and console in the audio control booth. Apart from the creative considerations, we are concerned with power flow instead of signal flow. There is a basic routing system for getting power to a light.

This equipment varies greatly from one studio to another in both sophistication and capacity. Therefore, it would serve little purpose to attempt to describe all of the possible techniques of patching operation that would follow the many individual designs. This is best learned from the specific construction of the equipment in your own studio. As a frame of reference to that process, it may help to consider some fundamental functions common to all lighting control equipment.

When a light on a grid has been connected to the nearby numbered line or grid outlet, the electrical power to turn on that light is available from two different sources in most studio setups—either a nondimmer circuit or a dimmer circuit. If no intensity control over the lamp is needed, a patch is made from the grid outlet or *load circuit* to a numbered nondimmer circuit and turned on at the switch or circuit breaker. If intensity control is called for, the patch is made from the load circuit into the dimmer board for a controlled power source. Here the circuitry may vary according to the design of the board.

In most boards, multiple units of lights can be connected into a single dimmer circuit. There is, however, a definite limit to the amount of power that can be fed to any one circuit. This limit should be ascertained and always observed.

Safety Precautions and Disciplines

Safety is the responsibility of everybody connected with a television production. Any unsafe situation can be avoided by using common sense and observing basic precautions. Part of the *discipline* of television production is the habit and attitude of *thinking safety.* Every crew member, whether or not part of the lighting team, should be disciplined to think always in terms of avoiding or correcting hazardous conditions. *Think overhead.* Are all lights, mounts, and other equipment securely fastened? When heavy equipment is moved or repositioned overhead, is everybody warned and the area below the equipment cleared out? *Think electrical.* Is all equipment turned off before moving or inspecting it? *Think hardware.* Has the item of equipment been thoroughly checked out and is it ready for use? Has everything been connected? Tightened? Tested?

Whenever a lighting assistant is moving or aiming lights, there should be at least one

Figure 4-22 Two types
of dimmer board
installations. (Top photo
courtesy of KCET.)

person steadying the ladder from below. The person on the ladder should always carry a wrench (secured by a band or tie around the wrist to prevent dropping it on persons or equipment below) to tighten any lamps that have become loose from excessive turning. When making any adjustment on any lighting instrument, the safety chain or cord should always remain fastened, securing the light to the pipe or grid.

When changing the direction of a light, always loosen the thumb screw (swivel bolt) first. Do not mistake it for the bolt holding the lamp hanger to the clamp, as loosening that bolt will detach the lamp from the lighting grid.[4]

When moving a light (clamp, hanger, and housing), always make certain that there are no people or equipment below the area in which you are working. Be certain the power to the lamp is off. Just because no light is being emitted does not mean that there is no power coming to the cord. Damaged lights, burnt-out bulbs, and short circuits are all potential dangers. Again, be sure that the power is off at the lamp's new location before plugging it into the grid outlet or load circuit. When moving an instrument from one location to another, the safety chain is always the last item to be unfastened, and it is the first thing to be hooked up when the instrument is repositioned.

When moving or aiming lights, do not look directly into a light. A light that measures 200 ftc at thirty feet may approach 100,000 ftc at the source. Studio lights are bright enough to permanently damage or even blind the naked eye.

4. The most common type of lamp hanger is the *C*-clamp (see fig. 4-21). There is a bolt that holds it to the lighting grid and a bolt that holds the light holder to the *C*-clamp. This bolt (*Y*-bolt) should *never* be loosened. To turn a light, there is usually a thumb screw in the side of the clamp. Make note of this when studying lighting in your own studio.

A 2,000-watt lamp creates a dangerous amount of heat. After being on for only a few minutes, most studio lamps are hot enough to cause serious burns. Most studio lamps have handles. Use them! Lighting technicians should also be furnished with heavy-duty asbestos gloves. Special caution must be used when adjusting barn doors, as they are directly in the path of the light source at only a few inches and absorb a large amount of heat.

Before moving a lamp, whether a large studio model or a small portable light, let the lamp stand for ten to fifteen minutes. This will help the lamp cool, help prolong the life of the filament, and also lessen the possibility of lamp explosion or burn-out from the shock of moving.

Preproduction Planning

One final note about production *discipline* from the standpoint of lighting procedures. In lighting—as in every aspect of television production—it is imperative that as many details as possible be taken care of before walking into the studio for the production setup and rehearsal. Every minute counts in the studio. You cannot afford to start your planning once you reach the studio.

The lighting director must use a lighting plan or **light plot.** This plan will be worked out well in advance of the actual studio setup time. It will include a schematic layout of the primary staging areas and the lighting requirements for each one. It should indicate each lighting instrument to be used and the intensity ratios among the various instruments. Often there is a space for additional notes. Here the director will indicate which lights are to be placed together on dimmer circuits or what kinds of lighting effects will actually be used on the air. Figure 4-23 represents a sample lighting plan for a simple panel discussion.

In many production situations, the lighting director will also prepare a more detailed

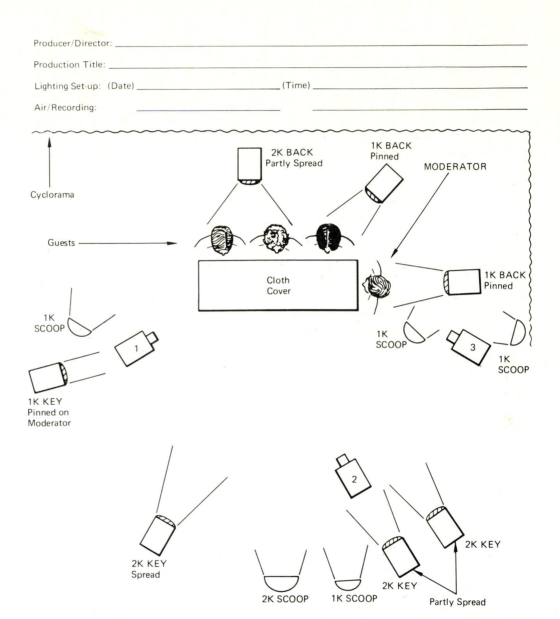

Producer/Director: _____

Production Title: _____

Lighting Set-up: (Date) _____ (Time) _____

Air/Recording: _____ _____

Cyclorama

2K BACK
Partly Spread

1K BACK
Pinned

MODERATOR

Guests

Cloth
Cover

1K BACK
Pinned

1K
SCOOP

1

1K
SCOOP

3

1K
SCOOP

1K KEY
Pinned on
Moderator

2K KEY
Spread

2

2K KEY

2K SCOOP   1K SCOOP   2K KEY
                    Partly Spread

Figure 4-23 Sample studio lighting plan.

The director of the television production would fill out a light plot on a form similar to this. Although the symbols are not to scale, these instructions indicate generally how the director envisions the production from the lighting standpoint: where the talent will be, how the numbered cameras will be positioned, and basically what lighting instruments would be used. The lighting director could then take this lighting plan and devise a more detailed lighting worksheet for the lighting crew to follow.

set of working instructions—a worksheet that lists, for each instrument to be used, the description of the light (spot, scoop); its size (500 watts, 2 KW [kilowatts]); the staging area it is to cover; its function (key, kicker); the grid outlet or load circuit it is to be plugged into; the dimmer or nondim circuit it will be patched to; and so forth. Again, the detailed preparation at this point will save valuable minutes of studio setup and rehearsal time later. The disciplined production person knows the importance of thorough **preproduction planning.**

Summary

As with audio considerations, lighting directors must be concerned both with technical (*basic illumination*) needs and with creative purposes. Basic illumination factors include establishing the correct amount of *base light* (usually determined by an *incident light* meter reading), working within an acceptable *contrast ratio* (established by *reflected light* meter readings), and maintaining the correct *color temperature* (3,000 to 3,400 degrees Kelvin). The creative lighting objectives include molding *shape* and *texture,* establishing a feeling of *reality* (or nonreality), and creating a *mood* or emotional setting. All of these functions are accomplished with *spotlights* that have a highly directional focused beam and/or with *floodlights* that give off a nondirectional diffused light.

Lighting a typical subject involves standard *three-point* lighting (key light, fill light, and back light). *Auxiliary sources* such as a side light (or a kicker) or background light may also be incorporated. As a starting point, lighting directors sometimes use a *basic ratio,* with the back light the strongest, then the key light, and the fill being the weakest source. Complete studio lighting procedures also include knowledge of various *mounting devices,* effective *lighting control* (by a combination of

dimmers and mechanical devices), adherence to fundamental *safety precautions* and the discipline of thorough *preproduction planning.*

All of the lighting considerations, of course, are but a means of creating the picture that will be picked up by the camera and its lens system. Camera/lens structure and camera operations are discussed in the next two chapters.

4.7 Training Exercises

Illustrate, on camera, the modeling effects of light upon the structure of the face by means of the following demonstrations.

1. From a straight-on position in line with the camera, direct a key light only upon a subject's face from angles of 60, 45, and 30 degrees from the horizontal. Note the generally uncomplimentary effect of shadows under the eyebrows, nose, and chin at the steeper angles.

2. Set the key at a 30- to 45-degree vertical angle, straight-on to the subject's face. Start with the camera position exactly in line with the direction of the light. Then have the subject slowly turn his or her face to the right. Have the camera make an arcing movement in the same direction, keeping a full-front face shot. Stop both of these movements at regular intervals, observing how the shadows created by the various lighting angles model the shape of the face. Note how the lines of the subject's forehead, nose, cheek, and so forth, are much more definite than with straight-on front lighting.

3. Set up a basic key, back, and fill light structure. Alternately take out and then put back one or even two of these basic light sources. This is most effective when the lights are on dimmers and the process is done gradually. Experiment with the various footcandle ratios among the three light sources by means of dimmer control.

4. With the basic key, back, and fill setup, use different subjects so that the variations created by hair, skin color, and clothes can be noted.

camera structure and lens design

5

With this chapter, we begin a look at the video system. It is a complex chain that includes lenses, cameras (and their mounts), camera control units and a synchronizing generator, a switcher, possibly an editor, usually a video recorder, and (ultimately) a transmitter. The next five chapters will be concerned with various components in this system.

5.1 Video Signal Flow and Control Functions

Just as we discussed the audio system in terms of audio signal flow, so also would it be helpful to think in terms of the **video signal flow** for the picture part of the television production. The same seven basic control functions introduced in section 2.2 can be applied to the video system. Figure 5-1 illustrates in simplified form the basic units in the video signal flow.

The first step, *transducing,* is accomplished by the camera itself. The camera, like the microphone, is a **transducer** that receives physical energy (light waves) and transforms it into electrical energy (video signals) that is suitable for electronic distribution. Although considerably more complex than the microphone, the camera performs this same basic function.

The video signal is then *channeled* directly or indirectly into the video switcher. Although no patch bay is as obvious as that in the audio system, cameras nevertheless can be patched or connected to different inputs in the switcher or to other points in the master control room.

The switcher (chapter 7), like the audio console, is the heart of the video signal flow. Here is where all video *mixing* occurs. Camera pictures can be slected and combined in a variety of ways.

Some amount of camera *shaping* also can occur at the switcher. This function, however, is controlled primarily through the **camera control unit (CCU)**. What most people think of as the camera is actually only part of a much larger unit known as the **camera chain.** Most of the equipment necessary for the control and shaping of the video signal is not located at the camera itself but at a separate point under the supervision of the video control operator. (On newer and simpler cameras—variations of the vidicon—controls are preset and do not need continual adjusting or attention.)

The *amplification* of the video signal occurs at several different points in the total system. Wherever the signal is distributed any

significant distance through the various camera cables, *distribution amplifiers* are used to boost the signal periodically.

Various types of video recorders (chapter 8) are used for **recording** and **playback** of the television signal. Usually, the signal recorded by the video recorder would be a combined video and audio signal of the entire TV production.

As with amplification, *monitoring* takes place at several different points within the system. In any regular studio production, the

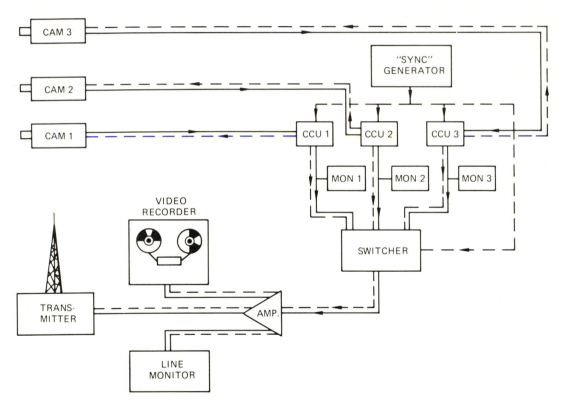

A portion of the synchronizing ("sync") pulse (dotted line) is sent out from the sync generator to each camera control unit (CCU) and on to each camera—keeping all cameras in perfect synchronization. The complete sync pulse is also sent to the switcher. Simultaneously, the picture information (solid line) flows from each camera to the CCU, where the video signal can be shaped

and altered. The composite signal (picture plus sync pulse) is then channeled into the switcher, with the picture information also being displayed on the video monitor for each camera. The one picture selected for the program or "line" is then sent from the switcher, through a distribution amplifier, to the line monitor, and into a videorecorder (or transmitter).

Figure 5-1   Diagram of the video signal flow.

camera operators will have a camera monitor to enable them to see what they are picking up with their cameras. The most conspicuous display of TV monitors is in the control room, where the director has a monitor for every camera and other video source being used in a particular program. In the simplest of studio operations this would involve three or four monitors. In ambitious network productions dozens of monitors might be used in a single control room. Video monitors and other monitoring equipment (**oscilloscopes** and testing instruments) would also be housed in the master control area for the use of the engineers.

It may now be worthwhile to look more carefully at the individual elements of the video signal flow, starting with the amazing device that actually picks up the electronic picture—the camera and its pickup tube.

5.2 The Camera Tube

At the heart of the entire television operation lies the camera **pickup tube**—that miraculous refinement of the cathode-ray tube that can transform (transduce) visual pictures into electrical signals.

Basic Television Pickup Tubes

The **image-orthicon (I-O)** tube was the first practical camera tube developed.[1] For many years, it was the standard of the professional industry for monochrome and color television. During the 1960s, however, the **vidicon** tube was developed and soon found its way into most applications formerly reserved for I-O cameras.

Although the I-O tube resulted in a good quality picture under a variety of lighting conditions, its expense, bulk, and tempermental nature could not compete economically and functionally with the vidicon tube and its many sophisticated offshoots. The vidicon is smaller and more rugged, and it can generally withstand a higher contrast ratio (section 4.2). A major operating advantage is that it is more stable; it warms up relatively fast and requires little operator attention. The I-O tubes, by contrast, were more sensitive; they tended to drift out of alignment and therefore required constant **video engineering**, or **shading**, to maintain a good picture. Also, vidicon tubes are not as susceptible to **burn-in** as were I-O tubes—especially as I-O tubes got older. Burn-in is a type of **image-retention** where the tube remembers the image of a picture it has been focused on (especially a high contrast shot that it has been sitting on for an extended period of time) and superimposes a negative image of that shot over succeeding shots the tube picks up.

One other major advantage of the vidicon tube is that it is less expensive and lasts longer than the I-O tube. Thus, this lower price tag—plus the lower operating costs (a video engineer is not needed in constant attendance)—have made vidicon technology the standard of both commercial and noncommercial television.

During the past few years, many refinements and improvements in the basic vidicon design have resulted in a wide range of advanced tubes. The **Plumbicon** tube[2] was one of the first to prove its superiority in color applications; it has long been the dominant tube in color broadcast operations. Today many other sophisticated versions of the basic tube such as the Saticon[3] and Newvicon—each of which boasts of its technical advantages in one area or another—compete for commercial dominance.

1. The first pickup tube developed was actually the **iconoscope** tube developed in the 1920s. It was never put into extensive use, however, as it was very insensitive to light, requiring large amounts of illumination to give a decent picture.

2. Plumbicon is a registered trademark of N. V. Philips.

3. Saticon is a trademark of Hitachi.

Principles of the Camera Tube

There are four primary principles that make the television picture possible. The first is the physiological phenomenon of *persistence of vision.* The human eye tends to retain images for a split second after the image has been removed. If about fifteen or more separate images per second are flashed before the eye, human perception will cause them to blend together, thus creating the illusion of motion. This persistence of vision is what makes motion pictures on film—as well as simulated motion on the face of a television tube—possible.

The second principle is the *electrochemical principle* of converting light into electrons and vice versa. Certain photoemissive materials give off electrons when exposed to light energy. This is what makes it possible for the pickup tube to act as a transducer, changing light waves into electrical energy. The opposite effect occurs at the receiver picture tube; when phosphors are bombarded by electrons, they give off light, thus changing electrical energy into light patterns. The picture tube in your home receiver is the final transducer.

The third principle is that of **scanning.** There had to be developed some way of picking up information from the face of the tube a tiny bit at a time, and then sequentially scanning the entire picture, gradually building up the picture from thousands of minute pieces of information—numerous times per second. This scanning procedure was developed using magnetic deflection of a single electron beam.

Fourth, the principle of *modulation of a radio carrier wave* is employed. This is the same principle that makes it possible to superimpose audio information on a carrier wave (section 2.2.1). With video information, however, much more information has to be modulated onto the carrier wave.

As these four principles were refined and combined, the theory of the television pickup tube became a reality. Figure 5-2 illustrates in greatly simplified form how the basic vidicon tube functions.

Light reflected from an object is focused through the **lens** onto the front of the pickup tube. The light-sensitive photoconductive coating of the tube transforms the light pattern into electrical charges. The charges are then picked up by the scanning beam being projected from the **electron gun** at the rear of the tube. The scanning beam is pulled across the face of the tube by deflection magnets, reading the varying electrical intensity of each spot on the tube. After the beam scans one line, it is momentarily *blanked,* or turned off, and pulled back to the other side of the tube and scans another line a fraction of an inch lower. The beam scans 525 lines across the face of the tube thirty times every second.[4]

The basic pattern of the electron beam is similar to that of your eyes reading across a line of type on a page and then jumping back to the left side of the page and starting on the next lower line—525 lines per page, thirty pages per second! The resulting electrical message is the video signal that has just begun its long and complicated path.

4. Actually, the electron beam does not scan 525 lines straight down the face of the tube. It scans every other line (for example, all of the odd-numbered lines) in one-sixtieth of a second; this is called one "field." It then starts at the top again and scans all of the remaining lines (the even-numbered lines); this is another field. These two fields, which total one-thirtieth of a second, make up the total picture that is referred to as a "frame." Thus, there are thirty full frames per second. This pattern of combining the two fields into one frame is called "interlacing." This whole process is described in more detail in section 5.3.

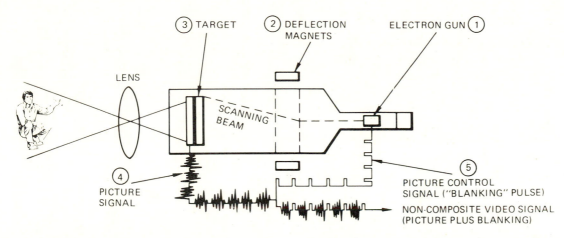

The electron gun (1) sends out a stream of electrons, all of equal charge; this scanning beam electronically "reads" the picture focused through the camera lens. The fields of force set up by the deflection magnets (2) pull the stream of electrons across each line and down to each subsequent line, creating the basic scanning grid structure. Several electronic elements, here grouped together under the term "target" (3), receive the focused picture from the lens. The image falls upon a photosensitive surface and is conducted to a signal plate. Here is where the beam scans the picture pattern created by the light energy and translates it into a continual line-and-dot pattern of electrical energy. This electrical information concerning the picture (4) as it is translated into the video signal is then combined with the picture control "blanking" information (5) which controls the timing of the scanning beam by turning the beam off as it retraces the face of the tube. This signal synchronizes the beam movement in the camera tube with all other electronic components in the video production and distribution system—including the home TV receiver. The rest of the synchronizing pulse is added to the signal at either the camera control unit (CCU) or at the switcher; from that point on the total signal (picture plus blanking plus sync pulse) is known as the "composite signal."

Figure 5-2 Simplified diagram of the vidicon pickup tube.

The Color Camera

The basic color television camera uses three pickup tubes. Virtually all color cameras use variations of the Plumbicon tube, which itself is an improved version of the vidicon tube. The first color cameras—which initially used I-O tubes—utilized a fourth tube to provide a black-and-white picture as a sort of skeletal structure for the picture. In the newer three-tube cameras, a combination of the three color tubes provides this luminance or brightness-darkness reference channel. Some portable cameras use two, or even one, pickup tube(s) for color pictures; however, the resulting picture is generally inferior to the three-tube cameras.

The basic principle of the color camera is to split the incoming light into the primary colors of *red, blue,* and *green*. The light is split into these three colors by means of special mirrors and color-selective filters; the red, blue, and green images are then sent to their respective pickup tubes and are translated into three separate video signals. Figure 5-3 illustrates one way that the light separation process is accomplished. In most professional cameras, the light-splitting structure is handled by one prism (or beam splitter) that houses all of the prisms, mirrors, and filters.

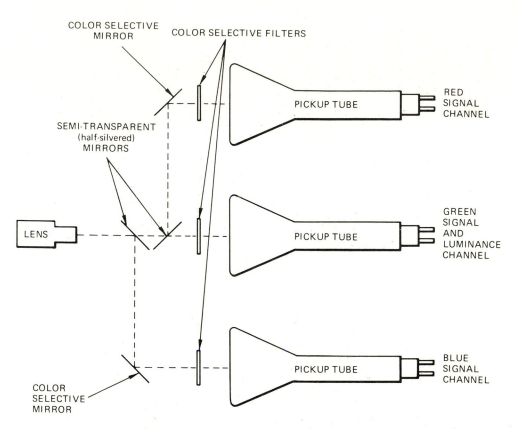

Figure 5-3 Diagram of a color pickup tube beam splitter.

By special dichroic (color-separating) mirrors and color selective filters, incoming light is split into red, green, and blue elements. These three separate signals are then picked up by their respective pickup tubes. The tubes themselves, of course, do not discriminate color; each tube just generates an electronic signal corresponding to the color information allowed to reach the tube through the beam splitter. The three video signals can then be transmitted and eventually recombined (at the receiver) to form the original full-color picture.

5.3 The Receiver Picture Tube

Just as the radio speaker resembles the microphone (the speaker's components are in reverse order of the microphone's signal flow), so is the receiver's picture tube the mirrored analog of the camera pickup tube.

Synchronizing Pulse

The **sync generator** is the key piece of equipment that produces the picture control signal, or **sync pulse,** that keeps all elements of the total video production-distribution-reception chain locked together in a synchronized pattern. In essence, there are different parts of the synchronizing signal that tell the camera scanning beam when to scan and when to shut off (**blanking**), when to skip down to its next line (**horizontal sync**), and when to jump up to the top of the picture to begin the next field (**vertical sync**). This sync pulse has often been called a system of *electronic sprocket holes* that keeps everything coordinated in a lock-step pattern.

The sync pulse—which is actually a complex pattern of several different signals—is produced by the sync generator and sent directly to the camera control units (CCUs) and to the switcher. After the picture signal is generated by the camera pickup tubes, the sync pulse is combined with the video signal at either the CCU or the switcher to form the **composite signal** (picture information plus the total sync pulse). The composite signal is modulated onto the carrier frequency at the transmitter and becomes an integrated part of the total broadcast signal.

Without the sync pulse, the elements in the system would not be scanning their respective pictures at the same time. Cameras could not be combined within a single program; the switcher could not process various incoming signals; the video recorder could not record a steady picture; and the home receiver could not lock into the transmitted signal.

The Monochrome Receiver

The television picture itself is composed of roughly 250,000 points of illumination on the picture-tube face. They are created when the electrochemical phosphors on the **kinescope tube** are bombarded by high velocity electrons. Each point, or dot as we shall refer to them, can be made to glow with varying degrees of brightness. In American systems (as well as those of several other countries, notably Japan), the dots are organized into 525 horizontal lines with each line containing slightly less than 500 dots. For a variety of technical reasons, some of the top and bottom lines are not seen on the face of the tube, hence our figure of roughly 250,000 dots. (See fig. 5-4.)

A picture is produced when an *electron gun* at the rear of the picture tube sends out an electron to each of the dots on the tube face. The electronic charge of each electron can vary and, as a result, each dot can glow variously from white, through shades of gray, to black. This procedure is accomplished by a scanning process that is controlled by the sync pulse and locked into the scanning pattern of the camera pickup tube. The pattern

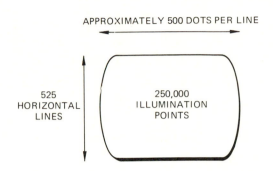

APPROXIMATELY 500 DOTS PER LINE

525 HORIZONTAL LINES

250,000 ILLUMINATION POINTS

Each line contains close to 500 phosphorescent dots that will respond to electrical charges given off by the electron gun scanning the tube. As the charge on each electron varies, so will each phosphorescent dot glow white, or a different shade of gray, down to black (for no signal at all). The face of the *color receiver* (kinescope tube) is coated with colored phosphor dots arranged in triangles, with one dot in every grouping for each of the primary colors—red, green, and blue. (See figure 5-6.)

Figure 5-4 Face of the kinescope picture tube.

starts with the furthest left dot of the top line, moving along that line to the right. At the end of the first line, however, the **scanning beam** does not go back to line number two immediately below. Instead, it moves down to line number three, then five, and so on, scanning the odd-numbered lines to the bottom of the picture. Each time, as the scanning beam returns from the right-hand edge to the left, its signal is blanked out, producing no effect on the screen. Figure 5-5 indicates how selected scanning lines would be represented on the monochrome picture tube.

When the scanning beam has caused all of the dots in the odd-numbered lines (one, three, five, and so forth) to glow with the necessary varying intensities, it has completed one **field**. The elapsed time from the top to the bottom has been one-sixtieth of a second. Immediately, guided by the sync pulse, the scanning beam moves back up and left to begin exactly the same process with lines two, four, six, and so forth; one-sixtieth of a second later it has completed another picture field. These two fields, when interlaced together, constitute

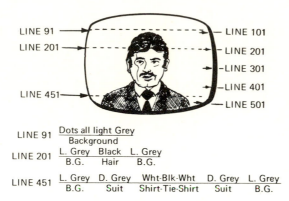

LINE 91   <u>Dots all light Grey</u>
           Background

LINE 201   <u>L. Grey   Black   L. Grey</u>
           B.G.   Hair   B.G.

LINE 451   <u>L. Grey   D. Grey   Wht-Blk-Wht   D. Grey   L. Grey</u>
           B.G.   Suit   Shirt-Tie-Shirt   Suit   B.G.

The subject is standing in front of an even-toned, light-gray background. His hair is black and his suit is dark gray. To produce the top of the picture, the electrons in the scanning beam cause the phosphor dots in the odd-numbered lines 1 through approximately 101 to glow with a light-gray intensity. Line 91 is shown as an example. Line 201 starts out with the gray of the background, then runs through the black hair of the subject, and completes the line with gray background again. Its middle section requires low intensity black dots as the beam scans that part of the line. Line 451 is somewhat more complex. At the appropriate times, light gray, dark gray, white, black, white, dark gray, and light gray dots must be used to produce the gray scale that corresponds to the background, suit, shirt, and tie. (On the color picture tube, every dot would be a triad of red, green, and blue pinpoints, each glowing with the proper intensity to reproduce red, green, and blue information. The human eye then would blend these primary colors into the appropriate hues to reproduce the illusion of brunet hair, skin tones, tan shirt, dark-brown suit, and so forth.)

**Figure 5-5
Representative scanning
on the picture tube.**

one complete picture **frame.** Now obviously this frame never exists as a completed unit, even for an infinitesimal fraction of a second. For that matter, neither does the field. What we have is the linear tracing of a point of light moving at an incredible rate of speed. Nevertheless, for a variety of technical purposes, television is said to have sixty fields per second, which are combined to produce thirty picture frames per second.

By scanning alternate odd-numbered and even-numbered fields and then combining them to produce the total picture frames, which is exactly the same pattern as that used by the camera pickup tube, the resulting picture has more of an even brightness. This interlace scanning, plus the phenomenon of persistence of vision, plus the fact that each phosphor dot tends to glow for a split second after it is "turned on" by the electron beam, all combine to give us a fairly steady picture with little perceptible flicker.

The Color Picture Tube

Turning the complex three-tube color signal into a picture on a receiving set is no small feat. The whole process operates on the principle that red, green, and blue colors can be added together in differing intensities to produce a relatively complete spectrum of all colors. The trick is to get the three different beams of electrons to activate luminescent agents of these three colors on the inside of the tube face.

An early and very successful system provides an easily understood example. (See fig. 5-6.) The inside surface of the tube is coated with approximately three-quarters of a million phosphorescent red, green, and blue dots. These dots are arranged to form triangles of the three colors. To keep the electron beams of one gun from hitting the wrong color dot, a mask is placed between the gun and the dots.

Other configurations have proved to be even more efficient in recent years, some involving the use of strips of luminescent materials. In the mid-1970s several variations were developed around the one-gun system. This process resulted in a sharper picture without having the alignment problems inherent in the three-beam-shadow mask system.

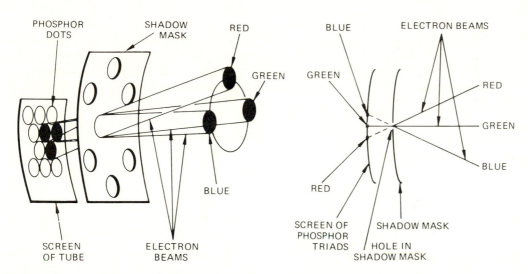

In this basic color picture tube system, the electron beams from the three color tubes would be focused through a series of carefully aligned holes in the shadow mask to ensure that each beam would hit only the colored phosphor dot intended for that color.

Figure 5-6 Shadow mask color receiver system.

5.4 Lens Characteristics

In conjunction with the camera pickup tube, the single most important element in the whole pictorial process probably is the lens. As illustrated in figure 5-2, it is the lens that focuses the picture upon the face of the pickup tube. A good lens can help the cheapest vidicon camera produce a sharp, clear picture. An inferior lens can turn the best Plumbicon camera's picture into blurred trash.

Today virtually all professional television camera work uses the zoom lens. Indeed, few TV-production students will ever see a **fixed-focus-lens** on a television camera. However, it is easier to understand the structure and function of the camera lens by studying the principles of the fixed-focus-length lens. After all, the zoom lens is nothing more than an arrangement of gears and lens elements that allow the operator to shift the lens elements (in relation to each other) in order to achieve varying focal lengths.

The characteristics of **focal length, focus, *f*-stop,** and **depth-of-field** are all simpler to grasp with a nonzoom fixed-length lens. It is much easier to comprehend the concept of a **long lens** compression of a picture or a **wide-angle lens** giving a greater depth-of-field if one visualizes the actual length and angle of the lens. In fact, any serious still photographer who has worked with fixed-length lenses will find it much easier to understand what a zoom lens can do—and why—than the photographer who started out with only a zoom lens. (One has only to compare a picture taken with a 200mm [telephoto] lens with that of a 25mm [wide-angle] lens.)

Therefore, this section will deal with lens characteristics using the fixed-focal-length lens as a reference point. Section 5.5 will deal specifically with the zoom lens.

Focal Length

The focal length of a lens is measured from the optical center point of the lens (when it is focused at infinity) to a point where the image is in focus. This focus point would be either the film in a film camera (movie or still camera) or the surface of the pickup tube in

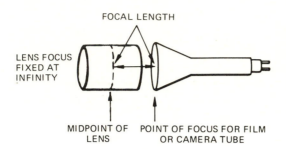

FOCAL LENGTH

LENS FOCUS
FIXED AT
INFINITY

MIDPOINT OF   POINT OF FOCUS FOR FILM
LENS   OR CAMERA TUBE

**Figure 5-7
Measurement of lens
focal length.**

With the lens focus adjustment set at infinity, the focal length is measured from the center of the lens to the point where the subject image is in focus on the surface of the pickup tube.

an electronic camera. (See fig. 5-7.) Focal length is measured in either millimeters or inches (twenty-five millimeters is approximately equal to one inch). The lenses used for 35mm film cameras are the same lenses that were used on most of the earlier professional image-orthicon cameras, and therefore provide a convenient reference point. Lenses used on vidicon cameras, on the other hand, are comparable to those used with 16mm film cameras.

Lenses of differing lengths are used so that more or less of a scene can be included in the picture. *The longer a lens is, the narrower its viewing angle will be, the less you will be able to get in the picture,* and therefore *the larger individual subjects will be.* Conversely, a short focal-length lens will give you a wider viewing angle, thereby allowing you to get more in the picture, but individual subjects will appear smaller than normal.[5] This *law of lenses* is

5. Because the face of the camera pickup tube is not processing *all* of the picture information passed through the lens, which is a circular scene, there is an apparent difference between the horizontal and vertical angles perceived by the camera. The electronically scanned picture is four units wide and three units high. The perceived angles, therefore, have the same 4:3 ratio. A one-inch focal-length vidicon lens, for example, will have a horizontal angle of about 27 degrees and a vertical angle of approximately 20 degrees. For most planning purposes, the horizontal angle is the most commonly used.

illustrated in figure 5-8. Long lenses, therefore, can be used to obtain closer views of objects. A long **telephoto** lens can get a relatively close-up view of an object from a great distance. On the other hand, a **short** (or wide-angle) **lens** will tend to increase distance and make things look farther away than they are. This fact can lead to distortion of distance.

A long lens (or a long-lens setting on a zoom lens) will *compress* distance. Two objects that are far apart from each other and at a great distance from the camera will be brought closer to the camera with a long lens, and consequently will seemingly be brought closer to each other. A common example is the baseball shot of the pitcher and batter as seen with an exceptionally long telephoto lens from center field. Although the pitcher and batter are about 60 feet apart, the camera is perhaps 400 feet away. Thus, the two players are brought much closer to the camera and, consequently, the distance between them is apparently compressed; on the home screen they may look as if they are only ten or fifteen feet apart.

On the other hand, a wide-angle lens (or a short-lens setting on a zoom lens) will *exaggerate* distance for exactly the opposite reason. The shorter the lens, the further apart objects appear to be spread. Small studios can be made to look immense by use of a wide-angle lens. The apparent force of a punch thrown at the camera will be greatly exaggerated with a wide-angle lens; if the person throwing the punch is only four feet from the camera, and the punch brings the person's fist three feet closer to the camera (so that the individual stops one foot short of the lens), the person has covered a great amount of viewing space by moving only three feet. The distance is exaggerated. Figure 5-9 illustrates how two lenses—one **narrow-angle** and one **wide-angle**—will vary the apparent distance between two persons.

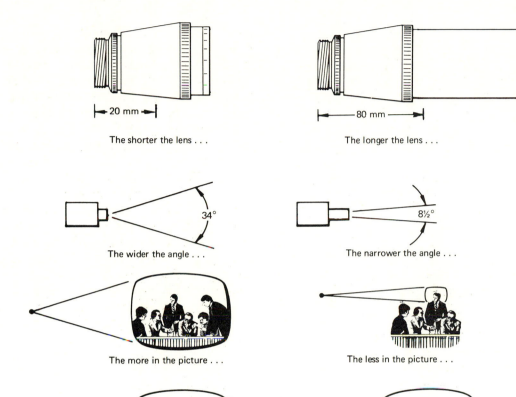

20 mm

The shorter the lens . . .

80 mm

The longer the lens . . .

34°

The wider the angle . . .

8½°

The narrower the angle . . .

The more in the picture . . .

The less in the picture . . .

The smaller the subject . . .

The bigger the subject . . .

Figure 5-8 Law of lenses.

In discussing the length of various lenses, it should be noted that the size (diameter) of the camera pickup tube will affect the apparent size of the picture obtained with a given focal-length lens. Because the older I-O camera had a larger surface area on the face of the pickup tube (either 3-inch or 4½-inch) than the smaller vidicon and Plumbicon variations (which range from ⅔-inch to 1¼-inch diameters), a 25mm vidicon lens would result in a picture approximately the same size (or focal length) as a 50mm I-O lens—although the 50mm lens is about double the actual physical length of the smaller vidicon lens.

Figure 5-10 lists the relative viewing angles of common sizes of vidicon lenses (or settings on a zoom lens), compared to the normal perception of the human eye.

Focusing Characteristics

Many fixed-focal-length lenses will have two adjustable rings. One will be the *f*-stop, or aperture opening, and the other will be the focusing ring. This focusing ring, which is common to all who have worked in still photography, can be adjusted anywhere from one or two feet to infinity. In most television studio work, however, this adjustment is seldom used.

Figure 5-9 Two subjects viewed simultaneously through different sized lenses. The monitor on the left shows them as seen by a narrow-angle (100mm) lens; note how close they appear to be. The right-hand monitor shows the same subjects as seen through a wide-angle (25mm) lens; note how the short lens exaggerates the distance. The woman and man are actually about fifteen feet apart.

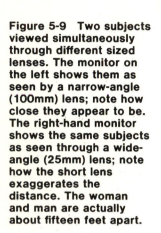

Lens Length	Viewpoint
10mm	Extreme wide angle
25mm	Wide angle
40mm	Normal
100mm	Narrow angle
200mm	Extreme narrow angle (telephoto)

Figure 5-10 Standard vidicon studio lenses.

The reason for this is that most older black-and-white TV cameras, which were designed to be used with fixed-length lenses, made the focusing adjustment by moving the pickup tube within the camera. This adjusts the distance from the lens to the surface of the tube, thus handling most ordinary focusing jobs within the studio. This physical movement of the pickup tube was accomplished by turning the focusing knob or handle on the side of the camera.

On color cameras, however, it is impossible to move the three pickup tubes back and forth. Therefore, all focusing is accomplished by the focusing ring on the lens and/or by rearranging the lens elements in the zoom lens. This adjustment is usually accomplished by remote control from the rear of the camera—often on the **pan handle.**

The *f*-Stop Aperture

As we mentioned when discussing lighting and contrast range (section 4.2), the television camera has a relatively narrow range of light tolerance as compared with the human eye. All camera lenses, therefore, have an adjustable diaphragm that can open or close the aperture. This lens opening is strictly to control the amount of light, within acceptable limits, falling upon the surface of the pickup tube; in no way can it affect the size of the picture the lens will pick up. (The size of the picture is strictly a function of the lens diameter and its relationship to the focal length of the lens.)

The size of the **aperture,** or lens opening, is given an *f*-stop number. Because of the complicated formula by which the *f*-stops are determined and identified, *the lower the f-stop number the larger the lens aperture,* and *the higher the f-stop number the smaller the lens aperture.* For instance, *f*-22 is typically the smallest aperture found on most television lenses. The widest opening usually may be anywhere from *f*-1.4 to *f*-3.5, depending upon the structure of the lens. (Longer lenses generally cannot "open up" as far as shorter lenses; they cannot let in as much light. More light therefore is needed when using long lenses.)

The most obvious application of *f*-stop adjustments is to enable the production technicians to adjust to varying light sources. If you are working under very poor lighting conditions, it might be advisable to open up to *f*-2 or even *f*-1.4. On the other hand, if you are working under extremely bright conditions (perhaps outdoors on a sunny day), you might want to "stop down" to *f*-16 or *f*-22.

Depending upon whether one is moving up or down the graded scale of *f*-stops, the amount of light permitted to enter the lens is either doubled or cut in half with each *f*-stop change. Let's take, for example, a given amount of light entering a camera with the lens set at *f*-5.6. By stopping down to *f*-8, the opening is made slightly smaller so that one-half as much light is now entering through the lens as with the *f*-5.6 opening. Conversely, moving from *f*-5.6 to *f*-4 doubles the amount of entering light. (See fig. 5-11.)

One word of warning about *f*-stop adjustments should be stated at this point. Generally speaking, the camera operator should not routinely think of the *f*-stop as a means to com-

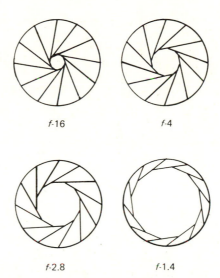

f-16   *f*-4

f-2.8   *f*-1.4

Each time the *f*-stop number is doubled or halved, the amount of light allowed through the lens is decreased or increased by a factor of four. For example, *f*-2.8 allows only one quarter as much light through the aperture as *f*-1.4. But *f*-2.8 allows twice as much light to pass through as *f*-4.

Figure 5-11 Diagrams of various *f*-stop openings.

pensate for bad lighting. The *f*-stops, together with the various electronic camera controls, should be set by the studio technician or video engineer and then left alone. Bad lighting or uneven lighting should be handled by correcting the lighting, not by tampering with the camera adjustments.

Depth of Field

One final consideration at this point is the depth of field of a lens on a particular shot. Depth of field refers to *the distance between the nearest point at which objects are in focus and the farthest point at which objects are in focus.* In a typical shot, objects close to the camera will be out of focus and objects too far away may be out of focus; the middle ground where objects are in focus is referred to as the depth of field.

Three different factors interrelate to determine the depth of field: *the f-stop* (the

The depth of field of a lens can be increased by altering any one of three different variables:

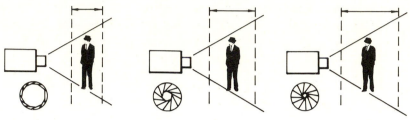

(a) by decreasing the lens aperture;

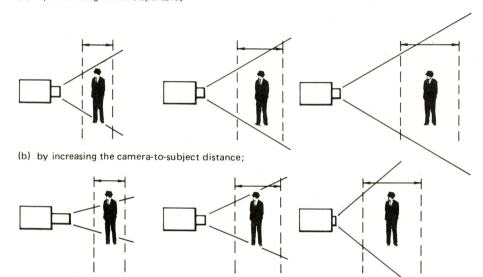

(b) by increasing the camera-to-subject distance;

(c) by decreasing the lens focal length.

Figure 5-12   Depth of field.

smaller the lens opening the greater the depth of field), *the distance from the subject to the camera* (the greater the camera-to-subject distance the greater the depth of field), and *the focal length of the lens* (the shorter the lens the greater the depth of field). Figure 5-12 illustrates these three variables.

Of these three factors, however, the only one that really gives you much flexibility is the *f*-stop. The camera-to-subject distance and the lens focal length are both related to the size of picture. You cannot alter either of these two variables without drastically changing your picture. In other words, if you have a given medium shot that you do not want to

change, and you want to increase your depth of field, you cannot increase your camera-to-subject distance (by moving the camera back) or you cannot decrease your lens focal length (by changing to a shorter lens) without changing your picture to a long shot. The only option left, therefore, is to stop down to a smaller lens opening; to compensate for that factor you will need to add more light to the scene.

Occasionally, beginning students arrive at the conclusion that the ideal lighting situation is one in which the lens can be stopped down to the smallest possible opening—thereby attaining the greatest depth of field (area of focus) possible. This, however, may not always be a desirable aim. First of all, for aesthetic reasons, the director may not want the background in focus, as it may detract from the foreground action of performers. Or the opposite may be true: the director may want the foreground to be out of focus (for example, he or she may be shooting through some defocused leaves of a tree) in order to concentrate on the action in the background. This is referred to as **selective focus**—when either the foreground or background is deliberately kept out of sharp focus.

Occasionally, for dramatic effect, the director may want the camera operator to **pull focus** or **rack focus** to shift a shallow depth of field from a foreground object to the background, or vice versa. For example, the director may want to open on a tight close-up shot of a half-empty glass close to the camera with the background out of focus; the camera operator could then change the focus (without otherwise altering the shot at all) to focus on the figure lying on the sofa while the foreground goes blurry.

Other factors may also necessitate a deliberate shallow depth of field. Perhaps the dramatic setting calls for low-key lighting, which means you have to operate with the lens aperture opened up. Another consideration is simply that of creature comfort; high-key lighting—solely for the sake of working with a greater depth of field—may not be worth the toll it takes on the performers working under the more intense lighting for a prolonged period.

5.5 The Zoom Lens

Except for some very limited applications, television cameras have never been operated with just a single fixed-focal-length lens. From the beginning of studio productions, professional cameras have been outfitted with a **lens turret** of four or even five lenses mounted so that with a simple spin of the turret any one of the several lenses could be immediately positioned in front of the pickup tube. (See fig. 5-13.) Thus, a typical studio complement of I-O lenses might include a 35mm, a 50mm, a 90mm, and an 8-inch lens. A facile and experienced camera operator could **rack** to any one of the four lenses and have it in focus within a second or two.

This still did not give production personnel the flexibility that they wanted. What was needed was some sort of variable-focal-length lens—one that would allow the operator to select any length wanted for a particular shot. And so the **zoom lens** was perfected and adapted for television.

When a **variable-focal-length lens** is **zoomed in** or **zoomed out**, the focal length of the lens is simultaneously being changed with the movement. By means of gears, the several lens elements within the structure expand and contract, changing the theoretical center point of the lens. Most studio zoom lenses have about a ten-to-one zoom ratio. A typical zoom lens for the vidicon camera, for example, might have a range from 17mm to 170mm. Figure 5-14 represents the angles of shots possible with a ten-to-one zoom lens. Smaller vidicon cameras might be equipped with just a four-to-one zoom lens, giving them the limited flexibility of, say, a 25mm-to-100mm range. For sporting events and other outdoor public event programing, most professional production units utilize twenty-to-one and even larger ratio zoom lenses.

In addition to giving the director and camera operator a wider range of lens lengths that are immediately available, the zoom lens also facilitates very smooth on-the-air movement. It is possible gradually (or quickly) to **tighten up** a shot, going smoothly and slickly from a **long shot** to a **medium shot** to a **close-up**. This

Figure 5-13 Lens turret on an older image-orthicon camera showing lenses of different focal lengths, any one of which can be rotated into the "taking" position in front of the pickup tube. (Photo courtesy of Jerry Hughes.)

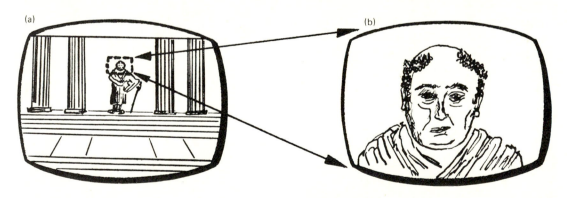

Figure 5-14 Range of a zoom lens.

These two views represent the extreme focal lengths of a 10 to 1 zoom lens: (a) Zoomed "out" to the shortest focal length, similar to a 1-1/2-inch lens, about a 50° angle; (b) Zoomed "in" to the longest focal length, equal to a 15-inch lens, approximately a 5° angle.

simulated movement is much safer and easier to handle than trying to move the camera physically. In addition, there are many occasions—especially on remote location productions—where it simply is not possible to move the camera. The movement of a zoom is not the same as the movement of **dollying,** however, and this distinction can make a subconscious difference in the reaction of the audience. (This area is discussed in section 6.1.) The convenience of the zoom can also be a drawback if it is not used judiciously.

There are also other drawbacks. The focusing characteristics of older zoom lenses tended to be a little soft. Because of the numerous lens elements in the zoom mechanism, it was difficult to obtain picture resolution as sharp as with a fixed-focal-length lens. To the naked eye, however, a truly high-quality zoom lens will result in a picture that compares favorably with fixed lenses.

With most zoom camera operations it is desirable to **preset** the focus so that the camera operator can zoom in or out on a given subject without having to readjust the focus during the zoom. If the focusing mechanisms are properly preset, the subject will remain reasonably in focus during the entire length of the zoom movement. On most black-and-white cameras the presetting operation can be quite precise. First, zoom out to the widest angle (a long shot) and adjust the camera focus by moving the pickup tube in relation to the lens. This is called adjusting the **back focus.** Then, zoom in to the tightest shot (close up) and focus with the zoom lens focus control (sometimes called the *front focus*). Now, slowly zoom back, checking the focus throughout the zoom, and readjusting the camera **tube focus,** if need be, when zoomed all the way out. (If the camera tube focus, or back focus, has to be readjusted, then the entire procedure must be repeated.)

With color cameras, the pickup tubes cannot be physically moved in synchronization; therefore, there is no way to move the tubes in relation to the lens to achieve a comparable means of camera focusing or back focusing. As a compromise, the internal optics of the zoom lens are set for a reasonably universal back-focused position. The only adjustment the operator has is the front focus or zoom lens focus control. Therefore, the presetting procedure is considerably simpler—if not as exact. First, zoom in all the way to the tightest shot you will want and adjust the lens focus. Now, zoom back slowly and check to make sure the subject is in reasonable focus throughout the entire length of the zoom. If not, the only slight adjustment you can make is with the zoom lens focus. Since there is no precise back-focusing possible, you may have to settle for a slightly softer (less sharp) wide shot than with a monochrome camera. But it is important to make sure that you preset your focus on the close-up.

As long as you have a few seconds and you are sure that the talent is not going to move or the director is not suddenly going to ask you to get a shot of something at some other distance from the camera, you should be able to get the zoom focus preset. But problems do occur—especially when you quickly have to get the unexpected shot that you were not prepared for.

One other small problem with the zoom lens concerns the *f*-stops. Because of the mechanical structure of a zoom lens, the lens aperture does not always produce as exact a gradation of entering light as does the fixed-focal-length lens. With the *f*-stop constant, a zoomed-in camera receives less light than when it is zoomed out. For this reason, a newer *T*, or *transmission, number* that more precisely measures the amount of light passing through the entire optical system is used on some lenses.

Summary

As with audio techniques and lighting considerations, a discussion of camera characteristics and operations could also be broken down into technical aspects and creative concerns. The sections dealing with the camera tube, the receiver picture tube, the lens characteristics, and the zoom lens have been concerned largely with *technical matters*.

The *video signal flow* can be seen as parallel to the audio signal flow. The same functions apply to both audio and video control: transducing, channeling, mixing, shaping, amplifying, recording (and playback), and monitoring. The transducing function is identified largely with the *camera pickup tube*: image-orthicon, vidicon, and Plumbicon. The four principles that led to the development of the television system are *persistence of vision, electrochemical conversion, scanning,* and *modulation of a carrier frequency*. The three-tube color camera splits the incoming light into the three primary colors of red, green, and blue—each one being channeled to its own pickup tube. The *receiver picture tube,* which can be thought of as the mirrored version of the camera pickup tube, is driven by the same sync pulse that keeps all elements of the video production-distribution-reception system locked together.

Mechanical and optical considerations of the fixed-focal-length lens include consideration of the *focal length, focusing characteristics,* the *f*-stop *lens aperture,* and *depth of field*. While the zoom lens has several advantages pertaining to *flexibility in selecting focal length* and facilitating *smooth movement,* it also has some potential drawbacks (especially in older models) regarding its possible *soft focus, focusing complexities,* and inconsistencies in the f-*stop designations*.

5.6   Training Exercises

In order to familiarize yourself with the cameras and focusing characteristics of the lenses in your own studio, work through the following projects.

1. Whether you have a zoom lens or a lens turret with fixed-length lenses, thoroughly acquaint yourself with the focusing mechanism. Set up two objects (or classmates) approximately two feet and fifteen feet from the camera. Using both a long lens (or a lens zoomed in tight) and a short lens (or a lens zoomed out all the way), how fast can you change focus from one to the other? Is it easier with the long lens or the short lens? Set up a well-lighted easel card a foot or so from the camera. Using both a long lens and a short lens, try to get as large a well-focused close-up as you can of a small card. You may have to manipulate both the camera tube focus and the lens focus. Is a long lens or a short lens better for getting good shots of very small objects? For future reference—in *your* studio conditions—determine how small an object or graphic you can use with your cameras. How long does it take to get such a shot?

2. Become familiar with *f*-stops and lighting conditions in your studio. Open up your lens to its widest aperture (lowest *f*-stop number). Using as little light as possible, get an acceptable picture

of a class model. Note the incident light meter reading. How does the picture look? Now, using every light possible, light the model as hot as you can in your studio; stop down the lens to its smallest aperture. Note the light meter reading. How does the picture look? Now, consulting figure 4-19, light the model, aiming for the ideal amount of illumination for your camera tubes. Carefully follow the suggested footcandle guidelines. What *f*-stop gives you the best picture with these base-light guidelines? How does this picture compare with the low-light picture and the intense-light picture? What would you conclude are the ideal base-light levels and *f*-stop standards for your studio conditions?

3. Experiment with varying depth-of-field conditions. Position and adequately light two classmates about ten feet apart in an almost straight line with the camera. Using a long lens, how close can you dolly in toward them and keep them both in focus? Try the same movement with a short lens. Keeping the lens constant, vary the light levels and *f*-stops accordingly. How close can you get with the lens opened wide? How close can you get with a smaller aperture? Practice some selective focus techniques. Set up an object on a pedestal, at camera lens height, about two feet in front of the camera; station a classmate about fifteen feet behind the object. With varying *f*-stops practice *pulling focus* from the foreground object to the person in the background. Reverse the process (pull focus from the background to the foreground object). Position the camera closer and further from the object. How does this change the impact of the change in focus?

camera operations and production techniques 6

Camera work is the result of the interaction of four elements of movement, functioning either in combination or singly: the angle and magnification changes made possible within the *lens* itself; changes in the *direction* a camera can be pointed or aimed; *elevation* changes achieved through the utilization of the **camera mount;** and changes of *camera position* accomplished by the movement of the mount itself.

6.1 Camera Movement

The first of these four elements—the angle and magnification characteristics of the lens— was introduced in the last chapter.

Movement of the Zoom Lens

The development of high-quality zoom lenses considerably changed the shooting patterns used on all types of television programs. Prior to this, directors and camera operators had to be well-versed in what eight or so basic fixed lenses could produce in terms of angle, magnification, and other optical qualities. Some directors were noted for plotting angle and distance for each shot with a military precision. The result was often excellent television. Unfortunately, this process meant that much of a camera's usable "air" time was lost in simply getting to and from specific locations and in rotating the turret to the correct lens.

With the zoom lens, of course, much of this lost time was regained. The camera operator always has the lens in position, and it is relatively easy to adjust the variable-focal-length zoom control (on the air as necessary) to obtain the exact viewing angle desired. With this ease of operation, however, also comes the tendency to get lazy and careless.

In the hands of a director and/or camera operator who is inexperienced, indolent, or both, the use of a zoom lens often results in dull, unimaginative camera work. It is easy to

107

fall into the trap of assuming that it is always possible to get a decent shot from any camera position at any time. Good camera work, however, requires that the director and camera operator always plot out each shot as carefully as possible, whether using a lens turret or a zoom lens. A large part of successful camera production *discipline* is related to this careful preplanning process. When truly creative people are involved, the zoom lens provides a versatility that amply compensates for the few limitations of the instrument.

The beginning camera operator soon begins to feel familiar with the production terminology. When the lens is *zoomed in,* the angle of the shot is made narrower and the degree of magnification is increased. The effect is that the viewer is *pulled in* to the subject. The reverse is true when the lens is *zoomed out.* The viewer is *taken out* from the subject.

An important consideration with any zoom movement is that of making sure that the lens focus is preset. The correct procedure for presetting the zoom lens (so that the subject is in focus from long shot to close-up) varies with individual camera design, the ratio of the zoom range (i.e., the relationship of the widest angle to the narrowest angle), the distance from the camera to the subject, and whether the camera is monochrome or color. General instructions were mentioned in section 5.5; specific directions are usually included as part of a camera's performance specifications.

Camera Head Movement

The second type of camera-lens movement— changes in the direction a camera can be pointed or aimed—is accomplished by the use of the **camera mounting head,** or **panning head.**

This pan head is used to attach the camera itself (with its system of lenses and the camera viewfinder) to the camera mounting or support. Thus, there are essentially three basic parts to the complete studio camera setup— the camera itself; the mounting or panning head; and the camera mounting. (See figure 6-1.)

The camera mounting head allows two kinds of movement: **panning,** which is a horizontal movement of the camera by rotating the camera mounting head; and **tilting,** which is a vertical movement of the camera by pivoting up and down.

There are two types of camera mounting heads that are most often used in professional studio operations. The *cradle head* balances the camera on a rocker mechanism that assures a fairly good balance of the camera during most panning and tilting moves. The *cam head* uses two cams, one placed on either side of the head, to provide even better balance than the cradle head, while enabling the camera a greater range of movement in tilting.

It should be noted that all instructions for a change in camera direction are given in terms of the camera operator looking toward the performance area. A new picture subject would be identified as being *camera right* or *camera left* of the operator. Thus, a *pan right* or *pan left* is a horizontal move of the lens of the camera in that same direction. (See fig. 6-2.)

For vertical movements, *tilt up* and *tilt down* are used to denote a change of shot framing in those respective directions. Although some directors may use the word *pan* to refer to a vertical movement, this usage can result in some momentary confusion on a busy intercom line and is not recommended. (See fig. 6-3.)

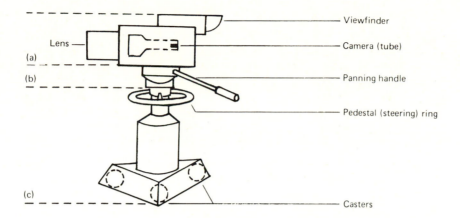

Lens

(a)

(b)

(c)

Viewfinder

Camera (tube)

Panning handle

Pedestal (steering) ring

Casters

(a) *Camera Head,* includes the camera tube and electronics, the viewfinder for the camera operator, and the lens (zoom lens or lens turret).
(b) *Camera Mounting Head,* with the panning handle which controls pan and tilt movements.
(c) *Camera Mount,* pictured is a "studio pedestal" with the steering ring and enclosed casters.

Figure 6-1 Three basic parts of the camera.

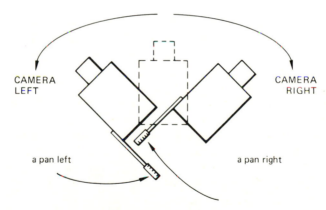

CAMERA LEFT

CAMERA RIGHT

a pan left

a pan right

In order to pan the camera in a given direction, the panning handle must be moved in the opposite direction. Thus, in order to effect a "pan left," the camera operator has to move the panning handle to the right.

Figure 6-2 Camera panning.

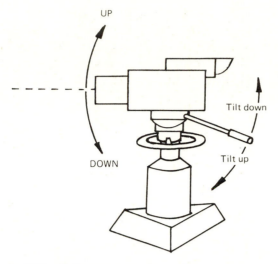

In "tilting" the camera up or down, only the camera head is pivoted. The camera mounting head (panning head) is not physically moved up or down with the camera mount.

Figure 6-3   Camera tilting.

Camera Mounts

Of the four types of camera-lens movements mentioned in the introductory paragraph of this chapter, the last two—camera elevation and camera position—are both dependent upon the camera mount.

The simplest and least expensive camera mount is the **tripod.** This three-legged stand usually is fastened to a dolly base consisting of three casters. The casters either can be allowed to rotate freely, facilitating quick and easy movement of the camera in all directions, or can be locked into a nonmovable position, which results in a steady camera unit for straight-line camera movement.

The tripod illustrated in figure 6-4 has a crank-operated pedestal that can be used to raise and lower the camera—although not

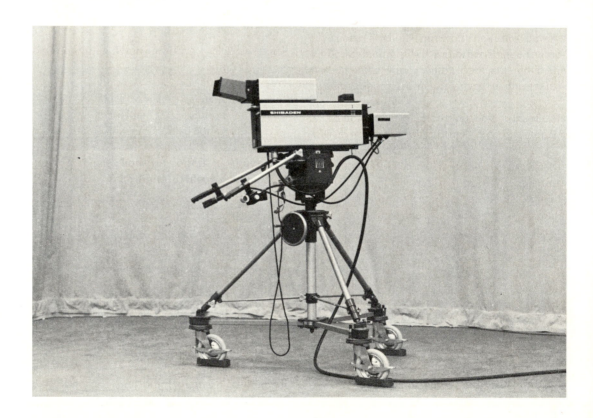

Figure 6-4   Camera mounted on an adjustable tripod.

smoothly enough to be used on the air. Most tripods, however, have no elevation adjustment other than the laborious process of mechanically adjusting the spread of the tripod legs. Thus, there is no real way to achieve any elevation repositioning during an actual production. The tripod, however, is lightweight and most models are readily collapsible. This makes the tripod a desirable camera mount for most remote productions.

A much more flexible type of camera mount is the *pedestal.* The simplest version is the lightweight *field-studio* pedestal. There are a couple varieties of this mount, which is basically a cross between a tripod and the heavier counterweighted studio pedestal described below. The field-studio pedestal, with its three larger casters, can be maneuvered like a tripod. Its distinctive feature is the central pedestal that can be raised or lowered, either by a hand crank or with compressed air. Although this method of camera elevation is not normally smooth enough to use on the air, it does allow for relatively quick elevation positioning of the camera between shots.

The counterweighted studio pedestal is a much more flexible and maneuverable studio mount. (See fig. 6-5.) It has two main features: a thick central pedestal that contains the counterweight (compressed air) system that enables the camera operator to raise or lower the camera smoothly on the air; and a steering ring that can control all three casters in a synchronized manner so that smooth on-the-air camera movements across the studio floor can be achieved. This ease and steadiness in camera movement have made the studio pedestal a popular workhorse in many studio situations.

Inherited from the film industry, the **studio crane** is the largest and most flexible type of camera mount. Although camera cranes come in a variety of sizes, they all have two elements in common: everything (including a

Figure 6-5   Camera on a compressed-air pedestal mount.

seat for the camera operator) is mounted on a large four-wheeled crane base; and the camera itself is mounted on a boom arm, or tongue, that can be moved vertically or laterally without moving the crane base. (See fig. 6-6.) Even though the studio crane provides the ultimate in smooth and flexible camera movement—for instance, the camera can be elevated from as low as two feet off the studio floor to more than ten feet high with the larger cranes—it does have the drawbacks of being relatively large and bulky and of requiring more than one camera operator. For these reasons, studio cranes are seldom seen in medium-sized studio operations.

Figure 6-6 Camera mounted on a medium-sized studio crane. (Photo courtesy of Chapman Studio Equipment.)

Camera-Mount Movements

There are several different ways in which the entire camera and its mounting can be moved about the studio floor. One of the most obvious is moving closer to or farther away from the subject; this is referred to as **dollying** the camera. With a lens turret of several fixed-length lenses, the physical movement toward or away from a subject was an important movement option for the director. It was the only way to get closer to or farther away from the subject without changing lenses. (See fig. 6-7.)

For the most part, the zoom lens has eliminated the need to rely extensively upon the *dolly in* and *dolly out* movements. There is a subtle difference between the types of movement, however, and a dolly is still preferred to the zoom for certain effects. The dolly move-

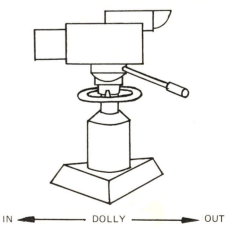

IN ◄────► DOLLY ────► OUT

In a dolly movement, the camera is simply brought closer to or farther away from the subject.

Figure 6-7 Camera dollying.

Dollying In. As the camera dollies past the foreground objects (or persons), the viewer is physically transported closer to the primary subject. The viewing angle is not changed; therefore, the viewer arrives at the subject with a relatively wide-angle view which exaggerates the distance between the picture objects.

Zooming In. As the camera zooms in to the primary subject, the viewing angle is narrowed down to exclude the foreground objects (persons). However, since the resulting picture has a relative-ly narrow viewing angle, the distance between picture objects is compressed, resulting in less "depth" to the picture. Also, the relationship between the picture objects remains unchanged.

Figure 6-8 Comparison of dollying in and zooming in.

ment physically moves the viewer past foreground objects, changing the relationship of various objects in the picture; the viewer's angle of vision remains the same, but physical elements are changed. With the zoom, on the other hand (as illustrated in fig. 6-8), the viewer's physical relationship with all objects in the picture is not altered; however, the viewer's angle of vision is narrowed down to exclude unwanted material; thus a sense of concentration is achieved without physically moving the viewer.

Lateral movement of the camera and its mount is known as **trucking**. A change of pic-ture is accomplished as the camera *trucks right* or *trucks left* because the camera moves sideways without panning to the right or left. (See fig. 6-9.)

It should be noted that both trucking and dollying movements are difficult to accomplish with a long focal-length lens or with a zoom lens that is zoomed in to a narrow angle. The slightest unsteadiness during the camera movement is exaggerated because the long lens, while magnifying the subject, is also magnifying the shaky camera movement. To a lesser extent, the same problem is apparent with panning and tilting movements. Generally, *the longer the lens, the more difficult any kind of camera head or camera-mount movement is going to be.*

A valuable camera movement is the **arc,** which is a combination truck and pan. As the camera circles, or arcs, to one side of the subject, the camera head is rotated so that it always points at the subject. The resulting picture maintains the same subject and the same sized shot, but the perspective or shooting angle changes as the camera movement is executed. (See fig. 6-10.)

While the tripod mount does not allow for any on-the-air adjustment in the elevation of the camera, most studio camera pedestals are designed to facilitate a smooth change in camera height. In this case, the word *pedestal* is

used as a command verb as the camera operator is asked to *pedestal up* or *pedestal down.* While such elevation changes may be limited to roughly two to four feet, this subtle change can be quite effective, especially at close quarters. (See fig. 6-11.) The pedestal movement can be thought of as a vertical equivalent to the truck. If the camera head is held stationary during a pedestal, then the picture subject will change as the camera is moved vertically. If the camera head is tilted during the pedestal movement, however (in a vertical analog to the arc shot), then the same subject can be kept in the frame while the angle and perspective will change.

In larger studios where the crane mounts or **crab dollies** are used, other movements are also possible. **Craning,** or **booming** (up or down), involves raising or lowering the crane or boom arm. The effect is similar to a pedestal movement, except that much greater vertical distances can be covered. A **crab** shot (left or right) is similar to a trucking shot, with the entire crane or crab dolly being moved sideways. One different kind of motion is the **tongue** move. With a large crane, the boom arm or crane can be tongued left or right in a lateral motion (while the base remains stationary).

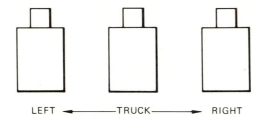

LEFT ◄———— TRUCK ————► RIGHT

In a trucking movement, the camera and mount are moved laterally without any adjustment of the camera mounting head.

Figure 6-9 Camera trucking.

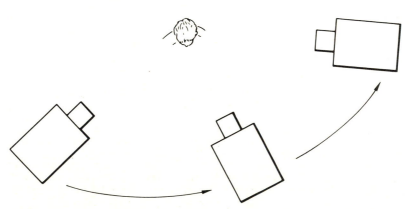

As the camera arcs to the right, the camera operator also has to pan left in order to keep the subject centered in the picture.

Figure 6-10 Camera arcing.

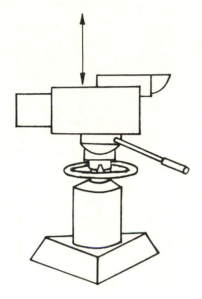
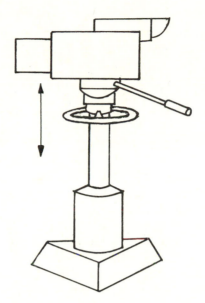

In a pedestal movement, the entire camera and mounting head are moved straight up or down, using a system of counterweights or compressed air.

Figure 6-11 Camera pedestaling.

6.2 Camera Perspectives

Before getting into specific camera operations, the beginning camera operator should be aware of the different ways that cameras can be employed in a television production.

The Viewpoint of the Camera

Generally speaking, the television camera can be used to represent one of three different perspectives: reportorial (or presentational), objective, or subjective.

Reportorial (Presentational) Perspective. This type of viewpoint is used to denote those uses of television when a presenter or reporter is speaking directly to the audience through the camera. The speaker establishes eye contact with the camera and talks directly to the lens. This approach is most often seen in newscasts, instructional TV lessons, sermons, some variety acts (for example, stand-up comedians), some political talks, demonstration programs, and so forth. Camera work in this kind of situation usually calls for a relatively close shot of the speaker—unless he or she has something to display or demonstrate for the camera. Basically, the camera work is simply to give the viewer a reasonably comfortable look at the person speaking.

Objective Perspective. The easiest way to visualize this use of television is to imagine the camera as an eavesdropper. The camera is standing back, taking an objective look at what is going on. No one is addressing the camera directly; the camera is just an observer of the action. This type of camera work constitutes the bulk of what we see on television: it includes virtually all drama, most variety and musical performances, talk shows and game shows (except when the host or announcer is directly addressing the audience through the camera), sporting events, and similar productions. Camera techniques vary tremendously for objective production. A wide variety of panoramic shots, quick reaction shots, leisurely camera movement, and rapid camera transitions are required for differing formats. Virtually all of the techniques discussed in the rest of this text are applicable to objective camera work.

Subjective Perspective. This particular camera use takes on special meaning when applied to dramatic productions. It refers to those occasional moments when the playwright-director wants to place the viewer in the position of an actor. The camera actually becomes (usually for only a scene) a participant in the drama. It interacts with other players, and it views the world from the individual perspective of the character it is representing. The camera, as the actor's eyes, is in the front seat of the car for the chase sequence; it is in the boxing ring, squaring off against the champion; it is trapped in the burning building, flames licking at the lens; it is drowning, with the waves lapping over the top of the camera-actor. These obvious filmic applications can also be applied—in a less sensational manner—in many types of studio television drama: the haggard hero looking in the mirror, the defocused glaze of the alcoholic lapsing into a coma, the scattered glances of the paranoid in a strange room, the intimate gaze of a lover seducing the camera, and so on. The subjective camera is a specialized technique, one that can have substantial impact when used judiciously. It also is a technique that requires the utmost in precision and concentration from the camera operator.

These three perspectives are intermingled in many television productions. The newscast mixes reportorial and objective perspectives as the newscaster turns from the camera to interview an in-studio guest. The drama mixes objective with subjective techniques, and a touch of the reportorial-presentational is thrown in as an actor turns to make a comment directly to the audience. The talk show jumps back and forth as the host and guests turn from their conversation with each other to talk directly to the viewer. As the camera operator is aware of these varying perspectives—and the production effects appropriate for each one—it is easier to achieve good camera work.

Field of View

At this point, the camera operator should be familiar with the various terms designating the size of the shot desired, or the **field of view.** Generally, most television shots can be related to three basic descriptions.

The Long Shot (LS). The long shot would be far enough away from a person that the entire body and quite a bit of the surroundings would be included in the shot. Often, the face of the person would be indistinguishable at this distance. If the person is so far away that he or she is hardly identifiable as a specific individual, then the shot can be labeled an *extreme long shot* (ELS or XLS). The label *wide shot* is used to denote a picture that encompasses the larger, external aspects of the program at a particular point in time. This **establishing shot** relates those people involved in a program not only to each other but also to the setting and circumstances of that program. The establishing shot is frequently used at the beginning of a program to establish the general locale or setting for the program or scene to follow. It also is often used as a closing shot to signal to the audience that we are pulling back from the action, out of the drama, as it comes to a close. Thus, the wide shot is generally used to communicate the broader elements that make up a program.

EXTREME CLOSE UP
(XCU)

CLOSE-UP
(CU)

MEDIUM SHOT
(MS)

LONG SHOT
(LS)

In addition to these basic shots, many other designations and modifications are possible, such as the "extreme long shot," "medium long shot," "medium close-up," and so forth.

Figure 6-12 Basic television shots.

The Medium Shot (MS). All of the shot designations are, of course, relative. What is a long shot for one dramatic segment may be considered a medium shot in another situation. Generally, a medium shot of a person would include most of the body, perhaps cutting the talent off slightly above or below the waist. The medium shot is probably the basic shot in standard television production. It is used to convey much of the dialogue in a drama and most of the action in talk shows, game shows, variety programs, and many other studio productions.

The Close-Up (CU). On the other hand, the close-up shot—with its sense of physical intimacy—can probe the individual and personal aspects of what a program is communicating. The eyes and facial expressions provide an important insight into the full meaning of a person's words. In many dramatic situations—as well as in many reportorial-presentational circumstances—the close-up is reserved for moments of high intensity and deep emotion. The close-up is usually defined as a shot consisting of the head and top of the shoulders of a subject. Of course, a close-up shot may be of objects other than a person; it may be a close-up of some item being demonstrated or of some picture being examined. Again, the term is relative. If even a

tighter shot is desired—say of just the eyes or of the eyes, nose, and mouth of an individual—then the shot would be labeled an *extreme close-up* (ECU or XCU). (See fig. 6-12.)

The process of alternating between the long shot and close-up aspects of a program is possibly the most important element in the communicative language of both film and television. This basic principle was discovered by pioneers such as Edwin Porter and D. W. Griffith during the early days of the motion picture. They realized that, by moving the camera into a closer position, they could accomplish what is automatically done by the eye and the mind. While the scope of human vision is almost 180 degrees, we immediately isolate and particularize the focus of our attention on a single person or object when the brain is motivated by a stimulus such as motion or sound. Cutting from a wide-angle to a close-up camera shot is much the same process, except that the distance factor is greatly reduced by lens magnification.

6.3 Picture Composition

Much has been written on the subject of picture composition and the related concepts that deal with the cumulative effect of a series of picture images. As in the motion picture, the main concern of television is usually the human element. Sets, props, and graphic arts have an important auxiliary function, but it is people we watch—the movements of their bodies and the expressions on their faces. When one considers the viewer sitting at some distance from a nineteen-inch or twenty-one-inch screen, the positioning of those faces and bodies assumes a critical importance.

As we discuss the following elements of framing, headroom, lead room, composition, and balance, keep in mind that these various "rules" that have evolved as part of the grammar of the medium should be considered *guidelines*—not federal regulations. Once the rules have been mastered, they exist to be modified or broken with proper justification and basis—dramatic motivations, artistic considerations, and so forth.

Framing

Television directors (borrowing somewhat from their older film cousins) have developed a simple terminology to describe to the camera operator the basic dimension of a shot. The scope of a shot is described in terms of that portion of the body that is to be cut off by the bottom edge of the picture. Thus a *full, knee, waist,* or *chest* shot quickly communicates the required *framing* of a person in the picture. Equally expressive are the terms **single** or **two-shot,** which describe the number of people to be included in the shot. For closer face shots, the precise terminology may vary somewhat with the individual director.

Other descriptive labels have evolved to specify certain kinds of desired shots. For example, an **over-the-shoulder shot (O/S)** might be called for in a situation when two people are facing each other in a conversation (such as a dramatic scene or an interview program). This means a shot favoring one person (who generally is facing the camera) framed by the back of the head and shoulder of the person with his or her back to camera.

Although it is largely a matter of subjective judgment and artistic "feel," it is important that the camera operator *always* be aware of the headroom on every shot. Too much headroom is as bad as too little.

Figure 6-13 Correct headroom framing.

Headroom

An important discipline for all camera operators is that of consistently maintaining an adequate amount of **headroom.** This term refers to the space between the top of a subject's head and the top of the frame. When this distance is not observed, the results can be somewhat distracting. (See fig. 6-13).

It is especially important that head room distance be uniform among all of the cameras on any production. A helpful guide for shot consistency is to place the eyes of subjects at the point of an imaginary line approximately one-third of the way down from the top of the picture. In close-up shots, the framing is best with the eyes slightly below the line. In wider shots, they would be slightly above the line. (See fig. 6-14.)

There is a very good technical reason why headroom distance is carefully watched by camera operators and directors. Due to several factors, most home television sets lose up to ten or fifteen percent of the picture area at the

As a general rule, with many exceptions, the longer a shot is, the more headroom you should have.

Figure 6-14 Correct headroom on different sized shots.

outer edge. As a result, framing that would appear to be adequate on the studio monitor will actually result in a **cropping** of heads or graphic art lettering on the home receiver.

Lead Room

When speakers or performers directly address the camera (reportorial perspective), they generally are centered in the frame, unless there is some foreground object or over-the-shoulder visual effect to be included in the frame. When subjects are speaking to one another, however, as in a dramatic presentation or a public affairs panel discussion (objective perspective), the framing is much more attractive if there is an added amount of **lead room** or *talk space* in the side of the frame to which they are speaking. By the same token, a distracting, crowded effect is created if the framing is such that the face of the subject is placed too close to the frame edge. (See fig. 6-15.)

The concept of lead room applies even more strongly to moving subjects. If a person is moving laterally across the screen, it is important to allow lead space in front of the person. Lead the talent; do not follow. (See fig. 6-16.)

BAD   CORRECT

BETTER

The camera operator should always intuitively give talent additional space in the direction in which he or she is looking.

Figure 6-15 Proper lead room or "talk space."

CORRECT   BAD

Whenever a person is moving across the screen, the camera operator should anticipate the flow of movement, giving the talent additional lead room in front of him or her.

Figure 6-16 Proper lead room for a moving subject.

Figure 6-17 Depth staging.

The over-the-shoulder shot (left) generally presents a more dynamic, interesting, and aesthetically pleasing picture than the flat two-shot (right).

By shooting the person behind the desk from an angle (left) a more inviting and vigorous effect can be achieved than with a formal head-on flat shot (right).

Depth Composition

Television is a two-dimensional medium. In order to simulate some feeling of depth, the director and camera operator can manipulate certain elements in pictorial composition. The feeling of depth is enhanced if some familiar background is used; it helps to give a feeling of scale or perspective. If a plain or abstract background is used, the viewer has no yardstick against which to gauge the distance from the subject to background.

Foreground objects can add significantly to the feeling of depth. By framing some nearby objects off to one side of the picture or along the bottom of the picture, the subject in the background is placed in greater relief. Care must be taken, however, not to force an unnatural effect for its own sake—as this will undoubtedly appear contrived to the viewer.

Whenever possible, depth composition can be achieved with the arrangement, or **blocking,** of talent. If several people appear in a scene, try to arrange them so that some are closer to the camera than others. Nothing is deadlier than three or four people stretched out in a straight line, all equidistant from the camera. Even with only two persons, an over-the-shoulder shot as a rule is preferred to a flat two-shot of a double profile. (See fig. 6-17.)

A feeling of depth can also be achieved by careful use of angles. If a shot calls for someone to be sitting behind a desk, the camera can get a much more interesting shot by trucking right or left and shooting the desk and subject from an angle. (Of course, the dramatic context might call for a formal head-on shot of a judge or stern employer.)

Balance and Other Considerations

There are many artistic elements to be considered in composing an aesthetically pleasing picture: balance, tone, unity, rhythm, proportion, line, mass, and others. It is beyond the scope of our discussion to try to treat these elements in this book.[1]

A few words about **balance,** however, would be in order. Many beginning camera operators try to achieve a pleasing composition by striving for **symmetrical balance.** They try to place the most important element directly in the center of the picture and/or try to balance picture components with equal elements

1. For a full discussion of all of the elements of picture composition, see Herbert Zettl, *Sight Sound Motion: Applied Media Aesthetics* (Belmont, Calif.: Wadsworth Publishing Company, 1973). See also Gerald Millerson, *The Technique of Television Production,* ninth edition, (New York: Hastings House Publishers, 1972).

Note how the two main focal points—the face and the hand holding the gun—are located at the intersections of the thirds. The table top, along the bottom third, helps to give the picture stability. And the floor lamp in the background, slightly off center, helps to balance the heavier right side of the frame.

**Figure 6-18
Asymmetrical balance
and the rule of thirds.**

equidistant from the center. This kind of mechanical balancing can lead to very stiff, dull, formal pictures.

A more dynamic kind of composition is **asymmetrical balance,** wherein a lightweight object some distance from the center of the picture can balance a heavier object closer to the center (similar to a seesaw with a light person at the end of the board balancing a heavier person seated closer to the center). (See section 10.1.)

Another way to avoid centralization of picture elements is to think in terms of the **rule of thirds.** Imagine the television screen divided horizontally and vertically into thirds. If major pictorial elements were placed at the points where the lines intersect, the result would be a more pleasing balance than if perfect symmetry were achieved. (See fig. 6-18.)

Movement

A final consideration of picture composition is the temporal and fluid quality of the medium. Since an important element of television is *movement* of one kind or another, pictures

rarely remain static for any period of time. Even in a discussion program, the guests will turn their heads as the conversation shifts to another person. In large musical or dramatic productions, the set and other background elements must be taken into consideration. For these reasons, proper composition involves a constant process of adjustment and an exercise of discretion in matters of balance and proportion.

6.4   Operating Techniques

At this point, the beginning camera operator should feel ready to start working with the cameras. A few words about some operating procedures—especially some safety precautions—should, however, be mentioned first.

Safety Procedures

There are several simple basic standard rules that every camera operator should always follow.

1. Put on your headset; make sure you are in contact with the control room before doing anything else.

2. If your camera is equipped with **lens caps,** check with the video engineer before removing them. Always ask for "permission to uncap." Unless you get this permission from the director or someone else in control, assume you are not yet authorized to use the camera.

3. Virtually every studio camera has provisions on the camera mounting head to lock the pan and tilt mechanisms. The pan and tilt locks should always be securely engaged whenever the camera is not in use. Release the locks, making certain you have a firm grip on the panning handle. Although all mounting heads should be balanced so that the camera head will not lurch forward or fall backward when unlocked, it is conceivable that something could go wrong and the camera could be

damaged. Once you have the pan and tilt heads unlocked, *never let go of the panning handle* without first locking the mounting head!

4. In all camera operations, always be alert to the possibility of an accident, which could result in the camera falling over or off its mount. Check all tripod leg adjustments; make sure the camera mounting head is securely fastened. Be especially careful, with lightweight tripods, of the possibility of tipping over the whole camera mount (for example, by stumbling over a camera cable).

5. Never stand on the camera cable. The **coaxial cable** consists of numerous individual strands of wire. Any unnecessary pressure on the cable can break some of these fragile wires.

6. After the production, reverse the procedures you followed in setting up the camera. Lock your pan and tilt heads before doing anything else. Cap up your lens and remove your headset.

7. Return your camera to its storage area and coil your cable in a figure-eight pattern.

Operating Hints

Aside from these rules, there are several operational techniques that will help you in most studio situations. Check to see exactly what procedures are followed in your studio.

Camera Setup (Prerehearsal).   Even before you are ready to set up your camera, see if you can help with other studio preparations. Can you be of assistance during the early stages of lighting and staging setup? In union studios, of course, this is not allowed; but in many university and educational closed-circuit operations, all crew members are expected to assist in all positions. Always be ready to help out wherever needed. This is part of the *discipline* of a successful team member.

With the consent and assistance of the video engineer, check out all connections, locks, adjustments, and controls on your camera. Make sure everything is in working order. Do not try to adjust the specific camera controls on the back of the camera (except for viewfinder adjustments) without explicit guidance or permission from the supervising engineer. Check your *f*-stop (or *f*-stops), but do not change or adjust them without higher authority.

Most camera mounting heads have adjustments that will apply a variable amount of drag or resistance to the pan and tilt controls. Depending upon the explicit production requirements, you may want your pan and tilt controls rather loose and free or you may want them tightened up. Adjust them accordingly.

Rehearsals.   In general, do not abuse the PL intercom (section 3.5). Quite a few production positions will be using the same line. Use it for speaking only when absolutely necessary. Use it for *listening* all the time. You never can be sure when the director or an engineer has to get you to react instantaneously.

During the early technical or blocking rehearsal, familiarize yourself as thoroughly as possible with the production and your role in it. Make certain you have floor assistance wherever and whenever you need it—someone to handle your graphics, someone to pull your cable in a difficult move. If you are working a boom or crane camera, make sure you coordinate all moves with your camera assistants. Practice all transitions and difficult moves; practice starting and stopping your pedestal and trucking moves; go over your difficult dollies. If you are using a zoom lens, make sure you know what all of your on-the-air zooms will be. Preset your focus for your various zoom movements. (Depending upon your position and the camera-to-subject distance, each zoom will have its focus preset differently.) Make sure you have plenty of cable to handle every move you may need to execute on the air.

On-the-Air Production. In general, be extra alert. Be prepared for anything. Anticipate the worst. (Your camera cable may tangle; your zoom lens may jam; your camera may get caught in a microphone cable.) Assume nothing. Again, this kind of alertness and sense of anticipation is what separates the disciplined professional from the "I'll get by" dilettante.

Prepare and anticipate all of your moves. Preset your zoom lens every time you get on a new long shot (and you should then be ready to zoom in, staying in focus, if called upon to do so). Make certain you are using a short (wide-angle) lens—or are zoomed out all the way—before attempting any camera moves (such as dolly, truck, arc, pedestal). If you are using a free-wheeling tripod, be certain your casters are set, all pointing in the correct position, before trying any camera-mount moves.

Always be ready for your next shot. Use your **shot sheet** (section 13.4) if the director is working from one; otherwise, anticipate your next shot based upon the rehearsal. Every camera should be equipped with **tally lights** on the front of the camera (for the talent) and by the viewfinder (for the camera operator); these indicator lights tell you when the camera is actually on the air. Watch your tally light; break to your next shot as soon as you are off the air, but not before.

If you are shooting an **ad-lib** or a semi-scripted program, do all you can to help the director. Anticipate shots the director may want. If you have the director's prior permission (or command), then "fish" for good shots. Do not, however, try to dictate to the director what shot to take. In many panel or interview programs, the director will not want you to move from your basic shot; do not presume to know more about the program than the director; stay with your assigned shot until you receive other orders. Watch the talent for signs that will telegraph any moves on his or her part. When the talent leans forward, shifts feet, looks toward the next set element, be ready to move with the first step or the rise from the chair. Again, anticipate; be alert.

At this point, you should be ready for your first camera assignment.

Summary

Camera movement can be divided into four classes: (1) movement of the lens (*zooming*); (2) movement of the camera mounting head (*panning, tilting*); (3) elevation and lateral movement of the camera mount (*pedestaling, tonguing, craning* or *booming*); and (4) movement of the entire mount—tripod, pedestal, or crane (*dollying, trucking, arcing, crabbing*). A zoom resembles a dolly except that when dollying, the viewer is physically moved while the viewing angle does not change; when zooming, the viewing angle is narrowed and there is not the same feeling of movement.

There are three different camera perspectives that can be employed: *reportorial-presentational* (the camera is addressed directly); *objective* (the camera is an eavesdropper); and *subjective* (the camera is an actor). The field of view of a camera can be thought of as consisting of long shots, medium shots, and close-ups—with quite a few variations and combinations.

In determining picture composition, shots are labeled descriptively—such as full shot, knee shot, waist shot, chest shot, single, two-shot, three-shot, and over-the-shoulder shot.

Headroom and lead room (talk space) are two important framing considerations. The illusion of depth in a television picture can be enhanced with proper background considerations, foreground objects, blocking of talent, and use of staging angles. Asymmetrical balance, which is generally more interesting than symmetrical balance, can be partially achieved by using the rule of thirds. Picture composition also has to be achieved in movement—as television is a temporal medium, constantly changing.

Before operating a camera, there are several safety procedures that the camera operator should follow. There also are a number of operating hints that the camera operator should be aware of during the setup period, during the rehearsals, and during the actual production.

Once the production crew member has mastered camera operation, the next step is to tackle the video switcher. Chapter 7 deals with the way camera outputs are selected and/or mixed to become the program video.

6.5   Training Exercises

1. Write a two-page analysis of how picture composition and camera movement were used during a thirty-second or one-minute television commercial that exhibited more than the usual slick or banal application of these disciplines. Choose one you have already seen several times. An audio recorder may aid in later recall of the more salient qualities of the commercial.

2. Set up a class practice session during which every member of the class has an opportunity to practice all of the lens and camera movements outlined in this chapter: lens movement (zooming or rotating a lens turret); panning and tilting; pedestaling (if your studio has studio pedestals); and camera-mount moves (dollying, trucking, arcing), plus crane movements if your studio is so equipped.

3. Stage five or seven class members in a manner similar to figure 6-8. Practice both a dolly in and a zoom in. Carefully note the differences. What are the emotional effects or subjective feelings of each movement? For what purposes would you use a dolly? a zoom?

the switcher: disciplines of the technical director

7

As outlined in section 5.1, the video signal flow can be traced in a pattern parallel to the audio signal flow. At the heart of the video signal flow system is the control room video switching unit—the switcher.[1] This video switcher, much like the audio console, has three primary functions. First, it is a *channeling,* or routing, device that can select a video source from any of several different cameras for signal output on the program line. Second, it is a *mixer* (the British term for the unit is the *vision-mixing desk*) that can combine different video sources by means of **superimpositions** and other **special effects.** The switcher also can be thought of as a *shaping* device, because some of the effects possible with the switcher do substantially alter the quality or shape of the video signal.

At the networks and top production houses, switchers are in use that carry these traditional functions to new levels of electronic wizardry. At this level the switcher is more often referred to as a **special effects generator (SEG).** When used in conjunction with a number of specific function modules, the unit can create and execute a wide range of video displays and transitions.

One of the most frequently used effects is that of a continuous movement (animation) of lettering or other elements of a *graphic.* In addition to familiar **dissolve** and **wipe** transitions, the picture can be made to **fold over,** which gives the effect of the turning of a page. Instead of a simple corner wipe with a separate picture in any given quarter of the frame, the **squeeze zoom** can reduce the whole frame to occupy the designated quarter-frame and at

---

1. The term *switcher* is confusing because it is commonly used to refer both to the piece of machinery (the video switching unit) and to the operator who pushes the buttons (the switcher who does the switching). To avoid confusion, in this text we shall follow industry practice and refer to the switching unit operator as the **technical director,** although the student occupying this position obviously is not a technical *director* in the professional sense of the word.

the same time fill the remainder of the screen with a new picture.

The graphics that one sees on television are less often the work of an artist with pen and brush than they are the electronic product of a creative artist-technician working with a **character generator** and a special effects switcher (see section 10.5). The display of a ballplayer's still picture and sports statistics is designed days in advance and programed into the unit for instant retrieval at game time. Effects that include timed transitions—such as an exact 2½-second (seventy-five-frame) wipe—can be similarly programed into the computerlike equipment for later precise execution. The digital technology that makes this possible is discussed in section 7.4.

7.1 The Principle of the Switcher

The switcher in a network television studio is indeed an impressive instrument. With its multiple rows of buttons, switches, levers, and lights, it is quite a formidable object. Despite all of its complexity, however, it operates on exactly the same fundamental principles found in the simplest units. Figures 7-1 and 7-2 illustrate two types of switching units.

While most educational institutions cannot yet afford special effects generators that can perform the video effects described, it is important to keep in mind that certain primary functions and their related operating principles are common to all switching units. When these basic functions are clearly understood, the well-trained student can master the equipment found in professional studios without difficulty. Differences in board configuration and capacity can be readily grasped if one is well grounded in the basics. Thus, this chapter has been written to treat switcher function and operation as generalized concepts that can be applied to the switchers found in most university studios.

Basically, the switcher can be thought of as a sophisticated *connection panel*—a means of taking video signals from several cameras and other sources (film chains, video recorders, remote feeds) and selecting those to be sent out as the *program signal,* or "program line out." There are two identical **banks** of buttons—identified in figure 7-3 as the *A* buss and the *B* buss. Each camera (and other source) has an input line that is fed to a button on the *A* buss and simultaneously each source is connected to a button on the *B* buss. There is also a **black** signal sent to a button position on each buss; this signal contains just the synchronizing pulses—no picture information—so it can be used whenever the switcher is to send out a blank (or black) picture.

Running beneath each row of buttons (out of sight within the switcher) is a **mix-buss** line. This functions much like the program mix buss in the audio console. (See fig. 2-6.) When one of the camera/source buttons is pressed, the signal from that camera (or other source) —for example, camera 2 on the *A* buss in fig. 7-3—is connected to the mix-buss line. Only one signal source can be connected to a given mix-buss line at a time; the buttons are self-cancelling so that when a button is pressed that action releases the previous connection. Therefore, each mix-buss line can have one camera signal punched into it at any given moment.

Each mix-buss line is then connected to a lever that functions just like a fader-potentiometer on the audio console. Each **fader arm** controls the amount of video signal flowing through the buss. When the *A*-buss fader is activated, the signal from the *A* buss is sent out the program line. When the *B*-fader arm is activated, the signal punched up on the *B* buss becomes the program output. The two fader arms are usually designed so that they can be physically locked together. In this manner when one fader is activated, the other

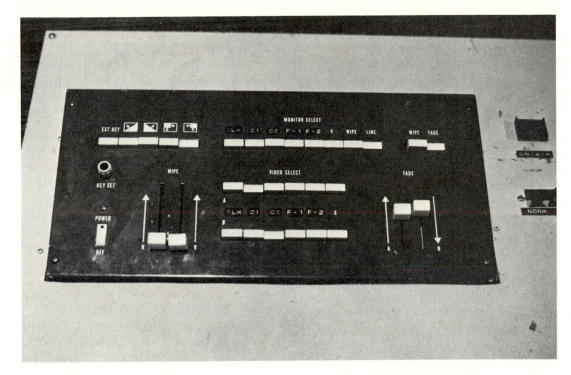

Figure 7-1 Relatively simple switcher with one mix buss.

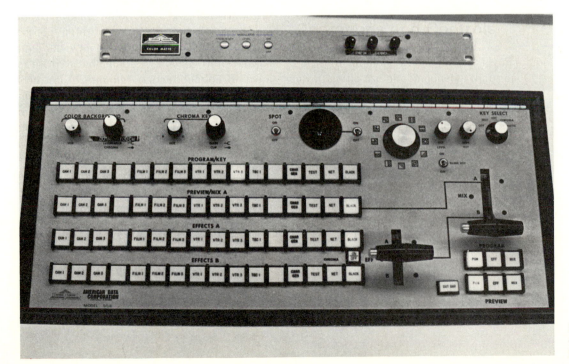

Figure 7-2 More complex studio production switcher.

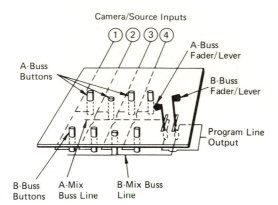

Camera/Source Inputs
① ② ③ ④

A-Buss Buttons

A-Buss Fader/Lever

B-Buss Fader/Lever

Program Line Output

B-Buss Buttons   A-Mix Buss Line   B-Mix Buss Line

Figure 7-3 Cutaway schematic drawing of two-buss switcher.

On the *A* buss, camera 2 is punched into the mix-buss line. On the *B* buss, camera 3 is punched into the mix-buss line. Thus—depending upon the positions of the fader arms—either the *A* buss (camera 2) or the *B* buss (camera 3) will provide the program line output.

will be automatically deactivated. Thus, when both fader arms are pushed up toward the *A*-buss position, the *A* buss will be activated and the *B* buss will be dead; when both faders are pulled down to the *B*-buss position, the *B* buss will be sending out its signal as the program feed and the *A* buss will be inactive. By keeping the two fader arms locked together—moving them up and down simultaneously—we will always have one buss activated (sending out the program signal) while the other buss is dead.

The simple switcher we have just described is the heart of every video switching unit regardless of how complex the equipment may be.

7.2 Cuts, Dissolves, Fades, and Supers

Moving pictorial expression utilizes two basic methods of changing from one image to the next. There is the direct cut, or **take**, in which the picture is instantly replaced by another;

and there is the **dissolve,** in which the picture is for a varying but brief period of time blended with the subsequent image. All fancier forms of electronic transitions—such as the wipe, the defocus, numerous pattern wipes, and digital-based transitions such as the fold-over and squeeze zoom—are but extensions of the dissolve.

Figure 7-4 illustrates the way in which either a **cut** (take) or a dissolve can be accomplished. With camera 1 pressed on the *A* bank (or buss) and both fader levers together in the *A*-bank position, the switcher would be feeding the picture on camera 1 to the program line. If the director wanted to instantaneously replace the camera 1 picture with the picture from camera 3, he or she would have the technical director simply press the camera 3 button on the *A* bank. The result is an immediate cut or take to camera 3.

If, for any one of a number of dramatic or aesthetic reasons, the director wanted to momentarily blend the images of two cameras in a transition, he or she could utilize a dissolve. Figure 7-4 shows the switcher set up for a dissolve from camera 1 to camera 2. With camera 1 punched up on the *A* buss and camera 2 on the *B* buss, camera 1 is on the line because both levers are in the *up* position, so all the video signal is coming through the *A* buss (camera 1). But as we begin to move both levers downward, we are decreasing the video signal from camera 1 on the *A* bank at the same rate that we are adding power to the picture (camera 2) on the *B* bank. When both faders are at the bottom position—fully activating the *B* buss and cutting out the *A* buss—we see only camera 2. But for a brief period we had the two camera pictures overlapping during the *dissolve* transition.

For years motion picture directors, working in the dramatic idiom only, used the *lap-dissolve* to denote the passage of time or the physical distance of one scene from the next.

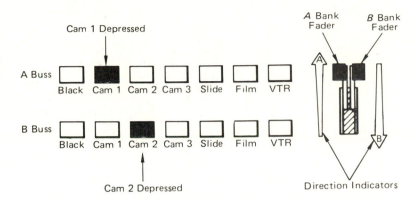

The arrows of the two fader arm direction indicators shows where the fader must be in order to activate its respective buss. Thus, the *A* fader must be *up* to activate the *A* buss; and the *B* buss is activated when the *B* fader is *down* at the widest part of its direction indicator.

Figure 7-4   Simple television switcher.

With the advent of television as a medium for many idioms—such as music, news, sports, documentaries, and so forth—the dissolve is often used in these program types as a connecting device.

If the director wishes to blend two images together and hold them in combination for a specific period of time, the result is termed a **superimposition** or, more often, a **super.** This is accomplished simply by holding the two fader levers midway between the *A* buss and the *B* buss, thus providing partial video display from both of the two busses (each with a different camera picture punched up).

Another type of video move—usually indicating a major program transition from one segment to another—is the **fade,** which is simply a dissolve using black in place of one of the cameras. Thus, a *fade in* to camera 3 is actually a dissolve from black to camera 3. A *fade out* is conversely a dissolve from the camera on the air to black.

When two pictures are *"in super,"* the brighter elements of both pictures dominate the resulting combination and the darker elements tend to disappear. An obvious question

might be, Why not separate the faders—activating both busses—and have the full value of both pictures? The best answer is that the resulting two-picture video level is usually far in excess of what the video control system can handle. The effect is a *blooming* (or white domination) of the brightness scale of the picture. In a super, however, where one picture has a weak brightness scale (such as a name card that is all black with white letters), it is possible to cheat somewhat and slightly separate the faders to reinforce the weaker signal. In this case, a prior word to the video operator is advised.

When two cameras are supered, it is possible to replace instantly either one of the pictures with any other signal source available on the switcher through a process called an **undercut.** As an example, in step 1 of figure 7-5 we have set up a super with camera 1 on the *A* buss, camera 3 on the *B* buss, and the faders in the midposition. In step 2, by simply pressing the camera 2 button on the *A* buss, the super instantly changes to camera 2 and camera 3 instead of cameras 1 and 3.

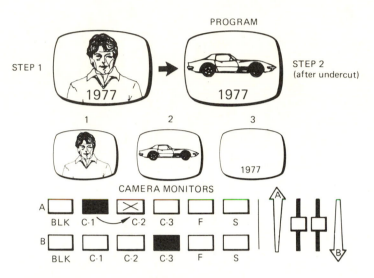

Figure 7-5 Undercutting while in super.

In this diagram, we have camera 3 supered over camera 1. By punching up camera 2 on the A buss—replacing camera 1 with camera 2—we have "undercut" to a new super, camera 3 over camera 2.

If two cameras are supered and the director wants to fade to black, the faders can be simultaneously *split* in those directions that kill their respective signals (in our illustration, moving the *A* fader down and the *B* fader up). Thus, both cameras would be faded out at the same time. For the most part, however, it greatly simplifies the process of learning the switcher operation if the faders are always locked together.

The usual method of fading to black is to use the black position on the inactivated buss as another camera and dissolve to it. For instance, in figure 7-4, if the director called for a fade to black, we would first have to punch up black on the *B* buss. Then we would move both faders down to the *B*-buss position. In actuality, we would be fading out the *A* buss with camera 1 on it while we are simultaneously fading in the *B* buss with black (nothing) punched up on it.

Monitors

In describing the undercut procedure illustrated in figure 7-5, we have shown what would appear on each of the three individual camera monitors and what would appear as the final super on the program line monitor. By this point in our study, most students will have become aware of a whole series of monitors in the video control room.[2] There may be up to a dozen different monitors, each performing an important individual function. Every video source should have its own monitor. Each studio camera, film chain (or telecine camera), and video recorder will have a small individual monitor. Other monitors, in

2. The video *monitor* is distinguished from the regular television *receiver* in that the monitor is usually a high-quality unit with ability to reproduce fine detail. It receives a direct unmodulated video signal, as opposed to a modulated radio frequency signal (see sections 2.2.1 and 5.1). Thus, there is no audio and no channel-selection capability.

a larger station operation, would include a network monitor (to indicate the actual network **feed**); an off-the-air monitor (a regular TV receiver tuned to the station's transmitter); one or more remote monitors (which can be used for a variety of auxiliary inputs, including remote on-location microwave feeds); and so forth.

In addition to the smaller monitors (they may range typically from seven-inch to twelve-inch tubes), there are a couple of other large monitors. The most crucial of all is the **line monitor.** This is the monitor that shows the actual picture coming out of the switcher that is being sent to master control for live transmission or video recording. The line monitor performs the final picture monitoring function in the video signal flow model (section 5.1)—analogous to the master audio speaker-monitor. This monitor, the one the director must be constantly aware of, serves as the final check on the program picture content.

The other large monitor in most control room configurations is the **preview monitor.** This is ordinarily set alongside the program monitor in an equally prominent spot. It can be used to preview anything the director wants to see. (Again, recall the audio previewing capability of the cue position on the audio console, section 3.4.) Typically, the preview monitor is used for one of two different purposes: *(1) To preview the shot that is going to be put on the air next.* As soon as the director **readies,** or **prepares,** the upcoming shot (section 7.5), the technical director can automatically punch it up on the preview monitor—letting the director preview the next shot before it is punched up on the air. (The advantages that the director gains by having shots previewed must always be weighed against the practical considerations of the increased workload that falls to the technical director.) *(2) To preview special effects or supers.* Usually

these shots will take some amount of adjusting before they are set up exactly the way the director wants them—so the preview monitor can be used for these special previewing purposes.

7.3 Preview and Preset Switcher Functions

The switcher model that we have designed up to this point—with two rows of buttons and one set of faders—would severely limit any but the simplest of productions. With just two more banks we can greatly increase the versatility of the switcher.

Program and Preview Busses

To accomplish the previewing function, we need to set up additional switching busses to feed the preview monitor. With only two mix busses there is no way to have a preview of a super—even if we had a second monitor to preview it on. One of the two mix banks must carry a full-strength picture signal. We cannot, at the same time, have our fader levers set in the midposition.

In figure 7-6 there is added a **program buss** that is, in effect, the final source of what goes out over the program line. When the *mix* button on the program buss is pressed, the program line is fed whatever has been set up on the two mix banks. The program signal would be a super if both faders are set at the midpoint (and each mix buss had a different camera punched up); the program signal would be a single camera (with the program mix button pressed) if the fader arms are at either the *A*-bank or *B*-bank position. (On the other hand, if the program mix button is *not* punched up—as in figure 7-6—then whatever camera button is engaged—camera 2 in the case of figure 7-6—would be the program signal.)

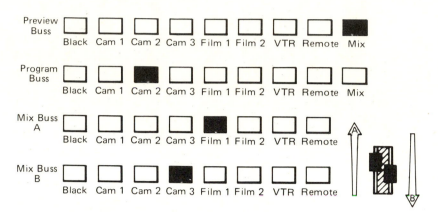

In this illustrated example, camera 2 is punched up on the program buss and is therefore being sent out directly to the program line. The preview buss has "mix" punched up which puts the A and B mix busses in the preview mode. On these two busses, we have film camera 1 selected on the A buss and camera 3 on the B buss. With the fader arms split between the two mix busses, we have both busses partially activated. Thus, we have a super of film 1 and camera 3 being adjusted on the preview monitor while camera 2 is being sent out on the air.

Figure 7-6 Basic four-buss television switcher.

If, as in figure 7-6, we also have a **preview buss** with an identical mix button—and that buss only sends a feed to the preview monitor—then we can have that preview of an upcoming super. In the simplest use of the term, we have a chance to *preset* (view and adjust) the super as well as to *preview* it.[3]

With this switcher layout, figure 7-7 illustrates how the preset and preview modes work in operational terms. With the switcher set up as in figure 7-6, the monitors appear as in stage 1. Camera 2 is feeding the program line through the program bank. Cameras "film 1" and 3 are in super on the mix busses and are feeding the preview monitor because mix is punched up on the preview bank. The

super can now be adjusted by manipulating the fader arms of mix-buss *A* (film 1) and mix-buss *B* (camera 3) until the desired balance is achieved. Then, in stage 2, we "take cameras 3 and film 1 in super" by simply pressing the program mix button.

In executing this operation, we have utilized the concepts of preview and preset and also employed a basic switcher principle of moving the continuing program feed from one area (buss) of the switcher to another. This principle of moving the program feed around to different banks of the switcher (or special effects generator) assumes much more importance as one works with switching units of more complex design. For now, however, let us look at another simple application of the basic four-buss switcher.

The monitors in figure 7-8 start out with the same setup as in figure 7-6 (and stage 1 of fig. 7-7), with camera 2 on the program

3. In many professional studios, there may be another preset monitor separate from the standard preview monitor that allows the technical director to view and adjust special effects as differentiated from the viewing of an upcoming shot.

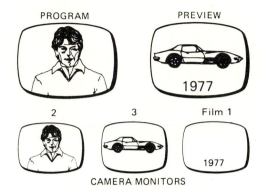

Stage 1: With the switcher set up as in figure 7-6, camera 2 is on the program monitor while a super of camera 3 and film 1 is preset on the preview monitor.

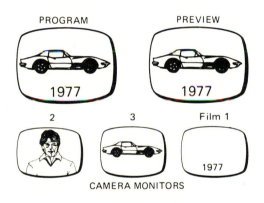

Stage 2: After adjusting the super (of camera 3 and film 1), the super is taken by simply pressing the mix button on the program buss.

Figure 7-7   Taking to a preset super.

buss (and monitor). In this instance, however, we want to cut first to the shot of the sports car and then gradually fade in the super of "1977." First, we cut directly to camera 3 on the program bank (stage 2). The command "set up a super of camera 3 and film 1" tells the technical director to adjust the super of film 1 (buss A) over camera 3 (buss B) by moving the fader arms to achieve the desired

balance. He or she would note where the levers are positioned—and then move them both down to buss B. By punching up *mix* on the program bank, the technical director has now rerouted the camera 3 signal from a direct feed through the program buss to a program feed going through buss B and the fader arms. The picture being sent out over the program line—camera 3—has remained unchanged. When the director wants to gradually fade in the super of film 1 (stage 3), he or she slowly pushes the fader arms back up to the previously noted desired (preset) positions.

Adapting to Individual Switchers

There are dozens of models of switchers in use throughout the industry. It would be futile to attempt to list the specific features and buss configurations of each of them. Some switchers have no permanently designated preview buss; any one of several different banks may be set up to serve preview functions. On some switchers, the preview function may be automatically transferred to the deactivated bank; for example, with mix levers at the B buss (on a standard four-buss switcher) the upcoming shot on the A buss is shown on the preview monitor; then—after a dissolve to the A buss—the preview monitor automatically "flip-flops" to show whatever is on the B buss. In more complex boards that use a *take bar*, this flip-flop feature may operate between the *preset* and *program* banks. The variety among switchers becomes even more overwhelming as the special effects generators (SEGs) become increasingly sophisticated and complicated.

By carefully reviewing the examples outlined, by concentrating on the fundamental concepts of *buss functions* and *preview/preset operations*—and by studying the analogy to the audio board—the student should be able to adapt these principles to any switcher. Keep in mind that professionals—especially those who free lance at a variety of facilities—go

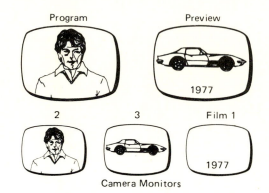

Program   Preview

2   3   Film 1

Camera Monitors

Stage 1: With the switcher set up as in figure 7-6, camera 2 is on the program monitor, while a super of camera 3 and film 1 is preset on the preview monitor.

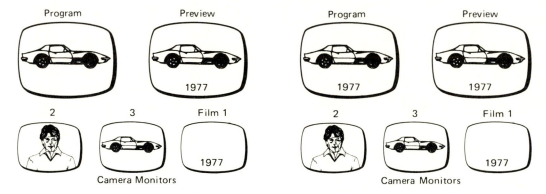

Program   Preview

2   3   Film 1

Camera Monitors

Program   Preview

2   3   Film 1

Camera Monitors

Stage 2: Camera 3 is punched up directly on the program buss (and monitor), while the super of camera 3 and film 1 is adjusted. When the desired balance is achieved, the positions of the fader arms are noted; then both levers are moved down to Mix Buss *B*. And the "mix" button is pushed on the program bank. The line feed (camera 3) remains the same. (We have just gone from a direct feed of camera 3 through the program buss to a feed of camera 3 through Mix Buss *B*.)

Stage 3: On command from the director, the fader arms are brought up to the preset positions, and the super of film 1 over camera 3 is accomplished.

Figure 7-8 Fading in a preset super.

through a similar process quite often. As long as one can trace the video signal flow, one can figure out how any switcher or SEG works.

Multiple Function Banks

Key and **wipe** effects are now standard on even the most basic types of production switchers. (These fundamental electronic effects are discussed in more detail in section 7.4.) The variety of moving design transitions based upon the principle of the wipe may number as many as several dozen on more elaborate units. The concept of the key, which along with the label of **matte** is variously applied to a number of related video effects, involves replacing a portion of a background picture with a solid keyed image (for example, white title lettering) from another camera source. As opposed to the ghostlike double image of a conventional superimposition, the key results in an opaque design being stenciled into the background image to form a solid mosaic.

On some switchers, these effects are generated only through banks that have been designated solely for that purpose. In less complicated switching consoles, either one or both effects may be created through busses that can be operated optionally as basic mixing banks.

One operational example of how *mix* and *effects* functions can be operated from the same banks is a basic three-buss SEG in which one bank may be the primary mix buss while other banks are designated as **effects busses.** In figure 7-9 we have illustrated a three-buss configuration with the lower buss (*C* bank) functioning as a mix bank. As such, it assumes the properties of a home-base buss, from which we can dissolve to the *A* or *B* bank picture in the usual manner, or from which we can dissolve to an *A* and *B* bank effects combination of two picture sources as produced in a key or a **split screen** (see section 7.4).

Let us first look at how we would set up a simple dissolve from the *C* bank to the *A*

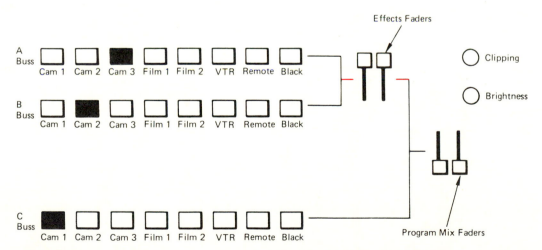

In this switcher the *program mix faders* determine the picture that is the program feed. An effect (a super, key, split screen, corner insert) can be set up on the "effects" banks (*A* and *B* busses)—using the *effects faders*—which can be mixed (dissolved) with the *C* buss. In the example, camera 1 (going through the *C* bank) is on the air, and the switcher is prepared for a dissolve to camera 3 (on the *A* bank)—or, if the *key mode* has been activated, we may be set for a dissolve from camera 1 to a key of camera 2 over camera 3.

Figure 7-9 Multiple function buss switcher.

bank. With this three-bank structure we must designate the *A* bank as the other operative buss in the dissolve by placing the *effects levers* in the upper *A*-bank position. We can then make the *C*-to-*A*-bank dissolve by moving the *program mix levers* from the lower (*C* bank) to the upper (*A/B* banks) position. (If the effects levers were in the *B*-bank position the dissolve would have been to that buss.)

By putting the program mix faders in the *up* position we have taken the first step in activating a two-buss effects subswitcher (*A* and *B* banks), which has its own control levers. It is with these two banks that transition effects such as the *wipe* are accomplished. The specific effect is chosen by means of buttons or rotary selection controls, and then the transition is made by moving the effects levers from one bank to the other.

With the less-complex special effects generators, one specific bank is usually structured as the effects completion bank. For example, a top-left *corner wipe* would always start with the original picture on the *A* bank. The new *B*-bank picture would gradually fill the screen as the levers are moved down to the *B* bank. (Moving the levers *from* the *B* bank to the *A* bank would produce the exact reverse corner-wipe effect.)

Effects such as split screens or corner inserts are produced by stopping the lever movement at the desired point in the transition between the two pictures. In order to accomplish a dissolve to any such preset effect, the preceding shot must be punched up on the home-base *C* bank. The mix levers must be *down* so that the *C*-bank shot is feeding the program line; then as the program mix faders are moved *up* (to the *A/B* banks) we dissolve into the preset split screen or corner insert.

Setting up and dissolving in and out of *key* and *matte* effects involves a slightly different set of operating techniques. Using these same three banks, and again applying the principle of designated function, we can set up a two-camera key effect—first in preview and then on the program line. In figure 7-9 we are back on the *C* bank, feeding the program line (since the mix faders are in the down position) with camera 1. On the upper two busses, one specific bank (either *A* or *B*) must be designated to handle the special electronic action necessary to achieve the white lettering *cut-out* keying effect. On some switchers the assignment of this function could be optional among two or more banks. On simpler units it is usually built into one specific bank. For our example, we will make it the *B* bank; therefore we will punch up camera 2—which is on the title card to be keyed—on the *B* buss. Camera 3, on the *A* bank, is on a wide shot of the set, which is to be used as the background scene for the key.

The ability to preview **brightness** and color levels is essential if the key effect is to be used at all. The levels of the two signal sources involved (cameras 3 and 2 in our example) must be kept within a narrow tolerance to function. Therefore, there must be a control that adjusts the level at which the keying action occurs. This control is sometimes called the *clipper* because when properly used it takes out or *clips out* extraneous video **noise** and *bleedthrough* effects. Depending upon the type of key being produced, there may also be a brightness control that can vary the lettering from pure white to solid black. On switchers with a color-generating component, the white lettering on the studio key card can at this point be replaced electronically with a properly contrasting color. Adjustment of these levels is accomplished with the preview monitor. (The *A/B* effects faders are not used in this electronic effects process; when the two banks are in the key mode, the fader levers are temporarily inoperative while adjustments are made with the clipping and/or brightness controls.)

What we have set up in our example (fig. 7-9), then, is a studio picture (camera 1) on the program line—being fed through the *C* buss—and a second studio picture (camera 3) being previewed in composite with a title key (on camera 2) on the *A/B* effects banks. When ready, the dissolve to the keyed effect (camera 2 over camera 3) is accomplished simply by moving the program mix faders to their upper position.

Instead of dissolving to the desired key effect (from camera 1 to camera 2 over camera 3), we also could fade in the key over the existing line picture. In this case, let us assume we wanted to gradually bring in the key camera (camera 2) over the shot we have on camera 1. Leaving camera 1 on the *C* buss (going out over the line), we would also punch up camera 1 on the *A* bank. We would then preview the effect and set the key levels—adjusting camera 2 (*B* buss) over camera 1 (*A* buss). Then, when ready for the effect, we would move the program mix faders to their upper position. As the fader arms are raised we gradually bring in camera 2 keyed over the camera 1 picture; in essence, we are dissolving from a solid picture on camera 1 (*C* bank) to a key of camera 2 over camera 1 (*A/B* banks).

To achieve the instant addition or removal of the keying signal from the composite picture, one would utilize the *black* button on the *B* bank. With the same camera punched up on busses *C* and *A*, preview the key effect (buss *B* over buss *A*). Then punch up black on the *B* buss and immediately dissolve from the *C* bank to the *A/B* banks; with this dissolve no change of picture will occur on the screen. (You are dissolving from a solid picture from the camera to a picture from the same camera with black—nothing—keyed over it). But, when the key camera is now pressed on the *B* buss, the key effect is then instantly punched up.

7.4 Special Electronic and Digital Effects

In addition to basic switching functions and simple camera transitions, there is a variety of special electronic effects that more complicated switchers and special equipment can handle. New processes and effects are constantly being developed. It is sufficient at this stage that the production student simply be aware of some of the basic effects and how they can be used; skill and refinement in using these sophisticated techniques can come at a later period in a student's professional development.

Indeed, there is a very real danger in getting too involved with elaborate electronic effects at an early stage. Too often they are used solely for the sake of playing around with the equipment. The student should learn to master the basic pieces of standard equipment before jumping unprepared into the world of electronic wizardry. A person must master the disciplines of communicating effectively with the medium of television before trying to exploit its full electronic potential. For this reason, we will not be concerned with diagrams and illustrations of how these various effects can be applied.

Specialized Transitions

Of course, even the *dissolve* is a type of electronic transition—a means of blending two different video images. Its use, however, has become so standard—as a result of its long ancestry as the lap-dissolve in motion pictures—that its function has become routine.

Most other electronic transitions can come under the heading of the *wipe*. With a standard wipe, one image is pushed off the face of the program monitor in a straight line as another image replaces the first one. The most standard patterns are the vertical wipe (similar to pulling down—or pushing up—a window shade) and the horizontal wipe (similar to pulling a sliding door across the picture).

Wipes are manipulated on the switcher by a special effects buss and another pair of control levers or faders. The desired pattern (left to right, bottom to top) is selected on one set of pushbuttons; the two cameras are punched up on the special effects busses (on some switchers the mix busses also serve this function); and the special-effects fader arms are moved to produce the effect. In a typical setup, one fader arm would control the vertical movement and one would control the horizontal movement.

On most simple special effects switchers, it is possible to combine the horizontal and vertical movement to effect a *corner wipe* that will have both a horizontal and vertical line. Other switchers may include a diagonal wipe.

More complicated SEGs will be able to produce a wide variety of patterns for the transition. Boxes, circles, diamonds, and stripes are common patterns. Most of these can be modified by adding any degree of *wiggle* desired. Color changes in *hue* and *tone* can be added to the effects. With a *wipe positioner,* or *joy stick,* these effects can be positioned to start anywhere on the screen.

Just as the superimposition is a dissolve that is held on the screen without effecting a transition, so can the electronics of the wipe be extended into a *split-screen* effect. The split screen is a means of combining two pictures with either a horizontal or vertical (and occasionally a diagonal) line separating the screen into two distinct areas, with a different picture (from separate cameras) in each part of the screen. By means of the special effects faders, relative sizes of the two pictures can be adjusted. By manipulating the horizontal and vertical special effects levers separately, it is also possible to achieve a **corner insert.**

This places one picture in any quadrant of the screen (say, in the lower left hand corner), with the video from another camera filling the rest of the screen. Again, the exact size and proportion of the corner insert can be easily manipulated by the control levers.

More sophisticated switchers and special effects generators have been developed with even greater refinements on the basic wipe and split screen. The *soft wipe* blurs the distinct line between the two images so that, at the actual line where the two (or more) images meet, there is a narrow superimposition; the result is a softening of the wipe effect. Another technical advance is the *multiple-source split screen.* With this device, it is possible to split the screen into a number of individual sections, each with a separate picture. Again, these separate divisions can be positioned and shaped to meet a variety of artistic demands—even resembling bordered snapshots in a photo album. The most conventional multiple-source split screen is probably the four-camera *quad split.* Another useful special effect is the *spotlight,* which enables the operator to darken the entire screen except for one circle of light, which can be shaped, changed in size, and positioned anywhere on the screen with a joy stick.

Keying and Matting

Several different keying and matting processes enable the switcher to use the video information from one video source to cut a pattern into another picture electronically. There are three basic, closely related types of keying effects—the *insert key,* the *matte key,* and the *chroma key.*

Insert Key.   The insert key is the most common and easy-to-use keying device. Often identified as the **internal key,** it is typically used for titling and written information. The

Figure 7-10 Two monitors illustrating the difference between a super and a key. The monitor on the left shows a black-and-white graphics card supered over the woman's face. The right-hand monitor shows the same card keyed over the woman's face.

key card is prepared the same as a super card (section 10.4)—white letters on a black card. Unlike a super, however, wherein the white letters are simply superimposed over another background picture, the key actually blocks out a portion of the picture from the background camera that corresponds to the white information on the key camera. The resulting composite picture is not a superimposition; the white lettering is solid and opaque, with no information from the background picture bleeding through. Figure 7-10 compares a super and a key.

Electronic keys—as well as wipes, split screens, and similar effects—all can be enhanced by the *border feature* found on many switchers. Bordering, or edging, can outline any key or insert to make its boundary distinct. The width, color, and softness of the border all can be altered electronically. The *edge key*, for example, will make keyed letters stand out in bold relief by edging each white letter with

a thin black line. This makes them more legible against a busy background. The *shadow key* can add a heavy shadow around two sides of each letter to give a solid three-dimensional feeling as it apparently stands out in front of the background.

Matte Key.   With an insert key, the electronic hole cut out by the keying camera is filled with the information supplied by that key camera—titles, graphic designs, or whatever. With a matte key, however, the electronic hole can be filled with information from any other video source—color, patterns, or picture information from another camera.

The **external key** uses the picture information from a third picture source to combine two other pictures. For instance, the key camera may be shooting a white circle on a black card; this determines the cutout pattern or shape the other cameras will use. When this is combined electronically with two other cameras, the picture from one camera is used wherever the key camera was shooting black (around the circle) and the picture information from the other camera is used wherever the key camera was shooting white (inside the circle).

The concept of keying is extended into *monochrome matte effects* whereby any black or very dark portions of a foreground picture are electronically cancelled when combined with some other background picture. The foreground image then appears to be a solid picture (not a superimposition) in front of the background scene.

Chroma Key.   Now one of the most common of the electronic special effects, the **chroma key** is a matting process that has become a staple of most color production. This is a technique in which a specific color—rather than a graphic design or pattern—is used as the electronic key to cut out part of the picture. (Any color can be selected by the switcher as the key; however, blue is most often used because it is farthest from any skin tones.) Wherever the foreground or key camera detects the designated hue, or *chroma,* in its picture, that video information is discarded and background picture signals are supplied from a second—or background—camera (often from the film chain, although it can be from another studio camera, a videotape, or any other source).

Thus, if the talent is standing in front of an evenly lit blue background and not wearing any blue item of clothing, this picture can be combined with any other background picture and the background will appear only where there was blue in the foreground picture. The talent can hence be placed in front of any other picture desired. This type of chroma key application is routinely used, for example, in newscasts where the picture information for a particular news story is keyed in behind the

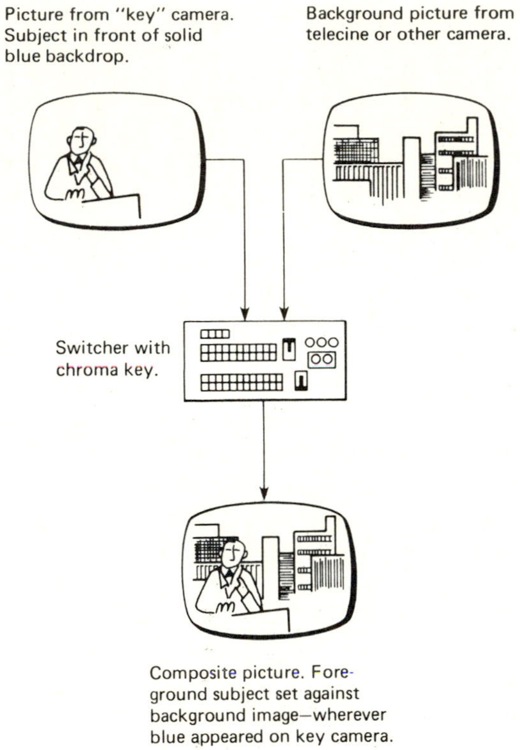

Picture from "key" camera. Subject in front of solid blue backdrop.

Background picture from telecine or other camera.

Switcher with chroma key.

Composite picture. Foreground subject set against background image—wherever blue appeared on key camera.

Figure 7-11   Chroma key.

newscaster. (See fig. 7-11.) This matting technique also has obvious applications for dramatic formats, instructional programs, variety shows, and virtually every other type of production.

Although the use of chroma key is widespread, it is not without numerous potential difficulties. The electronic equipment has to be delicately adjusted; lighting of the color background of the key camera has to be perfectly even; considerable attention must be given to selection of costumes and scenery. Slight problems in any of these areas lead to conspicuous troubles such as tearing of the foreground image, an obvious border around the foreground figure, discoloration, or indistinct contours.

Single-Camera Effects

In addition to the electronic transitions and keying and matting effects, certain other single-camera electronic effects should be briefly mentioned here. These are devices for image manipulation that do not involve the use of a second camera.

The video engineer has the ability to effect several changes through manipulation of the camera control unit (CCU). **Sweep reversals** can electronically reverse the scanning process of the camera. *Horizontal sweep reversal* reverses the left and right directions of a picture, creating a mirror image. This can be useful when shooting through a mirror for special angles (for example, shooting up at an overhead mirror to get a view of a table top, and then reversing the horizontal sweep in order to counteract the mirror reversal). On the other hand, *vertical sweep reversal*—turning a picture upside down—is usually only for obvious spectacular or comedic effects.

On black-and-white cameras, a negative-like image can be created with **polarity reversal.** This changes all of the blacks to white and whites to black. This has some fascinating artistic possibilities as well as some practical uses (for example, projecting negative film from which no positive print has been made).

High-contrast images can be achieved a couple of different ways. One is through **debeaming.** The video engineer can turn down one of the CCU controls (the intensity of the scanning beam), which reduces the image to stark white and black contrasts. A similar effect can be achieved with the internal key on the switcher. By keying a picture over black and adjusting the *clipper,* a strong high-contrast image can be created with all of the grays removed.

Just as it is possible to get audio reverberation or an echo effect by recording and playing back almost simultaneously a given sound source (section 3.4), so is it possible to achieve a form of **video feedback.** By feeding a camera's signal into a floor monitor and then using the same camera to shoot the face of the monitor, a wide variety of bizarre video effects can be obtained. The picture in figure 1-5 was achieved by keying over black and then using video feedback.

Most of these effects are especially applicable for monochrome television. (Some are not possible on color cameras at all without a lot of difficulty, for example, sweep reversal and polarity reversal.) One area where color television is especially exciting, however, is in the possibility of **colorization.** This process involves a special colorizing generator—also referred to as a *color video synthesizer*—that can add various colors to black-and-white pictures, create various abstract patterns, and even produce color images without the use of a camera at all. Such artistic applications take us out of the realm of basic communication and into the arena of video art (section 1.3).

Digital Effects

One of the most exciting frontiers of video imagery is in the area of digital manipulation. With digital technology it is possible to expand the creative and production capabilities of television far beyond what had been possible up to the mid-1970s.

The audio and video signals described in chapters 2 and 5 are *analog* systems; that is, variations in electrical current actually represent and define the sound and picture. With *digital* coding, on the other hand, the video information is transformed into a series of binary numbers. (See fig. 7-12.) Each of the 500 dots that are spread across a single scanning line, for example (see section 5.2), is reduced to a brightness level on a **gray scale** from 1 to 256. The video signal can thus be translated into a series of binary numbers expressed as off/on blips. (A point registering at a brightness level of 155 on the gray scale, for instance,

(a) Representation of an Analog Signal.

Figure 7-12 Comparison of analog and digital encoding.

1-0-0-1-1-0-1-1/1-0-0-1-1-0-1-0/1-0-0-1-1-0-0-1

(b) Representation of a Digital Signal.

would be encoded as 1-0-0-1-1-0-1-1 in the binary system.)[4]

Once the television signal is encoded into a binary-digital format, the system has many advantages: memory or storage capacity can be significantly increased; the quality of the video information does not deteriorate as it is processed, amplified, channeled, and transmitted; and, most importantly, the signal information can now be manipulated, rearranged, enhanced, and augmented in ways that are impossible with analog information.

Digital Video Manipulator. Several marvelous television devices have emerged from the digital age so far: the **time-base corrector,** so important in restoring sync in editing and switching operations (see section 8.2); the *framestore sychronizer,* used for synchronization of all major network feeds and remote pickups. None, however, offers as much excitement as the **digital video manipulator (DVM).**

The electronic wonders described at the beginning of this chapter are a result of the DVM. Other advances include *contin-*

4. Binary encoding, of course, is what forms the basis for all digital computers and microprocessing equipment. It is built on the base-two counting system, which reduces all numerical information to a two-symbol number (using *zero* and *one*). Thus, all numerical data can be handled as a series of *off* (zero) and *on* (one) electrical connections.

uous image compression, which enables the switcher operator to compress the full-frame picture down to the size of a tiny circle (at any rate, to any size) and—with a joy stick—to place the shrunken image anywhere on the screen. This is what makes the squeeze zoom possible as a transition.

Image expansion allows the director to take any segment of the video frame and enlarge it up to four times its original size (beyond which point it becomes unintelligible). A combined phenomenon is *image stretching.* Any portion of the picture can be expanded or compressed in any direction; ratios can be altered; and graphics can be shaped to fit the picture.

Other transitional devices—in addition to the fold-over and squeeze zoom—include the *video split,* which literally can take a picture and pull it apart in the middle to make room for a new frame, and the *push-off,* which simply shoves a whole frame off the tube sideways while replacing it with another image (as opposed to the wipe, which does not move the two stationary frames involved in the transition).

The impact of many of these advances is with postproduction editing. (See chapter 9.) Once the basic video images have been recorded, the director can sit down with an editor and decide how to time each transition, when to compress this image and bring in another, whether to electronically zoom in on a particular frame, how to shape graphics as they are added later, and so forth. The video editor now has at his or her command more sophisticated and less expensive creative opportunities than film editors have ever enjoyed.

The switcher, the SEG, and the DVM have come a long way since the crude connection panel we started with at the beginning of section 7.1.

7.5 Commands of Preparation and Execution

In discussing audio production techniques (section 3.5), we stressed the difference between commands of preparation and commands of execution. Nowhere is this distinction more important than in giving commands to the technical director. Because the switcher operator has two entirely different physical operations to perform—depending upon which command is given—the commands of preparation must allow for sufficient lead time. Such commands, given over the intercom system, also give a warning to the operator of the upcoming camera.

One helpful rule is that the command of preparation for any straight take is "ready." The preparation for any dissolve, super, fade, or special transition or effect that involves getting something set or prepared on another buss, uses the command "prepare." (A few directors prefer to use the command of "set up.") Although some directors use the term "standby" as a preparation for both takes and dissolves, this can be confusing to the crew. The use of correct terminology immediately lets the technical director know whether he or she simply has to get ready to push a button on the same buss or whether it is necessary to prepare or set up another camera on another buss.

The command sequence for a direct take from camera 1 to camera 2 would be stated by the director as follows:

(Preparation):   "Ready camera 2" (or simply) "Ready 2"
(Execution):   "Take 2"

The word *ready* lets the technical director know that he or she only has to place a finger on the camera 2 button on the activated buss.

No matter how rushed the director may be or how fast-paced the program may be, the director should never skimp on the command of preparation. *Accuracy in getting the technical director properly prepared is the most important part of calling shots correctly.* If the director does not have time to give full commands, he or she should abbreviate the command of execution, not preparation:

(Preparation):   "Ready 2"
(Execution):   "Take it" (or simply) "Take"

If time is so short that even this much preparation is impossible (for example, shooting a game show, fast-paced panel discussion, or football game), the command of preparation still must be given priority:

(Preparation):   "Two"
(Execution):   "Take"

A dissolve requires a different-sounding command of preparation to allow the technical director time to prepare for a more complex series of actions. Considering that we already have camera 1 on the line, the correct commands for a dissolve would be:

(Preparation):   "Prepare a dissolve to 2" (or) "Prepare 2" (or) "Set up 2"
(Execution):   "Dissolve to 2"

For a super, the actions are the same so the commands are much the same:

(Preparation):   "Prepare 2" (or) "Prepare to super 2 over 1" (or) "Set up 2" (or) "Set up a super of 2 with 1"
(Execution):   "Super camera 2" (or) "Super 2 over 1"

We depart slightly from the basic pattern whenever two cameras are to be taken together in a super. While this effect also involves a movement of the control levers, the movement is not one of program execution. In other words, the result of the lever movement is not seen, when it is being done, on the line monitor or on the air. As previously outlined, the command of execution is a "take"—calling only for the pressing of the *line mix* output button or *take bar*. For this reason, the voice procedure in this case should be as follows:

(Preparation):   "Ready to take 2 and 3 in super"
(Execution):   "Take 2 and 3 in super"

The "in super" at the end of the command is optional, but does reinforce the intent of the command.

When the director wants to preview a super of two cameras prior to their use, there is no necessary command of execution that follows. The preparatory command must be given far enough in advance so that the technical director has a chance to set up the preview at a time most convenient during the ongoing program. The director keeps an eye on the preview monitor to see when the preview is ready. The preparatory command would be:

"Prepare a preview of cameras 2 and 3 in super"

Whenever we have two cameras supered together, there are two optional ways to remove one of those cameras from the picture. To gradually fade out the super, either one of two command procedures can be used:

(Preparation):   "Prepare to lose camera 2"
(Execution):   "Lose 2" (or) "Fade out 2"

Or the more definite and safer way:

(Preparation):   "Prepare to dissolve through to camera 3"
(Execution):   "Dissolve through to camera 3" (or) "Go through to 3"

In this situation, we are simply moving the fader arms as if completing a dissolve.

If we want instead to instantly remove part of a super—and we have a switcher with a program buss—then we can go full to the intended remaining camera with a simple take to that camera on the program bank. The same sort of command and response structure works if a take-bar system is employed:

(Preparation):   "Ready to take out camera 2"
(Execution):   "Take out 2"

Or better yet:

(Preparation):   "Ready to take to camera 3 full"
(Execution):   "Take to camera 3 full"

Commands that call for special effects keys and wipes will generally follow this same pattern—with allowances for some of the more complicated displays and setups. Even with such simple effects as a key, the director should always emphasize important information such as the signal source (by number) that has the title graphic:

(Preparation):   "Prepare a preview of a key of chain 6—with the graphics—over camera 2"

(Continued Preparation): "Prepare to dissolve to the key of 6 over 2"

(Execution): "Dissolve to 2 and 6" (or) "Dissolve to 6 over 2"

For a corner insert:

(Preparation): "Prepare to wipe in corner insert of camera 2 over camera 1"

(Execution): "Wipe in 2"

Finally, fades to and from black are handled in a manner very similar to the dissolve (as the fade to or from black is in essence a dissolve to or from black). At the beginning of a program, let's assume the director wanted to fade in from black with a slide on film chain 2. The typical commands would be something like the following:

(Preparation): "Prepare film chain 2" (or) "Prepare to fade in film 2"

(Execution): "Fade in film chain 2" (or) "Fade up on film 2"

And the closing fade to black would be simply:

(Preparation): "Prepare black"

(Execution): "Fade to black" (or) "Fade sound and picture out"

These, then, are the basic elements of television's visual language: camera takes, dissolves, supers, cameras taken together in super, cameras undercut while in super, and fades to black. In the creative sense, the important consideration is that the transitions be appropriate to the context of the visual idea the picture sequence is expressing. Technically, their use depends upon the operating capabilities of the switcher, which can follow only from a certain amount of hands-on practice and discipline.

Crucial to the successful operation of the switcher is the use of the proper preparatory commands: "ready" for a take; "prepare" or "set up" for a dissolve, fade, or super. This terminology is fairly standard throughout the country, and its use is essential to any good control room operation. Just the use of the word *prepare*—even before the camera is mentioned by number—starts a response pattern in the thinking process. This is an integral part of the discipline of the technical director.

Summary

The switcher is the key *channeling* and *mixing* device in the video signal flow system. In conjunction with the special effects generator (SEG), it is also involved in *shaping* the video signal.

The switcher can be thought of as a simple connection panel, with additional *busses* and *fader arms* added to increase the flexibility of the unit. The basic camera transitions and effects used on the switcher include the *take, dissolve, fade,* and *super*.

There are several variations of more complex switchers that, in conjunction with the various video *monitors,* enable the technical director to *preview* and *preset* certain effects. Special electronic effects include *wipes* and *split screens* and numerous *keying and matting* effects—including the insert (internal) key, the matte (external) key, and the chroma key. Single-camera effects include sweep reversals, polarity reversals, debeaming, video feedback, and colorization.

Effects available through the *digital video manipulator* (DVM) encompass image compression and expansion and image stretching—as well as transitions such as the fold-over, squeeze zoom, video split, and push-off.

Vocal command procedures stress the importance of the correct preparatory commands: the use of "ready" before any cut or take; and of "prepare" or "set up" before any dissolve, fade, super, or special effect.

This chapter has been concerned with the operation of the TV switcher and the techniques of live studio editing. In chapter 8 we will look at videotape recording.

7.6   Training Exercise and Class Production Project

Class Exercise

The following written exercise is designed to help the student think about the actual operating process of the control room switcher in preparation for its use in later production exercises.

First draw a sketch of the switcher in your own control room, with the appropriate identifying terminology. Consider that only the black buttons on all busses have been pressed and that the control levers are in the *B*-buss position.

Then, following each command of preparation or execution, write in the necessary sequence of operation, the buttons to be pressed, and the levers to be moved in order to accomplish the command request. Keep in mind that this exercise represents an ongoing series of actions, as in a program sequence. Each movement is done only in the light of what has just been done previously. A technical director must constantly ask himself or herself, Which buttons are already pressed, and what is the position of the faders?

If possible, each student should have the opportunity to run through the exercise at the switcher, with another student giving commands as the director. For contrast, title cards, as well as wide, waist, and close-up shots, can be used. If done also as a studio exercise, the sequence of commands can be altered in order to give some variety of action.

Command Sequence

Prepare to fade up from black to camera 2

Fade up on camera 2

Ready camera 1

Take camera 1

Prepare a corner wipe from bottom left to camera 3

Wipe to camera 3

Prepare to super camera 1 over camera 3

Super camera 1

Prepare to dissolve through to camera 1

Dissolve through to camera 1

Preview a key of cameras 2 and 3; camera 3 has a title graphic

Prepare a dissolve from camera 1 to the key of cameras 2 and 3

Dissolve to key of cameras 2 and 3

Prepare to fade out camera 3

Fade out camera 3

Prepare to fade to black

Fade to black

Class Production Project (Appendix D-2)

The first combined use of all production facilities is a rewarding but difficult step. For this reason, we have devised a picture-card production exercise that concentrates on the development of basic switcher and camera control techniques. Later exercises will expand upon this introductory work to include the lighting and audio techniques required for larger studio productions.

Seven photographs and one super title card are included in appendix D. At relatively small cost, these can be photographically enlarged to a width of at least two feet to provide for adequate camera use when mounted on a hard backing. Each photo offers both long-shot and close-up aspects of the subject material for the promotional sequence. Depending upon how one wishes to use the images, there is the opportunity for pan, tilt, and zoom camera work.

There is no one correct way to do the exercise. Each person should study the photos and decide upon a meaningful sequence of images. The production is designed to allow for a maximum of individual input in the selection of music as well as the direction of the pace and style of the announcer and related camera work. Promotional copy also is provided in appendix D. Students should be encouraged to rewrite the script with possible changes in the order of the pictures. The concluding section offers an opportunity to intercut a montage of several pictures used earlier or to undercut them with the title card. What students are working toward is a totality and unity of production in which the end result is more than equal to the sum of its parts.

function and operation of the videotape recorder

8

One of the last steps in the video signal flow is the recording (and playback) operation. This chapter deals specifically with the electronic and functional aspects of magnetic recording. We will examine the general concepts of electromagnetic videotape recording and playback—relating the various component functions to operational controls. The equipment involved in electronic editing will only be peripherally mentioned. Chapter 9 will extend the discussion of magnetic video recording with a careful analysis of editing equipment and procedures as we get into *postproduction editing*—especially as it relates to ENG/EFP single-camera production techniques.

In spite of the rapid development of the television industry during its first decade, there was no satisfactory way of recording the electronic camera picture until the mid-1950s. The *kinescope* process (developed in the 1940s) was a specialized technique that used motion picture film to photograph the moving image off a receiver (kinescope) tube; the result was a blurry, washed-out picture with degraded audio quality.

A way had to be found to record the electromagnetic signals that actually generated the television picture. The subsequent development of videotape technology has not only changed the nature and scope of video production, it has had enormous impact upon the whole telecommunications industry.

8.1 Principles of Videotape Recording

Before we can go any further into the basics of electromagnetic recording, it will be necessary to expand somewhat upon the camera and picture tube structure as presented in chapter 5 (sections 5.2 and 5.3). Although the student should carefully reread those sections before proceeding, a brief recap is provided here for reference.

The Electronic Basis of Videotape Recording

Both the camera and picture tube raster (display area) are organized into 525 horizontal scanning lines. Each line contains roughly 500 separate illumination points. A stream of electrons (scanning beam) is made to cover the successive points on each of the 525 lines by means of electromagnets located just forward of the electron guns.

The scanning process actually occurs in two phases. Starting at the top left of the picture, the odd-numbered lines are first scanned to produce a top-to-bottom picture field. Only one-half of the illumination points have been used to produce this picture. With this completed, the scanning beam then starts at the top left of the tube and scans all the even-numbered lines to produce another picture field. There are sixty of these one-half picture fields occurring every second, which are interlaced to produce the effect of thirty complete frames per second.

Horizontal and Vertical Sync. Examining this process in greater detail, we find that several additional factors are needed to ensure the stability of the picture. As the electromagnets in both the camera and picture tubes pull the stream of electrons left to right and top to bottom, it is imperative that the scanning process in both units be exactly synchronized. A series of specialized pulses, generated separately from the color and intensity portion of the video signal, are utilized for this purpose. There is a *horizontal sync pulse,* which activates the video system at the beginning of each scanning line and turns it off for a brief retrace period (blanking) as the beam returns to the beginning of a new line on the left side of the tube.

At the completion of each field there is a similar retrace period as the scanning beam returns to the top left of the picture. At this point a *vertical sync pulse* is used to coordi-nate the start of each new field. While there are only two vertical sync pulses for every 525 horizontal sync pulses, they must nevertheless be considered as an extremely important part of the video sequence. Because it denotes the beginning of a new picture field, the vertical sync pulse has an important application in videotape editing.

The Magnetic Basis of Videotape Recording

In earlier sections of the text, we have seen how sound waves (section 2.2.1) and light waves (section 5.2)—through a series of transformations (transducing)—can be put into an electromagnetic form that is suitable for broadcast. By utilizing these and other qualities of magnetism and electrical energy, this complex broadcast signal can be permanently "memorized" for later use. As youngsters, many of us demonstrated how a magnet on the underside of a piece of paper can align iron filings into a magnetic pattern. The principle involved in this action provides the basis for all audio and videotape recording.

The record-playback **head** on any tape machine is actually a magnet, and the tape is a polyester strip coated on one side with iron oxide particles. If electrical energy—organized into a broadcast signal—is fed into the head, the iron oxide particles in the tape passing in contact with the head will be aligned into a continuing series of magnetic patterns. Thus, in the *record mode* the resulting magnetic patterns are themselves a memory of the broadcast signal. (The patterns are physically visible only if the oxide is treated with certain chemicals.)

In the *playback mode* no electrical energy is sent to the magnetic head. As the tape moves, however, the interaction of patterned iron oxide particles in the tape and the magnetic head produce an electronic signal in the playback head that is an exact duplicate of the original input. (See fig. 8-1.)

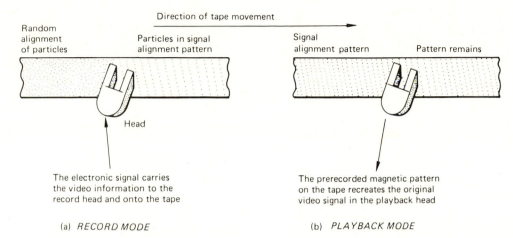

Direction of tape movement

Random alignment of particles

Particles in signal alignment pattern

Signal alignment pattern

Pattern remains

Head

The electronic signal carries the video information to the record head and onto the tape

The prerecorded magnetic pattern on the tape recreates the original video signal in the playback head

(a) *RECORD MODE*

(b) *PLAYBACK MODE*

(a) *Record Mode.* The electronic video signals sent to the record head activate the magnetized head to align the iron oxide particles on the tape to retain a permanent (until erased) pattern of the recorded electronic video signal.

(b) *Playback Mode.* The prerecorded video signals on the videotape generate a small amount of electrical current in the playback head which is an exact duplicate of the original video signal.

Figure 8-1 Video recording and playback heads.

It all seems simple enough until we remember that the video track must contain enough signal information to reproduce thirty 525-line pictures every second. With approximately 500 points of illumination per line, this amounts to roughly 250,000 bits of information per frame—or 7½-million bits per second! Just as in the camera-to-picture-tube signal process, great care must be taken to ensure the precise synchronization of the various elements of the video signal during the recording process. The cost of professional recording and editing equipment is directly related to the high degree of quality and reliability that are necessary for the maintenance of broadcast standards.

Development of the Quadruplex Videotape Recorders

In the fall of 1956 CBS in Hollywood broadcast its first program by means of a videotape recording. It originated from an Ampex machine that utilized a **quadruplex** video head assembly. The *quad head* recorder was named

for the four rotating video heads that vertically came into contact with a two-inch videotape. (See fig. 8-2.)

Some very impressive control signals and editing equipment were developed for the quad machines and these recorders became the industry standard for many years. They are still in use at many television stations.

It became apparent, however, that this format had some very definite limitations. Because of the basic elements of its design it could not produce a recognizable picture at tape speeds other than precisely 15 inches per second (ips)—or, with modifications, at 7½ ips. Slow motion as well as faster-than-normal search speeds were not possible. Also, the tape could not be stopped in order to produce a **freeze frame.** Not only did this make the editing process difficult, it also ruled out the production use of any stop-motion special effects.

Additionally, the quad-head recorders were very bulky and quite expensive—advanced models costing well in excess of $100,000 by the mid-1970s. Finally, the ma-

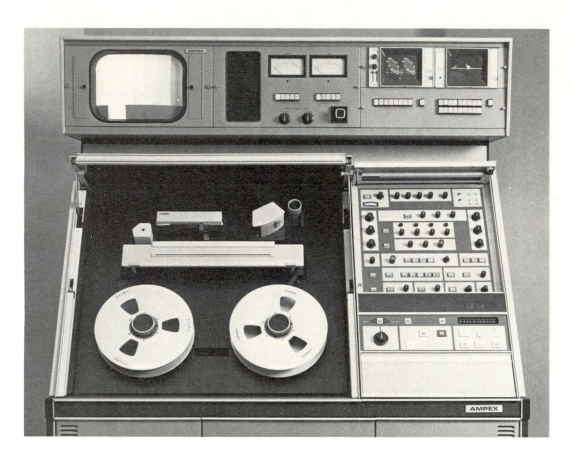

Figure 8-2 Quadruplex, high-band, color videotape recorder. (Photo courtesy of Ampex Corporation.)

chines were costly to maintain; they were delicate electronically and involved considerable engineering attention to keep the four heads aligned. (See figs. 8-3, 8-4, and 8-5.)

8.2 Helical-Scan Videotape Recorders

The answer to many of these problems was to be found in the **helical-scan,** or **slant-track,** videotape recorders (VTRs) developed in the late 1960s. Introduced originally as low-cost alternatives to the quadruplex machines, these helical-scan video recorders were rapidly adopted for nonbroadcast applications—school TV projects, hospitals, industrial training, and television production curriculums. (See fig. 8-6.)

Evolution of the Slant-Track Machines

With the helical-scan recorders, equipment costs are much lower, videotape is cheaper, there is less machine setup time and maintenance "down time," operating costs are smaller, and there is less need for highly trained operators. Despite the fact that the technical quality of early helical-scan VTR machines did not generally match the broadcast quality of quad-head machines, many closed-circuit systems and educational institutions choose to rely upon the helical-scan formats—for reasons of economy, reliability, and ease of operation.

During the late 1960s numerous manufacturers brought out competing formats and

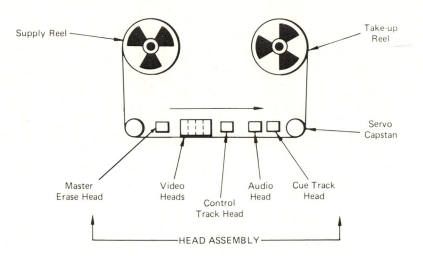

Supply Reel

Take-up Reel

Servo Capstan

Master Erase Head

Video Heads

Control Track Head

Audio Head

Cue Track Head

HEAD ASSEMBLY

As the videotape is pulled from the supply reel to the take-up reel, it passes first the master erase head—which is activated only when all of the information on the videotape is to be erased. The tape then passes the four revolving video heads which are used for both recording and playing back. The control track then puts on the neces-sary synchronizing information; the audio head records (or plays back) the sound portion of the program; and the cue track is used for various aux-iliary and editing information. The servo capstan pulls the tape through the head assembly at a con-stant speed during the playback and record proc-esses.

Figure 8-3 Head arrangement in a quadruplex recorder.

standards—utlizing tape widths from ¼-inch to 2 inches. Altogether there were close to forty different, noncompatible standards. Then, under the leadership of the SMPTE (Society of Motion Picture and Television Engineers), the industry adopted a ½-inch format that was picked up by most educational and training institutions.

In 1970 the ¾-inch U-matic videocassette system was introduced. Although there were earlier attempts to establish a standard cassette or cartridge system, the U-matic format was the first to become solidly accepted by educational and industrial users. With its many refinements and editing innovations, it became the workhorse of the closed-circuit television field.

After several abortive attempts to establish a consumer market with a home cartridge or cassette system, Sony finally succeeded with its Betamax format—followed closely by other manufacturers with the VHS system. Today, Beta and VHS dominate the growing home entertainment field.

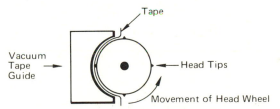

Tape

Vacuum Tape Guide

Head Tips

Movement of Head Wheel

As seen from the side, the videotape (which is being pulled past the head assembly) at this point is curved by the vacuum guide to fit the shape of the rotating head wheel—contain-ing the four heads—which is spinning at right angles to the direction of the tape movement.

Figure 8-4 Head assembly in a quadruplex recorder.

Even though the video signal of the early helical-scan recorders was inherently less sta-ble and reliable than the quadruplex format, the slant-track picture and electronic infor-nation could be significantly enhanced. By using a *time-base corrector,* the electronic in-formation from the helical-scan machine could be made virtually as stable as a quad-head signal. Time-base correction (in essence, upgrading the control track synchronizing in-formation) can greatly reduce picture jitters

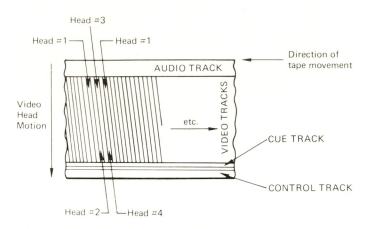

**Figure 8-5
Configuration of
quadruplex videotape
tracks.**

The four rotating heads lay down video information in bands or stripes that are transverse, almost
perpendicular, to the longitude of the tape. Each
head lays down every fourth video band.

**Figure 8-6   Helical scan
head assembly of a ¾-
inch VTR as seen from
above.**

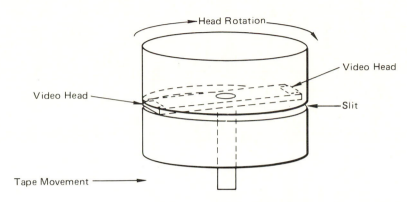

In order to attain the high "writing speed" necessary to record millions of bits of information per second, the video heads spin in the head drum at tremendous speeds. Most half-inch machines use two video heads in order to lay down enough video information.

Figure 8-7 Rotation of helical-scan video heads.

and drifting; several machines can be locked together for editing and dissolving between recorders without synchronization problems.

These technological improvements, plus the inherent advantages and simplicity of the **continuous field** helical-scan system,[1] spurred broadcast engineers on to find a slant-track format that would serve for open-circuit transmission. Finally in 1978, again with SMPTE leadership, the industry adopted the one-inch *type C* format, which has since become the standard of the broadcast industry. In addition to the lower operating costs and simpler maintenance requirements, the newer helical-scan recorders offer greater time-base stability, improvements in editing functions, still-frame, slow motion, faster-than-normal (or *jogging*) search speeds, and many other enhanced electronic refinements.

1. The continuous-field, or *nonsegmented,* recording format refers to the ability of the helical-scan recorder to record one complete electronic field at a time—as opposed to the quad-head format, which records the video picture in different bands or segments.

The Helical-Scan Video Head Assembly

Figure 8-7 illustrates the basic head assembly of a helical-scan machine as introduced on the earlier reel-to-reel models—essentially a drum with a slit around the middle. Inside of the drum there is a rotating bar with a video head on one or both ends. The head protrudes through the slit to come in contact with the slightly angled path of the tape, which produces the characteristic slant track seen in figure 8-8.

With the newer videocassette formats, the entire top half of the drum is a rotating wheel with the video heads attached to the outer circumference. This is because the tape itself cannot be angled with cassettes, so the drum must be tilted to produce the slanted track, as illustrated in figure 8-9.

With the head wheel rotating rapidly in one direction and the tape moving in the opposite direction, a ¾-inch cassette machine will achieve a *writing speed* of 700 inches per second even though the tape itself is moving

As the videotape winds around the circular drum, the tape is slightly higher at one end than at the other. The resulting pattern laid down by the rotating head is in the form of a helix, thus forming a helical line on the videotape.

Figure 8-8 Helical-scan record tracks.

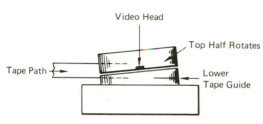

The playback/record heads are attached to the rotating top half of the tilted head assembly.

Figure 8-9 Helical-scan videocassette drum assembly.

through the unit at only 3¾ ips. In some of the formats the videotape wraps around slightly more than half of the drum. In the broadcast type C format designed for special effects editing and sophisticated production, the wrap goes around almost the entire circle of the drum at a slant-track angle of a little over 2 percent from the horizontal line of the tape.

The half or full-circle head sweeps that produce one picture field make possible an important feature of all the helical-scan machines. Each one of the parallel scanning lines contains enough electronic information to record and reproduce one complete 262.5-line top-to-bottom video *field*. The relationship between the one long slant-track scan of the video head and one complete field is very significant because it means that a stable picture field can be maintained when the tape itself is motionless on the video head drum. If the tape is in the "hold" position while the heads

are in motion, then the same line—representing one video field—will be scanned over and over again. The result is a freeze frame, which is invaluable both for editing and for special effects. On larger professional models the machine processes this information and actually fills in the other 262.5 missing scanning lines to recreate a complete frame. This is why slow motion, faster-than-normal (jogging) search speeds, and even reverse-motion viewing are possible with the helical-scan formats. The scanning process can be totally independent of the speed at which the tape passes the head assembly area.

The video drum is but one of several magnetically activated heads within the transport section of a tape machine. In some of the new professional equipment there may be six or more heads that perform various video, audio, control cueing, and erase functions. The configuration will vary with the complexity of the recorder. One can get an idea of this basic structure, however, from figure 8-10, which shows the arrangement of a VHS cassette unit.

"Upstream" of the video drum (before the moving tape reaches the drum) there is a full erase head. "Downstream" there is a unit that contains two separate heads—one for the control track (see below) and one for audio. Figure 8-10 also shows the way in which the two movable rollers engage the tape and pull it out of the cassette into the play/record position. They move along two grooved metal tracks (dotted lines) to put the tape into contact with the heads. (There are several other guides and rollers not shown in this figure.) The ¾-inch U-matic cassette machines operate in a similar fashion—although they are much more complicated. A large loop of tape is pulled out of the cassette, wound around the drum, and put into contact with the other heads.

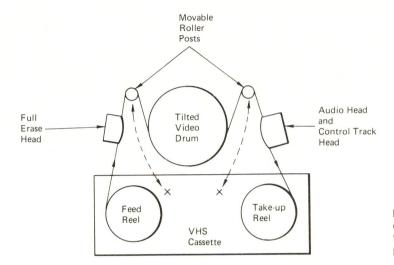

Figure 8-10 labels: Movable Roller Posts, Full Erase Head, Tilted Video Drum, Audio Head and Control Track Head, Feed Reel, Take-up Reel, VHS Cassette

Figure 8-10 VHS cassette engaged by transport system for play/record mode.

8.3 Video Recording Formats and Functions

Before proceeding with a detailed discussion of VTR operating controls and characteristics, it may be helpful to review the formats and basic recording functions of video recording.

Video Recording Formats

Virtually all of our discussion in this chapter is centered around the reel-to-reel recorder and the cartridge/cassette machines.[2] With the reel-to-reel VTR, the open reels (one supply reel and one take-up reel) are placed on

2. As with self-contained audio sources, the term *cassette* refers to a two-reeled unit in a semi-closed case; the videotape is not exposed to human handling. Once the cassette is inserted into its loading deck, the player mechanism automatically engages the tape around the recording head assembly. A *cartridge,* on the other hand, refers to a single-reel container that is, in effect, a sealed supply reel; the take-up reel is enclosed in the player mechanism. When the cartridge is inserted into the player, it is automatically threaded; again, human hands do not become involved in the loading and threading operation.

the VTR machine and the videotape is manually threaded through the recording head assembly. The cassette and cartridge formats eliminate the necessity for manual threading and loading of the machine. For this reason, cassette and cartridge recorders were initially devised as playback equipment; virtually anyone could handle the equipment and drop in a cassette or cartridge without being mechanically minded.

Because of the ease and convenience of operation, however, both the ¾-inch U-matic cassette and the ½-inch cassette formats have also become popular as recording media. Some of the elaborate production models have become as sophisticated and complex as the better quality reel-to-reel models. It was the production and editing capabilities of the U-matic cassette, for example, that led to the breakthroughs in ENG techniques.

Despite the several different formats for ½-inch, ¾-inch, and 1-inch cassette, cartridge, and reel-to-reel video recorders, there are several common functions and operational characteristics that apply to all video recorders.

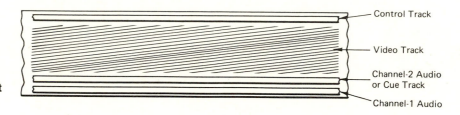

Control Track

Video Track

Channel-2 Audio
or Cue Track

Channel-1 Audio

Figure 8-11
Configuration of ¾-inch
U-matic videotape format
(not to scale).

(It should be noted in passing that many stations still use 2-inch quad cassettes for commercials and PSAs—public service announcements—and there is also, in the developmental stage, a ¼-inch longitudinal video recorder that records in a straight line like an audio recorder.)

Videotape Track Functions

As discussed above, the videotape contains more information than just picture signals. Figure 8-11, for example, is a representation of the four tracks that are used by the U-matic format. Other VTR formats will use a slightly different configuration to achieve similar functions.

The Video Track. The video track occupies approximately 80 percent of the surface of most VTR formats. Here is where the basic information for picture signal, color, and brightness is carried—more than 125,000 bits of electrical data on each individual slant track. To protect against any signal crossover from track to track there is a small unused "protection" strip between each of the basic tracks. A similar separation between the parallel slanted video tracks has been minimized almost to nothing. (The six-hour, slow-speed recording capacity on the VHS format was achieved by having the two heads that scan the tape touch the surface at slightly different angles—thus reducing the chance of one head picking up the other head's signal.)

The Control Track. The signal on the **control track** performs an important synchronization function so that the machine is able to process this incredible amount of video information. In the record mode a signal, which is partially derived from the vertical sync pulse (one per field), has been placed on the control track. During playback this signal is used to coordinate the speed of the video drum head and the servocapstan, which pulls the tape through the head assembly. This helps to ensure that the video head will sweep (sometimes the term *scan* is used) the vertical video track at the exact same rate as when the track was created. The overall process of video synchronization is greatly aided by the fact that all of the components are energized by a common sixty cycle-per-second electrical power source. This current is stabilized, refined, and otherwise modified, but its oscillation rate (the same as in your home) serves as the backbone of the video sequence. Because it records the sync pulse for each new field, the control track also plays an indispensable role in the editing process (see chapter 9).

The Cue Track. On most VTR formats the **cue track** can be used either for a second audio track (for stereo broadcasting or for a second language audio track) or as a *cueing* track—so named because it was originally used to record either verbal cues or high-frequency tones as cues for early editing systems. One of its most important functions today is for the **SMPTE time code.** This invaluable location

Hours — Frames
Minutes — Seconds

The SMPTE Time Code information (so named because the technical standards were established by the Society of Motion Picture and Television Engineers) is recorded on the cue track. As it is not part of the regular video picture information, it is not permanently displayed on the face of the monitor; it is seen only when the VTR operator or editor chooses to display it.

**Figure 8-12 Display of
time code information.**

system produces a clocklike numerical address for each hour, minute, second, and frame recorded on the videotape. It can reflect the "real time" at which the tape was being recorded or it can be added later, showing time elapsed from the beginning of a production or from some other reference point on the tape. The readout, as seen in figure 8-12, is displayed on the picture monitor by a process similar to the way titles are matted over any picture source.

In advanced editing systems (see section 9.3), a computer can "read" the unseen time code to locate predetermined edit points for the execution of cuts, dissolves, and special effects. The system is used on virtually all productions at the network level. Time-code referencing is especially important for programs such as "Wide World of Sports"—or the Olympics—where tapes from many recorders in many different locations must later be edited together in precise chronological synchro-

nization. Newer tape formats—such as the type C standard—have two audio tracks *plus* the cue track, so that the time code can be utilized in conjunction with a stereo production or a dual-language sound track.

The Audio Track.   The audio track hardly needs further explanation. The technology involved is exactly that of conventional sound recording. It must be noted, however, that the quality is somewhat less than that of professional audio equipment that is used in recording studios. The television industry is just beginning to take advantage of its capacity for stereo and high-fidelity sound—up to the 15,000 Hertz level now heard on FM radio. As more home receivers are sold with this capacity, stations and cable systems will begin to make the necessary modifications. Most VTR machines designed for educational and industrial use have a 5,000 Hertz limitation and cannot be easily upgraded.

8.4 Video Recorder Operations and Controls

The setup and operation of any VTR machine involves the use of components that generally fall under three headings: *connectors, control mechanisms,* and *visual indicators.* The arrangement, appearance, and even terminology may vary with the manufacturer—but once one knows what to look for, these basic components can be identified on any video recorder.

First, since videotape machines work in conjunction with other electronic units (cameras, switchers, microphones, other recorders, speakers, receivers, editing equipment, and so forth), we must be able to make such hookups as a primary step. Second, we must learn how to manipulate the collection of knobs, switches, levers, and push buttons that are used to start, stop, or change the basic audio and video functions of record, playback, and editing. Third, we must be able to use and understand the set of components that tell us whether or not the machine is operating the way we want it to—feedback provided by things such as indicator lights and meters.

Connections

The first set of connections we need to be concerned with are those that get incoming signals into the VTR machine to be recorded. In order for a video recorder to record picture and sound from a production studio it must be hooked up to the switcher and audio board outputs known as *program line feeds*.

These two separate signals—which have been amplified and in other ways processed between their sources and the final cable outputs—are plugged into VTR receptacles labeled *audio in* and *video in*. There will also be a pair of matching receptacles for *audio out* and *video out*. The corresponding plugs are usually *UHF, RCA, Mini,* or *phone-type* connectors. Occasionally a *BNC* coupling will be used. (See fig. 8-13.) The feeds from these outputs will go to speakers, video monitors, and other tape machines.

Some studio-type cameras are designed so that their signals can be plugged directly into the *video in* (line) connection on the recorder. Most lightweight EFP field cameras must use a multiple pin (often a ten-pin) connector so that the cable can carry camera remote control information and sound as well as the basic video signal. Cameras utilizing these kinds of connectors are compatible only with a very limited range of VTR recorders—usually from the same manufacturer. One must use caution in attempting multiple-pin connections.

The home television set is designed to operate by means of a combined audio and video

"F"-Type Connector for RF Cable

UHF-Type Plug for Unmodulated Line Video

RCA-Type Plug for Audio and Video

Sony Mini-Type Plug for Audio

BNC-Type Connector for Patch Bay and Equipment Connections

"Phone" Type for Audio.

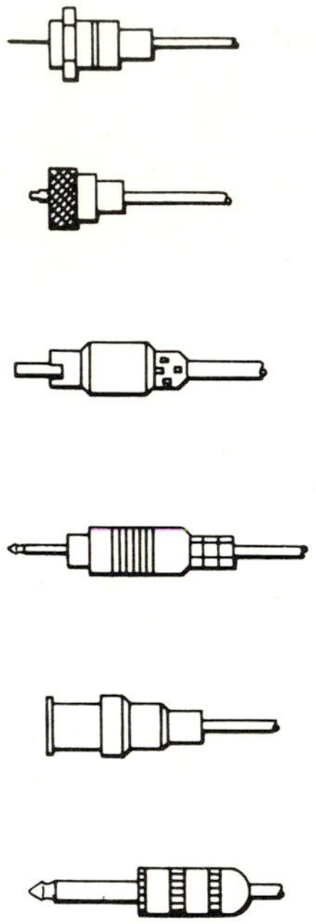

Figure 8-13 Commonly used audio and video plugs and connectors.

signal known as **radio frequency (RF)**.[3] This is the broadcast signal that the home antenna picks up and sends to the set. In a slightly altered form it is also what comes down the wire from the cable-TV company. Those VTR machines that have an RF output must have a converter unit that takes the unmodulated line feeds, decreases their strengths, combines the audio and video, and modulates them onto a carrier frequency (for example, some common VHF channel). The RF-out receptacle on

3. A pure unmodulated audio or video "line" signal can be distributed only over a cable or closed circuit. In order to be broadcast, the signal must be modulated (see section 2.2.1) and superimposed onto a carrier frequency—radio or television. It is then known as a radio frequency (RF) signal, capable of being decoded (demodulated) by a home receiver—radio or television.

older models is now being replaced by a *type F* (cable-TV) connector. On Beta and VHS home recorders the *VHF out* (with a type F connector) is actually an RF signal.

Many TV receivers have a rectangular eight-pin receptacle. It is most often used in Japan to connect the video recorder with specially equipped television sets as a two-way RF interconnection. In the United States it is used for portable field units that utilize RF monitors.

By examining a number of different video recorders, one can find quite a variety of connection provisions for auxiliary equipment. Additional video and audio inputs and outputs are the most common. The ¾-inch cassette machines have the capacity for two separate channels of audio as well as a receptacle for an earphone. Home videocassette (VCR) units have two different remote control inputs that should not be confused. One allows the camera operator to start and stop the recorder. The other component lets the viewer change channels in the tuner as well as start and stop the recorder. The receptacle for unamplified microphone input is an indication of the impedance level for the correct mike (see section 3.1). Adapters must be used with caution.

It is not uncommon to find an AC power outlet receptacle mounted next to the 110-volt power input. Most technical manuals will list a 5,000-watt limit when this outlet is used for lights or other equipment. It is important to note that the rounded third prong on an AC plug is a safety grounding device. If an adapter is used to go into a two-pronged wall receptacle, the ground wire on the adapter should be connected to the screw that fastens the wall socket plate to its wall box—or to some other suitable ground connection.

No connection area at the back of a recorder can be called "typical." Various units are designed to perform a wide range of diverse

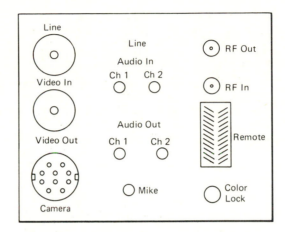

Figure 8-14 Video recorder connection area (composite illustration).

functions. A home VCR recorder will have a different structure than a professional model designed to function with an editing unit. Figure 8-14 is a composite of the sort of connector area that one would find on professional recorders used for educational, industrial, and local news operations.

Controls

Regardless of the age or simplicity of design, every video recorder will have at least five basic operational controls: *Play* (or forward), which moves the tape forward at a designated speed for either recording or playback purposes; *record*, which activates the record head while moving forward in the play position (because there is the possibility of accidentally pressing the record button at the wrong time and inadvertently erasing information on the tape, the record control is usually interlocked with the play button so that it can be activated only when they are both pressed at the same time); *fast forward*, which moves the tape forward at a fast rate (producing no usable video picture); *rewind*, which similarly moves the tape backward at a fast rate; and *stop*, which will halt both the take-up and supply reels. Most VTR designs require the unit to be in a neutral or stop position before going into any of the play, fast-forward, or reverse modes.

Many older video recorders operated the mode selection control by means of a mechanical function lever, which is to be pointed at the desired function. With the later generations of VTR machines the basic functions of tape movement (transport) are controlled by one or more panels of push buttons.

Many additional features are found on virtually all contemporary machines. The **pause mode** enables the operator to **still-frame** or **freeze** a single field on the screen for a short duration—by stopping the tape transport while the rotating head(s) continue to scan a single field. Generally, the tape should not be held in the *pause* mode more than a few seconds because this tends to wear down the tape oxide in a given spot. Prolonged use of this mode can cause tape damage and head wear and clogging—especially with old or inexpensive tape. Most VTRs also will have *variable speed* controls that facilitate slow or speeded-up motion, either forward or backward. Allowing the tape to creep slowly forward (or backward) in the *variable speed* mode will cause fewer problems than holding the tape in the pause mode.

On many recorders, there will also be simple electronic editing controls. Although some are relatively basic and result in a somewhat "noisy" edit, others are very efficient and trouble-free. These editing controls can be used for both **assemble** and **insert editing.** The *audio dub* button is used to make audio-only edits, inserts, or corrections. These editing functions are discussed in detail in chapter 9.

As indicated in figure 8-15, cassette machines not having a loading and unloading lever will have an *eject* button for cassette removal.

Most video recorders are designed to function with a variety of different types of inputs such as a *camera,* the tuner in a *receiver/monitor,* or a studio *line* feed. There must therefore be an *input selector switch* that differentiates among the various levels and/or sync sources of these inputs. The advice of a studio technician may be needed to determine proper switch position. Whereas a camera signal from the studio switcher would feed through the line input, a single camera might utilize some other selector position.

On some machines there is another switch that separately controls the use of internal or external *sync sources.* (On several VTR makes the alternative to the external position is labeled "defeat.") This *internal sync* position allows the recorder to "strip off" any incoming sync signal and utilize the synchronization pulse from the machine itself during the recording process.

The path of the tape around the video drum is crucial in the playback of a proper picture. Bands of noise distortion can result when a tape recorded on one machine is played back on another with a slightly different horizontal alignment. This problem can usually be corrected by an adjustment of the *tracking knob.* When the top portion of a videotape picture bends to the left or right, it is often caused by an incorrect amount of tension as the tape goes through the transport assembly. Tape that has been stretched (or has shrunk) can produce the same effect. If the problem is not too serious the twisted picture can be straightened out with a left or right adjustment of the *skew knob.* Both the tracking and skew controls have a marked *normal* operating position as set by the factory or the studio technician. The knobs should be returned to these positions for each new recording.

Two other controls relate to color operation. In transferring a black-and-white tape to a machine having the capacity for color, the *black/white-color option switch* must be used to avoid picture distortion. If this switch is not placed in the black-and-white position, the machine will attempt to find the color portion of the monochrome signal and, in the process,

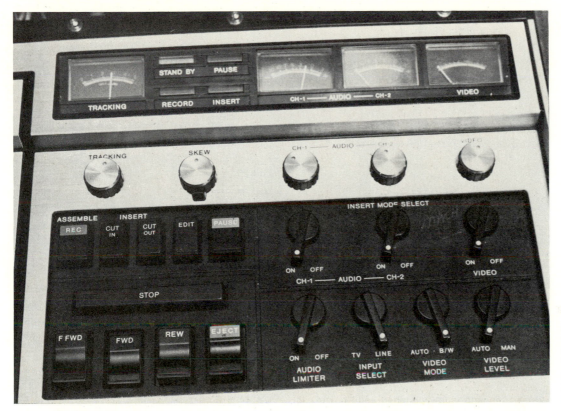

Figure 8-15 Portion of the control panel of the Sony 2850 ¾-inch VTR. The controls shown here are typical of units produced by several manufacturers.

do strange things to the picture. Finally, the *color lock control,* usually located at the back of the recorder, should be left in its normal position and only adjusted on the advice of a trained technician. This control should never be used in an attempt to fix what is actually an improper color signal coming from another part of the system.

Visual Indicators and Meters

Our final area of concern is with visual monitoring and feedback indicators. Although these will vary from machine to machine, there are a number of controls that group together in operational units and directly relate to a visual readout—starting with the *pilot light* that indicates when the *power on/off* switch is activated.

For example, on some ¾-inch recorders designed for editing there will be an *on/off video record switch,* another on/off switch to activate the *automatic gain control* (AGC)— also known as the limiter—the *potentiometer,* which manually controls the video levels, and the *volume unit* (VU) *meter,* which displays the video level changes. (Portable recorders usually have AGC for video, but none of the controls for manual override.)

For audio there are the same basic control units and monitors. On some popular models, for instance, there is an on/off switch to control the line feed, a pot, and a VU meter for each of the two audio channels. The on/off switch for AGC works for either or both channels being used. Controls are not necessarily grouped together into their operating units;

generally all VU meters are in one area, pots in another, and so forth.

Every VTR machine has a numerical *counter*, which helps the operator locate previously noted positions of taped segments. On top-of-the-line professional models, the numbers indicate hours, minutes, and seconds. On many older reel-to-reel machines these numbers count each revolution of the feed reel. On newer cassette recorders the counter indicates revolutions of the take-up reel. Since the circumference of the tape on each reel will change as the reels unwind and wind, the operator must keep in mind that a given number of revolutions will indicate differing amounts of tape footage.

Many video recorders have a *memory* device. At any point in the reel the *reset button* can be pressed to reset the counter to the zero (000) position. On rewinding, the machine will automatically stop at this point, however, and not go all the way back to the actual beginning of the reel.

Operation Mode Indicators.
The several color-coded lights on the control panel provide important feedback on the operational status of the VTR machine. The *record* and *pause* lights reassure the operator that the recorder is functioning in the requested mode. (The *insert* indicator light relates to editing and will be discussed in chapter 9.) When the VTR is put into one of these modes or asked to perform an eject or fast-forward function, a large number of circuits are sequentially activated. The clicking sounds one hears at this point are the opening and closing of relay switches. The yellow *stand by* light is a warning that this sequence is still in operation; and to introduce a new command signal at this time may jam the computerlike circuitry of the equipment. While some recorders have components that can delay and properly sequence command signals, no machine is completely fail-safe.

Successful Performance and Maintenance.
The key to successful operation of the videotape recorder—whether a complex broadcast-quality machine or a simple **backpack** for basic location recordings—is *familiarity* and *practice*. Instructions and specific controls will, of course, vary significantly from machine to machine. Become familiar with the ones you have access to. Make certain you have taken full advantage of the instructions and directions for the particular models you will be working with. Especially, follow the recommended care and maintenance instructions; this is particularly important for routine cleaning of the video heads. And then practice. Become familiar with the recorder. Under the guidance of a trained technician or instructor, work with the machine; experiment with it. Find out what it will and will not do. And then you should have the confidence and discipline to handle any video recording and playback assignment given to you.

A major part of your professional discipline will be care and respect for all production equipment; and the video recorder is one of the most expensive and delicate machines you will handle. Everyone will benefit if you follow a few common rules of preventative maintenance.

1. Videotape recorders require a constantly renewed supply of clean, cool, dry air. Heat, moisture, and cigarette smoke are damaging to all electronic equipment—especially VTR machines. Never place books, cassette cases, or papers on top of the recorder; it seriously inhibits the flow of air. Liquid containers and ash trays—anywhere adjacent to video recorders—are simply a disaster in the making.

2. Place a dust cover on the machine when it is not in use—but only after the unit has had time to cool off.

3. When a video recorder is moved, be extremely careful not to bump or jar the unit.

Delicate components are easily damaged by slight shocks. Do not attempt to operate a recorder immediately after it has been moved from a cold to a warm environment.

4. Videotape should not be left in the recorder when the unit is not in use. Tapes should be rewound and properly stored in a cool, dry place.

5. Keep the recorder and tapes at a distance from other equipment that may be generating strong magnetic fields.

6. Do not tinker with various controls and functions without a clear purpose and idea of what you are doing. Do not fool around, for example, with the color lock control and other critical mechanisms. Maintenance personnel who are unaware of these misadjustments may spend hours trying to find and correct the resulting problems.

7. As the videotape operator, always allow yourself time to carefully think through all connecting and patching procedures—as well as the basic disciplines of machine operation. The time spent always pays off later in time saved.

Summary

Video recording encompasses both *electronic principles* (such as the horizontal and vertical sync pulses) and *magnetic principles* (the electromagnetic properties of an electric current rearranging iron oxide particles) to record a video signal on videotape.

The first VTR machine, introduced in the late 1950s, was the *quadruplex videotape recorder,* which utilizes four revolving video heads to record video information transversely

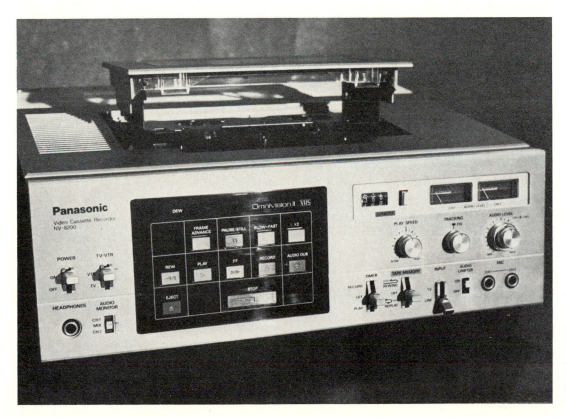

Figure 8-16 This Panasonic NV 8200 ½-inch VHS format VCR is designed for educational and industrial level playback and editing applications.

Figure 8-17 The RCA TR-800 type *C* one-inch videotape recorder. The unit shown here is in a configuration that includes an edit control panel and display screen, waveform monitor, and picture monitor. (Photo courtesy RCA.)

Beta and VHS home formats) have videotape configurations that include space for picture information, control track, cue signals, and audio track(s).

Operational functions for VTR machines include three considerations: *connections* (with cameras, switcher, line feeds, microphones, other recorders, speakers, monitors, editing facilities, and so forth); *controls* (for all operating modes such as play, record, fast forward, rewind, stop, pause, variable speed, dubbing and editing, input and sync selection, tracking and skewing adjustment, and color controls); and *indicators* (lights, VU meters, counter, and so forth).

This chapter has only briefly alluded to editing considerations. In chapter 9 we will look specifically at VTR editing functions—especially as they relate to single-camera ENG/EFP production techniques and post-production editing procedures.

8.5 Training Exercise

Ideally, each student should be able to go through the following exercise individually. If time or facilities do not permit, then students may be assigned in pairs.

On the videotape recorder(s) available in your facility, go through every step mentioned in the chapter. Thread the VTR machine and work with it in every function: play, fast forward, rewind. Record some sample programing from the studio. Use the pause-hold modes; experiment with any variable speed controls. Carefully, with engineering supervision, familiarize yourself with other adjustments such as tracking and skewing.

to the path of the two-inch tape. The bulky and expensive quad-head machines have largely been supplanted by the *helical-scan video recorder,* which wraps its narrower tape around a cylindrical head drum in a slant-track pattern.

Both *reel-to-reel recorders* (such as the broadcast-quality one-inch type C machines) and the *cartridge/cassette recorders* (like the professional ¾-inch U-matic and the ½-inch

production and editing procedures for single-camera video

9

In previous chapters we have been dealing with video production that is for the most part accomplished by means of **real-time editing.** The multiple-camera technique requires considerable preproduction planning and rehearsal of camera shot assignments. Program elements must be carefully timed and organized into their projected sequence. During a live broadcast, the task of the director is largely that of making a series of precise editing decisions. The technical director uses the switcher to connect the succeeding elements of the program by means of takes, dissolves, and special effects such as wipes and mattes. Prerecorded segments on disc, tape, and film are combined with the live camera inputs—all within the time disciplines of the continuous production operation. The spontaneous aspect of real-time production gives sports, news, and even game shows an important sense of immediacy and realism.

These benefits notwithstanding, there are also some serious difficulties that arise from working within the time constraints of the live or live-on-tape technique. The director, working in a moment-by-moment decision process, must also be constantly alert for unforeseen production difficulties. When the director is forced to solve production problems while on the air there is a good chance that the overall quality of the production will suffer. Some types of programs simply do not fit well into this studio concept of television production. In this chapter we will study the production options that have been made possible by a new generation of video equipment.

9.1 Postproduction and Preproduction Editing

Those persons who worked to develop the early TV equipment and production methods were quick to realize that a whole new range of production techniques were possible with the development of the videotape-based recording

Figure 9-1 A modern postproduction editing studio. Notice that the facility has been designed with "human engineering" factors in mind. Easy access to equipment, soft lighting, and comfort are important when editing sessions may last twelve hours or more. (Photo courtesy Pacific Video.)

and editing capability. The term *postproduction editing* refers to a number of techniques that in many ways resemble the way filmmakers have worked for years. The various program elements, be it a continuous five-minute dramatic scene or any of the smaller bits and pieces of an opening or closing format, are shot out of sequence in a stop-and-go process. High standards can be maintained because retakes are possible. The work is done on a production schedule that is convenient for the availability of facilities and talent as well as other budget considerations. Once the main production work has been completed, the post-

production unit takes over and puts the show together. On many programs there may be a separate company that is hired on a subcontract basis to do this final assembly. (See fig. 9-1.)

This method of operation has had an impact on almost every type of video production. The nationally syndicated celebrity talk shows now use editing to "sweeten" a program. Minor errors and slow-moving segments can be taken out to improve the pacing of the show. Prime-time situation comedies—which are usually shot in continuous three-to-five-minute segments with multiple cameras—do later retakes of close-ups and other inserts that have not played correctly on the main run-through. These—along with sections available from the taped dress rehearsal—are combined with titles, credits, and other elements in the postproduction assembly.

Some situation comedies and dramatic programs utilize a different technique. Each of the four cameras takes an assigned series of shots as the scene is run through. Each camera's picture is fed to its own separate video-tape recorder, and all of the editing is done later by means of a multiple-screen viewing technique.

This **isolated-camera (iso)** technique got its start as directors discovered the postproduction editing benefits of having one totally separate camera in operation during a traditional three-camera live-on-tape production. The director can concentrate on "cutting" the program through the switcher while the associate director (section 12.1) keeps an eye on the prearranged shots on the iso camera. Figure 9-2 shows the signal feed configuration of a commonly used technique combining several of these production methods.

The soap operas are one major type of program to utilize editing as a basic part of the production operation. For many years these shows all ran one-half hour in length and were shot with a continuous live-on-tape multiple-camera technique. Usually two different directors would split up the five shows in the week. When the first "soaps" expanded to a one-hour time period, the whole approach to production had to change. Many of the segments are now shot out of their eventual program order. Sometimes two different directors will work on various elements of the story during the same shooting day. Postproduction assembly is typically done a little over one week prior to air date.

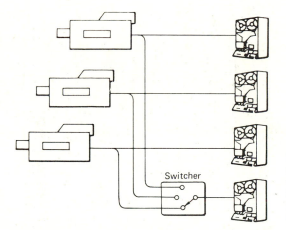

Figure 9-2 The diagram shows how three studio cameras are connected to the switcher and to their own "isolated" tape machines.

Preproduction Editing

The ability to record and edit videotape has had a similarly important effect upon those programs that air live—especially news. (See figs. 9-3 and 9-4.) Prior to the late 1970s, television news relied heavily upon film segments that had been edited prior to air. Lead time in terms of film developing and transportation had always been a problem. In 1975 CBS News decided to do a trial run of an electronic newsgathering (ENG) system at KMOX TV—its owned and operated station in St. Louis. There were no film cameras. A whole new staff structure was designed around the use of the electronic camera and videotape editing equipment. The **preproduction editing** techniques that they pioneered are now commonplace at most stations around the country.

One to two hours of production time on the out-of-studio elements of a major news story can be saved when videotape is used instead of film. There is no delay while the film is being developed. Segments can be immediately microwaved back to the station for editing—or the news team can go on the air live from the field as the story unfolds. The transition from the film-based news unit to ENG—also called EJ (electronic journalism)

Figure 9-3   An ABC-TV network news crew is shown here covering a still very active forest fire. Based at stations owned by the network, these units must be ready to go anywhere in the world with very little notice. (Photo courtesy ABC News.)

Figure 9-4   A network editing and operations control center hastily constructed in a hotel room for coverage of a major news story in a foreign country. Note clocks and monitors for incoming feeds. (Photo courtesy ABC News.)

and EFP (electronic field production) in various professional circles—has been a gradual one at most stations; but there can be no doubt as to the use of electronic cameras in the future.

Those working in related fields of corporate training and information processing have been equally quick to grasp the industrial and educational applications of this new technology. More and more industries now have their own video production units. A visit to any of the major equipment exhibitions such as that at the NAB (National Association of Broadcasters) convention will attest to the scope of professional nonbroadcast video. One of the more interesting aspects of this so-called video explosion has been the private use of video not only by individuals in the home but also by groups of people who are exploring the possibilities of communication and artistic expression through the access channels of local cable systems (section 1.3).

9.2   The Electronic Transfer Edit Concept

The earliest videotape editing techniques were in many ways a copy of long-standing film-based procedures. The tape was cut and edit-points spliced together, but the results were very crude, time-consuming, and expensive. Engineering leaders decided, therefore, to take advantage of technological advances and developed a whole new system upon the concept of an *edit transfer* of the audio and video signal from the original master to a second edited tape copy. A straight transfer of audio and video from one tape to another is known as a **dub.** If we are transferring a series of black-to-black segments—while rearranging their sequence we are, in effect, doing a simple form of editing. For the most part the term *editing* refers to the transfer connection of the picture and sound *tail* segment to the *head* of another

segment. Each time this electronic joining process is accomplished, a series of creative and technical considerations are brought into play. The end result of the process is called an *edit decision.* The term **on-line editing** is usually applied when, as with television news programs, the original footage is transferred directly to the edited air tape. The term **off-line editing** refers to a more elaborate procedure involving intermediate work print copies that lead to a final edited master.

Assemble Editing

Let us examine some of the basic operational techniques of editing by means of a simple editing problem.

Figure 9-5 shows three segments as recorded on tape on the original master. The first two segments have black on either end and the third contains audio and video material, which is available for optional use, at the beginning and end. Figure 9-6 shows how these segments could be edited together on the record machine as what would be called the *edited master.* These two illustrations are a simple example of the kind of planning that takes place before the actual editing session begins. (In studying these illustrations, keep in mind that the direction of the videotape is left to right; therefore it is necessary that you follow the action from the head of the tape, on the *right,* to the end of the tape, on the *left.*)

Much machine time can be saved if the director and/or producer preview the original master tape and plan the approximate inpoint and outpoint for each segment in advance. The process of progressively editing segment to segment in program sequence is known as the **assemble** mode of editing.

With segment #1 transferred, we face our first edit decision in deciding exactly where to **butt edit** it to the head of segment #2. The

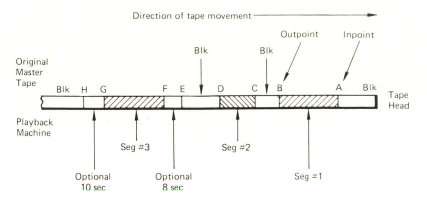

In this example, there are three segments of program material which are to be "assembled" in the same order: A-B, C-D, and F-G. The editing task is to remove the unwanted material between the segments: B-C, D-F, and G-H.

Figure 9-5 Recorded segments on the original master.

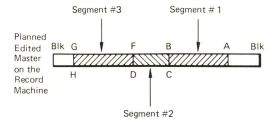

As the program segments (from figure 9-5) are assembled, the outpoint of segment #1 (B) is butted against the inpoint of segment #2 (C); the outpoint of segment #2 (D) is butted against the inpoint of segment #3 (F); and the outpoint of segment #3 (G) is edited to the final segment of black (H).

Figure 9-6 Program segments recorded on the edited master.

precise locations of outpoint B and inpoint C must be selected with several factors in mind. Let's say that in our example segment #1 consists of a single shot of an interviewer talking to camera. Outpoint B is the end of a sentence introducing a second person who will appear with the interviewer at the beginning of segment #2. Our edit must allow for a proper time lapse between the end of one sentence and the beginning of the next. Too short or too long a pause between sentences would be un-

natural and as a result would distract the viewer. We would therefore have outpoint B occur at a point that would allow for another half to one second of picture following the completion of audio. We would also allow for up to one second of establishing video prior to the beginning of the first word of segment #2 at inpoint C.

We must, at the same time, look carefully at the video of the two segments before making our edit decision. If the interviewer was making a small hand gesture at the end of segment #1, then that gesture should be completed before the edit is made. Similarly, if there was any movement at the beginning of segment #2, then that movement should be seen from its beginning or entirely eliminated. To edit to a movement that is in progress is a possible viewer distraction. Obviously this process of precisely adjusting the in-and-out edit points is possible only if extra video is available prior to and following the announcer's words in the segment. (The in-and-out points in figs. 9-5 and 9-6 are meant to be only approximations and therefore do not indicate any exact location of video in relation to audio.)

A good director will always include this video **pad** when recording separate segments of a program. During assemble editing any extra video ahead of the selected inpoint is eliminated when the edit transfer is made. The pad at the end of the segment, however, still is needed and is included in the transfer to the record tape. When the edit decision has been made for the subsequent segment, the excess video is erased as the new edit is made. The basic principle involved here is that of having overlapping source video available in order to provide for optional edit points. Without these options it is difficult to make edits that maintain a natural flow of picture and sound. Technical requirements relating to this pad material will be further discussed in section 9.4.

9.3 Machine-to-Machine Edit Transfer Using an Intermediate Editor Unit

The current state of the art in the electronics field has been made possible by a large number of individual advancements. Two important developments are especially significant in the field of video—the *silicon chip,* and the *helical-scan video head* described in the previous chapter. Using integrated circuits, tens of thousands of transistor units can be linked together on one chip. Using very small amounts of energy, the tiny transistor does the work of the old vacuum tube—amplifying and in other ways modulating the electronic wave form. Electronics gear that would fill a large room thirty years ago can now be miniaturized in a silicon chip the size of a person's thumbnail. One can begin to appreciate how this equipment functions in the editing process if one thinks in terms of a mini-computer that is able to mark and "remember" a series of precise locations on a continuous tape. The unit has the ability to use these location points to start

and stop the record and edit process with a sixtieth of a second accuracy. The delicate sequencing of all of the mechanical operations that start, stop, pause, and move the tape itself are controlled by this programed circuitry. If an operator punches control buttons too rapidly, the unit is able to slow down the command signal input and keep it in the proper sequence.

The process of transferring segment #2 to the end of segment #1 (fig. 9-6) would have been a slow and inexact operation in the early days of electronic editing. Many of these difficulties have been solved by the use of the editor unit, which simultaneously controls playback and record functions on two or more machines. As we come to the first step in our edit-transfer process, this component is immediately put to use. We must move our record machine back and forth to locate the exact planned outpoint of segment #1 (outpoint *B* in fig. 9-6). This is accomplished by the forward and reverse variable speed joystick control or by a *search dial* on some machines. On newer units the single joy-stick can be made to alternately move either the playback or record machine. (See fig. 9-7.) Some units will have two separate joy-sticks while others will function with a simple push-button control.

We again use the joy-stick to locate the beginning of segment #2 (inpoint *C*) on the playback machine. During this operation the two playback and record monitors provide the all-important visual feedback necessary to the search process. With both tapes stopped in the pause mode we can now simultaneously view a freeze frame of outpoint *B* shown on the record monitor #2 on the right (a medical scene "teaser") and inpoint *C* on the playback feed monitor #1 on the left (opening title) (fig. 9-8). Figure 9-9 shows how the two tapes have been positioned on their respective machines.

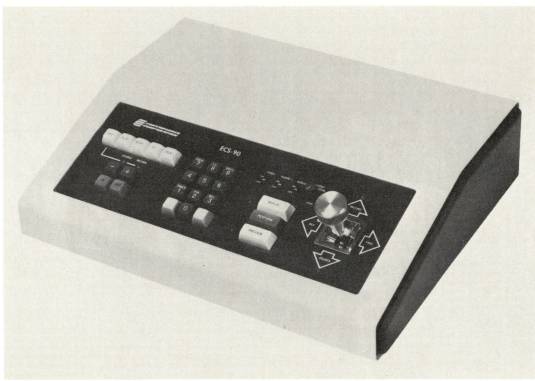

Figure 9-7   The ECS 90 Editing Controller. (Photo courtesy Convergence Corporation.)

The single joy-stick control can be used to alternately move tapes on the playback (source) or record machines. Note keyboard used program SMPTE time code.

Playback   Record

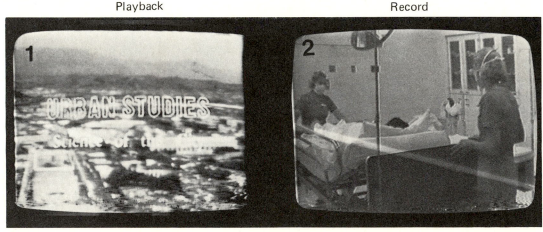

Figure 9-8   A simultaneous display of picture information from both the playback (original source) and record (edited master) machines.

The operator watches the picture on the playback machine on the left while searching for the starting point of the next segment to be recorded. When located, the machine is put into the pause mode as seen here. During this search, the last frame of the previously recorded segment can be viewed as seen here on the monitor on the right. The operator can easily compare these two pictures while making the edit decision.

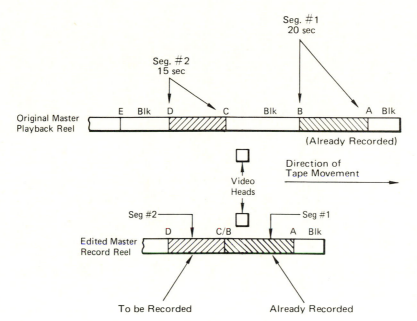

Figure 9-9 Playback and record tapes as they would be positioned relative to the video heads.

The relative position of the material on both tapes can be more easily kept in mind if one thinks of the two video heads as being locked together at a constant point in space and time.

The next step in achieving edit point *B/C* is to activate the *cue-set* control. This tells the editor memory component that the positions now in *pause* on both machines constitute the next edit decision. With the more sophisticated equipment the editor uses a typewriterlike keyboard to program the computer with SMPTE time code readouts of the edit points. In simpler equipment the unit keeps count of vertical sync pulses and other control track information to remember a designated edit point. In most edit formats, pressing the cue-set button also activates an automatic rewinding of tapes on both machines to a point (usually set for five seconds) forward of the planned edit point. This new position allows for the pre-edit roll period necessary for proper tape speed. (See fig. 9-10.)

The machines are now set up to perform an edit. At this point, however, most editors prefer to preview the point at which the sound and picture transition between the two segments will take place. This can be done without any actual transfer of the signal to the record tape. On command both machines are put in motion but as the tapes reach edit points *B* and *C,* the record monitor (showing the tail of segment #1) switches over and shows segment #2 from point *C* on. With smaller units this preview period may run only five seconds. At this point the unit automatically stops both machines and returns them to the pre-edit roll position. With other equipment the operator has manual control of these functions.

If the sound or picture transition point does not seem quite right, the operator can repeat the preview process as necessary and then make adjustments in the relative position of either of the tapes. For example, more of

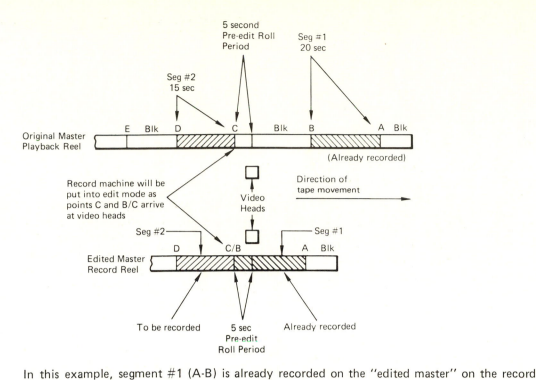

Figure 9-10 Tapes on the playback and record machines in position for the pre-edit roll period.

In this example, segment #1 (A-B) is already recorded on the "edited master" on the record machine; and the objective is to assemble segment #2 (C-D), from the original master on the playback machine, on to the record machine at point B. Thus, the edit point will be B/C on the record machine. Therefore, both recorders are rolled back exactly five seconds before point C (point B/C on the record machine). Both recorders are not started simultaneously, and precisely five seconds later (when the playback machine reaches point C and the record machine reaches point B) the record machine is put into the "edit" mode. The butt edit of segments 1 and 2 has been accomplished at point B/C.

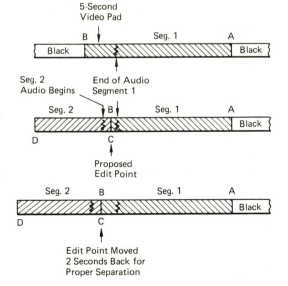

Figure 9-11 Segment as transferred from playback to record machine.

Figure 9-12 Preview of tight edit shows not enough audio separation.

Figure 9-13 Edit as completed on record machine.

a pad at the end of segment #1 (see fig. 9-11) can be used to slightly delay the beginning of segment #2. Had the edit shown in figure 9-12 been made without preview, there would not have been sufficient separation of audio between the two segments. It is also important to keep in mind that making the edit incorrectly would have erased most of the five-second pad at the end of segment #1. The operator would have to go back and retransfer segment #1 in order to correct the mistake.

By seeing and hearing the edit previewed, the operator knows that input C must occur two seconds later toward the end of segment #1. The operator would accomplish this by using the joy-stick control to move the *playback* machine tape two seconds *forward* and then programing a new cue for the edit point relating to both machines as shown in figure 9-13. When a second preview shows the edit to be acceptable, the unit is given the command and both machines will reverse and roll back to the points from which they will start the five-second pre-roll. (See fig. 9-10.)

To make any professional transfer edit, it is imperative that both machines be locked together with a common sync pulse. This is another thing that the editor unit (and its related components) does. At the exact moment when the edit transfer starts, both machines must begin a new field. This necessary synchronization can only be maintained if several other factors have been observed. During the pre-roll period and during the transfer itself there can be no interruption of the vertical sync pulse on the control tracks of either machine. On the playback machine a "clean" five-second pre-roll period means that the camera operator on the original recording or *shoot,* should roll black or picture video for a full ten seconds ahead of the planned audio beginning for any segment.

To ensure a continuous, clean record tape it has now become standard to record a sync black control track signal throughout the entire tape on which the editing is to be done. This is done by putting the machine into the edit/record mode and running the tape for whatever length of time is needed for the final edited program—or to the conclusion of the reel.

Even though we may be following what has been described as the assemble edit procedure—placing segment after segment in a planned sequence—we are in effect each time doing what is called an **insert edit.** We are inserting segment #2 between segment #1 and recorded sync black, which is upstream on the tape. With this in mind, the concept of *insert editing* should be easier to understand. Close to 90 percent of all EFP editing is accomplished in the insert mode.

Insert Editing

As an example we will again use our editing problem as outlined in figure 9-6. Let's say that we have gone ahead and edited segment #3 (points *F* to *G*) to the end of segment #2, and the interviewer has made a definite reference to the object of the discussion—a large bridge that has thus far been seen only in the background of the two-shot. The director has decided that the reference to the bridge calls for an information full shot of the bridge itself. At the end of the reel the director has taken just such a *protection shot* for later editing purposes.

The director would ask that the editor set up for a seven-second *video-only* edit covering the last five seconds of segment #2 and the first two seconds of segment #3. This two-second overlap of the old edit is easier to accomplish than to try to coincide the outpoint of the insert with edit point *F/D.* The playback and record tapes would be set up on the machines as shown in figure 9-14.

The Dissolve in Editing

Machine-to-machine edits as described to this point can be used only when the desired effect is that of an instantaneous *take* between pictures. Obviously for any kind of a dissolve transition between pictures, the levers and mix banks of a switcher must be utilized. As in any dissolve, this means that there must be two simultaneous sources of video signal. Also, when mixing various video sources, the time-base corrector (section 8.2) is used to guarantee that all video signals will lock up with no picture breakup.

If we had wanted to dissolve between segment #1 and segment #2 of our editing sample as shown in figure 9-5, we would need to set up separate tape feeds on *A* and *B* machines

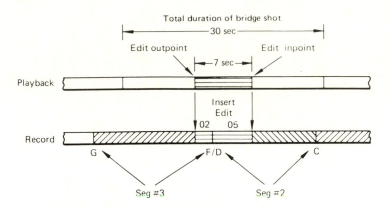

Figure 9-14 VTR machine set up for an insert edit.

The material to be inserted is designed to start five seconds before the original F/D edit point and end two seconds after the former edit point. Both machines are rolled simultaneously, and the "edit" (insert in) and "edit out" (insert out) buttons are pushed at the appropriate points seven seconds apart.

for playback. The technique is somewhat the same as in traditional *A* and *B* roll editing for film, where a final composite film is automatically printed from two specially edited film rolls. In television this system can either be set up for automatic computer control or be done manually at the switcher during the edit session. The basic principles involved in setting up the tapes are roughly the same in either situation.

When a dissolve between segments is planned, it is imperative that there be sufficient extra video pad following the outpoint of the first segment and the inpoint of the second. If in our example we establish edit point *B/C* as the midpoint of a two-second dissolve, then both playback machines must feed a video signal to the record machine throughout the duration of the dissolve. While only two seconds of pad from each segment would actually be needed for the two-second dissolve overlap, it is always advisable to have extra protection source video available. Most professional di-

rectors and technical directors would not feel comfortable without a working margin of at least three seconds added to each segment. Figure 9-15 shows how the video pad should be utilized in the setup of *A* and *B* roll tapes for dissolve edits.

A sequence in which all of the segments are to be connected by dissolves must be planned in order to be recorded from beginning to end. For all practical purposes there is no way in which the record machine can be stopped to set up the next dissolve without doing a butt edit. (An emergency matched edit technique is difficult to achieve and need not be discussed here.) Our three-segment sequence would call for two dissolves. Setting up the pre-edit roll periods on the *A* and *B* playback machines for a *B/C* dissolve edit poses no real problem. Note, however, that to continue recording, segment #3 must be in such a position on the *A* reel tape as to be available just prior to the end of segment #2. Segment #2 is of such short duration that there is no time for

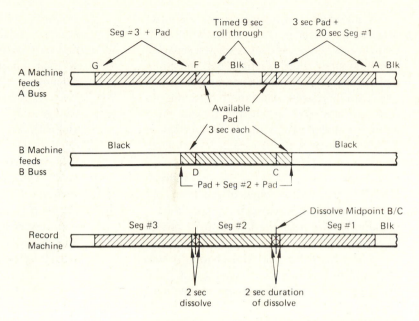

In preparing the A and B playback videotapes, care must be taken to ensure that every segment and each "roll through" (blank space) is precisely timed—including the exact pad that is wanted. As the two playback tapes are fed into the switcher, the actual dissolve edits are accomplished simply by using the fader arms.

Figure 9-15   Three VTR machines set up for a dissolve edit.

the operator to stop and re-cue the A roll. The solution to the problem is to have recorded segment #3 on the A roll in a precisely timed position. After the dissolve to segment #2, the A tape continues to roll and is available for the next dissolve.

If our segments had been at least two minutes in length, then there would be time for the operator to locate each upcoming segment and set up the pre-edit roll period. In this situation, markings on the tape or beep tones on the cue track are important to the operator. In any case, the use of A and B rolls for dissolve edits must of necessity involve a carefully planned pre-edit transfer session just for the preparation of the playback tapes.

9.4   Preproduction Planning

You may ask why material on editing has been presented prior to the sections dealing with single-camera production as a whole. Obviously a project must be planned and shot before it can be edited. For an answer to this question, let us take a brief look at the planning and production sequence itself. In a live or live-on-tape multiple-camera program, the on-the-air editing done by the director provides a time-oriented structure for production operations. This is made possible by an earlier planning stage when camera shots and other insert materials are blocked out in their intended sequence. The editing plan develops as the program comes together.

With single-camera operations a similar process takes place—but in a slightly different sequence. When assembly occurs at a separate and final stage of production, both planning and camera work must be done with the eventual editing process constantly in mind. As each separate scene is shot the director must be aware of those shots that will precede and follow it. With the single-camera technique the director has the luxury of shooting several alternatives for a later edit decision. It follows, therefore, that an awareness of the basic concepts of editing are necessary to any understanding of the planning and camera phases of production.

The concepts of pictorial continuity and shot transitions discussed in sections 13.1 and 13.2 also apply to single-camera production.

Crew Structure

The day when video completely replaces film as the medium for full-length *dramatic* productions lies somewhere in the future. Budgetary considerations have made the all-electronic system attractive to more and more producers of television *commercials.* There is no longer any doubt about the predominance of the electronic camera in television *news, public affairs,* and *documentary* work. Most of the newer *industrial* and *educational* production houses are totally committed to the all-electronic system.

The crew structure for this single-camera production work can range anywhere from two to ten or more people—depending upon the budget, union restrictions, and the scope of the assignment. There may be considerable variation in what is actually expected of a person who is functioning within a given job title. Most production groups divide their areas of responsibility into the following job descriptions. (See also chapter 12.)

1. *Producer:* Overall financial and creative responsibility. The person who makes it possible for everyone else to do their job at the highest level of efficiency.
2. *Writer/Researcher:* Basic source of background information for graphics and final script.
3. *Director:* In charge of studio and/or field production from a creative standpoint. Usually responsible for edited version of project.
4. *Production Assistant:* Works directly with either director or producer or both. Keeps production notes, shot log, etc. Handles many important details.
5. *Camera Operator:* Chief technical person. Usually involved in all technical decisions. Supervises lighting.
6. *Sound Operator:* Audio recorder. Technical backup. May do lighting.
7. *Editor:* Responsible for final assembly, including a strong creative input.

With larger budgets the crew structure will increase. Assistants are added to some of the described positions. Lighting will often require a separate person in any of the more complicated types of production. On the other hand, when the organization is small each person may wear several hats. A small-format or student production group (fig. 9-16) might have the following configuration.

1. *Producer,* also writer/researcher
2. *Director,* also editor
3. *Camera Operator,* also editor assistant, maybe lighting
4. *Production Assistant,* also sound operator, maybe lighting

As with most task-oriented working groups, an efficient operation must have a clearly established plan for areas of responsibility and authority.

Figure 9-16 This small-format student production crew worked out its own configuration of assignments under the leadership of the producer.

Script Preparation

Principal camera work on a project should only be started after completion of a script or at least a detailed outline of shot continuity. More than one student production team has found that all of those great ideas just seem to disappear into thin air upon arrival at the shooting location. The very act of putting things down on paper is an important test of the feasibility of the operational plan.

Fundamental Elements of the Audio/Visual Vocabulary. The three-to-five-minute mini-documentary is a staple of both local and network newscasts. It differs in many ways from the format of the breaking news story and its necessary deadline. With the *mini-docs* the

production disciplines are more those of background research, balanced presentation, and thorough preproduction planning. Even with a scheduled air date there is lead time to put together all of the essential ingredients. This format borrows much from educational and industrial films and tapes—as well as from the traditional film documentaries of the past sixty years. In rather general terms, these are the main production elements that they all share.

1. *Host/Reporter/Narrator.* There is usually a central figure who is used both on- and off-camera to accomplish several important things. This person sets up the basic background information. The audience must initially be

made aware of what the presentation is all about and what they can expect to learn. When the information is complex or has negative connotations, the host/reporter/narrator must be viewed by the audience in an authoritative yet neutral perspective. He or she introduces new segments of information and gives them meaning in terms of what is to come. Ultimately there must be a summary of material presented and a conclusion as to its overall meaning to the audience. This is usually done in the form of a verbal and visual recapitulation of the highlights of material presented. Used properly the host/reporter figure lends an important personal element that can give both credibility and continuity to the content.

2. *The Actuality*. News people refer to material that comes directly from an event or situation as an *actuality*. No news story is complete without at least one of two essential ingredients of the actuality: the *scene* itself—the fire in progress, the site of a plane crash, or even the lobby of the bank long after the robbers have fled; and the *interview*—with the citizen eyewitness or some authority figure such as a fire chief or corporate officer. As the very name implies, documentaries—whether for industrial training or for classroom instruction—need the same sort of device to establish the credibility of the information. Productions designed for instructional purposes often will have the authority figure assume a dominant role. The actuality may be the operator of a certain piece of equipment on location in the factory itself. In a medical production, the doctors and nurses may provide the bulk of the information presented.

3. *Titles and Graphics*. It is essential that a production and its subsequent segments be carefully titled. A few well-chosen words that can be quickly read by the audience can be very efficient in establishing the main concept of the production, its location and position in time, and its basic subdivisions. Name and title identifications by supers or keys are crucial. A good deal of other key information can be presented by means of graphic displays—either full frame or keyed over portions of the video. Numerical relationships are very difficult to grasp if they are only heard. They can have a very strong impact when presented on a bar graph or pie chart in which the drawings become a visual analog of the relative value of the numbers. Special effects animation has reduced the time/cost factor that previously limited the use of artwork visuals.

4. *Stock Footage*. When there is no cost-effective way of shooting footage that is essential to a presentation, most professional producers turn to commercial sources. The price is high (a minimum fee of $300 is not uncommon), but those companies that supply stock footage have a large supply of videotape and film to cover a wide variety of situations. News departments that used to discard their old news stories now carefully index and file everything they shoot for possible later use. Students who cannot afford professional help should first examine the resources of their own university. Large companies that turn out numerous public relations films will often allow usage of portions of footage if credits are given. The copyright laws that govern the use of all stock footage are rather strict and should always be observed.

5. *Musical Score.* Music, carefully used, can add an important dimension to almost every kind of visual presentation. Here also there are commercial libraries where one can pay for the use of copyrighted material. The scoring of most professional films and tapes is usually done by production houses that specialize in the selection and editing of a complete musical background for a project.

Students, however, can take advantage of the fact that after a specified period, musical recordings and compositions become part of the *public domain* and can be used without charge in most cases. Another interesting possibility stems from the fact that Russia and the United States do not have any reciprocal copyright treaty. Though limited in availability and scope, Russian records can be used freely with legal impunity.

Final Scripting. Taking all of these elements into consideration—the host, the actuality scene and interview(s), needed graphics, availability of stock footage, music, and so forth—the producer/director/writer must think in terms of the entire scripting process. Depending upon the complexity and sophistication of the production, several steps may be followed in preparing the final shooting script. A rough draft or outline of the content should certainly be drawn up at the outset. This should include a detailed statement of general and specific objectives for the program. Try to answer the questions, What do I really want to accomplish in this production? and, What content elements have to be included to meet those objectives?

Perhaps a storyboard may be essential to your production. Lay out in cartoon or visual outline form what every shot should look like. This will force you to think pictorially and

A series of rough sketches, plotting every camera shot, will serve as a guide both for recording and for editing.

Figure 9-17 A sample storyboard.

establish visual **continuity** for the entire shoot. These rough sketches, no matter how crude your artistic ability, will help immeasurably in setting up your shots once you get out into the field. It also facilitates determination of precise in-and-out points for your later editing. (See fig. 9-17.)

A final shooting script should indicate all of the important audio elements as well as each camera shot. Every word of an interview segment obviously cannot be written out in advance—but it should be outlined. Important introductions and transitions should be scripted before arriving to set up equipment. Like the major multiple-camera studio production, every hour spent in preproduction planning and scripting will save countless hours of valuable crew time on the shoot. (See chapters 13 and 14.) Careful script preparation and preproduction planning is perhaps the most crucial *discipline* involved in single-camera production.

Preproduction Location Survey

If at all possible the shooting-day production schedule should be drawn up only after the producer (preferably accompanied by the director and camera operator) has made a personal inspection of all shooting sites. Draw up a floor plan of the location. Use Polaroid shots of the scene. This is the point at which any difficulties should be worked out—not on the day of production. If A.C. power is to be used, its location must be determined. Are extension cables needed? Is there available access to all locations? If not, who has the keys? What about transportation and parking?

Do scheduled events at the location conflict with the shoot? If the crew is shooting on campus, for example, will the end of a class send large numbers of people walking through the shot? Are there telephones in an office that will ring and interrupt the shot? What about those campus chimes?

Make a comprehensive checklist of everything to be taken care of on the shoot day; an inventory of all equipment (what backup gear should be taken?); all necessary permissions and clearances. Do you need to arrange for field maintenance?

Once this information has been added to the planning process, an efficient schedule can be put together. Certain priorities begin to emerge. Since we are shooting out of the eventual program sequence, some of the more flexible shot requirements can be rearranged to fit into an optimum sequence of operations. The wise producer will still build in a few alternatives for the inevitable changes that do occur. If rain is a possibility on the day of an outdoor shoot then optional locations or alternate shooting days must be available.

9.5 Production and Postproduction Planning

Many of the important elements to be considered in preplanning and the location survey also have to be treated in terms of production and postproduction concerns—for example, lighting, camera, and audio problems.

Lighting.   Attention should be given to any potential lighting problems during the advance survey. If available light is to be used then it must be checked with the shooting time of day in mind. A perfect setup for a morning shoot can mean shooting into an impossible glare in the later afternoon. Available artificial light can be used as an effective source of fill if it is of the right type and strength. (Flourescent lighting should be avoided if possible. It casts an unflattering blue tinge to faces and may create a hum or buzz on the sound track.) Enough lighting equipment should be brought to the location to ensure that a basic key light source can be established at the 3200-degree Kelvin minimum. Below this point the picture begins to take on an orange tinge (section 4.2). No amount of later adjustment can restore the proper flesh tones. When light levels are considerably below minimum base-light standards the darker areas of the background will produce a dark green effect full of video noise.

Camera.   Most of the newer industrial-type cameras are equipped with a *white balance* control unit that adjusts the strength of the basic video level to suit the light that is available for an individual shot. When this is properly set (with the color control knobs in their respective *fix* positions), the operator can have some confidence in getting a proper color balance. (See fig. 9-18.)

The *f*-stop setting has an important relationship to the balance of the various colors in any picture. A shot with perfectly adjusted colors can be considerably distorted by the

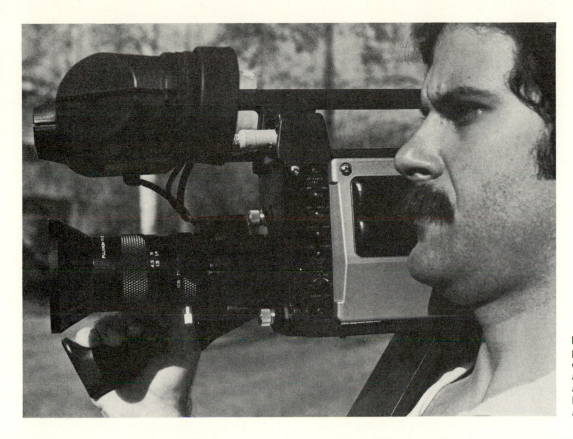

Figure 9-18 A
professional camera
designed for educational
and industrial
applications. Note the
location of white balance
and lens controls.

change of one or two f-stops. This can become a problem when the script calls for the camera to zoom in or out. When the lens zooms in, the focal length of the lens is continually changing. As it becomes a high magnification lens it allows considerably less light to get to the tube than when it was a wide-angle lens; thus, what had been a proper f-stop setting can become an insufficient one. On most of the newer cameras this problem has been solved by an automatic iris control that continually adjusts to the amount of light hitting the tube. If this feature is not available, the operator should rehearse the zoom—checking the resulting picture in order to make a manual f-stop adjustment.

The high level of activity and unanticipated problems on any location production occasionally mean that some of the usual equipment precautions may be temporarily forgotten. Cameras, recorders, and tapes are very vulnerable to the careless treatment they may be given on location. The camera operator must take special pains that no one points an open lens toward the sun or other hot light source, for example. The lens should be capped or closed between shots. Shock, moisture, dust, and heat and cold extremes can cause considerable damage to all.

Audio. The sound operator must be alert to a number of special location problems. Background noise, for example—which to the human ear might seem to be at the proper level—can be exaggerated by the mike and interfere with spoken dialogue. A good set of earphones and careful attention to the quality

PRODUCTION Campus Parking
SHOOTING DATE 8 Nov

PAGE 2
PRODUCER Evans

Slate	Count In	Count Out
Univ. Sec. Off. Seg 3 Shot 4 Take 3	Lt. Jones. 253 "My Job	270... this problem."
Sec. Off. Intro. Meyer Seg 3 Shot 1 Tk 1	275 "Lt. Jones ...	287... no parking."
	Cassette #2	
Parking Lot student #1 Seg 4 Shot 1 Tk 1	025 "Well everyday....	037... no spaces."
Parking lot student #1 Seg 4 Shot 1 Tk 2	045 "Everday....	051... really mad."
Parking lot student #2 Seg 4 Shot 2 Tk 1	059 "I don't see	071 ... parking ticket."

Figure 9-19 Production log sample.

of sound being recorded can do much to prevent any such problem. The operator must also be careful to keep the sound levels of all recorded materials within a consistent range so that they will match when edited. Use of the automatic gain control (AGC) is not always the solution to this problem. Actually, AGC can be the cause of another serious audio problem encountered with outdoor audio. When no one is speaking, the sound level of the background is automatically amplified producing a hissing or roaring effect. Because there is a built-in delay factor of a second or so, the effect is most noticeable at the beginning of segments or during long pauses. Attempts to erase this unwanted sound involve a risk of upcutting program audio. One solution may be to have the announcer say a few words up until two seconds prior to program sound.

During camera production, the director should be thinking of the audio as well as the video aspects of the editing job to come. Will there be a need for a *wildtrack*—separately recorded sound from any of the location shots? For example, a narrator may be standing next to a machine important to the story line, which has a distinctive sound. In the final program, shots that include the machine are to have a voice-over narration that is to be recorded later in the studio. If the director wants to have the sound of the machine as a part of the background under the narration, then it must be recorded for a later audio mix. Good sound operators will make a practice of recording numerous pieces of wildtrack sound as protection against unforeseen editing problems.

The Production Log

The importance of keeping an accurate record of production activities cannot be overemphasized. Important details that seem unforgetable at the moment somehow fade from memory at the end of a long, hard day. The log is an important way of keeping the production day organized. It should be used for essential information in brief form. (See fig. 9-19.) Additional notes should be written on the shooting script or attached to it. All of this information together becomes the script for the editing process.

The Postproduction Edit Sequence

There are several important steps that should be undertaken before the actual assembly process can begin. Even though basic operating procedure requires that each shot be checked during camera production, followed by an additional viewing of all of the **dailies** at the end of each shooting session, there is one more review that serves an important function. In this meeting, the producer—along with other members of the crew—must take an overall look at the footage and make some practical decisions about how special editing problems are to be solved. For example, if a tentative plan has been made to key titles and credits over camera footage, that footage must be selected with care. Unless specialized equipment is available, the usual procedure must be to produce a second generation tape combining the picture and the keyed lettering. This, of course, means that the final edited tape will be a third-generation transfer copy. The degree to which picture quality is diminished depends largely upon the quality of color, luminance, and resolution on the original tape. It is often wise to do the editing work on these and similar dissolve and special-effects segments before the main editing sequence is begun. Then, if problems develop, there can be time to work them out without delaying the whole project.

Audio Editing. The audio aspects of the editing process should also be carefully planned before any actual work is begun. Let's use the example of the wildtrack sound of the machine that is to be combined with the studio-recorded voice of the narrator. Using the studio facilities, these two sources are put together in an audio *mix track* on a separate videotape work cassette. Now the editor has two working options. He or she can first assemble-edit the video for the sequence and then later do an audio-only dub to match it; or the mixed audio track can be transferred to the master tape as an audio-only track with the video later put down to match it. Laying down an audio track and then editing video to it (the second approach) is often used when a picture montage is being matched to a particular piece of music. With this method, video shots can be edited to cut precisely with the rhythm of the music. (See fig. 9-20.)

There is an entirely different procedure that can be used when music or some other continuing sound background is to be added after the basic picture and sound have been recorded. The original sound should be put on the second audio track of the VTR recorder. Later, back at the studio, the VTR machine is patched to feed this track (#2) into the audio board. The music is set up to be fed into the console through a separate pot so that a balanced mix is produced on the program line output. This audio line output is then patched back to channel one on the same videotape machine that is feeding channel two. At the VTR recorder, we then set the controls for a playback of the video channel and audio channel two and a simultaneous audio dub on to channel one. There are numerous production applications for this system. Its utility is further enhanced by the fact that the video monitors at all locations can be used for cueing purposes.

Once these and similar techniques have been worked out, the editing can proceed with a maximum efficiency. Even after sufficient testing to check machine operation, the first few edits should be carefully checked. Audio, video, and control track levels should be continually monitored in order to provide consistent levels throughout the editing process. This is of special importance when editing takes place over a period of several days.

For student projects, an editing team structure of responsibilities should be worked

Figure 9-20 For students a two-person editing team can be a very efficient way to work. Most professionals, however, prefer to work alone whenever possible.

out. Much time can be saved when people are assigned to various aspects of the operation. While the editor is executing one edit decision, the producer (or director) with the script and log should be setting up details of the upcoming edit. If the work is being done from material that is on several tapes, a well-kept log will prove invaluable. The group should not be concerned if the work seems to progress slowly at first. A careful, thorough approach is much more important than any consideration of speed.

Summary

During the last few years the development of smaller, high-quality cameras and portable VTR recorders—and the evolution of sophisticated computer-based editing equipment—

has resulted in a new era of *single-camera* or EFP (electronic field production) techniques.

Postproduction electronic editing processes allow TV producers to use videotape the same way that filmmakers have been using celluloid film for decades—shooting single-camera scenes out of sequence, setting up for each separate shot, and shooting retakes as needed. Another technique that evolved was the *multiple-camera/recorder* method in which each of three or four cameras covering a continuous performance is recorded as an *isolated camera* on its individual VTR—for later editing decisions.

Preproduction editing of material to be inserted into live (or live-on-tape) programs evolved from ENG (electronic news gathering) pioneered in the mid-1970s. Prevalent throughout commercial broadcasting, these methods also permeate educational and corporate video technologies today.

Electronic editing is based upon the *electronic transfer* of audio and video information from the original master to a second, edited videotape. *Assemble editing* consists of adding desired shots in the proper sequence on the edited tape—joining the head of one segment to the tail of the preceding segment. *Insert editing* involves dropping in a video segment to replace previously recorded material.

With newer *electronic editors*—using microprocessors, SMPTE time code, joy-stick or search-dial frame locators, and precise synchronization—it is possible to set up an edit decision, preview the moving edit, and then execute the edit with single-field (sixtieth-of-a-second) accuracy. *Dissolves* and other *special effects* in editing can be accomplished by tying in the editor with a switcher or SEG.

Preproduction planning for single-camera location shooting—which involves crews anywhere from two to ten persons—is as crucial as planning for multiple-camera studio productions. Script preparation must include consideration of elements such as the *host/narrator*, *actuality* scenes and interviews, *graphics, stock footage*, and *music*. Scripting stages encompass setting forth precise *objectives*, drawing up a *storyboard*, and compiling a *final shooting script*.

Production and postproduction considerations include special problems concerned with *lighting, cameras*, and *audio*. The *production log* is a crucial record of all production-day activities—especially the length and location of all actual recorded segments. The *postproduction edit sequence* requires considerable preplanning and coordination—especially with any special *audio dubbing and mixing*.

In chapter 10, we will be concerned with important scenic and graphics elements that apply to both single-camera and multiple-camera studio production.

9.6 Training Exercises

The first exercise below is an individual assignment that should be carried out by each member of the class. The second exercise is a class project that should involve everyone in the decision-making steps required.

1. Plan a simple, single-camera location production. Start with a precise statement of objectives, draw a simple storyboard, and write a final shooting script. Prepare a checklist of the items that you would want to include on your preproduction location survey.

2. As a class, record the segments necessary for editing a simple, single-camera location actuality. This should consist of the following four shots:
   a. An opening statement or introduction by a host/narrator.
   b. A field interview with a simulated expert on any subject chosen (furniture making, automotive repair, pottery, or any other topic).
   c. A summary by the host/narrator.
   d. A *wild shot* (silent) of the item being discussed in the interview (table, carburator, or vase).

Assemble edit the first three segments together—following all due considerations of visual and audio continuity. *Insert edit* the wild shot into the appropriate spot in the interview.

pictorial elements: sets and graphics

10

In this chapter, we want to examine some of the actual scenic elements that make up the picture of the television production. What are the principles of design that should be applied to the use of sets and the construction of graphics? Although the student of production is initially concerned with the technical aspects of reproducing sound and picture—the hardware of microphones, cameras, lights, switchers, and recorders—we must also concentrate on the pictorial elements of what the cameras are looking at. Without a decent setting and without intelligible graphics, the best mechanical reproduction of video components can result only in a technically sharp program with no meaningful content.

10.1 The Concept of Pictorial Design

There are several elements of pictorial design that apply both to sets and to graphics. Although these two topics will be discussed separately in the remainder of this chapter, it may be helpful to consider some of the common elements first.

Functions of Design Elements

In discussing audio production and lighting techniques, we mentioned that there was both a *technical consideration* and a *creative aspect* to the use of these elements. To some extent we have a parallel consideration in examining pictorial elements. Here, however, instead of thinking in terms of technical and creative criteria, it is more applicable to consider the differences between *informational* functions of design and *emotional* or *psychological* functions of design.

First, the *informational aspects of pictorial design* must be considered. They are concerned with conveying appropriate information cues to the audience as accurately and efficiently as possible. In the case of a dramatic

191

setting, we ordinarily want to tell the audience as much as possible about the time and locale of the action. Where is the scene taking place? What historical period are we in? What time of day is it? We may also want to give other pictorial cues. What is the status of the main character? Where does he or she live? (Of course, there are many dramatic programs where this type of information is deliberately concealed from the audience for purposes of suspense or dramatic surprise.)

Nondramatic programs also need to convey this kind of information data. Are we in a newsroom? Are we on a stage in front of a live audience? Are we in a pulpit? How much do we need to tell the viewers about where they are and what should they know about their surroundings? All television staging considerations should start out with these types of questions.

With graphics, the informational considerations are even more important. The overwhelming use of graphics—especially for simpler productions and basic formats—is to convey information. What is the name of the program (title card)? What is the name of the person talking (super card)? How much of our tax dollar goes to education (pie chart)? What does the race course look like (diagram)? How does the piston work (animated graphic)? How bad was the accident (photo)? In designing graphics, the need for clarity is paramount. The director must always be asking, How can I get this information across as clearly and efficiently as possible? Most of the discussion in sections 10.4 and 10.5 is concerned with this question.

Second, the *emotional* or *psychological functions of pictorial design* must be considered. There are many subtle messages that the total production design can convey. All of the scenic elements—sets, props, graphics, furniture—combine to give a "feel" or "image" to the program. In a news program, do you want the image of an advanced technological communications center, of an abstract setting (fig. 10-1), or of a working newsroom (fig. 10-2)? In an instructional TV program, do you want the image of a typical academic setting or of a research lab? In a religious program, do you want the image of a traditional church service or of an avant-garde contemporary movement? In a variety program, do you want the image of a conventional stage presentation or of an electronic collage of entertainment happenings? Again, it is important that the director and designer begin with these types of questions before any decisions are made regarding the construction or assembling of set pieces or graphics.

In dramatic programs, of course, the overall *atmosphere* or *mood* is very important. Staging elements—combined with lighting—will tell us much about the mystery of an event, the state of mind of the hero, the lurking tragedy, the atmosphere of a family gathering, the majesty of an accomplishment, the power behind a particular move, the potential danger behind a closed door, the emptiness of a certain thought. The designer should always be concerned with maintaining or building the mood or feeling of every particular scene.

The emotional function of design would also include creating a given *style* or *continuity* to a program—helping to maintain a unity throughout the entire production. In the use of graphics, for instance, it would be jarring to establish a pattern of cartoons to illustrate a certain process and then suddenly switch to a series of detailed photographs. Several years ago, a church group produced a syndicated variety program dealing with the broad theme of the family. It was a composite of serious vignettes, vocal numbers, comedy sketches, talks, and dances, and featured many different performers and guest stars.[1] The pro-

1. *The Family and Other Living Things*, produced by the Church of the Latter Day Saints, 1976.

Figure 10-1 Abstract news set for local news program. (Photo courtesy of KABC-TV, Los Angeles.)

Figure 10-2 Two views of working newsroom used as actual on-the-air background for news set. (Photo courtesy of KNXT-TV, Los Angeles.)

duction very easily could have fallen apart into many mini-programs, however, the entire production was held together by its scenic design. Every segment of the program was staged on and around one scenic unit—a large, white, abstract open set combining several different levels, platforms, and stairs. Because it had a scenic unity, the production had a continuity that it otherwise could have lost.

Thus, every pictorial design should serve both an *informational* function and an *emotional* function. The set should not only tell us what time of day it is, but also give us a hint as to what is going to happen this day. The chart should not only tell us the information but emphasize how important the information is.

Elements of Pictorial Design

Artists and critics discourse long and eloquently about the many different factors that constitute aesthetic criteria—unity, harmony, texture, color, rhythm, proportion, and so forth. It is beyond the scope of this book to get into any detailed treatise on aesthetics of the still and moving picture.[2] The beginning production student should be aware, however, of at least three fundamental elements of pictorial design: (1) balance and mass; (2) lines and angles; and (3) tone and color.

Balance and Mass. The concept of balance was introduced in section 6.3 in connection with camera work. Asymmetrical balance is generally preferred over formal symmetrical balance. The larger a mass, the nearer it must be to the center of the scene in order to preserve a sense of balance with a smaller mass (fig. 10-3). In addition, the placement of mass

2. For a good discussion, see Gerald Millerson, *The Technique of Television Production* (New York: Hastings House Publishers, 1972), chapter 15. *See also* Herbert Zettl, *Sight Sound Motion: Applied Media Aesthetics* (Belmont, Calif.: Wadsworth Publishing Co., 1973), especially chapters 4–6.

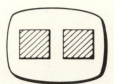

(a) Symmetrical balance results in a rigidity and formality that is usually not desired—except for certain occasions.

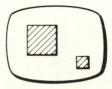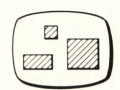

(b) Asymmetrical balance usually is more interesting and dynamic—resulting in a more fluid and creative mood, while just as well balanced aesthetically.

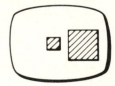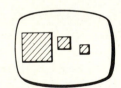

(c) An unbalanced picture can result, however, if care is not taken to position the asymmetrical elements with respect to their weight and mass. Temporarily, this may be desired.

**Figure 10-3
Symmetrical and
asymmetrical balance.**

within a scenic element will tend to affect the stability of the picture. A heavy mass in the bottom part of the picture implies firmness, solidity, support, importance. A heavier mass in the top part of the picture projects more instability, suspense, impermanence (fig. 10-4). These considerations of balance and placement have strong implications for the design of sets and graphics as well as for camera composition. A title card with lettering in the bottom of the frame projects a solid, strong

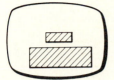
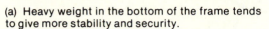

(a) Heavy weight in the bottom of the frame tends to give more stability and security.

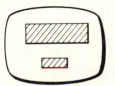

(b) If the top of the picture contains more mass than the bottom, the result is a feeling of uneasiness and suspense.

Figure 10-4 Location of mass in the picture.

(a) Horizontal lines are restful, inactive, stable. Vertical lines suggest solemnity, dignity, dominance. Diagonal lines represent action, movement, impermanence.

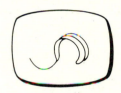

(b) Curved lines generally imply change, beauty, grace, flowing movement. With an upward, open curve there is a feeling of freedom and openness. A downward, open curve has more of a feeling of pressure and restriction.

Figure 10-5 The effect of straight and curved lines.

opening. A scenic unit with heavy ornamentation near the top implies a feeling of uneasiness, suspense.

Lines and Angles. The use of dominant lines is one of the strongest elements available to the scenic designer. Straight lines suggest firmness, rigidity, directness, strength; curved or rounded lines imply softness, elegance, movement. The direction of the dominant lines in a picture will carry strong connotations. Horizontal lines represent serenity, inactivity, openness. Vertical lines are dignified, important, strong. And diagonals imply action, imbalance, instability, insecurity (See fig. 10-5.)

Lines and angles can also be used to reinforce or exaggerate perspective, giving more of an illusion of depth. Painted on the studio floor, *forced perspective* lines can reinforce a great feeling of depth. *False perspective* lines can also be worked into other scenic elements. This kind of false perspective is limiting, however, in that the illusion works from only one specific camera location. (See fig. 10-6.)

Tone and Color. Working solely in monochrome television, variations in tone or gray scale value can have a substantial impact on scenic elements. The predominant tones determine, to a great extent, the overall emotional image of a production. Light tones result in a delicate, cheerful, happy, trivial feeling, whereas dark tones result in a feeling that is heavy, somber, serious, forceful. Tone also affects balance. A dark tone carries more mass, weighs more, and can be used to balance a larger mass that is light in color or tone. The position of various tones or blocks of dark and light mass in a picture also affect its stability and emotional quality. A dark mass at the top of a picture tends to induce a heavy, unnatural

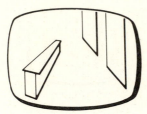 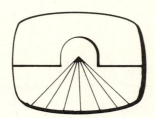

Figure 10-6 Lines and perspective.

A forced perspective can be created by careful use of scenic elements and even by painting false perspective lines directly on the studio floor.

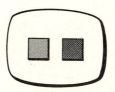 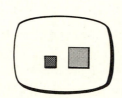

(a) A darker tone tends to imply more mass; thus the darker tone will overbalance the lighter mass (left). A smaller dark mass can be used to balance a lighter mass which is larger (right).

(b) A darker tone, or darker color, at the top of the picture or scenic element will tend to imply a top-heavy feeling of depression (left). The lighter tone, or brighter color, at the top gives more of a feeling of solidarity and normalcy (right).

Figure 10-7 Tone and balance.

feeling of entrapment and depression; heavier tones in the bottom of a picture give it more of a stable base. (See fig. 10-7.)

Color is usually discussed in terms of three characteristics. **Hue** is the actual color base itself (red, green, purple, orange, and so forth). **Saturation** refers to the strength or intensity of a color, how far removed it is from a neutral or gray shade. **Brightness** (or *lightness*) indicates where the color would fall on a scale from light (white) to dark (black).

Many of the considerations mentioned for tone also apply to color; for example, highly saturated colors (a vivid red) appear heavier—for purposes of balance—than unsaturated colors (a grayish red).

Various hues are also subjectively classified as *warm* (yellows and reds) or *cool* (blues and greens). Warm colors appear to be "heavier" than cool colors. Much of the secret of achieving good color balance is the art of mixing various hues that are compatible, balancing highly saturated colors with grayer shades, and selecting the right brightness of a particular hue (for example, baby blue rather than navy blue).

All of these elements of design—balance, line, tone—must be kept in mind as we look specifically at the elements of set design and graphics construction.

10.2 The Staging Design

As we begin to plan for scenery and staging, there are several different aspects we need to consider: staging styles, scenery elements, and staging requirements and considerations.

Staging Styles

One of the first decisions to be made by the director and designer concerns the style of staging that would be right for a particular program. Neutral, decorative, and realistic settings are three options.

Figure 10-8 Example of decorative or abstract setting.

Neutral Setting. One basic approach, which is appropriate for many different production purposes, would be the **neutral,** or *nonrepresentational* style. This is a **nonassociative** approach where there is no identifiable setting at all. All of the action takes place in **limbo** and there is no attempt to establish any locale. *Cameo* staging (section 4.3) would be an example of a neutral setting, as would some types of *silhouette* staging (although the latter usually is used only for a fragment of a larger scene). Most limbo settings, however, would be staged simply in front of a gray cyclorama or other neutral-colored plain background. In terms of overall production effect, the neutral staging might be used with the reportorial camera perspective (section 6.2)—for segments of a variety show, newscast, instructional TV lesson, and so forth.

Decorative Setting. If some elements are added to the neutral setting—purely for the sake of artistic gratification—then we would slip into a **decorative** (or even a *fantasy*) style. Some elements have been added, in an *abstract* setting, but there still is no attempt to suggest any kind of realistic location or identifiable elements. (See fig. 10-8.) Lighting effects and colors might be used; different scenic elements—platforms, steps, a podium—might be incorporated; but there still is no endeavor to represent anything recognizable. The various shapes, textures, colors, levels, and other scenic elements are used purely for their own artistic impact.

Again, many reportorial uses of television would be appropriate for this abstract kind of decorative setting, such as newscasts, talk shows, educational programs, and so forth. The biggest programing format to use this

Figure 10-9 Typical realistic setting with flats, set pieces, and furniture all contributing to a generalized atmospheric realism.

kind of staging, however, would be variety shows—dance numbers, musical performances, concerts, stand-up comedians, rock groups, singers, magicians, and others.

Realistic Settings. In dramatic programs, almost all staging is realistic to one extent or another. There are several levels of realism in stage and television setting. *Replicated realism* refers to the actual replication of a real locale—the Oval Office of the White House or the interior of Grand Central Station. Accurate down to tiny details, this style would correspond to the *naturalism* of the stage. For the most part, the approach is too detailed and cluttered for successful television production.

Much more common is *atmospheric realism,* where we are trying to convey a certain type of place—a Western saloon, an elegant drawing room, a busy office. (See fig. 10-9.) With this modified form of realism, we can use selected details and highlight certain ele-

ments that help to strengthen the drama. It is certainly realistic enough for virtually all dramatic purposes.

Another type of realism that is often employed is *symbolic realism.* In this staging style an open set is used. Rather than have a solid-walled closed set, the background is discontinuous—relying upon the viewer to fill in the missing pieces with *psychological closure.* In this staging style, selected symbols and props are used to represent the idea of the real thing—a table and two chairs comprise the kitchen, a tree trunk and tent make up the campsite, a desk and filing cabinet symbolize an office. There is no attempt to create an illusion of reality—just a suggestion will do.

Symbolic realism is often employed for brief comedy skits and slapstick sketches that are incorporated into a larger variety program, for example. Some abstract dramas may be staged entirely in symbolic realism. Nondramatic formats also make use of symbolic realism—the talk show with its desk and sofa, the homemaker program with a few kitchen appliances, and the illustrated lecture in front of a freestanding bookcase.

The open set gives the director much more freedom and flexibility in staging and shooting patterns. Blocking, camera movement, lighting, and microphone placement are all much easier to handle in the open set.

Scenery Elements

Regardless of the staging style, the director and the crew will probably find it convenient to think in terms of three broad categories of scenery and staging elements for purposes of ordering different items, constructing needed units, and considering storage and construction.

Settings. The term **setting** is usually used to refer to all of the major scenic pieces that make up the background and surrounding environment of the scene. This category would, in turn, include about three different kinds of scenic elements: **standard set units,** such as flats, two-folds, and other standing background pieces; **hanging units** including various cloth drops, hanging drapes, and the cyclorama (or cyc), which might cover two or three walls with a flat, neutral surface; and **set pieces,** which include pillars, steps and stairways, arches, platforms, wagons (platforms on casters), fences, lamp posts, and so forth. Many of the set pieces would be incorporated into realistic settings; others would be used in various artistic configurations in decorative or fantasy settings. The construction and use of some of the setting components are discussed below.

Set Dressings and Furniture. These terms, along with the label *stage props,* are used by different practitioners to mean slightly different things. Basically this category includes all

of those major items that are involved in *dressing* a set, filling out the naked setting represented by the flats and major set pieces. This would include all of the major items of furniture (desk, lectern, chairs, tables, appliances, and so forth) and large exterior stage props (bicycles, cannons, trees, and other natural or man-made objects). The term **set dressing** is often used to refer even more specifically to those smaller items that are used to make the set look lived in—lamps, ashtrays, pictures, books and magazines, household plants, vases, and other paraphernalia. Set dressings and stage props come from different sources, depending upon one's ingenuity and budget: a station's prop storage, the Drama department, secondhand stores, or one's own living room.

Hand Props. A specialized, but extremely important, category is that of hand **properties**—those items that are actually handled and manipulated as part of the television production. They include all those props needed for a dramatic production (telephones, bottles, kitchen tools, food, books, glasses, weapons), or for a commercial in a talk show (the box of cereal or can of dog food), or for an instructional program (globes, models, chemistry apparatus). Obviously some of these items overlap with other set dressings, the distinction being that hand props are actually *used* in the program, rather than being planted as *decoration.*

Staging Requirements and Considerations

At this point, before the director proceeds any further, there are several other considerations that must be given some thought. All of the staging and scenery elements will have to fit in with a total production design. Staging concerns have to meet other criteria also.

Camera Movement.   No matter what staging style is used, there must be provision for adequate camera movement. Several cameras will have to be free to have access from different angles in the setting. This usually would pose no problems with neutral or limbo sets; it generally is no major problem with decorative settings or the open set; but it could be a problem with some elaborate realistic settings. For this reason, sets are usually constructed as just two-walled or three-walled sets. The open wall (the missing side of the set) is used for camera access. In three-walled sets, the walls do not have to be set at exactly 90 degrees; they can be left open at oblique angles so that the camera can have even more access. In some sets (occasionally a four-walled set may have to be used), it is possible to position cameras behind the flats or other scenic elements and shoot through carefully masked camera peepholes—through a window, doorway, hole in a bookcase or fireplace, and other camouflaged openings.

Microphone Placement.   The setting also has to have provision for adequate microphone placement and, if on a boom, movement. Although the wireless microphone (section 3.2) is increasingly used in studio dramas—soap operas and situation comedies—the beginning audio operator must learn how to cope with staging concerns involved with wired microphones. For most *dramatic* productions—since lavaliers usually are not worn, hanging mikes result in bad audio, and hidden microphones are not encouraged—this does mean some sort of boom or giraffe or fishpole. This can lead to two kinds of problems.

First, if the set is small and the boom is large, there will be real movement and coordination troubles. Cameras also will have to maneuver around the boom and microphone cables. Adequate room has to be left open. Second, the mike boom can cause bad boom shadows. If the lighting has not been carefully

worked out with the precise boom placement in mind, there will be a strong possibility of unwanted shadows from the horizontal boom or fishpole. Ironically, this could be more of a problem in a neutral setting, with its plain background, than in a busy realistic set that may make a shadow less noticeable. In most cases, however, either the mike boom or the lighting instrument would have to be repositioned somewhat—or the light would have to be *barn doored* off of the boom (section 4.6).

Lighting Instruments.   Other lighting problems can be caused by certain kinds of setting arrangements. Occasionally, pillars or other foreground set pieces may be blocking crucial front lighting from a certain angle. Sometimes a strong key light might throw a very distracting shadow on a close-up shot of some small object. Or if the talent is lighted too close to the set (flat or cyc), the key light might throw too much illumination on the set. One of the most common problems, however, is the blocking of the backlight by a flat. If the flat is too high for the studio (a ten-foot flat might be high if the studio has a low ceiling), or if the flat is out too far into the studio from the backlight, or if the talent is standing too close to the flat, then it is going to be difficult to hit the talent with the backlight. (See fig. 10-10.) In this case, something—the backlight or the flat or the talent—will have to be moved.

Talent Movement.   Finally, the setting has to take into consideration all anticipated movement by the talent. How much action is required? Will several people be moving in the same direction simultaneously? How much space is needed for a certain movement (a dance step or tumbling demonstration)? Is there plenty of room for all entrances and exits? Will the talent be forced to maneuver so close to the set walls that part of their lighting will be cut off? Or, if the performers work too close to the set, will they cast unwanted shadows on the flat or cyc? Once the director is satisfied that there is enough room for talent movement, lighting instruments, microphone placement, and camera movement, he or she is ready to look at the functional aspects of using scenery.

10.3 Using Sets and Scenic Elements

Having considered several of the principles of staging design, we turn now to some of the practical factors connected with handling scenic elements and specific studio production techniques.

Handling Scenery

The physical manipulation and handling of all scenery units—construction, assembling, and storage—is a major study by itself. Television scenery is closely related to stage and film scenery; and anyone who has ever worked in technical theater or visited the back lot of a major motion picture studio has a feel for the scope of the scenery and props department. All we can do in this text is touch upon some of the basic elements involved in making scenery units, assembling them for studio use, and storing them for repeated use.[3]

Construction. The basic scenic unit for television, like that for the stage, is the **flat**—a cross-braced wooden frame faced with either canvas (which is lightweight, but too flimsy

3. For a full discussion of scenery construction and use, consult any good theater stagecraft text or manual, such as W. Oren Parker and Harvey K. Smith, *Scene Design and Stage Lighting,* second edition (New York: Holt, Rinehart & Winston, 1968), or Willard F. Bellman, *Scenography and Stage Technology: An Introduction* (New York: Thomas Y. Crowell Co., 1977).

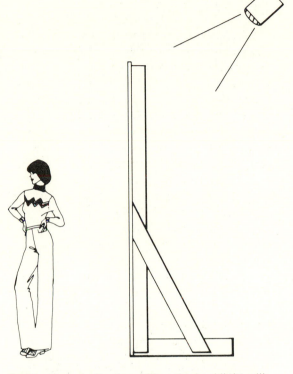

In this kind of situation, either the backlight will have to be repositioned closer to the flat, the flat will have to be moved back closer to the backlight, or the talent will have to move out farther away from the flat.

**Figure 10-10
Backlighting problems
with scenic flat.**

for repeated heavy use) or thin pressed board or plywood (which will take more abuse, although it is heavier to work with). Studios are increasingly turning to other rigid but lightweight materials, such as foamboard and corrugated feather board, for making flats and other scenic elements.

Typical construction for a flat is shown in figure 10-11. Flats can be made in any size, but common heights are ten feet for larger studios and eight feet for studios with lower ceilings. Widths also will vary, although they are seldom broader than five feet (the width that one person can comfortably handle with arms outstretched).

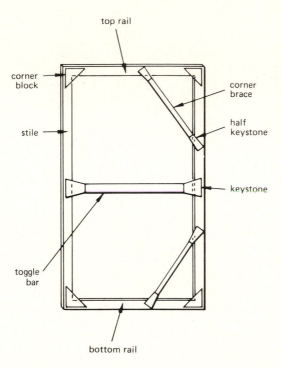

top rail

corner block

corner brace

half keystone

stile

keystone

toggle bar

bottom rail

Standard construction of a simple flat would consist of a frame made of 1″ × 3″ pine with 1/4″ plywood for the corner blocks and keystones. The front of the frame would be covered typically with canvas or with plywood (or pressed hardboard). (If a solid wooden front covering is used, then the corner braces would not be needed.)

Figure 10-11 Construction of an ordinary flat.

Cycs can be either a permanent solid cyc (faced with plywood or some other hard surface, which may tend to give audio problems) or a *cyc cloth* (canvas, duck, or gauze, depending upon the desired texture and reflectance quality desired). Cycs as a rule are designed to be used while stretched taut, giving a smooth limbo background; although they may be hung loosely in pleats to give the appearance of opened drapes. Drapes, which are usually of a heavier material and often darker can be either pulled taut or pleated, depending upon the desired effect. Darker, low reflectance drapes are effective backing for cameo lighting. Drapes usually are used in smaller widths than a cyc and can ordinarily be easily rigged or hung for specific applications. A cyc, on the other hand, usually is permanently mounted, covering two or even three walls of a studio.

Whenever wider widths are needed, flats can be hinged together semipermanently. Two flats hinged together would be known as a **two-fold.** Three flats similarly connected (seldom would you see more than three) would be known as a *three-fold*. When a wider span needs to be covered, the flat units are temporarily lashed or connected together. (See fig. 10-12.)

Construction of other set pieces (stairways, platforms, and so forth) is more complicated, requiring heavy bracing and sturdy framing for the amount of abuse and wear they will be subjected to.

Assembling.   Most flats are built with special hardware that facilitates easy temporary joining of two or more units. The stiles of the flats can be fitted with cleats so that a line can be used to lash two flats together quickly. (See fig. 10-12.)

Other methods of joining flats include the use of various metal fasteners (such as *L-plates,* which have drop-in fasteners and loose pin-hinges) and the use of large *quick-fix* clamps, which can be used to clamp the stiles of two adjoining flats together.

Most flats also have some sort of bracing or supporting unit so that they can be completely freestanding as a self-supporting unit. Several different types of stage braces are used. One of the most common is the **jack** or hinged wooden brace. (See fig. 10-12.) When the flat is in place, the jack is swung out behind the flat at right angles to the front of the flat and held in place with stage weights or sandbags.

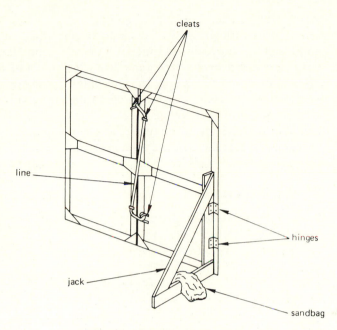

Cleats on both flats allow the units to be lashed together by means of the line (which is permanently tied onto one of the flats). The jack is a hinged stage brace which, when weighted, forms a good self-supporting unit.

Figure 10-12
Connecting and bracing flats.

Most set pieces are solid and freestanding units that need no special bracing when assembled for use in the studio. However, many of them—such as stairway units—do need to be fastened to other units or flats to make them as secure and immobile as possible. Door flats also need to be securely fastened to other set units to guarantee that the doorway will function properly without sticking or falling down when used. Some set pieces, such as *parallels* (collapsible platforms), can be partially disassembled and folded for storage. They must be carefully put together and securely set up before being used.

Storage.   In many small stations and educational institutions, scenery storage can be a serious problem. There is never enough room to house everything that is needed, and scenery storage always seems to be one area that suffers the most. This can be a particularly critical problem because so many of the flats and special set pieces can be reused over and over in a variety of ways—with different set dressings—in a number of configurations. Yet, they have to be stored somewhere and catalogued for easy retrieval.

Flats and other narrow units usually are stored in racks, which are simple frames designed to hold a number of flats in an upright position. Each rack can be designed and labeled to hold similarly matched scenic units (for example, living room flats, office flats, green-speckled flats, log cabin flats, and so forth).

Props and other small items can be stored on deep shelves in the storage area. Again, it is important that each shelf and/or cubicle be clearly labeled: telephones, dishes, bottles, and so on. Even furniture and other large stage props can be stored in multitiered shelves. Large overstuffed chairs, sofas, and heavy tables can be stored on the floor level; medium-sized chairs and tables can be stored on another level (four to five feet off the floor); and lightweight chairs and stools and small appliances can be stored on a third level (perhaps seven to eight feet above the floor).

Studio Techniques

In moving into actual studio usage, there are several other factors that the director and staging director need to be aware of.

Floor Plan.   First of all, as we have stressed throughout this text, the success of any television production is dependent to a great extent upon the discipline exercised in preproduction planning. As with the considerations of the lighting director, much valuable studio time and frustration can be saved by careful planning and plotting (section 4.6).

A good floor plan allows the director to make the most economical use of all studio and staging space. Sets can be planned efficiently; equipment can be placed with precision. The director can plan how best to take advantage, for example, of the *corner set*—a two-walled setting positioned in a corner of the studio—which provides good set backing for many types of productions (better than a flat backdrop), while allowing great depth and freedom of camera movement (more so than with a three-walled set).

A typical studio staging floor plan will include the placement of all flats and other set pieces and the exact location of all stage props and furniture. Other prominent studio facilities should also be included, as they are important to the production setting. It is important that all flats and furniture be drawn

to exact scale; otherwise the director's shooting angles, the talent's movement, and the lighting design will all be off. Figure 10-13 shows a typical plot plan, drawn to the scale of ⅛-inch to one foot. Once the accurate floor plan is drawn, it will be used by the director, staging director, staging assistants, floor manager, audio engineer, talent, and even the lighting director (to confirm and complement the lighting plot). It is therefore essential that the plan be prepared with as much detail and precision as possible.

Lighting Effects.   In addition to the regular lighting required for illumination of the production area, there are other special lighting effects that should be considered as part of the overall staging design. We have already mentioned the use of the cucalorus, or cookie, pattern (section 4.4) to cast various shadow patterns (venetian blinds, prison bars, Moorish lattice-work, and so forth) on the set wall. (See fig. 10-14.) Colored gels can be used to throw colored lights on a plain cyc or other surface. Subtle lighting changes (with the dimmer) can be employed to change color or shadowing as dramatic action unfolds. Other creative lighting effects (determining shape and texture, modifying reality, and establishing mood) were discussed in section 4.3. Staging and lighting must be considered as one integral production element; they cannot be looked at as isolated independent components.

Special Staging Effects.   There are several different kinds of mechanical and optical **staging effects** that can be used. Although some of the effects depend upon expensive equipment and elaborate arrangements, others can be adapted to most studio situations.

Large electric fans can create *wind* effects. Dry ice plunged into a tub of hot water creates *fog.* (Both of these effects cause studio noise that can be compensated for in a number

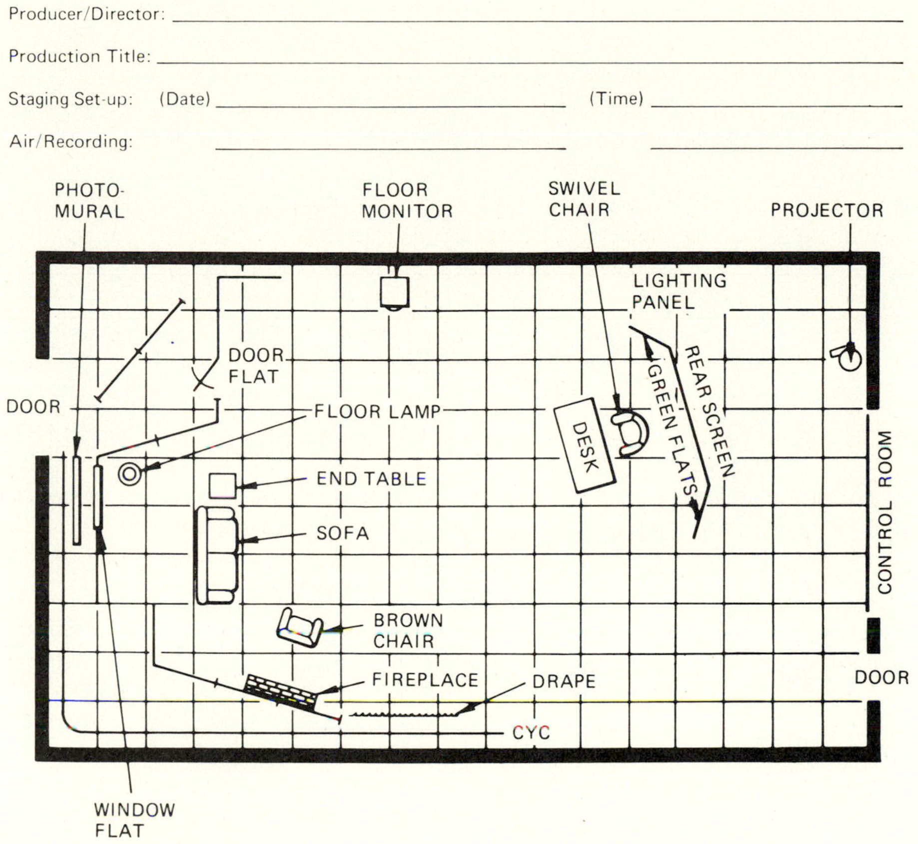

Producer/Director: _____

Production Title: _____

Staging Set-up: (Date) _____   (Time) _____

Air/Recording: _____   _____

PHOTO-MURAL   FLOOR MONITOR   SWIVEL CHAIR   PROJECTOR

LIGHTING PANEL

DOOR FLAT

DOOR

REAR SCREEN

GREEN FLATS

DESK

FLOOR LAMP

END TABLE

CONTROL ROOM

SOFA

BROWN CHAIR

FIREPLACE   DRAPE   DOOR

CYC

WINDOW FLAT

In this particular floor plan, the squares on the floor correspond to three-foot tiles actually on the studio floor. In other floor plans, a lighting grid or pipe battens might be superimposed over the studio plan.

Figure 10-13 Sample staging floor plan.

of ways, including sound effects records.) *Lightning* and *explosions* are best suggested by lighting effects (off set) coupled with sound effects.

To produce a *fire* effect, shake silk strips on a stick in front of a spotlight to create flickering shadows, or super film footage of a flame over the set (since flame is translucent the super effect works well). Again, use sound effects to present a total contextual effect. *Smoke* can be added by carefully pouring mineral oil on a hot plate.

Rain can be simulated by preparing a rain **drum** graphic—a continuous loop of black paper with white streaks splashed on it, attached to a studio crawl (section 10.5)—and rotating the drum; super a slightly defocused shot of the drum over the scene (with the actors in wet clothing). Again, add sound for a total effect.

There are several different kinds of optical effects that also can be incorporated into many kinds of productions. **Rear screen projection** can be used in many dramatic and reportorial

Figure 10-14 Use of a cucalorus pattern to throw a shadow pattern on the back wall of a set.

settings. Ranging in size from about four or five feet wide up to twelve feet across, rear screens can be used with regular slide projectors or, preferably, with special high-powered 4″×5″ projectors. They can be placed behind talent for newscasts or ITV lessons or they can be incorporated into a dramatic setting for outdoor locations or window backing. Special lighting and studio problems can occur, however. The use of the rear screen takes up quite a bit of floor space behind the set. Lighting is critical because no spill light (from the front or rear) can be allowed to fall upon the screen; lighting has to be from the sides or from very high steep angles.

Mirrors can be used in a variety of ways. For example, a large mirror suspended from a lighting grid can be used to get a shot looking straight down onto a demonstration table or into a cooking pot. Mirrors can also be used in musical productions. High and low shots can be obtained by using a double-mirrored periscope—for example, dancers' feet on a bandstand program.

Gobos are another handy staging device that enable a camera to frame a shot through some special foreground design. The gobo is a cutout (for instance, a simulated gunsight or keyhole) that is positioned several feet in front of a camera; it is an obvious stylistic effect that can be used judiciously to good advantage. Other optical devices using special filters and prisms also can be utilized in more sophisticated situations.

Production Problems. Finally, mention should be made of several common troubles that periodically plague even the best-planned staging plan. One is the difficulty of obtaining a consistent background from all angles. Whether a person is using a lighted cyc or a realistic set of flats, care must be taken to make certain that the set is evenly lit so that each camera, shooting from its particular angle, will be getting the same background shot. Also, care must be taken to ensure that the sets are wide enough—that there is enough cover at each end of the set—so that cameras shooting from outside angles will not be shooting off the set.

Troubles frequently occur with functional furniture. Chairs, stools, and sofas must be appropriately matched with talent. There are some common furniture problems: the *swinging swivel chair,* in which guests vent their nervous energy by rotating back and forth; the *precarious perch,* which involves sitting uncomfortably on top of a high, hard stool; and the *talent swallower,* overstuffed chairs and sofas that are so plush and soft that the person sinks down so far that the director is left with nothing but a shot of knees. Make sure you use solid furniture that is comfortable but firm.

One last production problem that has ruined many a final take is the forgotton prop. In any kind of production that relies on hand props (dramas, variety acts, demonstration shows, instructional TV), there is always the danger of failing to return a given prop to its starting point. The gun must be returned to the bedside table; the magician's paraphernalia must be repacked and checked; a new set of vegetables must be prepared for the cooking demonstration; the toys must be put back in the clown's sack; and so forth. Both the talent and the stage manager should double check, after the dress rehearsal, to determine that everything is in place for the final production.

10.4 Principles of Graphics Design

In this section we turn from the large picture of the entire setting to the area of television **graphics**—those two-dimensional visuals specifically prepared for television presentation. This definition includes items such as title cards, charts, drawings, cartoons, diagrams, photographs, maps, super (key) cards, slides, and the chalkboard.

Aspect Ratio

The first rule of graphics preparation is that all visual material must be prepared with a *three-to-four* **aspect ratio**—the television screen is three units high and four units wide. Nothing can be done to change that ratio: regardless of the size of a graphic, it still has to fit into that three-to-four ratio. (See fig. 10-15.) This is approximately the same ratio as a horizontal 35mm (2″ × 2″) slide. Most slides, therefore, can be used *horizontally* in the television format.

Vertical slides, of course, cannot as a rule be used successfully on the television screen. There are some exceptions when a graphic that is not in the three-to-four ratio can be used. A long horizontal card can be used as a **pan card**—that is, the camera can pan across the card, revealing part of the information at a time. Similarly, a tall narrow graphic can be used as a **tilt card**—with the camera tilting down (or up) the card, revealing only a portion of it at a time. Also, it is possible to use a tall card as part of a split screen (section 7.4), with the remainder of the screen filled by the talent or some other subject. Similarly, it would be possible to use a vertical slide if it were projected on a rear screen, and the rest of the television picture was filled with something else (like the talent standing next to the screen). In general, however, all television

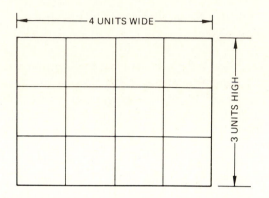

← 4 UNITS WIDE →

3 UNITS HIGH

Figure 10-15 Television aspect ratio.

Regardless of the size of the television graphic—whether it is four centimeters wide or eight feet wide—it must always be in the 3:4 aspect ratio.

material must be prepared to fit on the television screen with that three-to-four aspect ratio.

Scanning and Essential Areas

All material that is prepared on a graphic card will not be seen on the home receiver. There has to be some room around the border of the card for numbering and identification of the graphic, handling, smudge prints, and so forth. Let us call this the *border area* and assume that it will not be used for any information at all. The camera will never intend to shoot this area. To give ourselves plenty of room, let us assume that this margin should be about one-sixth of the total card: that is, if the card is twenty-four inches wide, we will take off one-sixth, or four inches, from each edge. This leaves us with a total usable width of sixteen inches. (See fig. 10-16.)

The remaining area that we have left is called the **scanning area.** This is the area actually to be scanned by the television camera. If we started out with a card that measured eighteen inches by twenty-four inches and reduced that with a border one-sixth the dimension of the card on all sides, we would now have a scanning area of twelve inches by six-

teen inches—still in the three-to-four ratio. (See fig. 10-16.)

Still, not everything in the scanning area will be transmitted through the entire system to reach the home TV set. The scanning system of the camera monitor may be slightly misaligned, so the camera operator will inadvertently cut off part of the graphic. The home receiver also will clip off, or crop, some of the picture. To be safe, we should decrease the total width of the usable scanning area by taking off about one-eighth on all sides. Starting with our original card twenty-four inches wide, we would now have a remaining width of about twelve inches (See fig. 10-16.)

The remaining area is known as the **essential area,** or the **critical area.** All of the essential information that we want to transmit through the system must be placed in this critical zone. This amounts to about one-half of the original card size. It is still a three-to-four ratio.

The information that is outside of the essential area but still within the scanning area (the shaded area in fig. 10-16) may or may not be seen on the home receiver. Depending upon the various components in the total transmission system, some of this information may reach the home set; some of it will be cropped. This information, therefore, must be part of the total graphic design, but it cannot be essential. Anything outside of the scanning area—on the border of the card—is technically known as *garbage,* and it is assumed that the camera will not try to transmit any of it.

Graphic Mask.   To assist you in the preparation of graphics, it may be helpful to make a template or mask as a guide in laying out standard graphic cards. One convenient size for graphics is eleven by fourteen inches (this is not only a convenient size to work with, it is also one-quarter of a standard sheet of 22″×28″ railroad or poster board). Take a piece of poster board eleven inches by fourteen

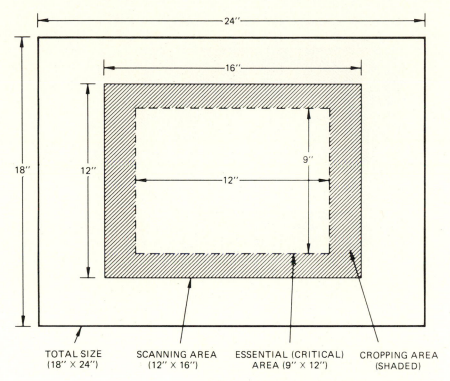

TOTAL SIZE
(18″ × 24″) SCANNING AREA
(12″ × 16″) ESSENTIAL (CRITICAL)
AREA (9″ × 12″) CROPPING AREA
(SHADED)

In this particular example, suppose we are working with a card that is actually 18″ by 24″. The scanning area is 2/3 of the total card size or 12″ by 16″ (which includes the shaded area). The essential (or critical) area is 3/4 of the scanning area (or half of the total card size) which is 9″ × 12″ (indicated by the dotted lines). The cropping area (shaded) is that portion of the scanning area which may be seen by the television camera but it may or may not be seen on the home television receiver.

**Figure 10-16
Relationship of scanning
area to essential area.**

inches and cut out a six-by-eight-inch rectangular hole in the exact center. This will give you a good approximation of the essential area for your graphic. The border is actually a little less than that recommended, but it is close enough to be functional. Also cut some slits in your mask 1 inch above and below the essential area, and 1⅓ inch to each side of the cutout. These mark the edges of your scanning area. Your mask should resemble the illustration in figure 10-17.

Quantity of Information

The amount of information that can be communicated on television obviously is limited. The quantity of data that can be successfully included in one TV picture is determined basically by three factors: the size of the symbols (lettering); the style of printing; and color and tonal contrast. Each of the three factors is discussed in the next three sections.

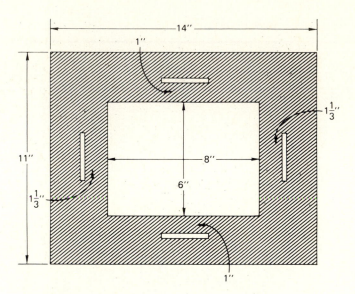

Starting with an 11″ by 14″ piece of poster board, and cutting out a 6″ by 8″ hole in the center, you will have a convenient guide or template for the preparation of 11″ by 14″ graphics. All information placed in the center cut-out area will be in the essential area. By making a slit 1″ above and below the central area, and 1 1/3″ to the sides of the essential area, you also have defined the scanning area.

Figure 10-17 Graphic mask.

As a rough rule of thumb, lettering on television should be *no smaller than one-fifteenth of the screen height.* If the critical area were fifteen inches high, that would mean that lettering could be no smaller than one inch. If the critical area is two inches high, individual letters would have to be a little over one-eighth-inch high. In the example of the mask constructed in figure 10-17, with a scanning area six inches high, the minimum height for each letter would be at least three-eighths of an inch. (Actually, it should be just about one centimeter.) Figure 10-18 indicates the amount of material that should be considered maximum for a typical TV graphic. If no line is less than one-fifteenth of the height of the critical area (and assuming some space is left between each line of letters), this would mean that *no more than seven lines of information*

should usually be included on a TV graphic card. Of course, artistic considerations—balance and arrangement of mass—might dictate that much less material be used. These guidelines must be considered a maximum.

Simplicity and Style

If there is one primary rule about the preparation of TV graphics, it is simply this: *Keep it simple.* All lettering. All design elements. All artwork. The screen is too small and the scanning lines are too blurry to permit any fine detail work.

This is particularly true with lettering styles. Letters should be bold, thick, well-defined, with a sharp, firm contour. Elegant lettering with fancy serifs and swirls must be avoided (except possibly for large stylized two-

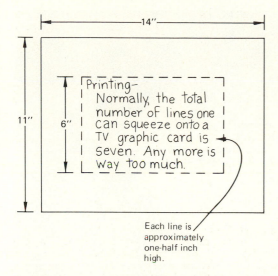

On a typical 11″ by 14″ graphic card, the essential area would be about 6″ high. This means that each individual letter would be about 1/2″ tall. The information on the card above represents the maximum amount that should be put on one card.

Figure 10-18 Quantity of information on a graphic card.

or three-word titles). Letters should be of even thickness throughout—both horizontal and vertical lines should be the same. (Thin horizontal lines, for example, can be obliterated in the scanning lines.)

Any other art work on a graphic card with lettering should also be kept simple. If it is too detailed, the audience will not get a chance to comprehend it; if it is too confusing and domineering, the audience will be distracted from the lettering.

All nonverbal graphics—pictures, cartoons, drawings, slides—must also be kept as simple as possible. Drawings or photographs showing a certain component or step in a process must show only what is absolutely necessary. One of the main troubles in trying to use visuals prepared for other media (for example, charts from a book or photos from a

magazine) is that they invariably contain too much detail. They are designed for a medium without the pressing temporal limitations of television. Usually they are visuals designed to convey as much information as possible in a single picture; they are designed for detailed study and comparison. Television, by contrast, may have to use three or four graphics sequentially to get the same information across.

This admonition is particularly true with *maps*. It is safe to say that no prepared maps (designed for non-television application) can be safely used on television. Any television graphic that tries to squeeze in more than twenty-five words is really too cramped and the information is too small (See fig. 10-18.) How many words are there on a typical map section that you might want to use? Maps have to be redone for TV. (See fig. 10-19.) Use only outlines of countries or natural geographical bodies and a few key labels or key locations. Use a series of maps if movement or detail is needed.

Color and Gray Scale Contrast

A third factor that can help determine the readability of a graphic and the quantity of information it can contain is color and monochrome contrast. Working with color graphics, it is important to use hues that contrast and complement each other without actually clashing. Artistic judgment and experience will help to determine which hues go well together. It is often very effective to combine different saturation levels of the same or closely related hues. Contrast in brightness levels also is effective in making certain segments of a graphic stand out.

In black-and-white television, you have to work for contrast within the gray scale. Avoid graphics that are all black and white (except for super and key cards, which have to be white letters on a black card). Two or three contrasting shades of gray generally help to

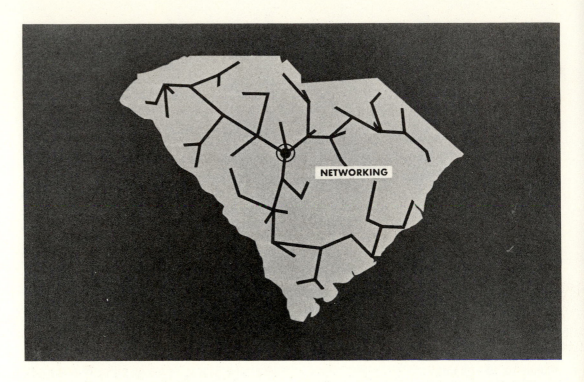

Figure 10-19 Example of a simplified map appropriate for a television graphic.

make a graphic card look appealing. In addition, video engineers like to have just a little white and a little black in a picture for reference points. Thus, a good graphic would be one that has two or three shades of gray plus a little white and black for sparkle and interest.

One problem to be avoided is the use of colors of the same brightness in preparing graphics for monochrome television. You may have colors of two different hues (for example, red and blue) and they may even be of strongly contrasting saturation (for example, a dull brownish red and a brilliant royal blue), but they still could have the same brightness level; in this case they will show up the same shade of gray on a black-and-white receiver.

Having considered these basic principles of designing television graphics, and keeping in mind some of the basic concepts of balance and line discussed in section 10.1, let us now look at some of the functional aspects of how TV graphics can be used in the studio.

10.5 Construction and Use of Graphics

In the actual preparation and use of graphics, several questions need to be answered about the way in which they are to be displayed, the ideal size for graphics, how they are to be constructed, and specific production applications.

Location and Display

Perhaps the first question to be asked about the use of a particular graphic is where and how it is to be displayed. There is one basic distinction that must be made. Is the graphic to be used on the set? Or is it to be an off-set graphic?

On-set graphics are meant to be displayed in front of the audience. Usually, a shooting pattern will be worked out that includes some shots of the talent and graphic(s) in the same shot. On-set graphics can be used on a floor easel or on a desk easel. They can be hanging as a decoration in the middle of the studio; they may be attached to freestanding poles. They might be mounted on a wall of the set. They can be used on a rear projection screen with the talent in front of the screen. In one way or another, however, they are designed to be used as an integral part of the set. The audience sees where and how they are used.

Off-set graphics, on the other hand, are never seen as an integrated part of the set. They appear out of nowhere. The audience has no reference point for them; for example, the audience would never know the actual size of the graphic. Off-set graphics can be employed in a variety of ways, but most often they are used on a graphics stand or floor easel. They also might be mounted on a drum or **crawl**— a large revolving drum that can be turned at varying speeds (either by hand or by an electric motor) with a long flexible graphic card attached to it. Off-set graphics might also be used as slides from telecine or the master control room film chain. This is often much easier and more convenient in that (a) the graphics are already framed and readily accessible without the chance of a slip-up on the floor, and (b) a camera can be freed for other studio work.

One reason that the distinction between on-set and off-set graphics is important is that you may design a graphic differently if it is to be an on-set graphic. For instance, conceivably you could use a vertical ratio—if you knew that the talent would always be standing in the same shot with the graphic. Or you might be able to design a graphic with more information than is otherwise recommended—if the talent will be talking at considerable length, with the aid of a pointer, about the parts of the graphic. In addition, color coordination and the use of mass and balance might be different if it were an on-set graphic, designed to be seen in the same shot with something else.

Whether a graphic is to be used on set or off set, if it is not firmly attached or stapled to some other scenic unit (such as a wall or a studio crawl), it must be firmly mounted. All graphics for easel stands must be either constructed directly on heavy poster board or firmly attached (glued) to heavy board.

Size of Graphics

To the viewer at home, it does not matter what size the graphic actually is as long as it is attractive and legible. For production purposes, however, size makes a difference.

On-set graphics have to be a reasonable size that balances with the talent and/or with other set elements. Size depends upon the purpose and the setting. A good average on-set size would probably be the full $22'' \times 28''$ poster board size. For simpler desk-top graphics, eleven-by-fourteen-inch size would probably be adequate. Seldom would on-set graphics be any smaller than that. At the other extreme, on-set graphics could be quite large—covering an entire wall or, as has been done, covering half the studio floor with a painted map.

Off-set graphics could vary considerably in size, again depending upon the exact use to which they are put. For most purposes, the ubiquitous eleven-by-fourteen-inches would be a good size. It is convenient, readily available, and easy to handle. When necessary, much smaller sizes can be used. Many cameras can focus in on a three-by-four-inch card without too much trouble. The smaller a graphic is, however, the more time and difficulty it takes for the camera operator to adjust focus; often the operator has to rack the tube focus (rear focus) to its extreme. It is possible, with many camera and tube complements, to get tight enough on a small area to use typewritten material on camera.

One general consideration to keep in mind is that the smaller a graphic is, the more every little camera movement is going to be magnified on the screen. With a three-by-four-inch card, the slightest camera jiggle will turn out to be a major movement on a twenty-one inch screen. Also, every little blemish on the graphic itself and every minor letter imperfection will be magnified. For these reasons, directors usually like to stay away from undersized graphics. In addition, if a camera is going to have to execute any movement on a graphic—panning or tilting, moving around on a map—then the bigger the graphic is, the smoother the movement will be. For these purposes, the 22″×28″ size is often utilized.

Graphics Preparation

There are quite a few methods for lettering on graphics. Depending upon one's artistic abilities, budget, and access to equipment, any one of the following might be appropriate. *Hand lettering* can be done with quite a variety of media and tools: pen, pencil, paint (poster paints, tempera), charcoal, chalk; felt-tip marking pens may be one of the fastest and easiest (for rough lettering). There are a number of ready-made, *ready-to-apply letters* that can be purchased: wax rub-on letters come in a variety of styles; large cutout, paste-on letters in various formats are available. Different types of *mechanical lettering aids,* stencils, and lettering sets can be effectively used in some applications. Specific *printing machines,* such as the hot press and other mechanical cold-press machines that use ribbon or tape acetate, can be very useful, if available.

The *typewriter,* as mentioned, can be considered for some jobs—under some conditions. In particular, if large primary type is available, with a good sharp carbon ribbon, the typewriter can prepare simple textual material. An ordinary typewriter, when magnified by the camera, as a rule does not look very satisfactory. Also, the camera runs into extensive production problems when trying to work with something as small as ordinary type.

Many newer lenses, however, have a close-up **macro lens** setting designed to make it easier to get tight shots of small objects.

In working with these various media and materials, take care to avoid—or work very carefully with—any highly reflective matter. Some of the cold-press acetate tape, for instance, makes letters that are very shiny. Be careful working with glossy photos too. Matte finishes are to be preferred, if you have a choice. Otherwise, lighting is critical in order to avoid glare.

One advantage to hand lettering and some of the ready-to-apply rub-on and paste-on letters is that you can optically space the letters. With most of the machine-generated letters, such as the typewriter and some character generators, each letter is mechanically spaced from the ones next to it—with a rigidity that is more convenient than artistic. (See fig. 10-20.)

One other hint to successful graphics preparation is to assemble your graphics in segments. Prepare your lettering—by whatever method—on appropriate shades of colored paper; and then cut the segments out in blocks and glue them onto your different colored basic board for the graphic. This accomplishes two things for you. First, it allows you to work more easily with blocks and masses. You can better control the balance and layout of each graphic. Second, the approach gives you more of an opportunity to work with varying textures and shades on one graphic. If you print black letters on a light gray paper and then cut out the blocks of paper and paste them onto darker gray poster board, you have introduced another tone in a rather pleasing and easy-to-handle manner.

Finally, those studios that have an electronic **character generator** (fig. 10-21) have a very handy, always available source for the quickest jobs of all. The character generator allows the operator to electronically type right

(METHODICAL)   (OPTICAL)

In the methodical spacing (left) each letter is spaced exactly the same distance from the one on either side of it. This results in an uneven appearance because those letters with a vertical line (such as the "I" and "N") appear very close together, while those with open space at the top or bottom (such as the "P" and "A") appear too far apart when next to each other. With the optical spacing (right) these variations can be taken into consideration as each letter is spaced visually according to its shape.

**Figure 10-20
Methodical and optical
spacing of letters.**

on the screen. Most models allow for quick retrieval of previously prepared material and flexible positioning and movement on the screen. The character generator, of course, cannot produce an artistic graphic card, but for many kinds of verbal displays its speed and efficiency make up for aesthetic drawbacks.

Computer-Generated Graphics.   Many major production studios, networks, and an increasing number of stations have added the computer to their art departments. Once a given graphic has been designed—whether from a hand-drawn picture or from a character generator—the electronic signals (video information) for that graphic can be stored in digital form in the computer's memory. From

**Figure 10-21 Character
generator with sample
video typed on the
screen.**

that stage on, the computer can retrieve the elements of that graphic (or generate any number of variations to create new graphics) and then—following previously programed instructions—use those signals for any pattern of digital manipulation desired.

The images can be stretched, squeezed, tilted, reversed, turned inside out, flipped upside down—at any pace or with any degree of distortion wanted—by the operation of a few simple buttons, knobs, and levers. These manipulations—the fold over and the squeeze zoom, for example—are also used as special effects transitions between camera pictures (see chapter 7).

Production Uses of Graphics

Finally, we want to mention different ways that graphics can actually be incorporated into a production. The innovative director will do much more with graphics than simply parade a number of similar static graphics before the camera.

There are many times, of course, when a *sequence* of graphics will have to be used. As mentioned above, because TV graphics have to be simple, it often takes a number of them to get across the same information that could be incorporated into one detailed visual in a print medium.

There are two different ways of sequencing a series of graphics. The smoother method is usually the *alternate camera* technique. Every other graphic is placed on each of two camera easel stands (all the odd-numbered graphics for one camera and the even-numbered graphics for the other camera). Then the director can simply take, dissolve, or wipe from one graphic to the next. *Single-camera sequencing* can also be used, although sometimes with less-than-satisfactory results. All graphics are set up for one camera, and, while that camera remains on the air, the graphics

are either flipped forward or pulled sideways. (Masking tape tabs on the sides of the cards can facilitate smoother pulls.) With practice—and a steady hand of the grip or floor assistant—this method can sometimes be effective.

An even smoother, more secure way of handling a sequence of graphics is to put them on *slides*. Then, by simply alternating between two different slide drums, the director and technical director have accurate control of the sequencing with fewer chances for a mishap—once the slides are set up properly.

In working with a graphics stand or camera easel, make certain that the camera is exactly perpendicular to the easel; otherwise the lettering will appear to be running uphill in one direction or the other, getting smaller as it goes. This effect is known as *keystoning*. To correct it, rotate the easel, bringing the uphill (or smaller) side of the easel closer to the camera.

Many production uses of graphics will involve *panning* and *tilting* large graphic cards. Ideally, if such moves are to be effective, the cards should be large enough so that the camera can get some distance back and still use a wide-angle lens for smooth movement. If the graphic is so small that the camera has to be too close, it will be hard to keep all areas of the card in focus as the camera lens moves closer and then farther away from the card during a pan. On the other hand, if the camera operator has to use a narrow-angle long lens on a small card, it is difficult to execute a smooth move without the magnification of every little shaky camera movement. With a good pedestal mount, *trucking* and/or *pedestaling* moves can be smoother and remain in sharper focus than panning and tilting.

In many situations, *animated graphics* can get a particular message across best. Although special effects and film animation can often do the job much better, there are still opportunities for actual live studio card animation. Different kinds of animation are possible. In some constructions, parts of the card can be made to move by means of wires or tabs manipulated from the side. In other versions, pull-off strips can be removed from the rear or pull-out inserts can be removed from the top or side (for example, to add color to a bar graph as each new figure is introduced). The ingenious designer will find other ways to make information appear or disappear while a card is on the air. Supers, of course, can be combined with other graphics cards.

Related to the animated graphic is what might be termed the *build-up* sequence. This is a production technique whereby additional information is sequentially added to a basic graphic. For example, a map with only one city indicated on it is shown first; then a second city is added without any change in the basic map; then a third city is added; then dotted lines are added to show relationships; then a county outline is added; and so on. Although this kind of build-up can be achieved live in the studio with clear acetate cells or transparent overlays, the execution of such an operation can be rather tricky and uncertain. A much more secure method of handling such a build-up is to shoot the successive graphics with a still camera on a good copy stand and then use the slides on the air, alternating between two slide drums as for the slide sequencing described previously.

Many other uses of graphics will be explored by the inventive director. Generally, basic productions do not take full advantage of the potential of good graphics. There are limitless possibilities in the use of graphics to reinforce and augment both verbal and nonverbal messages.[4]

4. For a fuller discussion of the possibilities of graphics in educational programs, see Beverley Clarke, *Graphic Design in Educational Television* (London: Lund Humphries, 1974).

Summary

Good pictorial design—for sets and graphics—starts with consideration of both *informational* functions and *emotional* functions of the picture. Emotional aspects include establishing an *image* for a program, creating *atmosphere,* and sustaining a *continuity* throughout the production. Basic elements of design that should be considered in every production include *balance and mass, dominant lines,* and *tone and color.* Color components include *hue, saturation,* and *brightness.*

In working on staging design, there are three basic staging styles that can be used— *neutral* setting, *decorative* or fantasy setting, and variations of a *realistic* setting. Scenery elements that we have to work with include *settings* (standard set units, hanging units, and set pieces), *set dressings and furniture,* and *hand props.* In designing a studio setting, we must also consider *camera movement, microphone placement, lighting instruments,* and *talent movement.*

In handling set pieces in the studio, we should know the basic *construction of a flat,* how flats can be *joined,* and the best way of *storing* flats, set pieces, and properties. Some other studio techniques involve the preparation of a staging *floor plan,* use of *lighting effects,* other special *staging effects,* and dealing with *basic problems* of backgrounds, furniture, and props.

Some of the important principles of graphics design are the *three-to-four aspect ratio,* the relationship of the *scanning area* and *essential area,* how much *information* can be included on a card, the *simplicity* needed and the basic *style of lettering,* plus the correct use of *color* and *tonal contrast.*

In constructing graphics, the first distinction to be made is whether the graphic is to be used *on set* or *off set.* The application will help to determine the best *size* for the graphic.

Graphics preparation, *lettering,* can be handled with a wide variety of tools and techniques, including hand lettering, ready-to-apply letters, lettering aids, printing machines, the typewriter, and the character generator. Computer-generated graphics are increasingly used by major production centers. There are several different production uses of graphics, including alternate and single-camera *sequencing,* the use of *pan and tilt cards, animated graphics,* and *build-up graphics.*

This chapter has been concerned with the nonhuman aspects of the television picture. Chapter 11 discusses the human element of the picture—the actors and performers.

10.6 Training Exercises

Both of the following two exercises should be carried out individually by each student in the class.

1. Using the dimensions and layout of your studio, design a basic staging plot for a standard dramatic scene. Be as realistic as you can in terms of the set elements, furniture, and set dressings that are available to you. Make sure everything is accurately done to scale, and include as much detail as you can.

2. Make yourself an eleven-by-fourteen-inch graphics mask, following the dimensions in figure 10-17. Using this mask, prepare two sample graphics. The first should be just lettering—a credit card (for the credits at the end of a mock TV production), using five or six lines of information. The second card should combine art work and lettering—some sort of diagram or chart with a written explanation or heading. On both of these cards, make sure you carefully follow the principles spelled out in section 10.4.

on-camera talent: the performer and actor

11

In television, anyone who appears in front of a camera is referred to as *talent*. This is a traditional use of the term whether the person is giving a cooking demonstration, reciting Tennyson, interviewing the mayor, running for mayor, singing a ballad, acting in *Hamlet,* teaching long division, or giving a weather report. In this chapter we are concerned about working with talent from several different points of view.

11.1 Working with Talent

What does the director have to know in order to direct actors? How do you control a rambling interviewer? How should the crew react to a nervous guest? How do you tell talent how to use notes or cue cards? How can you get the talent to relate to the audience? These are the questions that you, as a crew member and budding director, have to answer one way or another.

In this text *we are not concerned with training television performers and actors.* We cannot attempt to teach students how to become accomplished announcers, stand-up comedians, singers and dancers, dynamic interviewers, controversial reporters, or award-winning actors. What we *are* concerned with is how to work with these people.

One effective way to train people how to *work with talent* is to look at the topic from the perspective *of the talent*. This chapter, therefore, will be examining various performance and acting requirements that the talent must face. By gaining some insight into the talent's position, the director and crew members should better be able to cope with the talent's problems in various production situations.

At the same time, however, we are aware of the fact that many production personnel and station executives do have their turn in front of the camera. Numerous professional positions—especially in smaller stations— combine off-camera work (writing, producing, selling, managing) with some on-camera work (reporting, hosting, selling, interviewing). Therefore, it is helpful at this stage to have some insight into the world of on-camera talent. Also, realistically, in many types of production classes, the students will be performing the various on-camera roles. Production classes revolve around lab exercises in which all of the class members take their turns as newscasters, interviewers, TV lecturers, and actors. This chapter should be of direct assistance in helping you cope with these assignments.

In discussing on-camera activities, the distinction is often made between two groups: (1) those presentational or reportorial roles where the talent is serving essentially as a communicator, portraying no role except as a host or reporter; and (2) dramatic roles where the talent is portraying some theatrical character. The first category is referred to as *performers* while the second group is referred to as *actors*. Although the two groups share many characteristics and concerns, it may be helpful to look at them separately.

11.2   The Television Performer

The category of performer includes announcers, emcees, hosts, narrators, reporters, interviewers, demonstrators, TV lecturers, panel participants, and the like—talent who are communicating personally with the audience, usually addressing them directly. In examining the performer, it may be helpful to look at his or her role as it relates to others. Specifically, let us look at performers as they relate to the *audience,* to the *production crew,* and to *other performers.*

Audience Relationships

The primary responsibility of the performer is, of course, to the audience. In addition, the performer-audience relationship is crucial to the success of any television program.

Audience Concept.   Television is an intimate medium. It usually is received on a small screen, in the privacy of the home, as a rule by just a few people. The television performer is most successful when he or she conceives of the audience in that manner—three or four people sitting just a few feet away. The TV director must help the performer to think of the television camera as one close acquaintance. In the mind of the individual TV viewer, the aggregate audience of thousands or millions of people does not exist. It is basically a one-to-one relationship.

There are occasions, of course, when the TV camera is recording a performer who is playing to a large audience—the singer before a theater audience, the politican addressing his supporters, the minister preaching to a church congregation. In these situations, however, television is just an *objective* eavesdropper, covering an actual event. If the singer, politician, or minister is using television as a *reportorial* medium, addressing the audience directly and personally, then the director must help the performer adapt his or her style to a different audience relationship—more intimate, subdued, with direct eye contact, using a conversational tone of voice.

Speaking Voice.   The natural conversational speaking voice is one of the most elusive qualities the performer has to try to attain. The performer who can project the feeling of spontaneity and intimacy in his or her speaking style is on the way to capturing one of the most sought-after qualities of any television performer—*sincerity.*

This is not to argue that the performer should not exhibit enthusiasm or animation or exuberance (if that is the person's natural style). It is only to point out that the speaker's *desire* to communicate with three or four people on the other side of the camera is, perhaps, the single most important ingredient in successful performing. If the host-announcer-reporter-teacher *sincerely* and earnestly *wants* to communicate (without an obvious artificial eagerness), then he or she should succeed in that communication process. The director must also help the talent learn how to concentrate while on camera.

Eye Contact.   Just as important as vocal directness is the intimacy of specific visual directness—eye contact with the TV camera. In reportorial program formats where the performer (newscaster, TV lecturer, host, commentator) is speaking directly to the audience, the talent must attempt to maintain a direct and personal eye contact with the camera lens at all times, looking straight into the heart of the lens. In the case of a camera with a lens turret, the performer must know which of the four or five lenses facing him or her is the *taking lens*.

This direct eye contact is the secret of maintaining the illusion of a one-to-one relationship with each individual member of the audience. By looking directly into the lens, the performer is directly and personally addressing everyone who is in contact with the television receiver. A third-grade pupil was once asked why she was so enthusiastic about her television teacher, and the child replied, "Why, because he is always talking directly *to me*." The child's own live classroom teacher, of course, had to share her attention with thirty students at one time, but the TV teacher was talking directly to that one child—and to every individual viewer.

In maintaining the illusion of direct eye contact, the performer must be skilled, of course, in some of the artifice and techniques of the medium. The director must help in teaching some of these skills to the performer. In many productions the director will cut from one camera shot of the performer to another. The performer will have to reestablish eye contact with the new camera immediately. Whenever possible, the performer should be aided by the floor director's waving the talent to look at the new camera a split second before the camera cut is made. In some situations, the performer can make the transition look as natural as possible by momentarily glancing downward (or upward)—as if glancing at some notes or trying to collect his or her thoughts—and then immediately establishing eye contact with the new camera.

With the help of the director and stage manager, the performer should also be aware of what camera might be used exclusively for close-ups of some object he or she is demonstrating or discussing. If it is clearly explained to you (as talent) that camera 3, for example, will always be getting just a close-up of the globe, then you need not worry about looking at camera 3 every time the tally lights change on the cameras. You can maintain continual eye contact with the camera that has the medium shot of you. (See fig. 11-1.)

Distracting Mannerisms.   Because television is such an intimate, close-up medium, the talent should also be aware that any visually or vocally distracting mannerism will certainly be captured with full impact. Some nervous mannerisms, such as a facial twitch or the unconscious habit of licking the lips, may be hard to control. On the other hand, some fidgety distractions—such as playing with a pencil or pulling an ear lobe—can be corrected if

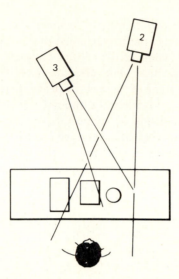

Figure 11-1 Camera pattern for shooting a close-up.

If the talent knows that camera 3 will be used only for close-ups of the objects on the table—and that camera 2 will always be getting the basic shot of the talent—then he or she will not have to worry about establishing eye contact with camera 3 every time the tally lights change. The talent can keep solid eye contact with camera 2.

the director or floor manager discreetly calls it to the performer's attention. Many an audio engineer has had a few hairs turn gray because a performer thumped his or her fingers on the table next to the desk mike or idly tapped his or her lavaliere while pondering a weighty question.

Vocal habits and mannerisms also can be distracting. The use of vocalized pauses (saying "um" or "ah") every time there is a second of dead air is a problem many of us share. The ubiquitous "I see" somehow always becomes part of the interviewer's basic vocabulary. (Why is it that in day-by-day conversation we seldom feel the need to say "I see" every time somebody makes a point to us, but as soon as we get on the air it becomes part of the interviewer's response pattern?) The talent also should be made aware of the tendency to state the obvious for the audience. While commenting on a series of slides with voice-over narration, there is no need to repeat, "Here

we are looking at. . . ." and "Here we see. . . ." Just explain simply, "This temple is one of. . . ."

Handling Scripted Material. Depending upon the specific function of the performer, he or she may be working fron a *full script,* speaking extemporaneously from a *semiscript* or full outline, or speaking spontaneously or *ad lib* with no preparation at all. Actually, aside from dramatic programs, there are only about three types of productions that call for working from a full script: (1) *Political talks* and other critical presentations or speeches (such as editorials) where it is extremely important to get every fact completely accurate, phrasing every comment on controversial issues precisely; (2) *commercials,* where the time element is so crucial that every second must be carefully accounted for with exact scripting; and (3) *news and sports reporting* (as opposed to ad lib, on-the-spot news coverage or play-by-play announcing), where—again—accuracy demands that every fact reported be carefully checked and worded and all elements be delivered in a precise sequence.

When working with a fully scripted program, you have a choice of several different means of handling the material. *Memorization* usually is required only for dramatic works, and is best left to the professionals. Seldom can typical television talent—unless they are exceptionally talented—deliver memorized copy without sounding too artificial and stiff. You are better off reading your copy—from a physical *script* in your hands, from **cue cards** held next to the camera, or from a prompting device such as the **teleprompter.**[1]

1. TelePrompTer is a registered trademark of the Teleprompter Corporation. It is a mechanical prompting device that attaches to the front of a camera. The prepared copy, on a long sheet of continuous paper, is projected onto a glass plate directly in front of the camera lens. Thus, the performer can read the copy while staring directly at the lens; and the lettering is too close to the lens to come into focus from the camera's perspective.

Reading directly from a script is satisfactory if you are somewhat familiar with the material and do not have to keep your eyes glued to the script. Some people can handle a script very well, glancing down only occasionally. Others, because of insecurity or nervousness, get completely buried in the script and never establish eye contact. If the talent has a tendency to fall into the latter category and read too much word-for-word, then the director would be better off using cue cards or—if it is available—a teleprompter. (See fig. 11-2.) If you, as director, do use a script, make sure you have the talent unstaple the script before going on the air and see that all of the pages are in order before starting the actual take.

If you decide to avoid the problems of working with a script, it will take some amount of extra coordination to use cue cards properly. Either the performer or some crew member will have to transfer the entire script onto large cue sheets (heavy oak tag paper or similar stiff stock). The cue-card holder also has to be trained to do a good job—holding the cards right next to the lens, reading along with the talent and raising each card to keep the exact line being read next to the lens, dropping each card silently, and positioning the next one. With a hefty stack of cue cards, holding them can become a very wearying and demanding assignment.

If you can enjoy the luxury of using a teleprompter, these tasks are taken care of with a minimum amount of trouble—and the exact spot on the script is always positioned directly in front of the lens (by means of mirrors) so that the reader's eyes cannot wander away from the lens. (The astute viewer will probably catch the eyes scanning back and forth, however, if you are using either cue cards or a teleprompter.)

Many performers think they have to work from a full script when they probably would

**Figure 11-2
Teleprompter mirror mounted in front of camera lens. (Photo courtesy of KABC-TV, Los Angles.)**

be better off working from an outline or a semiscripted format. This enables the talent to have enough of a solid outline to speak with confidence; yet, by composing the exact words on the spot—*extemporaneously*—one can add vitality and sincerity that is difficult to achieve with a prepared text. When speaking extemporaneously it is easier to use cue cards, because only one or two cards might be needed for the program outline. Many experienced performers prefer, however, to work from small note cards that they carry with them. It is a convenient and relatively unobtrusive way to handle material with confidence and ease. The talent can glance down at his or her notes when necessary but should not try to hide them from the audience. The talent can speak primarily and sincerely directly to the camera lens.

Many times the performer will be called upon to serve in specialized roles such as that of announcer, game show host, voice-over narrator, and so forth. Some of the functions come close to the dramatic talent needed as an actor—interpreting lines and/or assuming a certain type of role. We would just reinforce the general advice that talent should try to handle any such role with as much naturalness as possible, and avoid the temptation to try to sound like what one thinks an announcer or narrator should sound like. For more detailed assistance, there are several handbooks available.[2]

Crew Relationships

After examining the primary relationship the performer has with the audience, you should think about the relationship of the performer and the production crew. As talent, you will be working closely with many people who directly can affect your performance—helping you to look good and do your best job. If you inadvertently cause them trouble, however, they will not be able to do their best job; consequently, you will wind up walking out of camera range, speaking off mike, missing important cues, or finding yourself with nothing left to say and two minutes to fill. You should be thinking specifically about what you—as a performer—need to do in conjunction with the director and A.D., the camera operators, the audio engineer, and the stage manager.

The Director and A.D.   Up to the beginning of the actual on-the-air production, your closest relationship will be with the director and the **associate director (A.D.).** In virtually every kind of performance assignment, the director and talent must work closely on the prepara-

tion of the program—arranging segments, developing material, finding resources, designing graphics, working out cues, and so forth.

As a performer, you will find that the A.D. is probably your best friend as far as timing is concerned. In many formats—variety shows, interview programs, newscasts, ITV lessons—the program will be broken down into a number of timed segments. During the actual production, you will be receiving cues relayed from the A.D. to let you know how the timing on each segment is working out, when you need to speed up, and when you should slow down.

During the program, you will find that there are many times when you can help the director with some indirect signals. This is especially important on rather standardized nonscripted shows where you have not had an opportunity for a full rehearsal. You can aid the director with such cues as, "Now if we look at this through the microscope. . ." (setting up the first slide), or "Three elements are necessary for this demonstration. . ." (getting ready to walk to another area). The performer should avoid giving direct instructions to the crew, however: "Now, if I could just get a shot of this wristwatch!"

Camera Operators.   As a polished performer, you will eventually find that you can put yourself in the place of the camera operator—perceiving yourself from the camera's perspective. You develop a "feel" for how you should move, for instance. You know that you cannot make any big or sweeping gestures; the chances are that the camera has you on a fairly tight medium shot. You must be careful with facial grimaces; there is a likelihood that the camera has a close-up of you.

When you are ready to make a big move, you lean into it gradually, because you want to give the camera operator ample warning.

2. See, for example, Stuart W. Hyde, *Television and Radio Announcing,* 2nd ed. (Boston: Houghton-Mifflin Co., 1971).

Figure 11-3 Talent signaling his intention to rise by "leaning into" the move.

For example, you may be sitting in an easy chair and are ready to stand, turn, and walk over to the demonstration area. There are several telltale cues that you give to the camera operator. For example, you place both feet firmly on the floor, you lean forward, you put your hands on the sides of the chair, you now *slowly* lift yourself out of the chair. (See fig. 11-3.) The camera is able to follow you smoothly as you prepare the operator for your moves. The warnings are also of value to other members of the production crew, the boom operator, for one, who must follow the move with you. You also develop a habit of moving slowly as you go from one area of the set to another. Again, this gives the camera operator a good chance of moving with you gracefully. (And it always looks fast enough to the viewer.)

It does not take long before you also begin to get a feel for holding up objects for a close-up to the correct camera. In figure 11-1, the cameras are positioned correctly for a right-handed person to demonstrate something on a close-up shot. As you pick up or point to the object, it is automatically angled for a good close-up on camera 3. You intuitively position any object or graphic on your right side, aimed off to your left (camera right) for the close-up shot.

Most of the time, in the situation in figure 11-1, you would not pick the object up off the table. You would be certain the camera had a clear, unobstructed shot of the object on the table top; it is much steadier and stable to leave it on the solid table. If you must pick up the object, you move it slowly; you move it as little as possible; you rest your elbow on the table or steady the object with your other hand. You do not ask the close-up camera to hold a shot of the object while you are gesturing with it.

Intuitively, if you see that the director does not have a second camera free for close-ups and you want to get a good tight shot of the object, you pick it up and hold it next to your face, pointing it straight at your camera, holding your arm tightly against your body to steady the hand, as shown in figure 11-4. Now the director can get a good tight shot of your face and the object, using the single camera available.

Audio Engineer.   You also develop a feel for the positions and problems of other members of the crew. We mentioned consideration for the boom operator. You also help the audio engineer by making certain you do not abuse any of the mikes. Do not handle any of the microphones except hand or stand mikes. Avoid playing with the mike cords. Know the position of all microphones and avoid any sudden or explosive noises in their vicinity.

In addition, be sure you are consistent in giving the audio engineer your audio level when he or she is setting up the mikes and establishing proper mike levels. The audio person will ask you for a **level;** you are to speak into the mike so that the fader-pot levels can be determined. Some performers will mumble a relatively weak audio check and then boom out on the air with their best basso profundo. A few will do just the opposite—give a good strong audio test to set the level and then start out rather weakly on the air.

Stage Manager.   Finally, you will come to know your floor manager or stage manager rather well. Once the studio doors are closed and the production is underway, the floor manager is the one person assigned to be of general assistance. One of the stage manager's prime

jobs is giving you different cues (to speed up, slow down, move in this direction, speak up, and so forth). Generally, you do not have to acknowledge the cues that call for some sort of immediate action on your part; you just do as instructed. The floor manager, however, will also be giving you time-remaining cues (time left in this segment, minutes remaining until the end of the program). Occasionally you will want to acknowledge these cues to reassure the floor manager that you have received the message. One covert way of doing this (a nod of the head is too obvious for the audience) is with a prolonged blink. The audience will scarcely notice the blink, but it will be picked up by the floor director. (See appendix C for illustrations of the various cues and floor manager's hand signals.)

As talent you will not have to worry about where the floor director is. If you do not see him or her, it is because you do not *have* to see the floor manager at that moment. It is the job of the floor manager to be where you will definitely see him or her when you need to.

In some productions, however, the floor manager may get positioned so that he or she is always fully visible to the talent. For many performers, it is helpful to have the floor manager standing right next to the camera on the air, eagerly hanging on every word of the speaker—nodding encouragement, responding (silently), and reacting to the performer. This provides a sense of feedback and stimulation that many performers need. On the other hand, feedback can be distracting to some performers. One of the authors of this text recalls one production where the talent was so desperate for any live appreciation that every floor crew member had either to hide behind set pieces and cameras or, in the case of the floor manager, turn his back on the talent—in order to get the talent to look at the camera. If the performer could find one pair of eyes in the studio, he would address that single individual rather than the camera lens.

Figure 11-4 Talent holding an object close to his face for a close-up (when no second close-up camera is available).

Relationships will vary tremendously among performers and those in crew positions. Both the performer and the crew should try to be as sensitive as possible to the feelings and working patterns of others. This is all part of the *discipline* of the production crew.

Relationships with Other Talent

Finally, some mention must be made about the relationship that you—as talent—will have with other performers in the studio. As host, panel moderator, or interviewer, you often may find yourself in a position of organizing and controlling others. As a host-mod-erator-interviewer, one of your concerns will have to be with the comfort and emotional security of others, particularly guests at the television studio and inexperienced performers who may not feel at ease. One tangible aspect of this concern will be professional courtesy while you are off-camera. For the sake of the talent in front of the lens, you will be quiet, attentive, and as unobtrusive as possible.

You will get used to the idea of close physical proximity to other talent. For the sake of good camera shots, performers have to work very close together, especially in two-person interviews. You may feel uncomfortably intimate (and you may want to keep a good supply of breath fresheners handy), but to the audience the staging looks natural. One old television adage is, "If you ain't touching, you ain't close enough."

Interviewing Techniques. One prominent situation in which you, as performer, will frequently find yourself is the basic interview format. This may take many forms: the celebrity interview, the unprepared person-in-the-street interview, the factual interview (basically trying to present information to the audience), the controversial interview (with some outspoken public figure), and so forth. There are a few basic points to be aware of in preparing for a studio interview.

1. *Preparation.* Find out as much as you can about the guest. Research the background of the subject you will be discussing. Be familiar with what the guest has written, produced, or said about the topic. Go to other sources for outside opinions.

2. *Hospitality.* Be on hand to welcome the guest to the studio well before air time. Make the guest comfortable. Explain all of the studio procedures, the nature of the program, and the intended audience.

3. *Organization.* Determine with the guest what main points the interview will cover. Arrange the points in a well-organized pattern, keeping some material for the middle and end of the interview.

4. *Focus.* Remember that the spotlight should be on the guest. He or she is the one that the audience wants to learn more about—not you. Avoid the temptation to dominate the session by explaining all of your viewpoints and ideas on the topic.

5. *Questioning.* Ask questions requiring some solid comments and explanation (avoiding *yes* or *no* answers). Ask only one question at a time (avoiding double-barreled questions). With a controversial guest, do not compromise the integrity of the interview by avoiding awkward topics or hard issues; press on, courteously but tenaciously, for honest answers to honest questions.

6. *Transitions.* Keep the interview moving. Follow up on interesting answers, but do not get bogged down. Use answers as a transition to the next point. Summarize and clarify if necessary, but keep transitions short.

7. *Control.* Remember that, as host, you are in control. Do not allow yourself to be overwhelmed in the presence of a powerful personality. Be ready to take over entirely for

the last thirty seconds or so—to summarize, thank the guest, and bring the interview to a smooth close, right on time.

These are a few guidelines for the interviewer. As director you will be helping the talent to establish similar hints for other on-camera assignments—as lecturer, newscaster, demonstrator, and so forth.

11.3 The Television Actor

Although we cannot begin to present a separate treatise on television acting, there are a few points that should be made. Assuming that you, as a director, will be working with skilled or trained actors, we do not need to get into the basics of acting methodology in this book. Anyone seriously interested in television drama will, of course, be pursuing additional class work in acting and dramatic directing. Many actors who have been trained on the stage and may have some film experience, however, are not prepared for the adaptations they will have to make to the television studio.

Many of the observations made under "The Television Performer" apply equally to the television actor. Actors, too, must be concerned with their relationship with the *audience* (television is an intimate medium compared to the stage, or even to film); with the *production crew* (where everyone is immediately involved in the execution of the dramatic scene); and with *other talent* (all dramatic blocking is more compact and precise in the TV studio).

Television acting invariably is compared with other media, and actors must make adaptions as they move from one medium to another. The theater, film, and television stages all have their unique requirements and frustrations.

Theatrical acting is, of course, the ancestor of all other media. Furthermore, the stage is still where most actors begin. Live television

acting resembles the theatrical stage in that a continuous performance is presented. Actors have to create and sustain a characterization for a full sixty or ninety minutes, but the similarity stops there.

Film acting is, like television, a medium of the recording camera, and like television, there is no **proscenium arch.** There also are many differences. In discussing television acting, one should look at both *live* TV acting and *filmed TV* acting.

Live Television Acting

Live television acting includes all television drama that is produced in continuous scenes and recorded live-on-tape. (There is virtually no acting any more that is completely live at the time of transmission.) The daytime soap operas and an increasing number of situation comedies are recorded live-on-tape—often in short segments and out of sequence. There are four fundamental ways in which television acting differs from its stage counterpart.

First, and most obvious, there is *no proscenium arch:* there is no firm boundary separating the audience from the actors. The audience perspective is switched every time the camera is changed. The director can move

the audience 90 degrees with the push of a button. Even in a theatre-in-the-round, or arena theatre, each individual viewer is in one spot for the entire production; the viewer's perspective cannot be changed. In television, the viewer can be transported sideways, in or out, or (with the use of the subjective camera) into the mind of the actor. (Even when a live audience is in the TV studio watching the tape of a situation comedy, the action is staged for the cameras and the television audience; the live audience is just watching the production of a program.) Actors must learn to adjust to this concept of the moving audience perspective.

Second, actors must adjust to a *smaller scope of projection.* Instead of the exaggerated movements and sweeping gestures that must be seen in the back row of the theatre, the TV actor has to restrict all actions and movement to a camera only ten feet away. (See fig. 11-5.) Instead of projecting his or her voice so that every line is heard clearly sixty or seventy feet from the stage, the actor must restrict voice volume level—without losing emotion or intensity—for a pickup point only three or four feet away. Television is a close-up medium, and actors must adjust to this intimacy.

Figure 11-5 Differences exist in the scope of projection and gesturing. Shown are a large gesture appropriate for a theater, *left,* and an intimate version of the same gesture appropriate for television, *right.*

Third, actors must learn to work with a *physical precision* in television. Compared to the stage, television blocking is very precise; every move and tiny gesture have to be carefully planned and controlled. On the stage, each movement may be accurate to a few feet. In television, the action must be measured by inches. If the actor's head is tilted at the wrong angle, the framing for a given shot may be off. This is a discipline that many actors find difficult to accept.

Finally, television exists in a demanding and *nonflexible time frame.* Except for some programing on public television, all dramatic programs have to be squeezed (or stretched) into given time slots—multiples of a half-hour, minus requisite time for commercials. This means that an actor may have to adjust pacing and speed up or slow down delivery of lines or action. Again, this is a discipline that is not easy to adapt to.

Filmed Television Acting

For many years, most major television dramas have been produced and recorded on film, using production techniques common to the motion picture industry for decades. Many of the preceding comments apply to filmed TV drama also. There is no proscenium arch in filmed drama. Actors still must adjust to a smaller scope of movement and vocal projection—although outdoor locations and spectacular long shots may call for the grand gesture and loud cry (but there is less of this for *filmed TV,* the close-up medium, than for *theatrical motion pictures*). Physical precision still is necessary in filmed TV drama. (There is, however, less concern with the discipline of the inflexible time period from the actor's standpoint; the exact timing is worked out on the film editor's bench by cutting or augmenting silent footage, action shots, panoramic long shots, and chase sequences.)

There are two areas, nevertheless, where filmed TV drama differs even further from

stage acting or from other film drama. First, filmed dramas are almost always shot *out of sequence.* There is no continuity of drama from the actor's standpoint. All of the scenes in a given location are shot during the same setup. For example, once the camera, audio, and lights are set up for the drugstore exterior, every bit of action that takes place in that locale will be filmed—from the opening boy-meets-girl shot to the final boy-dies-in-gutter shot. This demands a great deal of concentration and training on the part of the actor.

Second, compared to the stage and to theatrical motion pictures, television drama (both filmed and live) is a *quick study* medium. Regular actors in a continuing series must learn up to an hour-long script every week—the equivalent of two feature-length motion pictures every month. For the actor in the daytime soap opera, the pace is even more demanding—up to a half-hour of dialogue every day!

Thus, from a variety of viewpoints, the task of the television actor is quite demanding and complicated. Your job, as a television director, is to make the transition as easy as possible for the inexperienced TV actor. The stage actor and the motion picture actor both will need some amount of guidance in adapting to the television medium.

11.4 Clothing and Costumes

Some attention also must be given to what the performers and actors will wear. There are a few general observations that are appropriate for a book of this scope.

Design Considerations

Many of the design criteria discussed in chapter 10 apply here also. In any color production, for example, the clothing and costumes of the performers have to be considered in conjunction with the color scheme of the entire setting. All designers certainly would consider costuming an integral part of the overall production design. Even in small station and educational closed-circuit operations, color has to be a major consideration. The hostess for a local talk show normally would not wear a red ensemble on her predominantly green set (unless it was for her Christmas program).

The same color factors that were discussed in section 10.1 (*hue, saturation,* and *brightness*) apply to clothing and costume design. Unless a spectacular, deliberately colorful, dazzling effect is advised, performers generally should be encouraged to stick to clothing of a dull saturation—choose muted aqua rather than chartreuse, tan rather than brilliant yellow. Brightness and tonal balance also should be considered in terms of the overall emotional effect that is desired. Would dark, somber grays and browns be more or less appropriate than lighter shades and pastels?

Line also is an important design consideration. Vertical lines tend to emphasize tall and slender proportions; horizontal stripes tend to exaggerate weight and mass. Performers who are concerned about appearing too heavy (and television has a tendency to make people appear a little heavier) should stick to vertical lines.

One other word of advice to the performer in street clothing: be natural. Do not try to emulate the latest fashions in order to make a striking television appearance. Avoid fads, extreme styles, and flashy finery, unless that is your natural inclination. If you step out of character for the sake of making a striking appearance, the chances are that you will wind up looking more foolish than fashionable.

Production Considerations

In addition to color, line, and style, there are some other practical considerations and potential problems that you should be aware of. Whether working in color or monochrome television, try to avoid high contrast and ex-

tremes in color brightness. Remember that the television camera has a relatively limited contrast ratio (section 4.2), which makes it difficult to handle white shirts under a dark suit. Try also to avoid high contrasts with skin tones. Dark clothes will make a pale person look even more pale; light-colored clothes next to a tanned complexion will make the skin appear darker. Blacks and other dark-skinned performers, on the other hand, should be careful of light-colored clothing that would tend to heighten the tonal contrast and wash out facial details in the dark areas.

Generally, finely detailed patterns should be avoided. Whereas clothing with a rich thick texture will photograph well on television, clothing with a fine pattern usually will not. The pattern often is too busy and distracting—fighting with other picture elements, including the talent, for the viewer's attention. Thin stripes, herringbones, and small checks also can create the **moiré effect**—a distracting visual vibration caused by the interference of the clothing pattern and the TV scanning lines.

Jewelry can also cause trouble. Highly reflective jewelry is more of a problem on monochrome television than on color TV. Too much flashy jewelry—even if it does not cause glare problems as a result of its high reflectance qualities—still can be distracting and needlessly gaudy.

There is one other minor production consideration with color TV. Be careful of blue outfits—even a blue tie—if any chroma key effects are to be used in the production (section 7.4). Any blue worn by the performer will form part of the keying pattern and the background picture will appear wherever the blue clothing is otherwise visible to the camera.

Dramatic Costumes

Again, all the points made for performer clothing (color harmony, line, tonal contrast, details, and jewelry) apply to theatrical costuming as well. In many respects, the use of color and style in a dramatic production is even more important.

Virtually all costuming considerations that apply to theatrical costumes apply equally to television: authenticity, historical accuracy, color, durability, and so forth. One aspect that needs to be emphasized more strongly for television than for the stage is *detail*. Although you may be able to get away with a few loose threads and a modern patch on the stage—where the nearest spectator is fifteen feet away—you cannot afford to try to fool the television camera, which brings the viewer only a few inches away. This is especially critical in costuming around the neck, shoulders, and chest areas, where the close-up picks up costume details with microscopic clarity.

11.5   Television Makeup

The field of television makeup is a specialized area that most production personnel seldom get into. The student should be aware, however, of some of the basic principles and major considerations. All television makeup is used for one of three functions: (1) to *enhance* appearance (improving the performer's basic physiognomy with color correction or emphasis on highlights); (2) to *correct* appearance (pulling back protruding ears or straightening a broken nose); or (3) to *create* appearance (building a new character such as Frankenstein's monster or Mr. Hyde). Ordinary television production situations rarely go beyond the first function; the last two areas are left for the specialist.

Principles of Basic Makeup

In many kinds of situations, little or no makeup will be called for. If a performer looks good on camera, there is no reason to consider any makeup at all. For many female performers, ordinary street makeup probably will be

all that is needed. For many male performers, a little powder to control perspiration or to reduce the shine on a bald head may be all that is necessary. Even in dramatic situations, little makeup may be called for. The object is to have the performer or actor look as natural as possible; and with the close-up lens any exaggerated makeup certainly would be perceived as unnatural. This is opposed to theatre use, where exaggerated makeup is necessary in order to highlight facial features for the last row of viewers.

For minor skin problems or blotchiness, a base or foundation may be all that is needed. It should cover uneven skin coloring, surface blemishes, beard shadow, and so forth. The foundation can be further used, if needed, to cover lip lines, eyebrows, and other features before a new formation is drawn in.

Some improvement in appearance often can be achieved by color correction. Depending upon lighting conditions, facial colors may need to be touched up in order to give a truer color rendition. Generally, cooler colors (those hues with a slight bluish tint) tend to emphasize facial shadows and dark areas. For this reason warmer colors (those with a reddish tendency) generally are preferred for the basic foundation. Care must be taken, however, that the Caucasian or Oriental skin tone is not tinted too pink and that the Black or Latin skin color is not turned too reddish. Although makeup companies will furnish detailed instructions and charts with their products (suggesting proper colors to use for different races and skin types), every individual skin tone will react differently under various lighting conditions and with diverse camera adjustments. Only by experimenting with each individual under actual lighting and camera conditions can the best color combination be determined.

Appearance also can be improved or enhanced by careful use of highlighting and darkening. Within prudent limits, localized highlighting will tend to enlarge the evident size and prominence of a facial feature; darkening will tend to reduce its size for the camera. Thus, it is possible to emphasize cheekbones with highlights or de-emphasize a prominent forehead by darkening it.

Basic Makeup Materials

The primary makeup element is the base, or **foundation.** This is the initial covering that usually is applied to the entire face or exposed area being treated (arms and hands and other parts of the body often need makeup treatment). The foundation comes in several different media. *Pancake* foundation is a water-based covering that is applied with a moist sponge; it is convenient to use and is preferred by many stations as the basic makeup treatment. *Cream-base* foundation usually is dabbed onto small areas and spread by the fingers; left unpowdered, it results in a noticeable sheen. *Greasepaint,* a theatrical standard for many years, is easily worked and occasionally used for major jobs. *Powder bases,* supplied in compacts, provide fair covering power for small areas and touch-up jobs.

Specific drawing tools and accessory items are then applied as necessary over the foundation: lipstick, mascara, eyebrow pencil, eye shadow, and so forth. The extent of the use of the accent items depends upon the need for remodeling and the individual taste of the performer. If extensive makeup treatment is needed, an after-powdering usually is applied to *set* the makeup and tone down any unwanted gloss or sheen.

Final Considerations

In addition to the basic makeup job, hairstyling and treatment need to be considered. Hairstyles with a definite shape or firm silhouette usually compliment the performer more than wispy, fluffy hairdos. Hair should be carefully combed because back light will tend to make loose strands stand out.

The performer should strive for as natural an appearance as possible. For this reason, fancy hair treatments and fresh permanents should be avoided. The performer should wear glasses if he or she ordinarily wears them; they should not be removed simply for cosmetic reasons.

For dramatic purposes, of course, much more makeup treatment is needed—getting into the third function of *creating* an appearance for certain characterizations. This includes hair pieces and wigs, *collodion* scars, nose putty, surface molding by plasticine and special waxes, and larger rebuilding jobs using latex prosthetics and face masks.

Aside from these extreme theatrical applications, the aim of good television makeup, like that of good costuming, is simply one of accentuating the natural appearance of the performer for purposes of more accurate rendering by the electronic camera.

Summary

Although the production student may not aspire to be a great television performer, he or she should nevertheless be familiar with the problems of on-camera performers and actors. Otherwise, it will be difficult to work with *talent* with any real understanding. Some on-camera experience and training is important for everyone connected with the production of programs. Generally, television talent is divided into two categories—*performers* (reportorial communicators such as lecturers, newscasters, hosts, announcers, interviewers) and *actors.*

The performer must be concerned with three kinds of relationships. The first is *audience relationships,* which include a concept of the intimacy of the audience and a feeling for sincerity as expressed by the *speaking voice* and *eye contact.* The performer also must be aware of the need to control certain distracting mannerisms. Problems in handling scripted material and extemporaneous material can be worked out for individual performers depending upon their own delivery styles and the requirements of particular production formats. The second is crew relationships, which include the director and A.D. (preparation of the program and on-the-air timing), the camera operators (how to move on camera, how to handle a close-up of an object), the audio engineer (treatment of equipment, establishing audio levels), and the floor manager (accepting directions and cues). The third is relationships with other talent, which include playing host to other performers, moderating panel discussions, and handling interview situations. Conducting an interview involves several basic factors—preparation, hospitality, organization, focus, questioning, transitions, and control.

The television actor usually has been trained for other media—the theatrical stage and/or film. There are quite a few differences between television acting and other media. The TV actor must be helped to adapt to these differences: lack of the proscenium arch; a smaller scope of projection (both gesturing and vocal); physical precision in blocking; the nonflexible time frame; shooting out of sequence (in filmed TV drama); and quick-study methods of preparation.

Clothing and makeup considerations are primarily to help present as natural an appearance as possible without creating any production problems. Clothing should adhere to the fundamental design considerations of color and line. High contrasts should be avoided and small patterns should not be worn. Other problems can be caused by jewelry and by blue clothing (for chroma keying). Dramatic costumes must pay special attention to detail for the close-up medium of television. For most television applications, makeup consists of little more than street makeup for the purpose of enhancing natural appearance. This includes covering skin blemishes, color correction, and some highlighting and darkening, with the use of a foundation, special accent items, and a powder set. Theatrical uses of makeup for corrective purposes and for creating characterizations are seldom employed in most station operations.

This chapter has been concerned with the people in front of the cameras. Chapter 12 explores in more detail the responsibilities and attitudes of those behind the cameras.

11.6 Training Exercises

The first exercise should be conducted for the entire class. The other two exercises may be considered optional, depending upon how much emphasis the class wants to put on costuming and makeup.

1. Set up three role-playing interview situations. For each one, assign one student to play the role of the interviewer; he or she is to do as good a job as possible. For each interview, another student is assigned as the guest; unknown to the interviewer each guest is instructed to manifest some particular negative trait that should give the interviewer considerable trouble in handling the situation. Each five-minute interview is conducted in front of the class. After each interview, the class should critique the situation and discuss what could have been done to handle that particular troublesome guest.

2. Select four or five class members and set up a camera demonstration to see how their street clothes look on television. Select those who are wearing clothing and accessories that may present specific problems—wide stripes, small patterns, high contrast, jewelry, and so forth.

3. Select one female student as a model. Have her remove all makeup. On camera, using a close-up, have her apply ordinary street makeup in sequence. Have her continue to apply what would be considered more than the usual amounts of accent items (lipstick, eye shadow, and so forth). Critique the results. If theatrical makeup supplies are available to the class, select a male model—one with a heavy five-o'clock shadow—and go through the same process on camera, emphasizing a good foundation base.

the production crew 12

Throughout this text we have touched on some of the duties and *techniques* of specific crew members as well as the development of a professional *discipline* among all members of the production team. At this point we want to look a little more carefully at some considerations and task responsibilities of various crew positions. We will be concerned with the lighting and staging personnel, audio engineer, camera operators, technical director, recording engineer, projectionists, and grips and floor assistants.

In particular, however, we will be discussing the jobs of the two key crew members that we have not had an opportunity to cover previously—the associate director (A.D.) and the stage manager (or floor manager or floor director). We have saved these positions for discussion at this point because their jobs are primarily people-oriented, and we have been looking first at the various crew positions that are equipment-oriented.

12.1 The Associate Director

If one were to think of the television director as the captain of the production team (with the producer, executive producer, sponsors, and network executives as the higher officers), then the two lieutenants would be the assistant director or *associate director* (A.D.) and the *stage manager*. The latter is in charge of virtually everything that takes place on the studio floor, while the A.D. is the director's right-hand person and surrogate in all other matters.

General Duties of the A.D.

In almost all respects, the A.D. is considered the director's top assistant—ready to handle virtually any task that the director may request. Depending on the actual production setup and the traditional organization of the studio/station, the A.D. might be labeled either the assistant director or the associate director.[1] The position often would carry quite a bit of responsibility for the production independent of the director's orders. In some network situations, the A.D. will be responsible for setting up all of the camera shots on the air.

In virtually every kind of studio operation, however, the A.D.'s primary job will be that of timing the production. The A.D. will time individual segments during rehearsals, get an overall timing of the program, if possible, and then be in charge of the pacing of the program—speeding up or stretching as required—during the actual recording. The details of timing a program are described below. Other duties of the A.D. can be outlined in terms of time periods before the studio rehearsal, during the rehearsal period, and during the actual program.

Before the Studio Rehearsal.   In any major production undertaking, the A.D. will work with the director well in advance of the actual production period—attending production conferences, working during **pre-studio rehearsals** with talent, and assembling props and other materials. During this pre-studio period, the A.D. may also be able to start getting some rough timings of the program.

Once the production moves into the studio, the A.D. often has several tasks before the rehearsals actually start. The A.D. might be in charge of the rest of the crew—checking to make certain that everyone is present and reporting this to the director. The A.D. may well be in charge of arranging substitute assignments, thus ensuring that every position is covered.

The A.D. would obtain all copies of the scripts and other production instructions from the producer and/or director and distribute them to members of the crew. He or she might also be in charge of distributing slides to the projectionist in telecine, graphics and props to the floor manager, and other materials to the proper crew positions.

If timing arrangements have not yet been worked out with the talent, the A.D. would at this point determine exactly what kind of time cues the talent would prefer (in other words, how many minutes warning the talent would want before the end of the program or before the end of each segment of the program). If there is nothing else to be done, the A.D. would remain at the director's side, ready for any requests the director might have.

During the Rehearsal Period.   The A.D. will time as much of the program as possible during the various rehearsals (technical rehearsal, walk-through rehearsal, dress rehearsal, and so forth), including individual segments, film inserts, and opening and closing elements.

During the rehearsals, the director will mention various production items that need attention before the actual take: the back lighting is weak in area two; the talent doesn't know the roll cue to the third film segment; the graphics are out of order during the map sequence; the guest's hair needs to be combed; and similar items to be cleaned up after the rehearsals. The A.D. will be jotting down the production notes as the director spots them. Additionally, the A.D. should be making notes of similar items that might have escaped the attention of the director. If the A.D. notices a major item, it should be called to the attention of the director before the rehearsal proceeds. Minor items are simply written down to be cleaned up later (note that it is the A.D. who has to make the distinction between minor items and those that are important enough to warrant interrupting the rehearsal).

1. The Directors' Guild of America officially refers to the position as *associate director*, because the *assistant director* title is traditionally used in the film industry.

The A.D. will be especially concerned with noting all of the script changes that are made.

Depending upon the production techniques of the individual director, the A.D. may or may not get involved with actually making production decisions. In some situations, the A.D. will be helping to compose shots for the director, giving direct orders to the camera operators. The A.D. also may be making other suggestions regarding talent moves, graphics, revisions, lighting problems, or whatever else needs attention. In other situations, the A.D. traditionally stays out of these kinds of directorial/aesthetic decisions and sticks pretty closely to the note-keeping and timing functions.

After the rehearsal and before the actual take, the A.D. will want to do several things. First, he or she must make certain that the director follows through on all production notes that were jotted down (fixing the back light, taking care of the talent's hair, and so forth. For minor corrections, the A.D. may take care of them without even bothering the director.) Next, the A.D. must make sure that everybody involved has all of the script changes marked down; as certainly as one person did not get a crucial script change, that omission will lead to an on-the-air mistake. Finally, the A.D. must remind the director of how much time is remaining before the program must get started on the air.

During the Program.   Just prior to production, the A.D. will read down the clock, letting the director know how many seconds until air. Once on the air, the A.D. should remain alert to any and all potential problems—ready to take any action needed or to call major troubles to the attention of the director; the A.D. must show initiative in this regard.

The A.D. should be following the director's marked script at all times, ready to give any assistance necessary. The A.D. will be alerting camera operators, audio personnel, projectionists, and other crew positions to any special cues coming up in the script. Depending, again, upon the production complexity and studio philosophy, the A.D. may help to get the camera shots lined up. In some network and station production situations, the A.D. will be giving the crew—including the camera operators—virtually all their instructions, based upon the director's script and rehearsals. The A.D. may even be giving "readies" and "prepares" to the technical director. This gives the director freedom to handle last-minute adjustments, make final artistic decisions, and call the actual takes on the air.

In many instances, the A.D. will at least be calling out shot numbers to the cameras. (In a thoroughly rehearsed production, the director will have every shot numbered in his or her script, and the camera operators will have a list of their shots by number. As the A.D. calls out the shot number on the air, all camera operators know exactly where they are in relation to the actual on-the-air shot.)

The primary job of the A.D., of course, is giving all time signals to the talent. The A.D. will have his or her script marked with all of the time cues and, either directly or through the director, tell the floor manager when to give each time signal to the talent. (See fig. 12-1.) Sometimes individual program segments will be timed. At the very minimum, time signals indicating the amount of time remaining in the program must be relayed to the talent. The A.D. will also be determining when the talent needs to be signaled to speed up or slow down (stretch).

Finally, the associate director will be ready to take over at any time. The A.D. is literally the standby director. Should the director be unable to complete the program, the A.D. will assume the responsibility for the calling of shots and the production will continue. (Once on a network program the director had a heart attack at the beginning of a

Figure 12-1 A.D. checking script timing with a stopclock.

production and the A.D. continued to direct the program on the air. The ambulance arrived before the program was finished, and the director lived.)

After the production is over, the A.D. will remind the director to thank the cast and crew; help to clean up the control room of extra scripts, notes, and other materials; debrief the director on any errors that occurred during the program, looking forward to the next day's program; and set up a schedule with the director for any postproduction editing or other postproduction problems that need to be cleaned up.

Timing the Program

As previously outlined, the A.D.'s primary job is timing the program—ensuring that the entire production ends on time. In carrying out this function, there are specific hints that the beginning A.D. may want to use.

Segment Timing Sheet.   The fundamental tool of the A.D. is, of course, the stopwatch. The A.D. also needs some way, however, of keeping track of the various timing notes and reminders. The stopwatch is not of much use if the A.D. does not have some organized way of writing down the timing information. One way is the use of a **segment timing sheet.** It may take several forms and be used in different ways. One sample format is shown in figure 12-2. In this particular example, there are five columns for the A.D. to use. The first column is for a brief description of each segment in the program. The next four columns are for timing notations of one kind or another. *"Unit"* means the actual *length of the individual segment or unit.* *"Cum"* is for the *cumulative time* of the program up to that point; it is the time in the program that each particular segment should (or did) end.

	SEGMENT (Description)	IDEAL (Unit) Cum.		REHEARSAL (Unit) Cum.		DRESS (Unit) Cum.	AIR (Unit) Cum.
1	TEASER	(:20)	0:20	:25		:25	:25
2	OPEN. TITLES	(:30)	0:50	:40		1:05	1:10
3	INTRO	(1:05)	1:55	1:30		2:15	2:20
4	CHART	(2:00)	3:55	1:50		4:00	4:10
5	DEMO.	(4:00)	7:55	4:45		8:15	8:30
6	INTERVIEW	(5:30)	13:25	6:00		13:45	13:30
7	WRAP-UP	(:30)	13:55	:20		14:05	13:55
8	CLOSE	(:35)	14:30	:45		14:50	14:30
9							
10				16:15			
11				(+1:45 over)			
12							

In this particular example, we have a demonstration/interview program with several segments—including a teaser, the opening titles, an introduction by the host, a two-minute chart talk, a demonstration, an interview, the host's summary, and the closing credits. The ideal times are entered in the first column. During the stop-and-go rehearsal, various unit or segment times are obtained. By totalling up these times, in the "Rehearsal" column, we can see that the program is likely to run 1:45 (one minute and 45 seconds) long. Adjustments are made—the interview segment is cut short—and the actual cumulative times are entered during the "dress" rehearsal and the actual "air" recording.

Figure 12-2 Sample segment timing sheet.

The *ideal* column is the estimated time that each segment *should* run; both the ideal unit-segment times and the ideal cumulative time should be figured out in advance of setting foot in the studio. The *rehearsal* column is for jotting down the unit times as various segments are worked through in a technical or stop-and-go rehearsal. It is difficult to get an accurate picture of the actual cumulative times at this point, but the total of the unit times should give the A.D. a rough picture of how long or how short the program is likely to be. The *dress* rehearsal column should give the A.D. a clear picture of how the actual cumulative times compare to the ideal times. The *air* column is filled in as the program progresses. It lets the A.D. know how much to tell the talent to *stretch* or—in this case—*cut* in order to come out on time. In this program, for example, we can see that several segments ran long, so the interview segment had to be cut short (from an ideal of 5½ minutes to an actual 5 minutes).

There are many variations of timing sheets. Some will include *time in* and *time out* cumulative columns. Some will work with only one or two columns. This sample, however, should give the beginning A.D. an idea of what is needed to get the program timed accurately on the air.

Program Time and Body Time. Time signals are given to the talent in terms of *time remaining*. Thus, as we approach the end of a program, the A.D. will have the stage manager signal the performer that there are "five

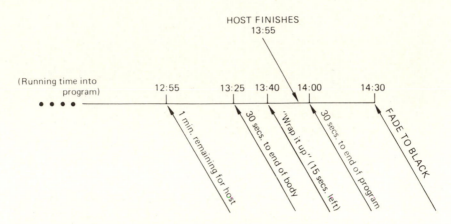

HOST FINISHES
13:55

(Running time into program)

12:55   13:25 13:40   14:00   14:30

1 min. remaining for host

30 secs. to end of body

"Wrap it up" (15 secs. left)

30 secs. to end of program

FADE TO BLACK

If the host is to be completely finished by 13:55, the "time remaining" *body-time* cues to the host are "one minute" (at 12:55), "thirty seconds" (at 13:25), and "wrap it up" (at 13:40). The *program-time* cue to the director would be "thirty seconds" (at 14:00).

Figure 12-3 Body time and program time.

minutes remaining," "three minutes remaining," "one minute to go," "thirty seconds left," and so forth (depending upon exactly what time cues the talent and A.D. had previously agreed would be used).

In many programs, such as the one illustrated in figure 12-2, the talent would need time cues remaining in specific segments. Thus—working from the *ideal* times—the host would get, for example, a "thirty-seconds remaining" cue at 3:25 into the program (as a reminder that there are thirty seconds left in the chart-talk) and at 7:25 (thirty seconds left in the demonstration). The talent might want time cues to get out of the interview segment on time (that is, a thirty-second cue at 12:55) or simply time cues to get through with the wrap-up summary on time (that is, a thirty-second cue at 13:25). Care must be taken that the talent clearly understands what these intermediate segment cues are so that they will not be confused with time remaining in the body of the program.

This brings up one other point of potential confusion. The A.D. must be concerned both with getting the talent wrapped up on time and with getting the program off the air on time. In figure 12-2 the talent needs a thirty-second cue at 13:25 because he or she has to be completely wrapped up and finished at 13:55 (leaving the director thirty-five seconds for the closing credits). Also, the director has to have a thirty-second cue at 14:00 in order to get the program off the air and into black at precisely 14:30. Thus, the A.D. has to work with both **body time,** the actual *length of the program content* including the host's closing summary but not the show's closing credits, and with **program time,** the *total length of the show* from fade-in to fade-out. Figure 12-3 illustrates this. Throughout the production, the A.D. has to be very careful to distinguish between *body-time cues to the talent* and *program-time cues to the director.* As can be imagined—solely from the standpoint of giving time cues—the A.D. has a very confusing and crucial role to play in any production.

12.2   The Stage Manager

The other right hand of the director is the stage manager (floor manager or floor director).[2] The stage manager is the director's surrogate to handle everything that happens on the studio floor. Actually, the stage manager's duties can be broken down into two very distinct areas: *handling the talent* and *managing all production activities* in the studio.

Working with Talent

Ideally, the floor director will have taken part in production conferences preceding the date of studio production. He or she has probably already met the principal talent and can anticipate the kind of problems that may exist. Once the production moves into the studio, the floor director is the primary contact the talent has with the rest of the world: the studio door is shut; the director is huddled with producers and technicians; all lights are focused upon the talent who is left isolated, facing the cameras alone—except for the support of the floor director.

There are two different kinds of talent needs that the floor director should be aware of and ready to minister to. First, there are *emotional-physical needs* that the talent may have. With inexperienced or exceptionally nervous talent, the floor director has to be especially sensitive in this area. Is the talent physically comfortable? Can you offer him or her a glass of water? Can you get the talent out of the lights for a few minutes? Does the talent need to talk to someone? Would he or she be better off left alone for a few moments of quiet reflection? What production mysteries should be explained to the talent?

2. The official Directors' Guild of America designation is *stage manager*, but all three terms are used in various stations and studio operations.

This last point is important. Because the talent is not tied into the P.L. intercom, he or she is not aware of what is going on most of the time. Explain to the talent why there is a delay (a result of the audio recorder malfunction); explain why all the crew is laughing (at the A.D.'s story—not at the talent's jacket). Try to put yourself in the position of the talent—isolated, in the spotlight, being stared at by the crew, and receiving no feedback as to what is going on.

With more experienced talent, this function becomes less of a priority. The routine production—with the continuing host/teacher/newscaster—can be done fairly smoothly without having to cater to the emotional needs of the skilled performer. A few wisecracks, a slap on the back, and the experienced talent is ready to proceed.

The other kind of talent needs are more tangible *technical-production* requirements. The floor director must work these out with the talent on a program-by-program basis. What props must be available and where? How will this movement be handled? Where is the talent to stand for this demonstration? What kinds of special cues might be needed? The details of each production must be worked out so that the talent is always sure of exactly what to do and the floor director is always sure of what specific tasks and cues he or she needs to execute to get the talent's job done. These types of production details are unique to each program; it is imperative that both the talent and floor manager are completely aware of what the other is doing.

One inevitable production requirement, common to every program, is the communication of information to the talent through various hand signals and/or flip cards (See fig. 12-4). The floor director—usually upon instructions from the director or A.D.—has to

Figure 12-4 Stage manager using hand cards to relay time signals to the talent. (Photo courtesy of KABC-TV, Los Angeles.)

be concerned with relaying quite a bit of material to the talent: stand by to start, begin talking, talk to this camera, get closer to the mike, speed up, slow down (stretch), get closer together, get further apart, move in this direction, everything is O.K., such and such number of minutes remain, thirty seconds to go, wrap it up (about fifteen seconds), cut, and so forth. (See appendix C for examples of the various hand signals.)

Production Management

In addition to handling talent, the other main job of the stage manager is that of handling all production details on the studio floor or stage. This includes broadly supervising staging and lighting setups and handling all staging and lighting changes during the program; coordinating all audio, camera, and other paraphernalia; directing all studio traffic; taking care of all graphics changes and movement; managing all talent movement; executing special effects; and every other production detail that might possibly occur.

The stage manager is ultimately in charge of virtually everything that happens on the studio floor, exercising dominion over all things technical—except the actual selection of shots for each camera. (In union situations, however, the stage manager may be restrained from crossing jurisdictional lines, such as giving orders to the lighting crew.) He or she must have a great deal of authority because virtually every other floor position is concerned with the production from only one specific viewpoint; for example, the camera operator, the audio engineer, and the lighting director all have their particular perspectives to take care of. Perhaps each of these three will have selected the same spot on the floor to position a camera, mike boom, and light stand. It is up to the stage manager to coordinate these needs and decide what goes where.

The stage manager does not work alone, of course. He or she will have a crew of floor assistants or grips, graphics flippers, cable pullers, rear screen projectionists, special effects operators, stagehands, lighting assistants, camera assistants, and so on. In a small-scale production, all of these positions and assistants may be combined in just one or two persons. In elaborate dramatic productions, the stage manager may have an assistant stage manager to coordinate the production activities of a floor crew of a dozen or so while the stage manager is occupied primarily with the job of talent managing.

As with the A.D., it may be convenient to think of the stage manager's responsibilities in terms of specific production periods: before the rehearsal period, during the rehearsals, and during the actual production.

Before the Studio Rehearsal.

Ideally, the floor manager will have been working with the director ahead of the production date, attending production conferences and contributing ideas to the production process. On the day of production, before the actual rehearsals start, the floor manager has several immediate tasks. He or she should obtain copies of the script and other specific instructions for various crew members and distribute them to everyone involved. The floor manager will assist the staging and lighting personnel however possible, assigning other floor people to help in the initial stages, coordinating set and light placements with the technical requirements for cameras, microphones, and so forth. The floor manager will obtain all graphics and props to be used in the production—making certain they are set up and arranged according to the script and the director's instructions. The floor manager, of course, will meet with the talent, cater to their comfort, and discuss any special requests.

Just as the primary tool of the A.D. was the stopwatch, the main tool of the floor manager is the clipboard. At this point in the production, the floor manager will have a pretty good idea of all that must be done before and during the program. He or she will have started to organize lists of key tasks and requirements—people to contact, props to secure, specific instructions to pass out, special effects to develop, talent needs, specialized crew problems, staging considerations, and so forth. The clipboard will have the master checklist that the floor manager will be working from during the rehearsal and production. This checklist will include all of the various action items that he or she must check on, supervise, or initiate during the production—arranging props, checking the sequence of graphics, securing water for the talent, checking the slides for the rear screen, closing the studio door, supervising the tricky camera move, setting up the lighting effect, ringing the buzzer, cueing the talent, changing the set piece, and on and on.

During the Rehearsal Period.

The floor manager must remain alert to the entire production process. He or she must try to anticipate problems before they escalate into crises, and constantly ask, What can I do to help the production? In addition, the floor manager must be especially sensitive to coordination problems among lighting, audio, special effects, staging, graphics, cameras, and other elements.

The floor manager will plan and coordinate all movement. What set elements have to be moved during the production? What props are to be placed where? What special effects will have to be cued? All graphics activity—moves, flips, pulls—will have to be planned and executed. Grips and floor assistants should be assigned to these various tasks so that each will know his or her cues and what to move when.

Working with cameras and audio on any special problems—camera and boom movements—is also the responsibility of the floor manager. Does the camera operator need an assistant for one particular trucking shot? Will the placement of camera and microphone cables affect other moving elements? The floor manager should always be looking ahead two minutes to see what problems might be averted by action now.

In addition, the floor manager gives the talent his or her undivided attention—always being in a position to be spotted easily by the performers. The talent should never have to turn his or her head to find the floor manager. All verbal instructions that come over the P. L. intercom from the director to the talent should be relayed clearly and tactfully, and all hand signal cues given promptly and forcefully. The floor manager will coordinate cue cards to ensure they are handled properly.

After the rehearsals and before the final take, there are several things the floor manager needs to check. All sets, props, graphics (and anything that is used during the body of the program) should be in place, ready for the beginning of the production; all consumables need to be replenished—water glasses, special effects, canisters. The chalkboard should be erased, and so forth. The stage manager should generally console and reassure the talent that everything is fine and that they are doing great. Assemble the crew, and make certain that everyone is ready and standing by for the beginning of the program.

During the Production. The stage manager must remain extra alert for any problems and doublecheck to ensure that all crew and talent are in their places, handling their moves, executing their cues. The stage manager will supervise all of the rehearsed moves and effects and make certain that all cues are clear and unambiguous. In general, he or she must guarantee that everything that was worked out during the rehearsal period is executed.

After the production, the stage manager supervises the strike, helps collect the graphics and props, assists the staging and lighting crew in getting their elements properly stored and taken care of, and generally polices the studio to see that everything is returned to where it belongs, ready for the next production.

In summary, the floor manager must think of himself or herself as *the* pivotal person in charge of the studio. The person is in complete control of all production elements. He or she must take the initiative in getting things done. *The floor manager* **gives** *orders; the floor manager does not stand around waiting for someone else to tell him or her what to do.*

12.3   Other Crew Positions

Throughout the text, we have had occasion to mention various duties of several crew members as we discussed equipment items. It may be helpful at this point to summarize some of these tasks and procedures of the key crew members.

Lighting and Staging

Lighting and staging personnel are usually the first to tackle their assignments in the studio. Depending on the scope of a production, all lighting and staging activity may be handled

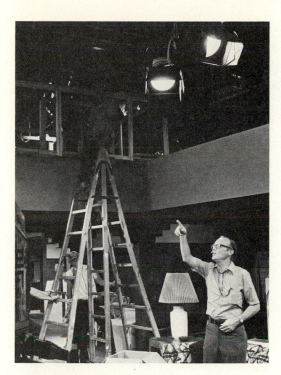

Figure 12-5 Lighting director giving instructions to lighting crew during production setup. (Photo courtesy of KCET and Hollywood Television Theater.)

by one lighting and staging supervisor, or there may be a lighting director and also a staging director. In any case, they would work closely together. (See fig. 12-5.)

Copies of the lighting and staging plots should be given to key crew members. Tools—hammers and screwdrivers, asbestos gloves and wrenches—should be distributed as needed. All major scenic units should be erected first—hanging units, flats, large set pieces. Then furniture and set dressings can be positioned as the lighting is being set up.

All lighting patches should be made with the current turned off. Instruments should be patched into the dimmer or nondim circuits as called for on the lighting plot and detailed lighting worksheet. Lights should be trimmed—aimed and focused—using talent or stand-ins of the same size and complexion. The finished lighting effect must be checked with both light meters and the control room monitors. A note of any malfunctioning equipment must be made and reported to the technical director, instructor, or supervising engineer.

After the lights are set and all ladders are put away, the set dressing and positioning of hand props should be completed. Someone should be assigned to work with the stage manager to execute any staging changes or lighting effects that are to take place during the program. After the production, lighting and staging personnel strike all set elements, return all furniture and props to their proper storage areas, unpatch all lighting instruments, and return the studio and control areas to their original condition.

Audio

The audio engineer (and any assistant) would select the proper microphones, plug them into the studio inputs, position them on stands or booms as required, and handle all patching in the audio control booth. All other sound sources (records, audio tapes, 16mm film soundtracks, VTR audio, cartridges) would be properly patched and threaded and checked out. Any equipment malfunction should be reported to the proper person. (See fig. 12-6.)

The audio operator would then obtain a level from the various talents, testing each one and setting a correct balance. If a musical production is involved, determining the best audio balance could demand quite a bit of time. All special cues are checked out with the director or A.D. During the production, the audio director must watch the VU meter, ride levels

Figure 12-6 Audio engineer during complicated television drama. (Photo courtesy of KABC-TV, Los Angeles.)

carefully, and listen closely for all audio cues from the director. Generally, microphones should be turned off except when they are actually in use. The audio director must also anticipate cues for film and VTR inserts.

After the production, the patch bay should be cleared, all switches and pot/faders returned to off or neutral positions, and all microphones, stands, and cables returned to their proper storage areas.

Cameras

The camera operator should attach the shot sheet (if they are being used) to the camera. After staging and lighting have generally cleared the area, the camera operator can pull the camera into its approximate position,

making certain to uncoil enough cable for estimated moves. He or she should then go through the uncapping and unlocking safety procedures as outlined in section 6.4, and report any apparent camera malfunction to the proper person. The pan and tilt drag should be loose enough for smooth camera movement, but not so loose that the operator's arm carries all the weight. (See fig. 12-7.)

The camera person should be attentive to all directions from the control room while working through the shot sheet. The zoom lens should be preset so that it maintains focus on major zooms. An operator should not leave a camera without permission and should lock the pan and tilt head whenever letting go of the pan handle.

Figure 12-7 Camera operator working with studio camera.

Figure 12-8 Technical director operating a complicated production switcher. (Photo courtesy of KABC-TV, Los Angeles.)

Composition is part of the camera operator's responsibility. If the picture has odd amputations, incongruous juxtapositions, confusing information, poor framing, and so forth, the operator is responsible. These things should be corrected before going on the air. If the shot is put on the air with bad composition, the operator may *cheat* (make slow minor adjustments that the audience will not perceive). The camera operator must always notice from the tally lights when the camera is on the air and not move unless ordered to do so by the director.

It is the camera person's responsibility after the production to cap up and lock up the camera, returning it to its studio storage area, and to wind the cable in a figure-eight pattern.

Technical Director

Unless given some other specific assignment, the technical director should report early to the switcher and put on the P.L. headset. While all other personnel are working around the studio in other capacities—setting up equipment, working with talent, and so forth—the T.D. is the one person who can be anchored in one spot in intercom communication with anyone else. The audio engineer, master control room, telecine, camera operators, and even the director can reach the T.D. from any other point to ask a question or to relay a message (simply by putting on a headset). Thus, until other positions are settled and the director gets into the control room, the T.D. can function as the director of all production operations. (See fig. 12-8.)

If the program is complicated or tricky from the switching standpoint, the director may want to have the T.D. go over the script and rehearse any complex transitions. Otherwise, the T.D. should need no special rehearsal. The T.D. should make certain, however, to check with the director about the speed of dissolves, fades, wipes, and so forth. During the production, clarification of the director's commands of preparation ("ready's" and "prepare's") can serve as an aid to the T.D., to camera operators, and to the video engineer. The T.D. should respond as accurately and quickly as possible to the director's commands, but not anticipate the director's orders and not try to direct from the T.D.'s chair.

Recording Engineer

As with other positions, procedures will vary tremendously from one production center to another, but there are several steps that recording engineers generally will have to follow.

The recording engineer must determine that the correct recording tape and the correct machine are being used. (If the facility has more than one of the same model, the instructor or supervising engineer may have some reason why a particular video recorder should or should not be used.) The recording engineer sets up all master control room patching and checks out all lines to verify that both the audio and video signals are getting into the recording machine properly. The audio engineer should send up an audio tone or some other signal at 100 percent of the audio board output so that the recording engineer can set the VU meter on the recording machine. (See fig. 12-9.)

If the program also has a video insert—to be played back on some other VTR machine—the recording engineer must make sure that it is patched up properly for a transfer. He or

Figure 12-9 Videotape operator, or recording engineer, supervising the taping of a studio drama. (Photo courtesy of KCET.)

she should play back a segment to the studio control room to verify that it is patched correctly, and clarify the exact cue points with the director so that the insert can roll properly. At the onset of the production recording, the recording engineer should make sure he or she *pushes the record button.* Many a program has been lost because one button was not pushed! After the production, the recording engineer is responsible for turning off all equipment, removing all the patches, labeling the videotape, and returning it to its assigned spot.

Projectionists

The job of the projectionist is to handle all film (8mm and 16mm) and slides (both two-inch format and three-by-four-inch format) and possibly even three-by-four-inch opaque *balop* cards (an adaptation of an opaque projector sometimes found on a film chain). The projectors usually will be clustered in a film island, with two or more projectors feeding into a single camera through a system of mirrors and prisms. One or more of the film chains will be found either in the telecine area or in the master control room. The projectionists must be completely familiar with the threading and loading procedures for all film and slide projectors. The instructions for different machines can sometimes be complicated.

Once the film and slides are loaded, the projectionist should check them out and then double-check to make certain that everything is set up right—that the film has the correct-sized loops and the right tension and that all of the slides are loaded right-side up in the correct order. The projectionist must make sure that all projection bulbs and exciter lamps are working and that all switches are turned on and prisms are set for the first projection. During the production—if the projectors are not controlled remotely from the studio control room—he or she must listen carefully for cues. (See fig. 12-10.)

Figure 12-10 Projectionist checking a slide in the telecine area of the master control room.

Projectionists will also be involved in rear screen (and occasionally front screen) projection in the studio. In this situation, standard film or slide projectors are likely to be used, with a live studio camera shooting the image off the screen. It may take some time to get the projector(s) and screen properly set up and aligned. Location of the screen and projector has to be carefully coordinated with the floor manager and camera operators. This can be a very critical setup from the standpoint of staging and lighting, especially with rear screen projection. Any light falling on the face of the screen can easily wash out most of the image. Once the screen and projector are set up satisfactorily, operation of the equipment should be no problem. In many studio slide applications, the talent—using a long remote-control cord—will be the one to advance the slides on the air.

Grips and Floor Assistants

Stagehands, floor assistants, grips, cable pullers, graphics flippers, and camera assistants are the people who actually get the work done. Although often relegated to the lowest position in the production pecking order, these people are crucial because they actually *do things* on the air. If their jobs are not handled well, the whole production looks and sounds bad. In fact, on the professional level, if you do not do well in these beginning positions, you are not likely to have an opportunity to show how well you can do at the higher echelons.

As the descriptive labels suggest, there are many different functions to be performed, under the supervision of the stage manager, by the grips or floor assistants. In some studios, depending upon union jurisdictions, some of these tasks might be engineering assignments, some might be labeled staging, and some might come under the jurisdiction of the Directors' Guild.

Cable pullers and camera assistants are concerned with helping camera operators make their moves as smoothly and effortlessly as possible. This includes manipulating camera booms and dollies; occasionally assisting in pulling the pedestal camera sideways for a trucking shot; or simply pulling cable so that the camera operator does not have to worry about running out of cable on a long dolly-in, or stumbling over his or her own cable during a dolly-back.

Graphics handlers are needed for simple off-air flips of graphics, for delicate on-air pulls and flips, and for some complicated animation effects. During a fast graphics sequence, the coordination between two cameras and their respective graphics flippers can be quite close. It is very easy to get out of sequence and throw a whole graphics segment out of order. Graphics handlers need to be sure-fingered and confident. After a rehearsal, the graphics handlers should check to ensure that the graphics on their particular stands or easels are all set up and in order for the beginning of the program. (See fig. 12-11.)

Other assignments for the floor assistants might include changing staging elements during a scene; handling special effects such as fog, wind, or shaking a fire-shadow stick; assisting talent in fast costume changes; any other special assignments; and the traditional **gopher** assignments (go-for a cup of coffee, go-for some paper towels).

In addition to being quick of feet, nimble of hand, and humble of heart, grips must possess two qualities of anonymity—they are not to be seen on camera or heard on microphone. To meet the first requirement they must always be careful never to cross in front of any camera or get their hands in a graphics shot. To meet the requirement of silence, grips must remember that almost anything can be done loudly if done carelessly. In addition to the obvious, such as talking on the air and knocking over set pieces, they must control the slightest noise associated with a particular assignment—even pulling cable or flipping

Figure 12-11 Floor assistant, or grip, handling graphics on a camera easel. (Photo courtesy of KABC-TV, Los Angeles.)

graphics can be done noisily. One final hint: grips should wear sneakers or work in socks. The studio floor is no place for hard-heeled shoes.

Regardless of the assignment, if a grip is really concerned about the success of the communication act and serious about his or her intentions in the field, he or she will carry out the assignment efficiently and conscientiously.

Summary

The *associate director* (A.D.) is one of the director's chief lieutenants and may get involved in almost every aspect of program design and execution from program planning to helping set up shots on the air. The major responsibility of the A.D., however, is that of *timing* the entire program—getting the director started on time, giving time signals to the talent throughout the program, and getting the director off on time.

The *stage manager (floor manager, floor director)* is the other chief lieutenant of the director. The stage/floor manager is directly in charge of everything on the studio floor. The duties generally can be divided into two areas: *working with talent* (attending to emotional-physical needs and to technical-production needs) and *production management* (supervising all audio, camera, staging, lighting, graphics, special effects, props, and projection elements).

In addition to these two key positions, every other assignment on the production crew has its own set of *techniques* and *disciplines* to master: those of the lighting and staging personnel, audio engineers, camera operators, technical director, recording engineer, projectionists, and grips and floor assistants.

In the final two chapters we will look at the one position that pulls it all together—the director's job.

12.4   Training Exercises

1. Using a stopwatch, time every segment of some talk show that you can watch at home. Start with a timing sheet similar to the one in figure 12-2. You will use three columns— "Segment," "Unit Time," and "Cumulative Time." You will need quite a few blank lines, however, as there will be a large number of individual segments. As the show progresses, write down every separate segment of the program—every commercial, every monologue, every demonstration, every station break, every musical number or variety act, every interview or discussion segment, and the like. Time each segment with a stopwatch, returning the watch to zero between every program unit; enter these times in the "Unit Time" column. Using your wristwatch or a clock with a second hand, keep track of the cumulative time in the third column. When you are through, you should be able to total up the unit times and arrive at the total elapsed time as indicated in your "Cumulative Time" column.

2. If you have the opportunity, visit a recording session of some studio television program. Pay particular attention to the job of the stage manager. Before, during, and after the production notice every task and responsibility of the floor manager. Keep a list of every specific job that he or she had to perform. What additional production and talent-liaison items might the stage manager have gotten involved with if the need had arisen?

directing your first tv production

13

This chapter and chapter 14 are designed to introduce the student to some of the concepts and techniques that are needed in directing one's first television production—principles of picture continuity, use of camera transitions, simple camera patterns, scripting formats, preproduction planning, rehearsal techniques, and control room disciplines. This is not designed as a complete text on television directing. It would take a much more voluminous work to present the student with an understanding of the many facets of directing different kinds of television productions. It is recognized, however, that many introductory production courses will involve the student in directing some basic programs. These two chapters, therefore, present several production exercises and examples of different kinds of production formats.

Most of the pictorial and editing concepts discussed in this chapter apply to both single-camera productions and multi-camera studio programs.

13.1 Principles of Picture Continuity

Early filmmakers quickly came to the conclusion that when one picture is immediately replaced by another an interaction occurs in the mind of the viewer that communicates something more than if each picture were viewed separately. This intriguing concept obviously can have direct bearing on the process of shot selection for any television program. Each shot must be thought of as being part of a flow of images, each with a relationship to the one that precedes it and the one that follows it.

Wide Shots and Close-Ups

The succession of pictures should be motivated by the basic tenet, "Give the viewers what they need to see when they need to see it." To a great extent this is determined by a juxta-position of establishing **collective** shots show-ing the whole picture—the relationship of all elements in the scene—and intimate **particu-larized** shots—giving the viewers the closer details they want. The generalities of a scene or program situation are established by the collective *cover shot*. Then the director cuts or dissolves to a series of medium or particular-ized *close-up shots* to examine the specific fac-ets of that situation. As the events of the program progress, the director again estab-lishes the broader aspects of the program, fol-lowed by another series of detailed particulars.

Even with the opportunity to preplan or *block out* the camera work, television's on-going production technique forces the director to make some rather quick, on-the-air editing decisions. A basic problem is that of always having the proper camera ready for a shot at the exact moment the situation calls for it. On the part of the director, this requires an ability to be able to think simultaneously on at least two levels—what is on the air and what is going to be on the air.

With a three-camera structure, the think-ing process might work something like this: Camera 1 is on the air. The director has the choice of using camera 2 or 3 for the next shot. Camera 3, however, has just been used on the previous shot. Camera 2, therefore, has more time to make a framing adjustment or even a change of position. (See fig. 13-1.)

By using the commands of preparation and execution properly (section 7.5), the di-rector can select the next camera to be used, allowing sufficient lead time to set the next shot.

It is accepted studio procedure in a three-camera setup to place camera 1 on the left, camera 2 in the middle, and camera 3 on the right. This setup allows the director to keep track easily of the relative positions of cameras on the floor and the angle of shots available to them.

Obviously, cameras usually are not em-ployed in a repeated 1-2-3-1-2-3 rotation. In order to observe the wide-shot and close-up shot requirements of any program, at least one of the three cameras at any given time will usually be designated as a wide-angle *cover shot* camera. This is especially important in shooting unrehearsed programs such as panel discussions where there are sudden changes in the person talking. The technique on such a program is to cut to a wide shot on the change of voice if a close-up of the new person is not immediately available. The director then has a chance to ascertain who is talking and call for the close-up. The most glaring error on any kind of television is for an unprepared director to be caught with a speaker or performer still on camera when that person is no longer speaking or performing.

In a rehearsed program, when the camera blocking has been worked out in advance, the director can temporarily commit all cameras to close-up shots, having planned to return to a cover shot at a later specific time. Generally, however, the wide-angle and close-up shot bal-ance requirements are such that at least one camera is always kept on a cover shot.

Shot Relationships

When changing from one shot to another the two pictures should relate to each other in both an informational and aesthetic setting. For example, the subject in two successive shots should be readily recognizable. You would not want to cut to such a different angle that the viewer would not immediately recognize the subject from the previous shot.

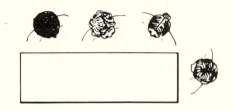

CAMERA 1
on the
air

CAMERA 2
Ready for
next shot

CAMERA 3
Has time to
adjust for
its next
shot

In this illustration, the director has just used camera 3 (before taking camera 1); therefore camera 2 probably would have had more time to get the next shot lined up.

Figure 13-1 Sequence of camera shots.

Jump Cuts. On the one hand, for aesthetic reasons, you should avoid taking or dissolving between cameras that have almost exactly the same or matching shots. The result is that the scene remains essentially the same, but the picture jumps slightly within the frame. On unrehearsed shows, two camera operators may inadvertently come up with almost identical shots, so that it is up to the director to watch carefully for this **jump-cutting** on the control room monitors.

Cutting Ratio. On the other hand, avoid going from one shot to another where there is too much difference in size between views of the same subject. Taking from a long shot to a tight close-up can be quite jarring to the viewer. (See fig. 13-2.) One good rule to follow is that you always keep your camera cuts within a three-to-one **cutting ratio.** That is, do not take to a shot that is three times larger or three times smaller than the preceding shot.

Position Jumps. Another problem to avoid is that of having a primary subject jump from one spot on the screen to another position in the next picture. This can occur, for example, if three people are lined up facing two cameras and each camera is getting a two-shot of two adjacent persons. The center person will be on the left of one picture and on the right side of the other camera's picture. (See fig. 13-3.) This position jump can be avoided by having one camera go to a three-shot before cutting or, conversely, cutting to a close-up single shot.

Axis of Action/Conversation

Another basic principle of continuity involves *screen direction.* In successive shots we want to make certain that all action is flowing in the same direction and that each screen character is facing in one consistent direction. If an imaginary line is drawn extending the path in which a character is moving, we can call

(a) In this example, the cut from the long shot to the tight close-up is jarring for a normal transition. Usually the director should not cut to a shot that is more than three times the size (larger or smaller) than the preceding shot.

(b) In this instance, the director has cut to an intermediate medium shot before going in to the close-up. The transition is much easier for the audience to take.

Figure 13-2   Three-to-one cutting ratio.

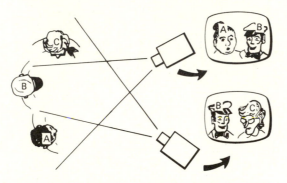

With both cameras shooting a standard two-shot, the central talent (Mr. "B") appears to jump from one side of the screen to the other as we take between the two-shots.

Figure 13-3   Subject jumping positions.

this the **axis of action.** As long as all cameras are placed on the same side of this axis, the action will continue to flow in the same direction. If cameras are placed on both sides of this axis of action, however, the apparent screen direction will be reversed when cutting between the cameras. (See fig. 13-4.) Directors, therefore, always try to avoid having cameras crossing the line. It is for this reason that all cameras covering a football game or basketball game must be placed on the same side of the field of action.

Closely related to the axis of action is the **axis of conversation.** If the imaginary axis is drawn through two persons facing each other, all cameras should be kept on the same side of this line. Otherwise the screen direction (in which a person is looking) will be reversed when you cut to the other side of the line. This imaginary line—the axis of conversation—will shift, of course, as performers move. Figure 13-5 shows two common errors in crossing the axis of conversation.

Other Principles of Continuity

All of these generalizations and principles have to be interpreted with flexibility. There are occasions when the experienced director will deliberately break some of the principles in order to create a certain effect—to disorient the audience intentionally, for aesthetic shock value, for exceptional dramatic impact, or whatever. Keep in mind, however, that before departing from any such guidelines one should have first gained a good understanding of the reason for the rule. The same can be said for the following four additional principles in planning picture continuity.

1. *Plan the camera sequence as a whole.* Every program or sequence within a program has a beginning, a middle, and an end. Design the image flow to capture the structural form of the performance or event, utilizing the collective and particularized perspectives.

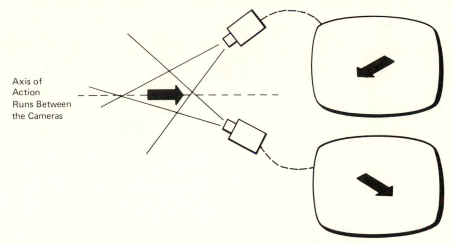

(a) *WRONG*. If cameras are placed on both sides of the imaginary axis of action, the screen direction will be reversed when cutting between the cameras.

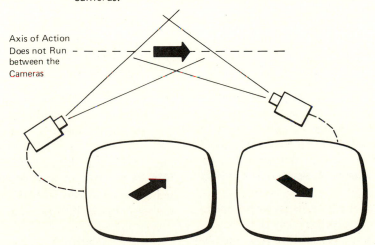

(b) *CORRECT*. When both cameras are on the same side of the axis of action, they will both perceive the action moving in the same direction.

Figure 13-4 Axis of action.

2. *Follow the action.* Be sure that motivating action or movement is picked up by the camera as it occurs. Nothing destroys the flow of ideas and images more than late camera work. The thought process of the entire crew must be such that it anticipates the progression of events in the program.

3. *Have the camera work be appropriate for the program situation.* Match the shot to the performance or action. A close-up shot denotes intimacy and personal expression. Extreme wide shots express a quality of "bigness" or importance. A superimposition serves to intensify further whatever is being expressed by the component images.

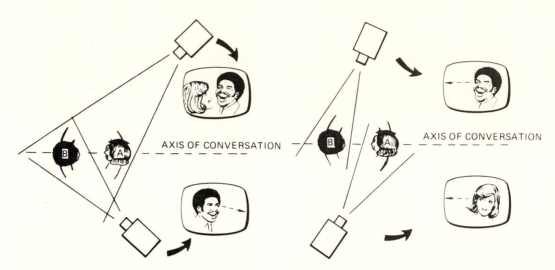

AXIS OF CONVERSATION

AXIS OF CONVERSATION

In the above illustration, Actor B changes screen direction as we cut from one camera to the other.

In this example, both actors appear to be looking in the same direction, making it difficult for the viewer to establish the relationship between the two.

Figure 13-5   Axis of conversation.

4. *Observe a consistency of style and pace.* Different types of programs require differing camera work, ranging from the subjective artistic to the reportorial pragmatic. Similarly, there is often a pattern to the frequency of camera change that stems from the program sequence itself. An effective series of fast camera cuts can lose its intensity if, for no motivated reason, a dissolve is suddenly used.

The essence of all television is movement, either physical or psychological or both. Pictorial composition and sequence flow must be designed to interact in such a way as not only to capture accurately but also to enhance further the events of the production sequence. The skills necessary for effective camera work require both study and practice as well as a great amount of judgment on the part of both the camera operator and the director.

13.2   Continuity and Transitions

Picture continuity refers to the sequential relationship of successive screen images. The mechanics of continuity are carried out by the actual camera transitions—the manner in which we change from one picture to another. This can be effected in several different ways, and we need to be aware of the how, when, and why of camera transitions.

Types of Camera Transitions

Without getting into sophisticated electronic switching devices, there are basically five different transitional methods for going from one camera to another. The director must be aware of the psychological and grammatical impact of each—when to use one and when to use another.

The Take. The instantaneous *cut* or straight take replaces one picture immediately with another. It implies that there is no change in time or locale. It happens right now. The audience is not moved anywhere, except to a different perspective of the same scene. The shots relate directly to each other as far as time and space are concerned. It is the basic transition. It is the device that the audience has accepted since the beginning of the motion picture film for changing a point of view without making any major dramatic change. In terms of grammar it is the end of a sentence—a period—and the beginning of a new sentence.

The Dissolve. The dissolve, simultaneous fading out of one picture and fading in of another picture, creates a temporary overlapping of images. Dramatically, this implies a change of *place* or a change in *time* (usually a lapse of time). It shows a relationship with the previous shot, but there has been a change; the audience has been moved somewhere else or somewhere later in time. Grammatically, the dissolve corresponds to the end of a paragraph or possibly even to the end of a major section of a chapter. In nondramatic television, the dissolve often is used purely for aesthetic reasons—a slow dissolve of a singer from a medium to a tight close-up profile, or a close-up of the dancer's feet dissolving to a long shot of the dancer. No change in time or locale is implied in this case—just a pleasant visual effect. In musical productions, the dissolve can be used as an artistic connecting or relating transition, whereas it has the opposite effect in dramas.

The Fade. A fade from a camera to black or a fade up from black implies a very strong separation. It is used in going from one segment of a program to another—from the juggling act to the used-car commercial.

Dramatically, the fade is the curtain falling—the end of a scene or an act. Grammatically, it would be the visual counterpart of the end of a chapter—or of the story.

The Defocus. One specialized transition that can be used with no fancy electronic effects is the **defocus;** the camera on the air defocuses and dissolves to a similarly defocused shot on another camera, which then comes back into focus. This is a specialized form of dissolve that has very strong overtones. It usually implies either a deranged state of mind or a transition *backward* in time. As do other specialized transitions, it tends to call attention to itself and must be used very sparingly.

The Wipe. Wiping one picture off the face of the screen and replacing it with another also calls attention to itself. It is a highly stylized method of going from one camera to another. As do other electronic transitions—the circle wipe, the starburst—the straight-edged wipe has to be used very cautiously. It has no special grammatical significance except to say, "Isn't this a fancy transition!"

Timing of the Transition

Understanding the different types of transitions helps to explain the *how* and *why* of changing cameras, but a word needs to be said about the *when*. Generally, camera changes must be adequately motivated; there has to be some reason for cutting at a particular point. The audience should want to see something else. ("Give the viewers what they need to see when they need to see it.") Unless the viewer feels a need for a change of camera, there probably is no reason to cut. Without proper motivation, you should avoid the temptation to change the picture just for the sake of change.

Cutting on Action.   One of the strongest motivations for cutting is to capture action. When the action starts, you need a wider view. When the talent walks to a new area, you need an establishing shot. When cutting on action, you should always try to cut *just prior to the action*—neither too long before it nor immediately after it. Ideally, as soon as the action starts, the audience needs to see the wider shot.

Cutting on Dialogue.   During an interview or panel program, the strongest motivation for cutting is when a speaker *starts to talk*. The audience wants to see who is talking. The ideal timing of the take is precisely between the two speakers—not three seconds after the second speaker has started. As a practical matter, cutting during an ad-lib discussion program will usually involve a delay of a second or so. To counteract this, the director has to be sensitive to the body language and facial expressions of all the participants (watching his or her off-the-air camera monitors). Who has his mouth open? Who has her eyebrows raised? Who just leaned forward? Who just took a deep breath? Anticipate who the next speaker is going to be.

Cutting on Reaction.   Include appropriate—judiciously spaced—reaction shots also. How are the listeners reacting? Which listener is especially animated? In timing reaction shots, *do not* cut at the end of an obvious statement or during a break in the speaking; it will look too much like a cut to the wrong participant. Reaction shots are most effective in the middle of a speech.

Cutting on the Beat.   During musical numbers, time your cuts to fit the music. (In slower tempos, purely for an aesthetic "feel," the transitions may better be dissolves.) The cuts should be crisp and clean, following a regular rhythmical pattern—cutting every four bars or eight bars—as the music dictates. See section 14.2 for an extended demonstration of camera usage during a musical number.

Cutting with Movement.   Generally, do not cut from a moving camera to a stationary camera. If the camera is panning a shot or zooming in or out, wait until it stops to take to another stationary camera. And vice versa; do not cut from a static shot to a moving camera. The effect is somewhat jolting to the viewer. It can be effective, however, to take or dissolve from a moving camera to another camera panning or zooming in the same direction—assuming there is a continuity in subject and tempo.

As with the rules given under "Principles of Picture Continuity," these guidelines can be interpreted in a flexible manner if you know what effect you are after. Exceptions can be made to the basic rules once the rules are mastered.

13.3 Basic Camera Patterns

In setting up the **camera pattern** for a multi-camera production, or blocking (positioning) the cameras for a scene, there are several principles to keep in mind.

1. *Cross your camera angles.* In most staging setups, the natural pattern will have two people facing each other—or a person facing a graphic or demonstrating an object. Shooting this situation with two cameras you can get the best head-on shots by having the cameras shoot across each other's angles; that is, each camera should be shooting the person or object farthest away from the camera. The camera on the right should be getting the shot of the person on the left and vice versa. (See figs. 11-1 and 13-6.)

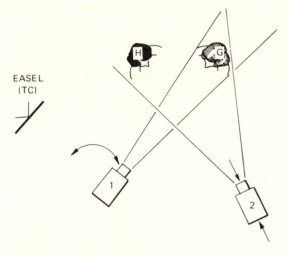

EASEL
(TC)

Camera 1: Title card (TC).
Camera 2: Single-shot (MS or CU) of host. Dolly back or zoom back to two-shot as guest is mentioned.
Camera 1: CU of guest (for the introduction) and CU of guest and two-shots favoring guest (during interview).
Camera 2: CU of host and two-shots favoring host (during interview). Dolly in or zoom in to single of host at end of interview.
Camera 1: Closing credits and title card.

Figure 13-6 Camera pattern for simple interview.

2. *Start blocking in the center of the program.* Pick the most crucial or difficult part of the production and figure out your camera pattern for that segment first. Once you know how that segment has to be blocked, you can figure backward to see how you will want to work your way up to that position. Continuing to work backward, you will be able to determine how you want to set up your cameras for the beginning of the program.

3. *Select your easel positions last.* As a corollary to principle 2, you should not figure out where you will place your graphics stands until all of the crucial camera blocking has

been taken care of. Once you know how the whole production is set up, you can best figure out the most convenient spot to place the easels. Too many beginning directors start by positioning the opening title card first, and then work their way into a bind from there.

Starting with these simple principles, let us see how some simple camera patterns could be worked out for a few basic formats.

Simple Interview

Following the principles outlined above, a two-person interview could be staged as indicated in figure 13-6. With the host seated on the left and the guest on the right, cameras 1 and 2 would cross angles so that camera 2 would get the basic shot of the host (and an over-the-shoulder two-shot favoring the host) and camera 1 would get the basic shots favoring the guest. Assuming that camera 2, on the host, would be the first camera shot in the body of the program, this means that camera 1 is free to get the opening title card (before breaking to the basic shot of the guest). We did not know, however, which camera would have been free to get the title card until after we decided on the camera pattern in the body of the show.

Simple Demonstration

The same basic pattern would hold true for a simple demonstration program. Figure 13-7 indicates how a demonstration sequence might be set up. In this case, working from the body of the program we might determine that the host, being right-handed, wants to work with the object to be demonstrated on his right side so that he can hold the object in his right hand. Crossing angles, camera 1, therefore, would get the basic head-on shot of the talent (and a two-shot of the host and object) while camera 2 would get the close-ups of the object.

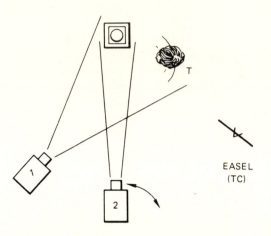

Camera 2: Title card (TC).
Camera 1: Single-shot (MS or CU) of talent. Dolly back or zoom back to include object to be demonstrated.
Camera 2: CU of object.
Camera 1: Two-shot of talent and object. Optional dolly in or zoom in to single of talent.
Camera 2: Closing credits and title card (TC).

Figure 13-7 Camera pattern for simple demonstration.

(Note the similarity to fig. 11-1.) This means that camera 2 would be the one that would be free for the opening title card.

Note that the camera pattern illustrated in figure 13-7 would be the same pattern that could be used for a graphics sequence in which the talent was working with an on-set graphic. In this case, the pattern is set up for a left-handed host; the easel is positioned on his right side in order to enable him to turn in towards the graphic and work with his left hand to gesture, point, or write on the graphic. For a right-handed talent, it is most comfortable to work with the graphic positioned on his or her left.

Demonstration-Lecture with Graphics

Following the same basic principles, let us see how a slightly more complicated camera pattern might be worked out. The talent is going to start by talking directly to camera with

nothing else in the shot (position *A*). She then walks over to her right to demonstrate an object (position *B*). She then crosses back to a graphics stand to go through some on-set graphics (position *C*); she is right-handed so we want the graphics stand to be on her left side. The basic title cards are on slides to be projected from telecine (camera 4), but there are super cards to be used at both the open and the close.

Where do we begin to block out the camera pattern? (See fig. 13-8.) The most crucial position probably would be at the graphics stand (position *C*); let us begin there. We will want camera 2 getting the cover shot of the talent, with camera 1 crossing angles to get the close-up of the graphics. This means that camera 2 probably would be the best camera to pan across with the talent on her move from position *B* to *C*. Working backward at position *B*, we therefore would want camera 1 on the basic head-on shot of the talent at position *B*; this means that camera 2, which is in the best location for the close-ups of the object, would have time to flip or zoom wide for the walk-over shot from position *B* to *C*. (Camera 2 is the best camera for the walking shot because it is a stronger move to have the talent walking toward the camera; she is walking away from camera 1.) Camera 1 would be the best camera for the walk-over shot from position *A* to *B*. (First, this would give camera 2 time to get prepared on the close-up of the object, and second—as mentioned above—it is stronger to have the talent walking toward the camera.) Having worked our way backward to the opening shots, we therefore see that camera 2 is the best camera for the opening shot of the talent at position *A* (we want to be able to take to camera 1 on the beginning of the action/walk-over shot to position *B*). Thus, camera 1 will get our opening super cards on an off-set easel placed to the camera left of the set (the easel stand is placed last). Camera 1 also will be free to get the closing super cards, but, since camera 1 will be positioned on easel

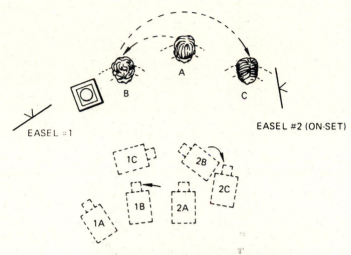

EASEL #1   EASEL #2 (ON-SET)

Camera 4: (Telecine) Title card (slide).
Camera 1: Super cards, easel #1, position A.
Camera 2: Single of talent, position A.
Camera 1: Pan with talent to position B. Cover shot, position B.
Camera 2: CU object, position B.
Camera 1: Two-shot, talent and object, position B.
Camera 2: Pan with talent to position C. Two-shot (cover shot), talent and easel #2.
Camera 1: CU graphics (easel #2), position C.
Camera 2: Closing shot, talent, position C.
Camera 4: Title card (slide).
Camera 1: Super cards, easel #2.

Figure 13-8 Camera pattern for demonstration-lecture with graphics.

#2 (for the on-set graphics sequence in position *C*), camera 1 can get the closing super cards on easel #2.

Although the explanation may seem complicated at first, if you read through it carefully, checking the illustration in figure 13-8, you should be able to see how all of the principles mentioned at the beginning of this section apply.

13.4 The Television Script

The television script is the basic working document of the TV director. Everything starts with the script, and the beginning director must learn how to interpret and break it down, as well as how to mark it for use during the actual production.

Scripting Formats

Basically, there are three different script forms that the director might have to work with: the *fully scripted program;* the *outline,* or *semi-scripted program;* and the *show format,* or *run-down sheet.*

The Fully Scripted Program.   Programs that are likely to be fully scripted include dramatic programs, newscasts, documentaries, commercials, station breaks, editorials, some talk programs such as political broadcasts, and similar productions where it is important that every single word and picture element be precisely controlled. Section 14.3 is an example of one kind of dramatic script format (appendix D–4). Section 14.4 is an example of the fully scripted station break and promotional copy (appendix D–5).

Although there are exceptions, scripts generally are constructed in vertical columns, with one column (usually the right-hand side) for audio and another column for video. On some scripts, the video column will be written in (section 13.5), and in other formats the video column will be left blank for the director to fill in. Some formats (see figs. 13-9 and 13-11) will have both the audio and video integrated into one column, with the other column left open for the director to use for markings.

The Outline, or Semiscripted Program.

Many kinds of programs do not have every word written out in advance. Among them are variety shows, educational/lecture programs, interview programs, and other formats where there is a good deal of ad-libbing and extemporaneous discussion.

Section 13.5 (appendix D–3) is an example of a semiscripted outline for a discussion program in which both columns are written out. Figure 13-9 is an example of an abbreviated script outline for a discussion program in which the audio and video elements have all been integrated into the right-hand column so that the left-hand (blank) column can be used for more extensive director's notes.

In figures 13-10 and 13-11 we have two different versions of the same program content. In figure 13-10, the ITV script outline utilizes both columns. In figure 13-11, exactly the same content is incorporated into the outline, but all the material is included in the right-hand column.

One technique that is used in some scripts, as in the previous examples, is to use upper- and lowercase letters for everything that is actually to be heard on the air. Note that all of the announcer copy in figure 13-9 is written

out, which is done in many semiscripted formats, and the summary of the host's remarks are also in upper- and lowercase. All other material (video instructions, audio cues) is put in uppercase letters only. This makes it easy to identify which is which.

In addition to writing out the announcer copy in full, most outline scripts also will write out exact roll cues to be used in facilitating correct timing into film and videotape inserts. The semiscripted format also will include a somewhat detailed outline of the content, together with fairly complete video information.

The Show Format, or Run-Down Sheet.

Many routine programs that are produced on a daily or weekly basis by a station will not even work from a complete semiscripted outline. The daily homemaker show, ITV lectures, regular interview programs, game shows, weekly panel discussions, and other programs—where the same talent uses the same format continually—may use only a **show format,** or **run-down sheet.** This would list just the order of the basic segments. Perhaps exact **roll cues** for film and VTR inserts might be included—along with times for inserted elements. Figure 13-12 illustrates a typical run-down sheet for a local variety show.

Once you, as director, have the script in hand, your job is ready to begin. Your task now is to break down the script, decide how each element is to be handled, block camera movement, prepare instructions for the key crew members and engineering staff, and mark the script for your own directing use.

Marking the Script

Almost all script formats are at least double-spaced. This not only makes it easier for the talent and others to read, but also facilitates the numerous notes and markings that the director will have to make on the script. It is the

(This column is left blank for the director's notes)	GRAPHIC: STREET SCENE
	MUSIC: THEME, ESTABLISH, AND UNDER
	ANNC (OFF CAMERA): Good morning, and welcome to . . .
	SUPER CARD (OVER "STREET SCENE"): "LIVE"
	ANNC: "Live," . . . a penetrating look at some of the issues and controversies surrounding the American scene. This fast-paced discussion is brought to you, live, . . .
	DISCUSSION SET, IN SILHOUETTE
	ANNC: . . . from the studios of KCSN-TV. Today's topic is "The Tax Squeeze on Middle America." Your host is _____ .
	HOST: Welcome, etc. Introduces each guest.
	BODY OF DISCUSSION
	(Points to be covered:
	Federal income tax
	State income and sales taxes
	Local property taxes)
	HOST: Summarizes. Thanks guests.
	DISCUSSION SET, IN SILHOUETTE
	MUSIC: THEME, SNEAK IN, ESTABLISH, AND UNDER
	ANNC: For the past fifteen minutes, you have been watching another stimulating program in the series,
	SUPER CARD (OVER SET): "LIVE"
	ANNC: . . . "Live," from KCSN-TV.
	MUSIC OUT
	BLACK

Figure 13-9 Sample semiscripted outline.

VIDEO	AUDIO
	Concept of green leaves as food factories:
CHART: DIAGRAM OF CYCLE	1. Oxygen--CO2 Cycle
	2. Water and Nourishment up from roots
SLIDE # 1	3. Manufacture of chlorophyll
	Role of chlorophyll in growth of vegetation
FILM: 1' 20"	FILM ROLL CUE: Now suppose we take a look at the inside of a green leaf and see for ourselves.

Figure 13-10 Sample semiscripted ITV lesson: two columns.

	AUDIO/VIDEO
	Concept of green leaves as food factories:
	1. Oxygen--CO2 Cycle
	CHART: DIAGRAM OF CYCLE
	2. Water and Nourishment up from roots
	3. Manufacture of chlorophyll
	SLIDE # 1
	Role of chlorophyll in growth of vegetation
	FILM ROLL CUE: Now suppose we take a look-- through a microscope-- at the inside of a green leaf and see for ourselves how the little dots of chlorophyll flow through the cells of the leaf substance.
	FILM: 1' 20"
	FILM ENDS WITH SHOT OF PULSING DOTS SLOWING DOWN TO A DEAD STOP

Figure 13-11 Sample semiscripted ITV lesson: single column.

```
                    "MOLLIE'S MORNING" (NO:  78-0314    )

                                    FAX:

                                    VTR:
```

VIDEO	AUDIO	
1. TEASER: MOLLY AND DOG	STUDIO: MOLLIE LIVE	(:30)
2. OPENING FILM	THEME MUSIC UP: S.O.F. MAG TRACK	(:45)
3. MOLLIE: MONOLOGUE	STUDIO: MOLLIE LIVE	(2:00)
4. INTERVIEW SET	INTERVIEW: JOHN LOOMIS	(5:00)
LOOMIS SLIDES (6 OR 7)	VOICE-OVER NARRATION	
5. MOLLIE, TO CAMERA	(ROLL CUE): One of the most enchanting things	
	about interior decoration is the impact	
	that simple ideas can have when done	
	creatively.	(:10)
6. FILM: THE WORLD OF JEAN JAMESON	FILM: S.O.F. OPTICAL	(2:25)
7. MOLLIE, TO CAMERA	BOOM #2: INTRO TO NELSON	(:30)
WALK TO LIVING RM SET		
8. LIVING ROOM SET:	INTERVIEW: HEATHER NELSON	(7:00)
DEMO: FABRICS		
7 OR 8 GRAPHICS		
9. MOLLIE, TO CAMERA	SUMMARY AND CLOSE	(:40)
10. CLOSING FILM	THEME MUSIC: S.O.F. MAG TRACK	(:30)

Figure 13-12 Sample show format.

director's task to decide what cameras will have to be used where, what instructions the technical director and engineers must have, where the audio cues will have to be, what cues the talent will need, and so forth. Preparing and marking the script is one of the most critical tasks the director has. On a major studio drama, it could involve numerous detailed drawings and hundreds of abbreviated cues and instructions and notes; with a fairly routine ongoing program (such as "Mollie's Morning"), script preparation may take no more than a few penciled reminders of unusual cues.

Standard Symbols. In preparing their scripts for production, most directors will use a system of shorthand symbols. Experienced directors have worked out their own set of symbols; each one is a very personalized system and does not have to make sense to anyone but the director. The symbols work if they are clear, easy to read, unambiguous, and do not take up much space.

There are some standardized symbols, however, that form the basis for most of the personalized systems the directors adopt. Some of these universal markings are indicated in figure 13-13. In using the symbols to

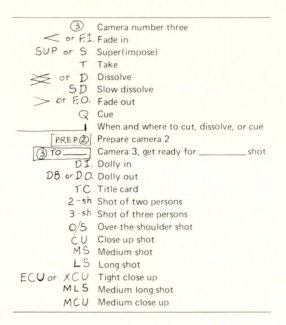

③	Camera number three
< or F.I.	Fade in
SUP or S	Super(impose)
T	Take
≶ or D	Dissolve
S D	Slow dissolve
> or F.O.	Fade out
Q	Cue
⌐	When and where to cut, dissolve, or cue
PREP ②	Prepare camera 2
③ TO ⎯	Camera 3, get ready for ⎯⎯⎯ shot
D.I.	Dolly in
DB or D.O.	Dolly out
TC	Title card
2-sh	Shot of two persons
3-sh	Shot of three persons
O/S	Over-the-shoulder shot
CU	Close-up shot
MS	Medium shot
LS	Long shot
ECU or XCU	Tight close up
MLS	Medium long shot
MCU	Medium close up

Figure 13-13   Standard script-marking symbols.

mark your script, you generally should use pencil. Once you get into rehearsal, there are script changes, camera positions that do not work, slides that did not turn out, and many other production modifications—some major and many minor—that will necessitate your changing your script markings. Therefore, it is always safer to start with pencil.

Generally, the script markings should remind you of every preplanned command you will have to give—to cameras, T.D., talent, audio, projectionists, floor crew, lighting, and everyone else. The marked script may indicate not only the necessary commands of execution but also the important commands of preparation ("readies" and "prepares") and other off-air directions. Figure 13-14 illustrates what a thoroughly marked script might look like. As directors become more experienced and comfortable with the medium, their scripts will not be marked this heavily. For the purposes of illustration, figure 13-14 shows virtually every command and preparation for the open and close of a discussion program.

Experienced directors will work with a less detailed marked script in order to concentrate on the camera monitors. Directors must be able to watch everything that is going on; they cannot be content just to keep their eyes glued on the prepared script, reading off all instructions in order.

Shot Sheets.   Once the director has the script completely marked, he or she can prepare detailed instructions for other crew members—for the floor director, for audio, technical director, recording engineer, projectionist, lighting and staging, and anyone else who might be handling a complex assignment. Some of these forms have already been discussed (lighting and staging plot plans). The prepared written instructions can save considerable studio time once the director is ready to set up and start rehearsals.

The most common form of these specialized instructions is the *shot sheet* for the camera operators—an abbreviated description of every shot that a particular camera has to get. It is compact enough to be attached to the rear of the camera where the operator can quickly refer to it. Shot sheets are particularly valuable for complex, fully scripted programs, such as dramas, where every shot has been carefully worked out by the director—and where the cameras will have to be moving quite a bit to get various shots as requested. In preparing the marked script for a drama, for example, once the blocking is firmed up and the director has every shot planned, each shot will be numbered; the shot sheets then list each camera's shot by number. Figure 13-15 shows the three shot sheets for a three-camera drama. In the illustration all three camera shot sheets are indicated on one page. In practice these three sheets would be cut out separately, and each camera operator would have his or her own shot sheet taped or clipped by the viewfinder.

① ON TC   PREP. ③ ON SUP

< ① / HIT MUSIC . . . UNDER
(OPEN MIKE)   Q ANNC

SUP ③/①

PREP ② ON COVER

LOSE ③   BREAK TO HOST

✗ ② – COVER – D.I.

LIGHTS UP

(MUSIC OUT)

Q HOST/T ③ MS HOST

DURING BODY { ③ ON HOST
      ① ON SINGLES
      ② ON COVER
        OR 2-SHOTS

(ON ③)   READY ② COVER

READY LIGHTS / MUSIC

T ② LIGHTS TO SIL.

HIT MUSIC . . . UNDER

(OPEN MIKE)   Q ANNC

PREPARE ① ON SUP
SUP ①/②

LOSE MUSIC / >

GRAPHIC: STREET SCENE

MUSIC: THEME, ESTABLISH, AND UNDER

ANNC (OFF CAMERA): Good morning, and welcome to . . .

SUPER CARD (OVER "STREET SCENE"): "LIVE"

ANNC: "Live," . . . a penetrating look at some

of the issues and controversies surrounding the

American scene. This fast-paced discussion is

brought to you, live, . . .

DISCUSSION SET, IN SILHOUETTE

ANNC: . . . from the studios of KCSN-TV. Today's

topic is "The Tax Squeeze on Middle America."

Your host is _____.

HOST: Welcome, etc. Introduces each guest.

BODY OF DISCUSSION

(Points to be covered:

   Federal income tax

   State income and sales taxes

   Local property taxes)

HOST: Summarizes. Thanks guests.

DISCUSSION SET, IN SILHOUETTE

MUSIC: THEME, SNEAK IN, ESTABLISH, AND UNDER

ANNC: For the past fifteen minutes, you have been

   watching another stimulating program in the series,

SUPER CARD (OVER SET): "LIVE"

ANNC: . . . "Live," from KCSN-TV.

MUSIC OUT

BLACK

Figure 13-14 Sample marked script.

CAMERA 1	CAMERA 2	CAMERA 3
2. GR #2	4. Wide sh., Kitchen, hi-angle, boom down	1. TC (GR #1)
6. LS, Mary in doorway	7. MS Mary. Follow her	3. Sup cards (A, B, C, D)
8. LS, David in doorway	15. 2-sh. Pan L as David crosses behind Mary	5. CU coffee cup, pan to ash tray
10. MS David (he walks into an O/S)	18. MS David. D.B. as he comes to her. Open to 2-sh.	9. MS Mary (she rises)
12. O/S David	20. CU Mary	11. O/S Mary
14. CU David	22. 2-sh (tight)	13. CU Mary
17. MS Mary (she sits)	24. (Crane up) Hi angle 2-sh D.I. & crane down to single of David.	16. MS David
23. Loose 2-sh (Mary rises)	28. Single David (wide) D.B., follow as he walks to Mary. Open to 2-sh.	19. MCU David (bust-shot)
25. O/S Mary (in doorway). She walks toward David. David turns to camera.	30. CU Mary's hands	21. CU David
27. CU David	34. MS Alice	26. 2-sh as Mary turns
31. 2-sh. Mary walks past camera. Hold on David	37. MS David (he sits)	29. (Hook wheels) 2-sh. D.I. to ECU Mary
33. MS David. Pan to door as Alice enters	40. ECU David	32. MS Mary
36. 3-sh, favoring Alice	43. (Crane down) Loose MS Alice. Follow her to table. Follow action w/cup. Crane up & D.I.	35. Loose 2-sh (Mary, David)
39. CU Alice		38. Loose CU, Mary
42. CU Alice		41. ECU Mary
45. Wide 3-sh, follow action		44. ECU Mary
		46. CU of knife

Figure 13-15
Representative camera shot sheets.

Summary

The successful television director must keep in mind the principles of picture continuity: the balance of *wide shots* and *close-ups*, correct use of *shot relationships* (avoiding jump cuts, extreme cutting ratios, and position jumps), observing the *axis of action* (and *conversation*), and other principles of continuity. He or she must also use different *types of transitions* knowledgeably and be careful with the *timing of transitions*.

In blocking cameras for a production, the director should *cross the camera angles*, start blocking in the *center of the program*, and position *graphics easels last*. The director must be familiar with *three types of scripting formats*—the full script; the outline, or semi-scripted program; and the show format, or run-down sheet. In preparing for the production, there are standard symbols that most directors use in *marking the script*. Directors should also prepare other production instructions such as *camera shot sheets*.

In chapter 14, we will summarize the scope of the director's job and look at the production requirements for a couple of specialized formats.

13.5 Production Project: The Discussion Program

While no single phase of production could be considered as the sine qua non of any successful television program, the process whereby the director plans the staging and camera blocking of a show is, for most programs, one of critical importance. Although most directors refer to it as their homework, this series of interrelated decisions usually continues beyond the final rehearsal.

In some programs—such as drama—this effort may entail plotting every performer movement

Figure 13-16 Typical setup for an *L*-shaped staging arrangement for a discussion program.

and camera shot. For programs of a more spontaneous nature, the director usually sets up a flexible shooting plan designed to cover all the various program contingencies.

Planning the Discussion Program

That sometimes maligned but nevertheless ubiquitous stalwart of television programing, the *talk show,* provides an excellent format for understanding the fundamental principles involved in staging and camera blocking. The absence of performer movement on such programs allows for concentration upon picture composition and clarity.

Staging.   The majority of talk shows utilize some variation of two basic staging configurations: an *L-shaped grouping* that places the host on the end facing down a row of other participants (fig. 13-16); or a *semicricle,* in which the host is generally placed in the center. This conformity of staging is not as much a lack of originality on the part of the directors as it is their recognition that these seating plans provide an arrangement whereby the guests can best relate to each other and the host and, at the same time, provide the director with the best camera angles of the participants.

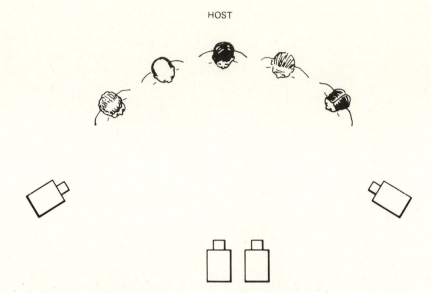

HOST

Figure 13-17   Camera pattern for semicircular staging.

In this typical "talk show" camera pattern, one center camera remains on a cover shot of the en-tire group while the other center camera holds a close-up of the host.

Figure 13-17 shows a very open semicircular seating arrangement similar to that used on several syndicated talk shows.

On these programs, four cameras are utilized. One of the center cameras holds a wide shot of the entire group at all times. The other center camera holds a shot of the host for use at all times in the program. On a three-camera show, one center camera would have to alternate between these two shots. Note the extreme angle to the set of the two outside cameras. Although both can provide shots of the entire group from these positions, their primary assignment is that of providing close-up shots of those persons facing in their direction—by crossing their angles (section 13.3).

On a musical or comedy-variety type of production, the performers generally face toward a stage-front camera and audience area as they would in a conventional stage show. In a discussion program, the participants relate not to the audience but to each other, and as a result face not to the front but in the direction of the persons to their right and left. Depending upon the role of the host-moderator, the other participants will tend to face in his or her direction during much of the program.

Lighting.   A suggested lighting plan for an *L-shaped* seating configuration has been presented as a sample lighting plot in figure 4-23. (Section 4.6). A review of that section of material will be of value in the preparation of lighting plots for any of the several main seating configurations. On a discussion program, care must be taken to ensure that the face, especially the eyes, is properly lit from all potential camera angles. The locations of the cameras provide a good guide to the location of the main lights in relation to the subjects. The amount of light reflected back from each subject to the camera must be individually balanced occasionally for equal intensity. Differences in hair, clothing, and complexion can produce unsuitably dark and light close-up shots. When taken in succession, such shots are noticeably objectionable.

Shot Continuity.   In section 13.1, reference was made to *wide-angle* and *close-up* shots in terms of their respective abilities to communicate collective or particularized program information. Wide-angle *cover* shots are used within a program sequence to re-establish the relationship of program participants to each other and to the elements of the set. It is the *collectivizing* view of all those production values that contribute to the program as a whole.

By contrast, the close-up shot is a *particularized* view of a person or object at a precisely appropriate point in the program sequence. As such, the information it conveys is selective and personal, even to the point of being intimate. The eyes and facial muscles add an important dimension to the total meaning of

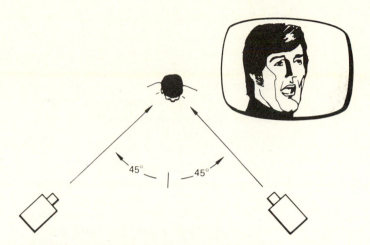

Any camera getting a close-up shot should be as perpendicular to the talent as possible. The camera should not be more than 45 degrees from a head-on shot for a good close-up.

Figure 13-18 Optimum angles for close-ups.

what a person is expressing in words. This is especially true of actors or other personalities who often speak in public or on television. For this reason, the most effective close-up shots are those in which the camera angle is not more than 45 degrees from a head-on position. (See fig. 13-18.) Close-up shots from profile angles, while extremely valuable on many types of productions, should be used with caution on discussion programs.

Transitions.   The most important production value on a discussion program is the precision with which the camera shots follow the spontaneous flow of the conversation. Each time a new person begins to speak, the camera on the air—whether a cover shot or a close-up—should include that person. To linger for more than a split-second on someone who has just stopped talking or to cut to the wrong person is very distracting to the audience.

Ideally, each change of voice would be accompanied by a change of cameras to a close-up shot or one that predominately features the person talking. On a three-camera show that features four guests and a moderator, this is not always possible. By carefully watching the panel for clues as to who may be speaking next (section 13.2), the director may somewhat improve the chances of having the shot ready.

Most directors solve the problem by having a cover shot of the entire group available for use at all times. When a close-up shot of a new speaker is not readily available, a take to the cover shot performs several important functions. Primarily, it gives the director a chance to be certain of who is speaking before assigning a camera to the shot. In a fast-paced discussion, this alternative is the only way the director can stay with the quickly changing flow of the conversation. Once the cover shot has been taken, the close-up need not be used immediately. The director can let the wide shot re-establish the collective aspect of the group while waiting for the end of a sentence as a convenient point to cut to the close-up.

During a discussion program, the situation often calls for shots other than a close-up or one of the total group. Shots including two or

three persons not only add pictorial variety but are quite useful when several people begin a rapid interchange of short statements or questions and answers. Smaller group shots have an added dimension, showing the silent but often revealing expression on the faces of persons other than the speaker. A brief close-up shot of someone moving his or her head in agreement or disagreement—a reaction shot—is especially useful when one person has been speaking for an extended period of time.

On the other hand, the director must be alert to group shots in which those persons who are not talking are looking away from the speaker. Whether or not intended, the visual effect is one of boredom and, as such, has a negative impact on the program as a whole.

Camera Blocking. The range of shots available to each camera in a program situation is dependent upon the two interrelated variables of camera and subject position. These factors must be considered together when plans for shot coverage are made. On a discussion program, where the staging options are somewhat limited, the director generally uses the seating arrangement as a starting point in the camera blocking process. Primary camera positions can then be selected on the basis of the best angles for the close-up shots and the important requirement of wide-angle cover

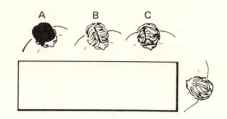

Plan A: *Camera 1* remains on a wide-angle cover shot. *Camera 2* gets close-ups of panelists as they face camera right and two-shots or three-shot of panelists. *Camera 3* gets singles of panelists as they face camera right and over-the-shoulder shots (with host in foreground).

Plan B: *Camera 1* gets close-ups of moderator/host, two-shot of host and nearest panelist, and singles and two-shots as panelists look camera left. *Camera 2* gets close-ups of panelists as they face camera right and two-shots or three-shot of panelists. *Camera 3* remains on a wide-angle cover shot.

Figure 13-19 Camera patterns for *L*-shaped staging.

shots. All of the shot possibilities for each camera should be plotted so that each camera operator can work within the parameters of established shot assignments. Graphic stands, the drum or crawl, and other off-camera visuals should be positioned for easy accessibility to camera positions—after the basic camera pattern has been established (section 13.3).

The use of a definite shooting plan aids in having critical shots available when they are needed and at the same time helps in holding down the talk on the P.L. intercommunication system.

The direction of conversational flow may vary at different times during a program. For this reason, directors usually develop several shooting plans to cover all

contingencies. Figure 13-19 shows two such plans that would be used in the coverage of an *L-shaped* arrangement. Plan A is designed to provide maximum close-up coverage of the three panel members, with the moderator being seen only on the wide shot on camera 1. Plan B is set up for situations in which the moderator takes a very active role in the program and, as a result, needs a close-up shot ready at all times, or for a period during which conversations develop between two guests.

Plan A has obvious limitations but has a basic utility in predictable situations such as a period in the program during which the host is bringing out individual responses from each participant.

The beginning and ending of discussion programs usually assume this structure.

A director would probably quickly shift over to Plan B during the more active phases of the conversation. By holding camera 3 on a cover shot, camera 1 is able to get a close-up shot of the moderator. Camera 1 also has the option of getting close-up shots of those who turn camera left for a two-person conversation. In this situation, camera 2 then has the option of a close-up of the other person or a two-shot of both speakers. The reverse structure is also possible with camera 1 on the two-shot and camera 2 on the single of the person facing camera right.

Taken together, these two shooting plans by no means exhaust the possibilities available within an *L-shaped* seating configuration. The use of camera 2 as a cover camera from either a left-side or right-side studio position opens up another series of coverage patterns. The suggestion of cameras 1 or 3 for cover shots stems from the fact that their angle to the set allows for a more interesting grouping of all participants in the frame. Each person's face occupies a larger proportion of the frame than in a wide shot from the center—which also results in empty space at the top and bottom of the frame.

In the press of a fast-moving program, the director often is tempted to give up the cover shot and use that camera temporarily for smaller group shots and close-ups. It is an option that even the most experienced directors use with considerable care. Invariably, when all cameras are committed to the three people who are dominating the conversation, the fourth (off-camera) voice suddenly starts speaking. It takes quick thinking to avoid five or more seconds of non-talking faces being aired or, worse, a wrong shot taken in haste.

Shooting in the Round.   Many directors of discussion programs have had considerable success in staging program participants in a full circle and shooting from all points outside that circle. There are several benefits to be derived from this camera arrangement and a goodly number of problems as well. Because of the varying angles involved, it is difficult to get "clean" close-ups or two-shots. Heads, hands, and whole bodies seem always to be in the way of the shot that is needed. It also is very difficult to position cameras to avoid seeing other cameras in the shot, unless the set is specially designed.

Depending upon the intended nature of the program, it is sometimes possible deliberately to use these crowded, poorly framed shots, taken from unusual angles, in an effective manner. The very roughness of the shooting technique is visually compatible with the sense of conflict created by varying points of view. The resulting *cinema verite* quality would be suitable for a program confrontation between activist and establishment representatives. Even the presence of cameras in some of the shots would communicate something of the reality of the total program situation.

Calling Shots.   In a discussion program, it is essential that preparatory commands always be used in conjunction with the commands of execution (section 7.5). An inexperienced director might be tempted to think that a needed shot could be put on the air instantaneously if only the command of execution were given. To do so, however, would be to increase appreciably the possibilities for error. The spontaneous nature of talk programs makes the command of preparation doubly important. The technical director needs this lead time to be certain of the switcher operation. Of equal importance is the possibility that the camera operators need this time for final adjustment of the framing or as a warning to hold a shot they might otherwise be in the process of changing.

A good procedure for the director on a fast-moving talk show is to give a "ready" for a probable next shot as soon as possible after the previous shot is on the line. This does not remove any option for a subsequent change in the upcoming shot; it simply aids the director in staying ahead of the action. An example of how the director can inform the crew of several probable courses of action would be as follows (fig. 13-19).

"Ready camera 3 . . . take 3" (cover shot). "Ready camera 2 on a close-up of guest C . . . camera 1, hold the moderator close-up, but be ready to move over to guest B."

In this situation, guest C has just interrupted the moderator. The director can afford to wait on the cover shot to see whether guest C will continue talking or whether the moderator will start talking again. At the same time, the director has noticed that guest B also is trying to break into the conversation.

Discussion Program Production Project (Appendix D-3)

The somewhat simplified opening and closing format in appendix D-3 is presented as an aid to an all-class production exercise. Practical experience in the utilization of cameras in a spontaneous program situation is valuable not only in itself but also serves as an important background to camera blocking procedures in more complex productions such as music and drama (see chapter 14).

A minimum running time of five minutes for each exercise is suggested so that each director has an opportunity to become familiar with the pattern of the conversational flow and the related continuity of camera shots. A realistic element can be added by having the A.D. and stage manager feed the moderator countdown cues for time remaining in the exercise. Directors should be prepared for the fact that the transition from the body of a program to the closing segment can be difficult unless cues and other instructions are given well in advance.

Discussion topics should be carefully selected so that the conversation does not lag. One way to ensure an active interchange of comments is to have the panel members role play assigned roles such as judge, police officer, and taxpayer. It often is easier to verbalize the supposed opinions of generalized cultural types than to express one's own point of view.

directing techniques for various formats

14

In this final chapter, we want to summarize some of the elements that the beginning director should keep uppermost in his or her mind. We also want to present some specific considerations for directing particular formats—a musical production and a dramatic sequence. Finally, we will introduce a concluding production project—in the form of an extended station break—that involves the beginning director in integrating a number of production elements (slide, film, studio, and videotape) in one short production segment. The scripted production model appears in appendix D-5.

14.1 From Planning to Postproduction

At this stage, it may be helpful for the student director to take a *chronological* look at the entire operation of putting a program together. Throughout the text, we have touched on many individual elements in the production process. In this section, we want to pull the ingredients together and add a few other considerations in creating a total perspective on the directing process.

Preproduction Planning

The discipline of thorough preproduction planning cannot be overemphasized. The success of every production is determined—to a very great extent—by the quality of the preproduction planning that the director has undertaken. For the purposes of organizing our thinking, it may be helpful to consider preproduction planning in five areas: *script familiarization, facilities and equipment, cast and crew, production requirements,* and *script preparation.*

1. Script Familiarization.   In many academic and closed-circuit settings, the director will also function as the producer-writer, and thus will have shaped the script from the beginning. In many other situations you, as director, will have the script handed to you and will take the production from there.

Your first concern should be to determine the *specific purpose* of the script. What is the objective of the program? What should happen as a result of this production? How do you want the audience to be different when this program is over? Then you can begin to think in terms of the overall "feel" and image of the program. What kinds of settings, lighting, graphics would be most effective in this particular *communication* process?

Next, there may be several immediate steps that need to be taken. Check the script for rough timing; read through it and get an idea of how long it might run. Is the length all right? Does it need to be cut? Does it need to be lengthened? The script should be put in its final television production format and duplicated for all personnel involved. Is any rewriting necessary? How many copies do you need? The script must be checked for any necessary copyright clearances. Can it be used as it stands? In a professional situation, this is when you must be working out a specific budget. How much money do you have for the production?

2. Facilities and Equipment.   Once you are completely comfortable with the script, you should be able to start specific *facilities planning*. In the case of a remote coverage of some event, you have to scout the location, of course. You must make arrangements for mobile equipment. In other professional situations, you may have to make arrangements for the rental of actual studio facilities. How large a studio do you need? What size sets will you be using? How long will you need the studio? This, obviously, is one of the largest items in your budget.

In most academic and training situations, the studio will be assigned to you for a definite period of time. In many institutions—even for training purposes—you still will have to fill out a Facilities Request Form, reserving a specific studio and control room(s), cameras, microphones, video recorders, lights, sets, graphics, and other requirements. The items are requested for a particular production date and time. Failure to attend to such paperwork carefully at this stage can result in costly problems and misunderstandings later.

3. Cast and Crew.   Again, in most academic situations, you may not have to be concerned with securing personnel. The technical crew may be assigned from your class or from some other cooperating class. There still may be some occasions, however, when you will be involved in selecting specific individuals for particular crew assignments. You should be familiar with the process of making out crew sheets to get the positions filled that you need for your production.

Casting for actors or other performers also may be done on an informal basis in the academic setting. You may work through the Drama or the Theatre Arts departments, or you may prevail upon your personal friends. In securing such volunteer help, make certain that you have a firm commitment; many a student production has been ruined because some friend or casual acquaintance backed out of a production at the last moment. In professional situations, of course, casting is quite an involved process. The producer will probably line up the major talent and the rest of the casting will be handled by a specialized casting director.

4. Production Requirements.   Production requirements are what the bulk of this text has been concerned with. Now comes the job of pulling it all together. In any kind of major production, the director should plan on hold-

Figure 14-1 Production conference with director, A.D., stage manager, T.D., and staging and lighting director.

ing one or more production conferences involving the chief production heads—set designer, art director, lighting chief, engineering supervisor, other key production persons, and, of course, the A.D. and floor manager. (See fig. 14-1.) Depending upon the nature and complexity of the program, there may be several different kinds of conferences: *script conferences* (involving writers and the producer), *art conferences, engineering conferences,* and so forth.

The director must now make sure that all of the necessary preproduction elements are properly requested and constructed. The *lighting and staging plans* are developed at this stage. If any special *costumes* or *props* have to be ordered or fabricated, they are initiated now. All *graphics* have to be ordered and produced; if you have access to an art department, graphics request forms will be turned in. Any

film or *still photography* has to be planned well in advance. Are station photographers available? How much will you do yourself? Will you have slides made of some of your graphics? Any *special effects* will have to be arranged. *Music* and *other special audio* selections must be chosen and/or ordered.

During all of this process, the director has to be working within a very tight interlocking schedule of *checkpoints* and *deadlines*. Many production elements cannot proceed until other items are taken care of first. Everything, therefore, must be scheduled days and weeks in advance. The exterior tape cannot be shot until the costumes arrive. Costumes cannot be designed until the overall color scheme of the setting is determined. Slides cannot be shot until the graphics are made. Set pieces cannot be constructed until the setting design is completed. And the graphics cannot be made until the talent decides what he or she wants to do.

To protect yourself, you will put in *pads* or *cushions*—a few extra days protection throughout the schedule. In major productions the intertwining complexities of the production schedule can become pretty awesome. You cannot wait until the last minute to get things started.

5. Script Preparation.   During all of this activity you also are concerned with your script breakdown and specific preparation for the day of production. You start with the basics—reminding yourself that your primary job is that of delivering a clear communicative *message* in an effective, interesting, and artistically pleasing manner. How are you going to use your cameras? What balance of wide *collective* shots and close-up *particularized* shots will you strive for (section 13.1)? What kinds of transitions will best move the program forward without ambiguity? What will be the pacing you want to achieve? In short, what images and sounds do you want to create to achieve your purpose?

This process, of course, takes into consideration all of the elements of picture continuity and transitions and camera patterns discussed in chapter 13. You prepare your script with specific script markings and instructions, and you prepare other written instructions for key positions on the production crew—camera shot sheets, audio instructions, and so forth.

Rehearsals

By now, the director has moved into rehearsals in one form or another. You should think in terms of several different kinds of rehearsals: pre-studio rehearsals, floor rehearsals, and control room rehearsals.

Pre-Studio Rehearsals.   For many extensive productions—especially dramas—you will want to have some rehearsals prior to coming into the studio. Studio time is too precious to start from scratch with basic blocking.

Using a rehearsal hall, an empty studio or warehouse, or a living room, you can begin working with actors. Specific areas can be measured off and marked with masking tape or furniture to represent major staging areas, and much of your blocking of action can take place—as well as quite a bit of the dramatic interpretation and working on lines.

For nondramatic productions there are also many good reasons for pre-studio rehearsals. Documentaries, educational programs, political broadcasts, and the like, can benefit from having an early **dry-run** session where the director and talent can work together.

Studio Floor Rehearsals.   When the director and production crew start to work in the studio, the director usually will spend some amount of time on the studio floor before assuming the director's chair in the control room. There are a couple of different ways that the director might profitably spend this rehearsal period. Depending on the type of production, either the talent or the technical crew might benefit most from your presence on the studio floor. If the talent is particularly insecure or if the technical coordination of a production is really complicated, you might spend quite a bit of your time on the studio floor. On the other hand, if the talent is in control of the situation and the technical elements are no special problem, you probably would benefit from getting into the control room as early as you can.

One of the first rehearsal techniques you would conduct from the studio floor would be a *walk-through rehearsal*. This might be either a *talent* walk-through (if they are not really sure of their positions and movements) or a *technical* walk-through (to explain major camera moves, audio placement, scene changes, and special effects. In many instances, the walk-through is a combination, taking both the talent and the crew through an abbreviated version of the production.

Control Room Rehearsals. The full rehearsals are usually conducted with the director calling shots from the control room. If time is critical or if technical problems exist, however, the director may elect to work longer on the studio floor. The initial type of full-facilities rehearsal would be called a *camera* rehearsal. For the first time the camera operators are behind the cameras and all other technical personnel are at their positions.

This first camera rehearsal usually is a *start-and-stop,* or *stop-start*, rehearsal. In this approach, you interrupt the rehearsal every time there is a major problem. You correct the trouble and then continue the rehearsal. This type of rehearsal procedure *may* be conducted from the floor if the director feels the potential problems need his or her immediate and direct supervision. It is quite a time-consuming process, although it can be effective if you have the luxury of enough studio time. Another approach to the first camera rehearsal is the *uninterrupted run-through*. This should almost always be conducted from the control room. In this approach, the director attempts to get through the entire production with a minimum of interruptions. If time is short—and if problems are minor—you keep on plowing through the rehearsal regardless of what happens (assuming that your A.D. is keeping thorough production notes about what needs to be corrected after you are through the rehearsal).

Finally, there is the *dress rehearsal*. Theoretically, this is the final rehearsal—a complete, uninterrupted, full-scale rehearsal after all of the problems have been straightened out. In practice, this stage is rarely reached. Realities of the medium are such that there simply is never enough studio time to do as polished a job as you would want. In many instances, the director will wind up with a combination start-and-stop and dress-rehearsal, stumbling through as fast as possible to try to complete at least one full camera rehearsal of some description before air time.

When time is short, the director must economize and try to make the most efficient use of the time available. Do not stand around waiting for others to finish their jobs before starting your rehearsal; you can rehearse even while the lighting crew is still trimming the lights and while the audio engineer is establishing levels. In an abbreviated walk-through rehearsal, at least make certain you get through all of the rough spots in the production; *rehearse the open and the close* and *the crucial transitions* that call for coordination of several kinds of movement. Pick your priorities; do not get hung up on small details (such as worrying about the possibility of a boom shadow) when you have only a few minutes to work out major problems (the talent doesn't know where he or she should move next). Before you know it, the A.D. will be telling you, "45 seconds to air."

Production and Postproduction

Finally, you are ready to start calling shots on your first production. As we pointed out in section 1.6, the director has three main functions—*planner, artist,* and *executor.* You have done all you can in the first two areas—as planner and as creative artist—and you now are ready to execute the program.

First, try to control your physical anxieties. Regardless of what might be churning inside, try not to let it show. Force yourself to sit down and present a calm facade. During the final minute before you go on the air, make a point of quietly and calmly assuring everybody that all will go well. Force yourself to sit back and take a deep breath; let it out slowly; and now coolly tell all of the crew and the talent that everything shall proceed confidently. Remember that the composure or anxiety you communicate to the crew will surely be returned to you in the same or even an exaggerated manner.

Give all of your commands and directions as clearly as you can. Refer to talent (when talking to the floor director) by name— "Cue Dr. Morgan," not "Cue him"—to avoid misunderstandings. Refer to camera operators, on the other hand, by numbers; you are less likely to slip up and get confused. Make sure you use correct and precise commands of preparation to the technical director (section 7.5) and to all other production positions; the commands of preparation are at least as important as the commands of execution.

Keeping the lag time of various equipment and personnel in mind, give your cues in a sequence designed to get things happening when you want them to. In opening your program, say "Hit music" and then "Fade in camera 2." It always takes a second or so before the music will be heard (if it is properly cued up), but the camera is there with the push of a lever. Similarly, always cue talent before putting his or her camera on the air. "Open-mike-cue-talent-dissolve-to-two" is often given as one command of execution. By the time the stage manager reacts and throws the cue and the talent takes a breath and starts to talk, the camera will be on the air.

Watch and listen to your monitors. Always be aware of exactly what is going out over the air—as far as picture and sound are concerned. If a picture is not what you want ("what the viewer needs"), then change it. The viewer watching his or her home receiver could care less about your sinus headache or your incompetent T.D. or your fight with the talent or the camera cable with the bad connection; all he or she knows is what comes out over the receiver, and, if it is bad, it is bad. Also, always check your camera monitors before calling a shot to be put on the air. You cannot afford to get buried in your beautifully marked script while ignoring the realities of the picture and sound you are sending out.

During the course of your program, always be looking ahead two or three minutes.

What possible problems lie ahead? What about the close-up we didn't get a chance to rehearse? Did the mike boom get repositioned all right? If something should go drastically wrong, tell yourself you are going to remain in control and salvage what you can. Camera 2 just went dead? Get a wide shot on camera 1 and keep going. The graphics easel fell over and mixed up all the graphics? The talent will have to explain the best he or she can. Whatever happens, it is your job to keep going. Do not give up until the producer or instructor tells you to throw in the towel.

Finally, no matter what else happens, television is a time-bound medium. Everything has to fit into scheduled slots. If you are directing a program that is supposed to be exactly 7:30 long, that means exactly seven minutes and thirty-seconds—not one second more or less. Listen to your A.D. and, when you are told you have five seconds to black, that means you fade it out and sneak out the music; you have no choice, unless, of course, you know you are working with a flexible time slot.

Once the program is off the air, use the studio address (talk-back) to thank the crew and talent. Assure them that everything went well. Keep your composure until you have a chance to collapse in private. Supervise the strike and make certain you clear the control room and studio of all scripts, graphics, props, and everything else.

If there is any postproduction editing to be accomplished, your job is far from done (chapter 9). If it is a simple matter of inserting a clean shot to cover the one bad blunder on the air, you may be able to get it done right away. If it is a major postproduction editing job of assembling video pieces from several different sources, it will take quite a bit of scheduling and lonely master control room sessions.

Figure 14-2 Director calling shots during a production, checking the camera monitors while following his script.

In the next two sections, we want to look at two specialized production formats—the musical and the drama—and examine camera blocking and other considerations for these production types. The student should read through and study the sections carefully—whether or not they are used as class production projects—to become familiar with these specialized situations.

14.2 Production of the Musical Number

The techniques used for shooting instrumental groups are, for the most part, based upon the same collective and particularized considerations previously outlined. Musical productions, especially jazz and rock, offer the director an opportunity to explore the use of extreme wide and close-up shots. Shots that include portions of an audience can be used very effectively. At the other extreme, tight close-up shots of the face of a performer can be used to a degree that would be unsuitable in another program context.

Camera Blocking.   The primary consideration in any musical production is that of consistently matching the visual aspect of the performance to the sound being heard. A "big" sound with the entire group playing and/or singing calls for an equally "big" look from a visual standpoint. The director would seek to achieve visual contrast and a sense of movement by tight and loosely framed group shots from various angles. Vocal and instrumental solos require a more intimate use of the camera. The director would explore the more particularized elements of the performance by means of close-up shots of the face,

Musical Production Script Example

"Beginnings" Chicago Transit Authority Approx. First Three Minutes

Time	Bars	Camera	Shot
00:00	6	1	XCU Guitar/hand zoom out to tight waist
06	2	2	Drummer solo
09	4		Zoom out to include Guitarist
13	4		Pan to include Bass
17	7	1	Group profile Brass foreground
24	1	2	Drummer
26	8		Zoom out to Group wide
34	8	3	CU Singer low 45° angle
43	6	1	Bust Singer zoom in CU profile
49	4	2	Group high angle 45° from left
54	8		Arm across to right dropping
1:02	8		to low 45° from right
1:11	4	3	CU Singer profile from right
1:15	4	1	Tight 45° Group
1:19	4	2	CU Singer 45° angle
1:24	4	1	Tight 45° Group
1:28	4	2	Waist Singer and arc across
1:37	8		to left
1:45	8	1	Profile Group
1:54	6	3	Low 45° Singer Drums Bass
2:00	4	2	MCU head on high angle zoom out wide
2:05	8	2 slow diss.	High wide
2:13	8	3	Super CU low 45° singles
2:22	4		Dissolve thru and zoom in
2:26	4	1	Group profile
2:30	4	3	MCU
2:34	4	1	Group profile
2:39	16	2	Low angle—bust
2:55	8	1,2, and 3 ad lib takes	Drum solo
3:05	8	1	Vocal to conclusion Etc.

hands, and the instrument itself. The close-ups would be interspersed with re-establishing full and waist shots to capture performer movement and to show the relation of the performer to his or her instrument.

The director must at all times seek to capture visually the intensity and mood of the performance. If, for example, the entire group is playing at a low sound level, the intent may be a mood of sadness or alienation. To produce a matching visual effect, the group could be shot in such a way as to produce a sense of isolation. This could be achieved by shooting the group in tight profile or extremely low-angle shots.

At the other extreme, there are those numbers that create a certain degree of excitement with high sound levels and a great deal of performer movement. The director can capture and even enhance the action by dolly and trucking movements of the cameras themselves. Two camera shots can be superimposed to further enhance the intensity of a performance. A close-up shot of the lead singer supered over a wide shot of the group might capture both the particularized and collective aspects of the "high point" of a big production number.

The musical structure of the number serves as the basis for the sequence of camera shots. In an ad-lib concert performance, the director is forced to attempt to predict the sequence of the action. In a rehearsed studio production, the director would have the leader provide a breakdown of each number. This usually is given in terms of the number of measures (bars) within four, eight, or sixteen-measure phrases. If the number is prerecorded and the musicians are going to mime and lip sync their performance, then the phrase groupings can be expressed in seconds. Remember that the exact timing of camera cuts or other transitions should always be on the beat (section 13.2).

Production Example

An illustration of both of these methods is given in the production script example of camera blocking for the first three minutes of "Beginnings" as recorded by the group Chicago.[1] The sequence of camera shots for the production model is based on the staging configuration and camera positions as shown in figure 14-3. The camera work has been planned to include a crane mount for camera 2. Cameras 1 and 3 have been kept in relatively static positions to be ready for a quick succession of shots.

This scripted production model has been designed to be used in two ways. By playing the record and envisioning the sequence of shots, the student is provided an opportunity to understand how the individual shots are made to fit together into a production whole. The script can also be used as the basis for a full class exercise. Class members can be placed in the indicated staging positions (using real instruments if possible) and the number can be shot as a production sequence. In this case, the script should be used only as a guide. Each individual director should be encouraged to attempt some degree of variation in both staging and shot selection.

In an actual production, the director, assistant director, technical director, and possibly the audio operator would work with a copy of the blocking script. Quite frequently—depending upon the type of musical production—the director and/or A.D. will be using the actual musical score as the working script. Each camera operator would be given either a copy of the full script or a shot sheet, which would list only the shots for that particular camera.

1. Columbia Records XSM-139684-CS 9809, Side 1, cut 3.

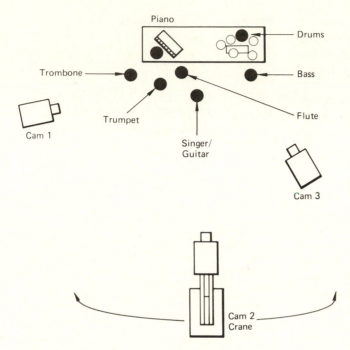

Piano

Drums

Trombone

Bass

Trumpet

Flute

Cam 1

Singer/
Guitar

Cam 3

Cam 2
Crane

Figure 14-3 Camera pattern for musical number.

This represents typical camera blocking with cameras 1 and 3 fairly stationary and camera 2, on a crane, available for major moves.

14.3 Production of the Dramatic Sequence

Contemporary directors of television programming have developed a diversity of shooting techniques for both film and electronic cameras. Some have gone so far as to reverse traditional patterns and use multiple film cameras, while others have explored the use of the single electronic camera. Many observers feel that during the 1980s a whole new generation of technology will emerge that will have an improved electronic camera as its basis. It is possible that several differently designed cameras will emerge, each suited to a particular type of production. This is already somewhat apparent with the development of the *mini* and *micro* electronic cameras.

While the sixty-minute or ninety-minute live dramatic production is probably a thing of the past, the return to the use of multiple electronic cameras on dramatic programs has been important. Soap operas, situation comedies, and even serious dramatic productions are using this production technique increasingly.

Camera Blocking.   The process whereby a television director plans the staging of actors borrows somewhat from both stage and single-camera motion picture techniques. The main difference between the older methods and those used for an ongoing television sequence lies in the fact that for television the director must continually relate the staging to three or more camera angles. The previously mentioned concept of the collective and particularized eye of the camera again serves as the basis for shot framing and selection. The wide-angle shot encompasses the totality of the scene at given points in the action. With this shot, the director establishes and, at later points, reestablishes the relationships of the actors to each other and to the elements of the set. The wide-angle shot shows the choreography of the characters within the set.

The more important dramatic elements of the story line are, however, more often portrayed by tighter shots involving two people or single close-up shots. The eyes and facial expressions may be as important in the actor's communication process as the lines themselves. In the use of the close-up, the director must be careful to position the camera and lights to reveal the expression of the face fully. The profile angle, unless specifically called for, usually is avoided.

The pattern of shots for a short, two-person sequence at the beginning of a longer scene could be as follows:

1. Camera 2. Wide-angle cover shot. Locates the actors within the set and establishes the set itself.
2. Camera 1. Closer two-shot, possibly over the shoulder of actor A into the face of actor B.
3. Camera 3. Close-up shot of actor A.
4. Camera 1. Close-up shot of actor B.
5. Camera 2. Medium two-shot.
6. Camera 3. Tight close-up of actor A.
7. Camera 1. Waist shot of actor B.
8. Camera 2. Medium wide shot. One or both actors move to new positions within the set.

The sequence of shots within a coherent scene usually is accomplished by means of an instantaneous camera cut or take. The director's decision to take to another camera and the framing of that subsequent shot is based on the structure of the lines of the performance and the related movements of the actors. A close-up shot points up the importance of any line or series of lines from an actor. A two-shot alerts the audience for some sort of verbal or even physical interaction between the actors. A wider shot allows for larger movements and can be used to permit the actors to physically express an emotional intensity. A widely framed two-shot can also be used to express an emotional separation or isolation.

The frequency of camera cuts in a scene is related to the sense of *pacing,* or intensity of action communicated by that scene. To cut too often and without motivation can, however, create a cluttered look in a scene and actually disturb the continuity of the performance. A director often will avoid changing cameras and will instead have the performers move within the continuing frame of the camera. A side-by-side two-shot can flow into a close-up of one foreground actor as that person moves toward the camera. That actor can then turn his or her back to the camera for an over-the-shoulder two-shot. The actor can then walk away from the camera, past the first actor, for what becomes a wide shot. The director has accomplished three differently framed shots—all on the same camera.

Production Example

The short situation comedy script in appendix D-4 ("It's A Date?") has been designed to present the kind of camera blocking problems common to most dramatic productions. The main difficulties are those that involve the handling of three or four performers. The staging of four people standing side by side should at all times be avoided. Whenever possible, actors should move both upstage and downstage, as well as in a line perpendicular to the camera. (See fig. 14-4.)

Figure 14-4 Rehearsal for a production of the script, "It's a Date."

The script can be used as the basis of a single class production exercise or as a series of individual student productions. If the latter method is followed, each student should be encouraged to rewrite the lines to provide a variety of characterizations and actions.

Various interpretations and characterizations can lead to entirely different production treatments of the same basic script. The blank space under "Video" should be used to write in the director's notes—camera numbers and shot descriptions.

14.4 Full Facilities Production Project

Most television productions include a wide range of program inputs in addition to those provided by studio microphones and cameras. A so-called *live* newscast, for instance, consists of a number of production elements that have been previously recorded in one form or another. Film and videotape segments, commercials, live remote *feeds,* slides, music, and even

announcer copy on cartridge may constitute one-third or more of a news program's content.

The scripted production model in appendix D-5 (Full Facilities Exercise) was designed to provide an introduction to the process of combining a series of short live and recorded production elements into an ongoing sequence. The format is that of an extra-long station break similar to one that would be viewed in the late afternoon hours. The techniques of production are much the same as those that apply to newcasts.

The coordination of roll cues for film and videotape inserts is one of the most difficult aspects of such a sequence. On network program feeds, a standard ten-second rolling period has been used to ensure that tape machines have achieved stabilization of the electronic signal. Newer equipment has been developed that allows for an almost instant start. A five-second advance rolling time for both film and tape is the standard at most stations for both film and videotape inserts or commercials.

The five-second delay between the roll cue and the precise moment at which the picture

Director

"Ready to take slide,
stand by music
and announcer
followed by film,
with sound, on 2 dissolve."

"Cue music, take slide."
"Stand by music under."
"Music, under, and cue announcer."
"Stand by to roll film."
"Stand by to take music out."

"Roll film."

"Music out."
"Dissolve film sound on."

"Stand by news announcer on camera one."
"Prepare a dissolve to one."
"Cue news announcer, dissolve to camera one."

D-5 Script for Full Facilities

	VIDEO	AUDIO
−:10		
:00	SLIDE, FRAME OF REFERENCE	MUSIC: ES
:05		BOOTH ANNC:
		Ban the sal
		Anderson is
		this import
		Saturday af
:10		
:15	FILM 16MM PUBLIC SERVICE	SOUND ON FI
:30		
:45	STUDIO NEW PROMO	NEWS ANNC:
		Have the la
:30		The availab
		from Washin

The verbal commands written out in the left-hand column are what might actually be used by the director for the "full facilities" production exercise. In practice; the director

would probably mark the script with the symbols discussed in section 13.4 (see fig. 13-13.).

Figure 14-5 Sequence of commands.

and sound must be put on the program line means that the command to roll film or tape must be given at an exact moment in the program continuum. That "five seconds to conclusion" point can be determined only by means of accurate timing of the preceding segment. If the preceding segment is copy done by a live announcer, the problem is somewhat different. The usual procedure is for the director to time the announcer on the reading of the last eleven or twelve words of the copy. The timing generally will run a little under four seconds. By allowing for a one-second margin of time to separate the announcer's words from the film or videotape audio, an accurate five-second roll cue can thus be established.

Figure 14-5 shows the sequence of commands for the first part of the Appendix D-5 exercise. Note the suggestion that the director reinforce the later film roll with an extra standby command prior to the beginning of the station break.

In preparation for the *full facilities* station break production, each student should carefully plan a complete set of director's instructions (section 13.4) and write the commands in an abbreviated form on the left-hand side of the script, as in figure 14-5. The student should then mentally rehearse the whole sequence, using a watch or stopwatch to approximate the pressures of the actual time frame. During class production of the exercise, it is suggested that the sequence of materials in the script be rearranged to provide a variety of production experience.

Note: Artwork that can be used to produce the *frame of reference* slide is available in appendix D. Spare film and videotape inserts are available in most localities at no cost; television stations receive numerous public service and promotional spots that they, in turn, usually make available to teaching facilities.

14.5   A Wrap-up and Summary

The traditional **wrap-up** is given to a performer about fifteen seconds before he or she has to get off the air. It means that there is very little time left to wrap things up, quickly summarize, and say good-bye. Perhaps it is appropriate that we wrap up quickly at this point.

This text has been concerned with the production *techniques* of handling audio, lighting, camera, switcher, recorder, editor, staging, graphics, talent, floor crew positions, and directing. If it has been successful, it has also gotten into the *disciplines* of handling these various elements. Discipline has been defined as many things in this text. As much as anything, it can be considered a matter of attitude.

Attitude toward learning and improving is one major ingredient of discipline. If you truly want to learn as much as you can about the business of television, you will gain quite a bit from this course. You will observe intently. You will try conscientiously. One of the most important secrets of learning in a course such as this is the ability to admit areas of temporary ignorance and then ask questions or seek experiences to fill in those areas. If you are unsure about audio patching, ask to have it explained to you. If you are insecure with the switcher, get all the experience you can as technical director. Do not try to bluff your way through; no one gets very far that way.

Attitude toward communication is important. Unless you have a strong feeling for the pursuit of communication—unless you really have a deep desire to want to succeed in communicating a message—then you are in the wrong field. Television is not just a business of glamor, or money, or excitement. It is the business of communication. For example, every program starts with a specific purpose— a clearcut idea of what is to be attained in the production. Until you begin program planning with this attitude, your productions may be slick and polished, but they most certainly will turn out to be meaningless.

Finally, *attitude toward a professional obligation* must be considered. The terms *professional attitude* and *professionalism* are bandied about with little thought as to their implications. We use the terms here to imply more than just a means of earning a livelihood (a profession is a vocation; a professional is one who gets paid—as opposed to an amateur). We also challenge the student to think of the professional in the original sense of the three learned professions (law, medicine, and theology), which carried a strong societal obligation. The true professional is one who is dedicated to high principles and a sense of community benefit. If you are committed to this kind of altruistic professionalism, you certainly will be more likely to leave your mark upon the field.

appendix a electromagnetic waves

The principles employed in the transmission of television picture and sound are extensions of several important discoveries made more than 100 years ago involving the related phenomena of electricity and magnetism. In 1856 James Clerk Maxwell further developed Faraday's concept of magnetic lines of force and expressed the theory that electrical energy existed within the universe in the form of oscillating waves. He further suggested that not only did these electric waves travel at the same speed as light but also that the waves were physically related to light itself.

By 1887 Heinrich Hertz was able to prove the existence of waves of electrical force by developing the equipment with which to generate them. His experiments revealed that the waves had varying lengths and differing rates of oscillation. It was further seen that these two factors interact with each other in a mathematical relationship also involving the wave velocity.

Before proceeding, it should be pointed out that while the vibrations that constitute natural sound in some ways resemble the qualities of the waves of the **electromagnetic spectrum,** present-day scientific thinking considers each of these to be a separate phenomenon, existing side by side within the physical laws of the universe. (See chapter 2 and appendix B.) Pressure sound waves can be transmitted only through the media of the atoms and molecules of solids, liquids, and gases; whereas electromagnetic waves can move also through the vacuum of space.

The analogy to water waves has developed as a convenient way of expressing the very complex properties of both of these forms of energy transmission. While sound pressure waves are relatively well understood, most scientists confess an inability to comprehend totally the nature of electromagnetic energy.

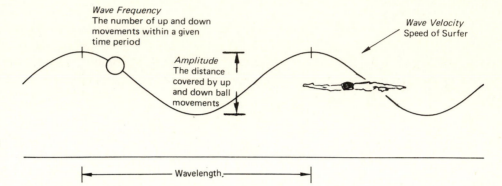

Wave Frequency
The number of up and down
movements within a given
time period

Amplitude
The distance
covered by up
and down ball
movements

Wave Velocity
Speed of Surfer

Wavelength

**Figure A-1 Relationship
of wavelength,
frequency, amplitude,
and velocity.**

In any case, let us use the water wave analogy as a means of understanding the properties of both types of oscillations. Think of a series of ocean waves as seen from a cutaway side view. In the water there is a rubber ball that floats up and down with the crests and troughs of the passing waves but remains stationary in relation to a fixed point on the sand beneath. Riding just in front of a wave crest is a body surfer. If the person moves in a straight line, he or she will indicate the speed at which the wave is traveling relative to the shoreline. In our hypothetical ocean, all of the waves come into the shore at the same speed. With this in mind, we can tell several important things by looking at the ball and the surfer. (See fig. A-1.)

First, we can measure the distance from crest to crest to determine the **wavelength.** We then notice that this wavelength has a definite relationship to the number of times the ball goes up and down in a certain period of time. This crest to trough-and-back-to-trough rate of oscillation is the measure of **frequency.** If the wavelength were shorter (distance between crests), the ball would go up and down more often in the same period of time. (Do not forget that our waves move through the water at a constant velocity.) This is an important quality of waves of electrical energy—*the greater the frequency, the shorter the wavelength.*

Watching the up-and-down movements of the ball over a long period of time may give us one more important piece of information. The ball may continue its same up-and-down movement at a consistent number of oscillations per minute, but as the hours pass we may notice that it is not going as far up and down. As in a real ocean, the height of the wave is often the result of energy expended by a storm out at sea. The height of the wave will decrease as the energy creating it decreases. In electrical energy wave theory, the *amplitude* or amount of oscillation is the result of the amount of energy applied to the wave.

The *velocity* of the wave is simply a measure of how long it takes the crest of a single wave to move from one given point to another. In the case of electromagnetic energy, this speed is constant—the same as the speed of light, roughly 186,000 miles per second. As with light, the direction follows that of a straight line. The complex exceptions to this general rule are such that they need not draw our attention.

The basic wave cycle that measures one complete oscillation from crest to trough and back to crest again is usually called a *Hertz* in honor of Heinrich Hertz, who did so much of the preliminary research in this scientific area. Because the number of cycles per second is so large in most scientific measurements,

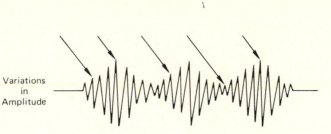

Figure A-2 Amplitude modulation.

Variations in Amplitude

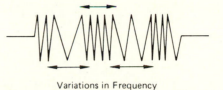

Variations in Frequency

Figure A-3 Frequency modulation.

figures are usually expressed in *kiloHertz,* or thousands of cycles, and *megaHertz,* or millions of cycles.

Looking at the AM radio, we see that the carrier frequencies utilized for transmission are those of 540 kiloHertz (540,000 cps) to 1,600 kiloHertz. Each AM station occupies a band of frequencies 10 kiloHertz wide. The station's call letters are identified with the midpoint of these frequencies. For example, KNX in Los Angeles, 1070 on the dial, actually utilizes 1,065 to 1,075 kiloHertz for broadcast purposes.

In AM (amplitude modulation) radio the broadcast signal is, in effect, added onto the carrier frequency, and in the process variously alters the amplitude of the signal. It is this modulation of the amplitude that the receiver translates back into sound. (See fig. A-2.)

FM (frequency modulation) radio uses much higher carrier frequencies, from 88 to 108 megaHertz. Here, it is the frequency of the carrier signal that is changed by the modulation process and, in turn, translated or demodulated back into sound. (See fig. A-3.)

As shown in figure A-4, radio and television occupy but a small part of the immense range of the known electromagnetic spectrum.

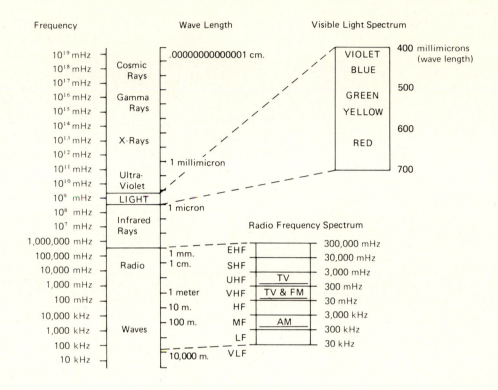

Figure A-4   The electromagnetic spectrum.

appendix b
the overtone
series

In the early chapters of this text, we explained in rather simple terms the process whereby the wave form of natural sound, known as pressure waves, is transformed for broadcasting purposes into the very different electromagnetic energy wave. The production use of microphones, speakers, and other audio equipment depends largely upon a good understanding of the qualities of sound itself. The water wave analogy used in appendix A is of considerable help in examining these qualities.

The factor that distinguishes the tone of middle C on a piano from its higher neighbor, D, is its frequency. Whether it is the string on a violin, the reed on a clarinet, or the vocal cords of the human voice, each instrument has an element that is able to vibrate at varying rates of cycles per second. The relative size of the vibration is the measure of amplitude. If more force in terms of air pressure is applied to the reed, the vibration is bigger and the tone therefore is louder. The frequency, however, does not change. The pitch of the note stays the same—until the apparatus producing the tone (the clarinet barrel or violin string) is altered in shape or length to change the frequency of the vibration.

The velocity, or traveling speed, of a sound wave is relative to the density of the form of matter within which it moves. In the air, altitude and temperature can affect this speed. In fairly average conditions, the velocity of sound is 1,120 feet per second. With the increased density of water, the speed is 4,700 feet per second. In solid steel, for example, the velocity is sixteen times that which occurs in the air. Such velocities are a very minor consideration in broadcasting.

Our primary consideration is the effect of a vibrating instrument upon the molecules of the air. Let us take the example of a middle C tone struck on a piano. Actually, three middle C strings are set in motion when struck by the hammer, but let us follow just the action

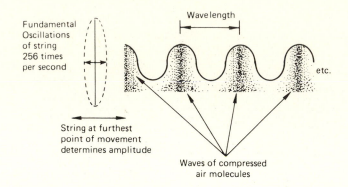

Figure B-1 Sound pressure waves.

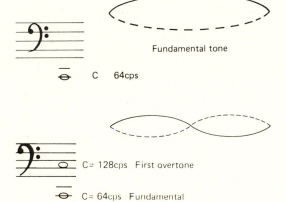

Figure B-2 Fundamental tone.

Figure B-3 First overtone.

of one. The string is set in motion at the rate of 256 cycles per second. Each oscillation presses against the molecules of the air and creates a moving pressure wave. When 256 of these pressure waves strike the ear every second, we hear it as middle *C*. (See fig. B-1.)

This simple example of the back-and-forth movement of the string is not a complete description of what is happening to the agitated string. Actually, a vibrating string further subdivides itself into smaller vibrating lengths that produce additional pitches or *overtones* or *harmonics* at higher frequencies. The main tone we hear is called the *funda-*

mental tone. As an example, we shall move two octaves down the piano keyboard to the low *C* just off the musical staff. As a fundamental tone, it vibrates at a frequency of sixty-four times a second. (See fig. B-2.)

Together with this main vibration of the string between its two endpoints, a series of smaller subdivisions occurs, each of which produces its own tone. The first subdivision divides the string in half and produces the first overtone. (See fig. B-3.) Each subsequent subdivision separates the vibrating string into quarters, eighths, sixteenths, and so forth.

The series of succeeding overtones are of far less intensity or loudness than the fundamental tone. Only the most discriminating ear even hears them as separate notes. Generally speaking, the lower overtones predominate, with the higher frequencies becoming almost inaudible. It is the resonating quality of each type of instrument that determines the presence or absence of overtones. The fundamental tone of *A*, 440 cycles per second, on a violin will resonate and thereby reflect certain overtone frequencies better than others in the series as a result of the very design of the instrument. A metal flute playing the identical tone will resonate an entirely different series of overtones. It is this differing profile of se-

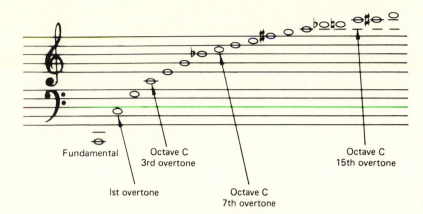

Fundamental

1st overtone

Octave C
3rd overtone

Octave C
7th overtone

Octave C
15th overtone

Figure B-4 Overtone series.

lected overtones from among the entire series that determines the distinctive tonal quality of an instrument.[1] The electronic synthesizer artificially creates tones closely resembling real instruments by manipulating the overtone series. In the same manner, it can create tonal effects previously unattainable on conventional instruments.

1. The equal-tempered scale of the modern keyboard instruments such as the piano has made necessary some minute compromises in the tuning of such instruments. As a result, several of the overtones on the piano, notably the sixth, tenth, twelveth, and thirteenth, are at slight variance as to the exact number of cycles per second. A well-written description of the development of the modern keyboard scale is contained in the book *Science and Music,* written by Sir James Jeans (New York: Dover Publications, 1968).

appendix c
hand and arm
signals

In a production situation, the hand and arm signals of the stage manager are simply a visual extension of the director's commands. Most of these gestures were developed during the early days of radio. A few have been altered somewhat for use in television production. The following examples show the signals most generally in use today.

TELEVISION HAND SIGNALS

CUE	MEANING	DESCRIPTION
STAND BY 	Ready to start show Ready to record Quiet on the set	Stage Manager raises hand in air, with fingers pointing upward
YOU'RE ON TAKE YOUR CUE 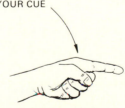	Start talking Talent is on the air	Points to performer or live camera
GET CLOSER TOGETHER 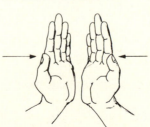	Talent, performers or reporters too far apart Get closer together Get closer to object of interest	Stage Manager plays an invisible accordian, bringing palms together repeatedly

CUE	MEANING	DESCRIPTION
GET FURTHER APART	Talent too close together, opposite of above	Stage Manager moves hands together, back to back, then spreads them sharply apart

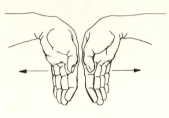

CUE	MEANING	DESCRIPTION
STOP **THAT'S FAR ENOUGH**	Close enough or far enough, stop moving together or apart	Traffic cop's signal, similar to stand-by signal

| **TALK TO THIS CAMERA**
CAMERA CHANGE | Changing cameras | Stage Manager swings hands through a wide arc from camera that is on the air to the camera that will be on the air |

| **GET CLOSER TO THE**
MICROPHONE OR
SPEAK LOUDER | Audio level too low
Get closer to the mike | Stage Manager moves hands toward himself/herself or toward the mike |

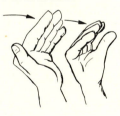

| **GET FURTHER FROM**
MICROPHONE OR
SPEAK LOWER | Opposite of above | Opposite of above |

| **KEEP TALKING**
STRETCH | Too much time left
Fill in | Extend thumb and forefinger horizontally, move them like the beak of a bird |

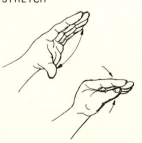

CUE	MEANING	DESCRIPTION

**STRETCH IT OUT
SLOW DOWN**

Talking too fast

Move hands as if pulling taffy apart or stretching rubber bands.

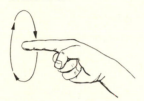

SPEED IT UP

Talking too slow
Running out of time

Move forefinger in circles

**ON THE NOSE
PROGRAM ON TIME**

Program is running right on time, no problems

Stage Manager touches nose with foreginger

**O.K.
ALL IS WELL
YOUR POSITION IS
FINE**

Well done
Stay right there

Form an "O" with thumb and forefinger with other three fingers raised

CUE	MEANING	DESCRIPTION
FIVE MINUTES TO GO TWO MINUTES TO GO ONE MINUTE TO GO	Time cues to end of show	Raise hand with corresponding number of fingers spread apart or raise flash cards

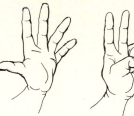

HALF A MINUTE TO GO	Time to end of segment or end of show	Cross forefingers or forearms at midpoint

WRAP IT UP	10 seconds left Come to a conclusion	Rocking or shaking of clenched fist

CUT FINISH OFF THE AIR	Segment or show is over	Stage Manager slashes own throat with forefinger or edge of hand

STATION BREAK (I.D.)	Commercial	The motion of breaking a twig is made with clenched fists

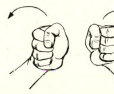

appendix d production projects

D-1 Class Audio Production Project (Chapter 3)

COPY: "INTEGRATED SOUND CORPORATION" COMMERCIAL

MUSIC: UP FULL FOR TEN SECONDS AND UNDER

ANNC #1   THE <u>INTEGRATED SOUND CORPORATION</u> OF MANHATTAN

                    CORDIALLY INVITES YOU TO A PREVIEW PRESENTATION OF

                    THE NEWEST DEVELOPMENTS FROM THE <u>OLYMPIA</u> LINE OF

                    FINE SOUND REPRODUCTION SYSTEMS. FOR THE NEXT

                    WEEK, ALL TEN <u>INTEGRATED</u> STORES IN NEW YORK CITY

                    AND NEW JERSEY WILL BE DEMONSTRATING STEREO

                    COMPONENTS DESIGNED TO PRODUCE A FULL FREQUENCY

                    RESPONSE HERETOFORE HEARD ONLY IN PROFESSIONAL

                    SOUND RECORDING STUDIOS.

MUSIC: FADE UP FULL TEN SECONDS AND UNDER

ANNC #2   <u>OLYMPIA'S</u> GREATEST ADVANCE IN THE PAST TWENTY

                    YEARS HAS BEEN MADE POSSIBLE BY THE NEW HORIZONTAL

                    FIELD EFFECT TRANSISTOR, WHICH PRODUCES A CLEAN,

                    UNCOLORED SOUND POWER OF INCREDIBLE DIMENSION.

                            (CONTINUED)

MUSIC: FADE UP FULL TEN SECONDS AND UNDER

ANNC #1   THE OLYMPIA T-E-A 850 STEREO AMPLIFIER, WITH 100

                    WATTS PER CHANNEL, REPRODUCES FREQUENCIES AS LOW

                    AS 20 CYCLES PER SECOND UP TO 20,000 CYCLES PER

                    SECOND. THIS ENCOMPASSES A RANGE OF TONES THAT ARE

                    LOWER THAN THE LOWEST NOTE ON THE PIANO KEYBOARD

                    UP TO THE HIGHEST OVERTONE FREQUENCIES THAT ARE

                    WITHIN THE RANGE OF HUMAN HEARING. THE RESULT IS A

                    LIFELIKE "OPEN" SOUND QUALITY PRODUCED WITH SOLID

                    STATE HIGH STABILITY AND RELIABILITY.

MUSIC: FADE UP FULL TEN SECONDS AND UNDER

ANNC #2   SEE ALL OF THE COMPONENTS IN THE EXCITING NEW LINE

                    FROM OLYMPIA THIS WEEK AT ANY OF YOUR INTEGRATED

                    STORES IN NEW YORK CITY AND NEW JERSEY.

MUSIC: UP FULL FIVE SECONDS AND OUT

The seven photographs and one super card included in this appendix are to be photographically enlarged and used in the class production projects for sections 7.6 and 14.4.

D-2 "The Magnificent Burden" Visual Materials (Chapter 7)

VIDEO	AUDIO
CARD, CONVENTION	<u>MUSIC</u>: ESTABLISH THREE SECONDS AND UNDER <u>ANNC</u>: WHAT QUALITY OF MIND IS IT THAT WOULD MAKE A MAN OR WOMAN WANT TO BECOME PRESIDENT OF THE UNITED STATES? STATURE? . . . POWER? . . . OR WEALTH?
CARD, PARADE	MOST OF THE MEN WHO ARE SERIOUSLY CONSIDERED FOR THE OFFICE HAVE ALREADY ACHIEVED MORE THAN ENOUGH OF THESE TO LAST MOST OF A LIFETIME.
CARD, ROOSEVELT	FRANKLIN D. ROOSEVELT, WHO SERVED THROUGHOUT A MAJOR DEPRESSION AND A WORLD WAR, EXERCISED MORE POWER FOR THE GOOD OF HIS COUNTRY THAN ALMOST ANY OTHER PRESIDENT BEFORE HIM. HE LED WHILE FACING PHYSICAL HANDICAPS THAT WOULD HAVE EASILY DEFEATED A LESSER MAN.

(CONTINUED)

VIDEO	AUDIO
CARD, KENNEDY	MANY SENSED IN JOHN F. KENNEDY A DEEP FEELING OF RESPONSIBILITY TO THE PEOPLE OF ALL THE WORLD. AFTER EARLY ERRORS HE SHOWED INCREASING STRENGTH, AS WAS EVIDENCED BY HIS HANDLING OF THE CUBAN MISSILE CRISIS. HE WAS GIVEN ONLY A THOUSAND DAYS.
CARD, JOHNSON	POWER ALONE IS INADEQUATE TO COMPLETELY EXPLAIN EXPLAIN THE EXERCISE OF AUTHORITY THAT CIRCUMSTANCES CAN PLACE UPON OUR NATIONAL LEADER. LYNDON B. JOHNSON, A MAN WHO HAD USED POWER LONG AND WELL IN THE CONGRESS, FOUND HIS STRENGTH DILUTED AND BLOCKED DURING HIS LAST MONTHS IN OFFICE.
CARD, NIXON	THERE ARE TIMES WHEN CIRCUMSTANCES APPEAR TO OVERWHELM THE MEN WHO HOLD THIS GREAT OFFICE. A FINAL FAIR AND MEANINGFUL JUDGMENT OF THE PRESIDENCY OF RICHARD M. NIXON WILL PROBABLY NOT BE COMPLETELY WRITTEN FOR AT LEAST A DECADE.

VIDEO	AUDIO
CARD, CAPITOL	THE LONELINESS AND ISOLATION OF HIGH OFFICE, COUPLED WITH A TREMENDOUS PRESSURE OF DECISION, MAKE THE ACHIEVEMENTS OF THESE UNIQUE INDIVIDUALS SEEM TRULY REMARKABLE IN THE JUDGMENT OF HISTORY.
CARD, TITLE, SUPER OR KEY	OUR PROGRAM, ""The Magnificent Burden'', PROBES THEIR VICTORIES AND THEIR DISAPPOINTMENTS . . . SUNDAY EVENINGS AT NINE.
FADE TO BLACK	

D-3   PRODUCTION PROJECT: DISCUSSION PROGRAM (CHAPTER 13)

OPENING AND CLOSING FORMAT

VIDEO	AUDIO

WIDE ESTAB. SHOT CAM 2	MUSIC: ESTABLISH FIVE SECONDS AND UNDER
	ANNC: "Frame of Reference," an information service program designed to explore the multifaceted issues that affect us, both as individuals and as members of an increasingly complex society. Here with our guests is the "Frame of Reference" moderator, _____ .
	MUSIC: OUT
MCU, CAM 1	MODERATOR: Our area of examination today is _____ _____ .
	MODERATOR: (CONTINUED) To help us in gaining a greater understanding of the problems that are involved in this issue are three people who hold somewhat differing views on the solutions to
CU CAM 2	those problems. Seated next to me is _____from _____ .

VIDEO	AUDIO

CU CAM 3

Our second guest is _____

who represents _____ .

CU CAM 2

Our final guest, who is from _____ ,

is _____ .

WIDE-SHOT
CAM 1

As a way of establishing the background to today's

issue, I would like to ask my first question of

_____ .

(BODY OF PROGRAM)

CU MODERATOR
CAM 1

MODERATOR: With that last point we must, for now,

conclude our discussion of _____ . The

issue is a large one and our program time is,

unfortunately, limited. I would like to thank our

ZOOM OUT TO
TIGHT 4 SHOT

guests, _____ , _____ ,

and _____ for joining us today and for

measurably adding to our collective knowledge of

this controversial issue. This is _____ .

Good-bye until next week.

EXTREME WIDE-
SHOT CAM 2

MUSIC: ESTABLISH FIVE SECONDS AND UNDER

(CONTINUED)

VIDEO	AUDIO
(SUPER CREDITS)	<u>ANNC</u>: As a program, "Frame of Reference" makes no attempt to establish any final solutions to the problems under discussion. Our goal is that of presenting well-informed opinion leaders to our viewing public so that each individual can come to his or her own conclusions. Next week our "Frame of Reference" will encompass the matter of _____ _____ . Be sure to join us then. <u>MUSIC</u>: UP FULL TO CONCLUSION
FADE TO BLACK	<u>MUSIC</u>: FADE OUT

D–4   Production Exercise: "It's a Date?" (Chapter 14)

VIDEO	AUDIO	(APPROX. 4:00 MIN.)

HARRY: (TALKING TO NANCY, WHO IS OFFSTAGE) I see where old Harold Osgood is fighting with the university again.

NANCY: (ENTERING FROM CAMERA RIGHT) What, dear?

HARRY: Councilman Osgood objects to the fact that taxpayer's money is being spent on a college course called "The Crisis in Human Sexuality." He says that it's part of a plot to destroy the morals of American youth.

NANCY: Oh, it's probably just one of those courses that teach people how to get along with one another.

HARRY: (SARCASTICALLY) Yeah, I'll bet it is.

NANCY: Oh, Harry, it's not that. Those kind of classes just help people to establish their personal identity . . . you know, who they really are.

(CONTINUED)

VIDEO	AUDIO

HARRY: Well, when I was in college no professor had to tell me who or what I was.

NANCY: I remember very well what kind of a guy you were. (KIDDING) You were a big <u>wolf,</u> that's what you were.

HARRY: (SMILING) Oh, come on, Nancy, I was just a normal red-blooded American boy.

NANCY: Well it just might have done <u>you</u> some good to have taken one of those courses. Things are different now with men and women, Harry. We're no longer in the Dark Ages.

HARRY: Yeh, a lot of good it's done . . . a bunch of so-called liberated females running around. . . .

NANCY: (INTERRUPTING) Harry, they don't run around. They do a lot of constructive things. Why only last week. . . .

VIDEO	AUDIO

KIM: (INTERRUPTING FROM OFFSTAGE) Daddy, what time is it? (ENTERING SOMEWHAT BREATHLESSLY) Richard will be here any minute.

HARRY: (STERN BUT FATHERLY) It's seven twenty-five, and who's Richard?

KIM: He's only a really neat guy, that's all. And don't be so uptight, Daddy.

NANCY: Kim, you know that your father always thinks of your dates as being direct descendants of Attila the Hun.

KIM: Well he's not. He's really nice. He writes on the school newspaper and he's really into broadcasting.

HARRY: If he has somehow made you suddenly aware of the discipline of time, he can't be all bad.

KIM: Well, he's very . . . you know, intellectual. He knows all about music and things.

(CONTINUED)

VIDEO	AUDIO

HARRY: Yes, I can imagine. I remember that football player friend of yours. He spoke English like a second language.

MUSIC: ROCK AND ROLL MUSIC UNDER THE CONVERSATION AS IF FROM OUTSIDE THE HOUSE.

HARRY: (CONTINUING) The only trouble was that he didn't have a first . . . . say what's that noise?

KIM: Oh, that must be Richard. Will you go to the door? I'm not ready! (EXITS)

NANCY: Well, we should be thankful that Richard at least comes to the door . . . not like the boy who sat in the driveway and honked. (SHE EXITS CAMERA RIGHT)

(HARRY PUTS DOWN THE NEWSPAPER AND SLOWLY STANDS UP SHAKING HIS HEAD.)

VIDEO	AUDIO

NANCY: (OFFSTAGE) Hello, I'm Kim's mother. You must be Richard. Won't you come in? She will be right out. (ENTERING FROM CAMERA RIGHT) Harry, this is Kim's friend, Richard. I'm afraid that Kim hasn't told us your last name.

RICHARD: Uh, Richard's O.K.

(THERE IS AN AWKWARD FIVE-SECOND PAUSE WHILE ALL TRY TO THINK OF SOMETHING TO SAY.)

NANCY: Well, it's so nice.

HARRY: (OVER NANCY'S LINE) Is that music coming from your car?

RICHARD: That's my van. It sleeps two.

(HARRY STARTS TO SAY SOMETHING, THINKS BETTER OF IT, AND QUICKLY TRIES TO COVER HIS STARTLED EXPRESSION.)

RICHARD: (CONTINUING) Like, I do a lot of camping. It's really great with my tape deck out in the woods.

(CONTINUED)

VIDEO	AUDIO

HARRY: (STRAIGHT BUT WITH A TOUCH OF SARCASM)
Yes, I guess you could really get back to nature.

(NANCY CROSSES TO HIM, TAKES HIS ARM AND GIVES IT
A WARNING SQUEEZE.)

RICHARD: That's Wretched Yellow playing "Boogie
'Til Nineteen Eighty-five." It's their big hit.
Great guitar. (HE MOVES SLIGHTLY WITH THE MUSIC)

NANCY: Kim tells us that you write for the school
newspaper.

RICHARD: Yeah, I write a column called "Diggin'
the Discs." They wanted me to call it "Pickin' the
Platters," but I thought it sounded kinda' corny.

HARRY: You're right, it just doesn't have the
same ring to it.

(NANCY GIVES HARRY ANOTHER WARNING SQUEEZE.)

RICHARD: What do you do, Mr. Olmstead?

HARRY: Well, I . . . uh . . . I work at the bank.

VIDEO	AUDIO

RICHARD: Oh yeah, Kim told me. Well, I guess everybody has to do something.

HARRY: (REACTING) It may seem sort of quaint, but in today's society. . . .

KIM: (INTERRUPTING AS SHE ENTERS FROM CAMERA LEFT) Hi, Richard. (SHE CROSSES TO HIM.)

RICHARD: Wow, you are some kind o' looker.

KIM: Richie, I just love your jacket. It's really neat. Hey, we better go.

NANCY: Wait a minute. Where are you two going?

KIM: To the movies. We can either see a musical, The Monster on Lead Guitar or My Secret Swedish Summer. They say it's a beautiful, artistic movie about this couple in love. . . .

HARRY: I don't think I want to hear . . . I can already guess.

(CONTINUED)

VIDEO	AUDIO

NANCY: Isn't there something else playing?

RICHARD: Yeah, but they're just like what's on television. Kim, let's go to the monster movie. They say that Lulu Bash is fantastic in the death scenes. She does karate moves while playing the love theme from the movie on her guitar.

KIM: Super. Well, we better go. See you later. (EXITING) Everybody at school has seen it by now. We just have to go.

NANCY: Don't be too late, dear.

KIM: I won't. (OFFSTAGE) Bye-bye.

(WHEN THEY ARE GONE, THERE IS A PAUSE AS NANCY AND HARRY LOOK AT EACH OTHER.)

HARRY: (LAUGHING RUEFULLY) Where did we go wrong?

NANCY: Oh, he's a nice boy, Harry. He's just at that age.

VIDEO   AUDIO
_____

HARRY: I guess you're right. I hope so anyway.

Say . . . how would you like to sneak off and see

My Secret Swedish Summer?

NANCY: (LAUGHING) Let me think about it.

MUSIC: Briefly fade rock music up full and out.

D-5 Script for Full Facilities Production Exercise (Chapter 13)

VIDEO	AUDIO
SLIDE, "FRAME OF REFERENCE"	<u>MUSIC</u>: ESTABLISH, FIVE SECONDS AND UNDER <u>BOOTH ANNC</u> (OFF CAMERA): Should the United States Government ban the sale and manufacture of DMSO? Kenneth Anderson is joined by experts on both sides of this important question on "Frame of Reference," Saturday afternoon at four.
FILM: 16MM PUBLIC SERVICE :30	<u>SOUND ON FILM</u>
STUDIO NEWS PROMO :30	<u>NEWS ANNC</u>: Tonight on the six o'clock news we have the latest statement by the President on the availability of Middle Eastern oil. . . . A report from Washington that the plumbing in the Watergate Hotel has sprung its own leak. . . News from Detroit that thousands of new cars have been recalled before they ever got off the assembly line . . . and sportscaster Stan Dilbeck has a report on the Matadors and their chance for a winning season.

VIDEO	AUDIO
STUDIO HOST	HOST (ON CAMERA): Tonight at nine our program series "The Magnificent Burden" presents an account of the triumphs and defeats of Lyndon B.
CARD: JOHNSON	Johnson. As a man forced to assume power in a time
CARD: MATTE "THE MAGNIFICENT BURDEN"	of crisis, he was often admired for the way in which he took over the responsibilities of leadership. Many of his proposed social reforms were, however, sacrificed to the demands of a war that seemingly could not be ended. "The Magnificent Burden" tonight at nine.
STUDIO	HOST (ON CAMERA): Coming up in just a moment we have something in a lighter vein on "Campus Rock." Host, Charlie "Red" Stewart, presents The Grass Valley Boys singing "Pure Pleasure," Bonnie Street does her version of "The Sadness of My Life," and that new group, The Electric Car, performs their hit, "Turn on the Lights." They get it all together, next on _____ TV.
VTR	SOUND ON TAPE

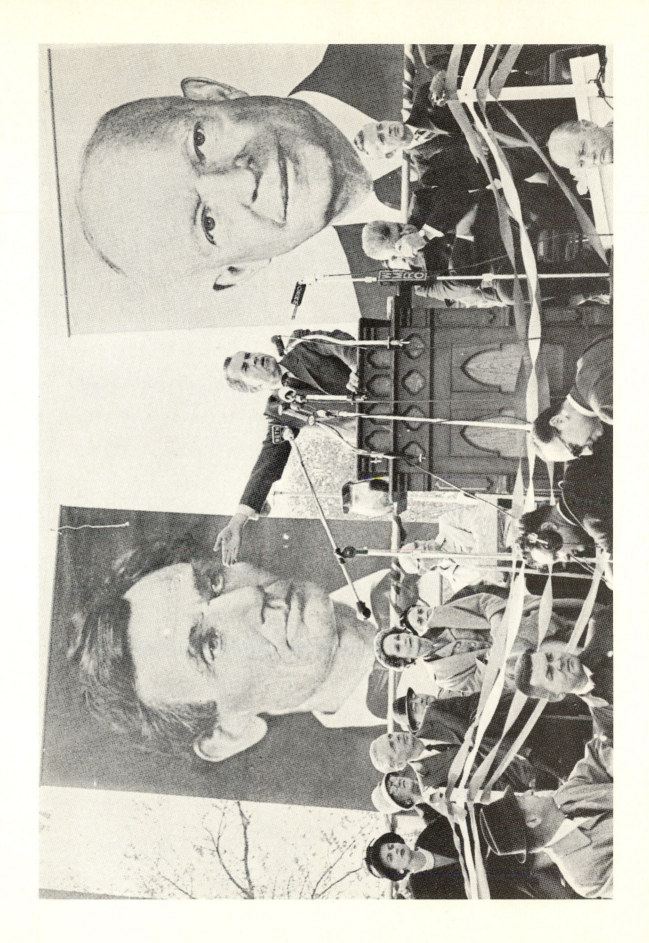

THE MAGNIFICENT BURDEN

Sundays, 9:00 pm

glossary

above-the-line costs The creative and performing personnel (such as the producer, associate producers, writers, artists, musicians, actors, and others) and other administrative elements (such as office space, rehearsal halls, studio space, and so forth).

A.D. (associate director, assistant director) A key production assistant—usually responsible for timing of the program—who may be delegated any other key responsibilities by the director.

ad-lib Dialogue or action that is completely spontaneous and unrehearsed.

amplifier A device that can magnify an electrical signal—either audio or video—for mixing, distribution, and transducing purposes.

amplitude Measurement of the intensity of an electromagnetic wave.

aperture The opening in the camera lens that determines how much light will pass through.

arcing A combination trucking, panning, and dollying movement, in which the camera is moved in an arc around a subject while the camera head is always pointed towards the same subject.

aspect ratio The ratio of the height of the television screen (three units high) to its width (four units wide).

assemble editing Creation of a television production by adding various segments sequentially in the final program order.

asymmetrical balance An informal arrangement with an important object placed close to the center of the picture balanced by a lightweight object some distance from the center.

attentuator *See* Potentiometer.

audio The sound portion of a television production.

audio compressor An electronic device used to bring weak audio levels up to an averaged volume.

343

audio control room (audio booth)   The room where all audio signals are controlled and mixed; all audio inputs (microphones, prerecorded tapes and records, and the like) are centrally controlled and then sent on to a master control room, video recorder, or transmitter.

audio signal flow   The theoretical schematic model that sequentially traces every step of the audio path from the microphone (or other audio source) to the home radio or TV receiver.

axis of action/conversation   An imaginary line that (1) extends the path in which a character is moving or (2) connects two persons talking to each other; all cameras should remain on the same side of this line.

back focus   *See* Tube Focus.

background light   *See* Set Light.

back light   A highly directional light coming from above and behind a subject, adding highlights, shape, and separation from the background.

backpack VTR   *See* Portapack.

balance   1. In audio, the achievement of the correct ratio among several sound sources. 2. Visually, the relative composition and stability among elements in a picture.

bank   *See* Buss, definition 2.

barn doors   Movable metal shutters, attached to the front of a lighting instrument, which are used to limit the area of the projected light.

base light   The basic lighting needed for adequate illumination to achieve a technically acceptable television picture.

beam splitter   The optical device in a color camera consisting of special mirrors and lenses, which separates the incoming visual image into the primary colors of blue, red, and green.

below-the-line costs   The technical and production personnel (such as the engineers, camera and audio operators, stagehands, and others) and other production equipment, facilities, and services.

black   Technically, a synchronized video signal that contains no picture information—a blank screen.

blanking   The process of momentarily turning off the scanning beam while it retraces its path before starting to scan another line.

blocking   Careful planning and coordinating of all movement and positioning of talent and production equipment.

body time   Time remaining in the body of the program—not including closing credits and titles—indicating the time signals that must be given to the talent.

boom (mike boom)   Any device consisting of a movable base, an adjustable stand, and a long arm for suspending a microphone above and in front of a performer.

booming (craning)   Moving the boom arm or tongue of a camera crane up or down. (*See* Crane, definition 2.)

brightness (lightness, value)   1. The intensity of the picture on a television tube. 2. An indication of where a color would fall on a scale from light (white) to dark (black); corresponds to the gray scale for monochrome television.

broad   A floodlight with a large rectangular, pan-like reflector.

broadcasting   *See* Open Circuit.

burn-in   *See* Image Retention.

buss   1. A common audio circuit that collects signals from several audio sources and feeds them into one source (for example, a mix buss feeds the combined audio signal to the master potentiometer). 2. The row of buttons representing various video sources on the switcher (also called a *bank*).

butt edit   The editing of two segments together so that the end of the first is immediately followed by the beginning of the second.

cameo lighting   Lighting the foreground subject with carefully controlled, directional light; the background is kept dark.

camera chain The electronic camera plus associated equipment such as the sync generator, camera control unit, and so forth.

camera control unit (CCU) Electronic control equipment, usually located in the master control area, which regulates all of the engineering functions of each camera.

camera head (camera) The electronic picture pickup device, which includes the lens (or lenses), pickup tube (or tubes), and viewfinder; the camera serves as a video transducer that converts incoming light energy (pictures) into electrical signals.

camera mount The support arrangement that holds the camera mounting head and the camera itself—usually a movable tripod, pedestal, or crane.

camera mounting head (pan head) The mechanism that connects the camera itself to the camera mount; it allows the camera head to be tilted vertically and to be panned horizontally.

camera pattern The basic positioning and blocking of studio cameras and subsequent movement of the cameras for a particular program sequence.

cardioid pattern *See* Unidirectional.

carrier frequency A specific portion of the electromagnetic spectrum assigned, by the Federal Communications Commission, to a radio or television station for transmission of its modulated broadcast signal.

cartridge An audiotape or videotape recording and/or playback unit that uses a self-contained single-reel case that can be cued up automatically.

cassette An audiotape or videotape recording and/or playback unit that contains both a supply reel and take-up reel in a self-contained case.

catwalk A system of walkways suspended below the studio ceiling that allows lighting personnel easy access to lighting instruments.

C-**clamp** A metal clamp with a pivot adjus for attaching lighting instruments to a lighting grid.

CCU *See* Camera Control Unit.

channel selector key An audio channeling switch, usually located adjacent to a pot, which can send the audio signal out through either of two or more line-out channels.

character generator A special electronic effects device, with a typewriterlike keyboard that can produce letters and numerals directly on the television screen.

cheat Making minor on-the-air adjustments that the audience will not notice: (1) adjusting camera composition; (2) angling a performer toward a camera.

chroma key A special effects color matte whereby a specific color (usually blue) is used as a key to determine what picture information is to be cut out of the picture with the foreground image.

closed-circuit (CCTV) Television distribution between points connected by cable—anything from a simple two-room hookup to a multichannel statewide interconnection.

close-up (CU) View of a subject from a relatively short distance.

coaxial cable (coax) Standard camera and video cable with a central insulated conducting wire and a concentrically arranged outer wire.

collective shot A wide shot showing the collective effect or relationship of various elements—an establishing shot.

colorization The use of a special color video synthesizer to produce abstract color effects.

color temperature The relative reddish or bluish quality of a light source, as measured in degrees Kelvin.

comet-tailing *See* Lag.

composite signal Electronic signal that contains both picture information and the sync pulse.

condenser microphone   A high-quality microphone whose transducer consists of a vibrating condenser plate and a fixed backplate.

console (audio board)   The control panel or *mixing board* where all audio signals can be amplified, combined, shaped, and channeled.

continuity   *See* Picture Continuity.

contrast ratio   The ratio of the brightest area to the darkest area in a given camera shot, as determined by reflected light readings.

control room (video booth, studio control room)   The room where all video signals are mixed; the director and T.D. control all program elements from this location; sometimes audio and lighting control will also be incorporated into the same area.

control track   Portion of a videotape that is used to record the synchronizing pulse.

corner insert   A split screen with one camera inserted into a specific quadrant of the picture.

cover shot   *See* Establishing Shot.

crabbing   Moving the crane or crab dolly base sideways, similar to a *trucking* shot.

crab dolly   A small studio crane, first developed for film camera movement.

crane (studio crane)   1. Large camera mount with an extended boom arm or tongue for the camera, with everything—including a seat for the camera operator—placed on a large, four-wheeled dolly or crane base. 2. To move the boom arm up or down.

crawl   *See* Drum.

critical area   *See* Essential Area.

cropping   Cutting off the edges or border of a picture.

cross-fade   1. An audio transition in which one sound is faded out while another is simultaneously faded in (similar to a video dissolve). 2. A video transition in which one picture is faded out and another picture is immediately faded in from black (similar to an audio segue).

cucalorus (cookie, kook)   1. A special metal cutout pattern that can be inserted into an ellipsoidal spotlight to achieve definite shadow effects. 2. A cardboard or wooden cutout pattern that is placed in front of a spotlight to produce a shadow effect on a scenic background.

cue   1. To give a signal to a talent to start or to perform a certain action. 2. To prepare an audio source (record or audiotape) for a precise start at some predetermined point.

cue cards (idiot sheets)   Large, lightweight cards, containing either script material or content outline, held next to the camera for the talent to read.

cue position (audition position)   A position on most audio pots and faders that connects the audio source to a separate nonprogram *cue* amplifier and speaker to enable the audio operator to listen to the source without interfering with the program audio.

cue track   Portion of a videotape that is used to record electronic or audio cues, the SMPTE time code, or similar information.

cut   1. To eliminate some program material, leave out part of the script. 2. To interrupt a rehearsal. 3. *See* Take, definition 1.

cutting ratio   The relationship between the size of an object in two successive shots; ordinarily this ratio should not be more than three to one.

cyc (cyclorama)   A large, continuous, smooth backing—usually made of cloth—that may cover two or three walls of a studio.

cycles per second (cps)   *See* Hertz.

dailies   The videotape or film footage shot during a day's production sessions.

debeaming   Turning down the intensity of the scanning beam, resulting in a high-contrast picture that gradually deteriorates into a faded gray image.

decibel (Db)   A unit of measurement of sound that compares the relative intensity of different sound sources.

decorative setting An abstract style of staging with nonrealistic elements added purely for artistic effect.

defocus dissolve A camera transition in which the on-the-air camera defocuses and the switcher then dissolves to a similarly defocused camera, which then focuses after it is on the air.

depth of field The distance between the nearest point at which objects are in focus and the farthest point at which objects are in focus.

depth staging The use of foreground and background elements in order to give a feeling of depth to the television picture.

diaphragm 1. The vibrating element in a dynamic microphone that responds to the compressed air molecules of sound waves. 2. The adjustable mechanism that controls the size of the lens aperture.

digital recording An advanced form of video and/or audio electromagnetic recording wherein picture and/or sound information is converted into computerlike off-and-on bits of data.

digital video manipulator (DVM) An electronic control device that can manipulate video signals—once they have been converted into digital information—to achieve a wide variety of pictorial effects.

dimmer board A lighting control unit, operated on the same principle as a rheostat, which determines the intensity of a light by controlling the amount of electric current flowing to the instrument.

director The person in charge of actual production and editing operations—everything that takes place in the studio or on a remote—directing all picture and sound elements to create a final program.

disciplines Those learned and acquired attitudes and habits, developed over a period of time, which comprise an internalized system of professional behavior—such as responsibility, self-control, respect, and initiative.

dissolve A simultaneous fading out of one picture while fading in another picture, thus effecting a gradual transition between shots with a momentary overlapping or *superimposition* of images as one strengthens while the other weakens.

dollying Moving the entire camera mount closer to (dollying in) or farther from (dollying out) the subject.

downcut During either production or editing, the loss of a small amount of audio and/or video material at the end of a segment—usually occuring at the point of transition between program elements from two different sources.

dress rehearsal Final, full rehearsal before the actual production take—using all sets, props, and costumes—designed to be conducted straight through without interruption.

drum (crawl) Large cylindrical graphics-mounting device (similar in appearance to a bass drum) that can roll a long vertical graphic up a television screen.

dry-run rehearsal Rehearsal—either in a rehearsal hall or in the studio—without any technical facilities.

dubbing The electronic duplication of a videotape onto a second tape.

dynamic microphone A rugged microphone whose transducer consists of a diaphragm connected to a movable coil.

editing Putting together pieces of program either by physically splicing film or tape or by arranging program elements by means of electronic transfer.

effects *See* Special Effects *and* Staging Effects.

effects buss The switcher buss that is used for special electronic effects such as inserts, keys, and wipes.

electromagnetic spectrum The entire range of electromagnetic energy wavelengths (and frequencies), which include everything from cosmic rays and visible light to broadcast waves.

electron gun The device, in the rear of the camera pickup tube, that shoots out the electron scanning beam.

electronic editing Joining together program elements on videotape by sequential signal transfer from an original (playback) tape to a second (record) tape.

ellipsoidal spotlight (leko) A specialized spotlight with a highly defined beam that can be further shaped by means of metal shutters and the insertion of a cucalorus pattern.

ENG (electronic news gathering) The use of a high-quality, portable broadcast camera to record news events and other actualities; it is a single-camera technique (replacing a film camera with an electronic camera), resulting in a fast and mobile professional operation.

equalizer An electronic device used to increase or decrease the levels of different audio frequencies.

essential area (critical area) That center portion of the *scanning area* of a graphic card that contains all of the critical or essential information that probably will be seen on the receiving set.

establishing shot (cover shot) An all-inclusive long shot that, by its collective nature, establishes the relationships of performers and other elements in a given scene.

extemporaneous Speaking from a semiscripted format or outline—broadly prepared but not written out word for word.

external key An electronic keying effect whereby a third camera furnishes the keying (or stenciling) image used in combining two other video signals.

fade 1. The gradual bringing in or taking out of an audio source. 2. The gradual transition from black to a picture (fade in) or from a picture to black (fade out).

fader (slide-fader) *See* Potentiometer.

fader arm On the switcher, a small lever—operating on the same principle as a rheostat—that controls the amount of video signal flowing to a specific buss.

feed A program signal, audio and/or video, brought into a mixer (audio console or switcher) from some outside (nonstudio) source, e.g., a remote location or a network line.

feedback 1. In audio, a high-pitched squeal that results from accidentally feeding a program monitor into a live microphone, causing an instantaneous overamplification of the system. 2. A video effect caused by re-entry of a video signal into the switcher with subsequent overamplification.

fidelity The ability to reproduce a given tone, with all of its overtones, accurately.

field One-half of a television picture, consisting of alternate scanning lines, lasting one-sixtieth of a second.

field of view Size or scope of a shot, indicating how much is encompassed.

fill light An unfocused and diffused (nondirectional) light used to complement the key light, coming from the side opposite the key, filling in dark areas and softening the shadows.

film chain (telecine) A film island where various picture sources (16mm film, 8mm film, slides, opaque cards) can be mixed through a multiplexer and fed into a television pickup camera.

filter An audio device that can be used to eliminate selected low-frequency or high-frequency overtones.

fishpole A small, lightweight pole to which a microphone is attached, to be handheld by an audio assistant outside of the picture frame.

fixed-focal-length lens A simple lens that is one specific focal length.

flag A rectangular cloth-covered frame placed in front of a lighting instrument to produce a precise shadow on one side of the light beam.

flat A standard staging unit, constructed of a wooden frame covered with cloth or hardboard, often used to represent walls of a room or the exterior of a building.

floodlight A lighting instrument that produces a highly diffused, nondirectional source of light.

floor manager (floor director) *See* Stage Manager.

floor plan A scaled plan of the studio floor indicating where all scenery and staging units are to be placed.

focal length The distance from the optical center point of a lens, when it is set at infinity, to a point where the image is in focus (that is, the front surface of the camera pickup tube).

fold-over A digital-based electronic transition in which one picture is squeezed and apparently flipped over (revealing a second picture) to simulate a turning page.

footcandle A unit of light measurement equivalent to the amount of light falling upon a surface one foot away from a standard candle.

foundation make-up The make-up base upon which more detailed accent items are constructed.

frame 1. One complete television picture, consisting of two fields, lasting one-thirtieth of a second. 2. To compose a picture artistically within the frame of the television screen.

freeze frame *See* Pause Mode.

frequency 1. The number of cycles per second of a given tone—which determines the basic pitch of that tone (the greater the frequency, the higher the pitch). 2. Measurement of the number of oscillations per second (Hertz) of an electromagnetic wave of a given wavelength (the greater the frequency, the smaller the wavelength).

frequency range The total scope of frequencies or pitches (and overtones) that a microphone, ear, loudspeaker, or transmitter is able to discriminate and/or reproduce.

Fresnel lens A lightweight spotlight lens developed by Augustin Jean Fresnel that uses a system of concentric ring-shaped steps to achieve its focusing effect.

***f*-stop** A notation that indicates the size of the lens aperture; the higher the *f*-stop number, the smaller the opening; the lower the *f*-stop number, the larger the opening.

gain control *See* Potentiometer.

gel (gelatin) A thin, translucent, colored material such as gelatin or plastic that can be mounted in front of lighting instruments to produce specific color effects.

giraffe A medium-sized mike boom, consisting of a tripod base and a telescoping arm.

gobo A scenic cutout unit that is positioned several feet in front of a camera to provide foreground design, depth, and framing interest.

gopher An assistant who is asked to "go for" specific items—coffee, scripts, tape, paper, and so forth.

graphics Two-dimensional visuals specifically prepared for television presentation—charts, drawings, photographs, maps, slides, and the like.

gray scale A theoretical scale, representing several shades of gray from TV white to TV black, that can be readily distinguished by a camera pickup tube; most good camera systems can be relied upon to reproduce only a seven-step gray scale.

grip A floor assistant or stagehand, especially one who is concerned with scenery and set dressing.

hanging mike A microphone suspended by its cord from a lighting grid or catwalk.

hanging units Any background pieces that are hung or flown in the studio—such as drapes, cloth drops, and the cyclorama.

harmonics *See* Overtones.

head The small electromagnet—on either a video recorder or an audio recorder—that puts the electromagnetic information on the tape (records) or erases the signal from the tape or reads (plays back) the information that is on the tape.

headroom Space between the top of a subject's head and the upper edge of the camera frame.

headset The apparatus (consisting of an earphone and mouthpiece) worn over the head that connects all production personnel on the intercom network.

helical-scan (slant-track) VTR A videotape recording format that lays down the video information in a long, slanted, helical pattern on the tape.

Hertz (Hz) Basic unit of frequency measurement for electromagnetic waves—named after Heinrich Hertz—replacing the older term of *cycles per second;* broadcast frequencies are often measured in terms of kiloHertz (kHz) and megaHertz (mHz).

high-band recording High quality video recording, recorded in a high-frequency range, featured in most quality color recorders.

high-key lighting Overall intense illumination, with a fully lit background.

horizontal sync pulse The portion of the synchronizing pulse that controls the horizontal sweep of the scanning beam.

hue The actual color base, such as red, green, orange, and so forth.

iconoscope No longer used, this was the first practical electronic camera pickup tube.

image-orthicon (I-O) A particular type of camera pickup tube, long the standard of the broadcast industry for monochrome production.

image retention (burn-in, sticking) A phenomenon, characteristic of older I-O tubes, where the tube superimposes a negative image of a shot (especially a high contrast shot) over succeeding shots the tube picks up.

impedance Resistance to the flow of an audio signal in a microphone cable.

incandescent light The conventional lamp, housed in a glass bulb, that produces light by the glow of a heated filament.

incident light Light coming directly from the source of illumination.

input selector switch The switch found on many audio control boards (either a toggle switch or a push-button connector) that will connect a specific patch bay input to a particular microphone position on the console.

insert editing Electronically inserting a new program segment into the middle of a previously recorded production; the new material (video and/or audio) to be inserted is locked into the existing control track.

intercom network (P.L.) A closed-circuit intercommunication audio network connecting all production personnel with headsets.

interlacing The process of combining two picture fields to produce one full frame.

internal key An electronic keying effect whereby one of the two cameras involved also furnishes the key (or stenciling) signal.

I-O tube *See* Image-Orthicon.

isolated (iso) camera A camera that is patched directly to its separate video recorder—which can be used either for instant replay (in live productions) or for postproduction editing.

jack 1. A socket or receptacle (female) for an audio connection. 2. A hinged stage brace attached to the rear of a flat.

jump cut A take between two cameras—or a badly planned edit—that results in connecting two shots that have almost identical views of the same object; as a result the object appears to jump slightly for no apparent reason.

key A special electronic effect, where one camera cuts in with a solid image into the background picture produced by another camera.

key light The primary source of illumination falling upon a subject, highly directional, producing a definite modeling or shaping effect with well-defined shadows.

kicker Additional light, usually a spotlight, coming from the side and slightly to the rear of the subject.

kill To turn off equipment (such as microphones, lights).

kinescope recording The process of using a specially adapted film camera to record a television program from the face of the kinescope tube.

kinescope tube The television receiving tube.

kook (cookie) *See* Cucalorus, definition 1.

lag (smear, comet-tailing) A cometlike tail that follows a moving image across the screen, characteristic of the vidicon tube at low light levels.

lavaliere (chest mike, neck mike) A very small microphone that can be worn around the neck on a cord or clipped onto an article of clothing.

lead room (nose room, talk space) Additional framing space in a camera picture on the side toward which a subject is looking or moving.

leko *See* Ellipsoidal Spotlight.

lens 1. The optical glass disc, usually having one or both surfaces curved, used for focusing rays of light coming from a spotlight, for example, plano-convex or Fresnel. 2. The optical elements that make it possible to focus visual (light) images onto the face of a camera tube.

lens cap Protective covering that can be placed on the front of a camera lens.

lens turret A round metal plate on the front of a camera, holding three to five lenses, that can be rotated to place any one of the lenses into position in front of the pickup tube.

level Sound volume or intensity from a specific source or talent.

lighting grid A permanent arrangement of pipes suspended below the studio ceiling, upon which lighting instruments can be hung.

light meter A photoelectric device that measures the amount of light falling upon a specific area.

light plot A floor plan that indicates the lighting requirements—location, type, and function of each instrument—for every staging area in the studio.

limbo A neutral setting, often set against a plain backdrop with no staging elements in view.

limiter An electronic device used to cut off audio levels when the volume is too strong.

line monitor The master program monitor that displays the final program picture that is to be recorded or transmitted.

live-on-tape production Program that is recorded on videotape in its entirety, or in long complete segments; the viewing audience watches the performance, unedited, as it actually took place earlier.

live production Studio or remote production where the program is transmitted (either broadcast or closed-circuit) as the action takes place; the viewing audience watches the performance as it actually is happening.

long lens A long focal-length lens with a narrow viewing angle; it includes relatively little in the picture, but tends to compress distance.

long shot (LS) View of a subject from a relatively great distance.

looping An audio technique whereby a single loop of audiotape can be repeated endlessly on either a reel-to-reel recorder or on an audio cart machine.

loosen up (loosen a shot) To decrease the size of an object in a picture, either by dollying back or by zooming out.

low-key lighting Selective lighting, with an overall low level of intensity and a dark background.

luminance channel A monochrome signal, in color cameras, that is derived from the three color pictures; it is used to provide the correct contrast for the color signal as well as to produce the compatible black-and-white picture for monochrome receivers.

macro lens Special wide-angle lens designed for close-ups of small objects at short distances.

master control room Primary engineering control center where all video and audio signals are ultimately channeled; program input (both studio and network feeds), camera controls, video recording, and transmitter distribution usually are all handled from this location.

matte A special electronic effect whereby two cameras are electronically keyed together, with one furnishing a foreground image and the other the background.

medium shot (MS) View of a subject from a comfortable medium distance, between a long shot and a close-up.

microphone (mike, mic) An audio transducer that converts sound pressure waves (sound energy) into electrical signals.

mix busses The switcher busses, with fader arms, that are used for on-the-air fading and mixing of video sources such as supers and dissolves.

mixer 1. An electronic control unit for selecting and combining audio or video signals from more than one source and forming a new program signal—such as the audio console or the video switcher. 2. *See* Potentiometer.

mixing 1. The combining and balancing of two or more audio sources through the audio console. 2. The combining of two or more video sources through the switcher.

modulation The alteration of a carrier frequency—either by amplitude modulation (AM) or by frequency modulation (FM)—in order to superimpose a video and/or audio signal for broadcast purposes.

moiré effect Distracting visual vibration caused by the interaction of a narrow striped pattern and the television scanning lines.

monitor 1. An audio speaker used to check the actual sounds being mixed. 2. A video display device that features a high-quality television picture that has not been modulated to an RF signal; it is ordinarily used in studio and control room applications.

multiple-camera production Conventional television production situation—either in a studio or remote on-location origination—where several cameras are used simultaneously to pick up the action or performance; whether transmitted live or recorded, the pictures from the various cameras are edited instantaneously as the program progresses.

multiplexer A system of mirrors and prisms in the film chain designed to direct the various projected images into the television camera.

narrow-angle lens *See* Long Lens.

neutral setting (nonassociative style) A setting with no identifiable elements at all.

noise 1. Any interference that distracts from the communicative act. 2. Specific audio interference (unwanted sounds or static) or video interference (electronic disturbance or snow).

nondirectional *See* Omnidirectional.

normalled Having a certain output on an audio patch bay permanently wired to a given position on the console so that a patch cord is not needed to make the temporary connection.

nose room *See* Lead Room.

objective perspective Use of a camera as an observer or eavesdropper; no one addresses the camera directly.

off-camera Any sound or action that takes place out of the camera's view.

off-line editing Any of several sophisticated electronic editing techniques involving intermediate steps—such as first-stage trial assembly or production of special effects—where the final editing is typically computer-controlled using the SMPTE time code.

off-mike The audio quality resulting from a sound source that is a great distance from the microphone or out of the pickup pattern of a unidirectional mike.

off-set graphics Graphics, such as title cards and slides, that are never seen in or on the set; the audience has no idea where they are originating.

omnidirectional (nondirectional) A microphone pickup pattern in which sounds are received equally well from all directions.

on-line editing Electronic editing technique involving the direct transfer of materials from an original tape to a final program master.

on-set graphics Large graphics and display devices designed to be integrated into the set.

open-circuit (broadcasting) Television distribution through the ether or open space; a specific carrier frequency is modulated with video and/or audio signals and then transmitted from an antenna to receivers that are not connected by wire or cable to the origination point.

oscilloscope Engineering evaluation instrument that displays various electronic patterns on a video screen.

outline script *See* Semiscripted Outline.

over-the-shoulder-shot (O/S) Camera shot looking at one person framed by the back of the head and shoulder of another person in the foreground.

overtones (harmonics) Acoustical or electrical frequencies that are higher than the fundamental tone.

pad 1. Extra video material that is recorded before and after a program segment to facilitate a margin of judgment during editing. 2. Extra script material that may be used if the program begins to run short.

pan card A long horizontal graphic designed to be panned on the air.

pan head *See* Camera Mounting Head.

panning Turning the camera horizontally by rotating the camera mounting head.

panning handle (pan handle) The handle extending toward the rear of the camera with which the camera operator controls movement of the camera.

pantograph A scissors-like spring, counterbalanced lighting mount that enables lights to be quickly pushed up or pulled down to any height.

particularized shot A close shot showing the important aspect of some specific object.

patch bay (patch board) A board with numerous terminals (inputs and outputs) through which various audio, video, or lighting signals can be connected by patch cords to other channels or circuits.

pause mode (still frame, freeze frame) Repeated scanning of a single video frame—while holding the videotape stationary—resulting in a still frame during playback.

pedestal 1. Heavy camera mount that facilitates easy raising or lowering of the camera head, usually with a counterweight system or with compressed air. 2. To move the camera head up or down with the pedestal mount.

perambulator boom A large boom on a dolly base, having a platform for the mike operator, with a long counter-weighted boom arm.

performer Any talent who is addressing the audience directly, as opposed to an actor portraying a dramatic character.

perspective 1. In audio, the quality of matching visual and sound distance. 2. In scenery, the illusion of distance caused by several lines converging at one point on the horizon.

pickup tube The transducing element of the camera that receives the visual image and converts it into an electronic signal.

picture continuity The relationship of visual images from one shot to the next, involving flow of action, screen direction, composition, cutting ratio, type of transitions, motivation, and similar considerations.

pin Concentrating or narrowing the beam of a spotlight by moving the bulb-reflector unit away from the lens.

P.L. (private line) *See* Intercom Network.

plano-convex lens The basic, relatively heavy spotlight lens—with one flat surface and one convex surface—from which the Fresnel lens was developed.

playback The process whereby the recorded magnetic information stored on the recording tape is picked up by the playback head to recreate the original video and/or audio electronic signals.

Plumbicon A lead-oxide version of the vidicon tube, used extensively for color cameras. (The word *Plumbicon* is a registered trademark of N. V. Philips.)

polarity reversal Reversing the black and white aspects of a picture, thus attaining a negative image.

pop filter A protective shield attached to a microphone that filters out air blasts from plosive consonants such as *p*'s and *t*'s.

portapack (backpack) Small, portable, battery-operated, lightweight video recorder—typically using ½-inch or ¼-inch tape—used for small-format television.

postproduction editing Electronic editing process that takes place after the individual program segments have been produced and recorded.

potentiometer (pot) A volume-control device that is manipulated by either a rotating knob or a sliding *fader*.

preamplifier An electronic device that can magnify the low signal output of microphones and other transducers before the signal is sent to a mixing board or to other amplifiers.

"prepare" (or "set up") The standard command of preparation preceding a fade, dissolve, super, or special effect that involves preparation of another buss.

preproduction editing Electronic editing process whereby individual program segments—especially in news and sports coverage—are edited in advance for later insertion or assembly editing into a finished production.

preproduction planning All of the preparation and careful planning that a director must complete before starting studio rehearsals.

presence The audio phenomenon of performing very close to a microphone, with a consequent intimate quality resulting from a lowered pitch, breathiness, and subdued tone.

preset 1. On a lighting board, to prearrange a given lighting setup so that it can be automatically executed when needed. 2. Adjusting a zoom lens so that a given object is in focus at all focal lengths. 3. Using the switcher preview buss and preview monitor to set up a given effect before punching it up on the air.

pre-studio rehearsal Rehearsal with talent (e.g., actors) in a rehearsal hall or other location before coming into the studio.

preview buss The switcher buss, connected to the preview monitor, which is used for setting up any special effects or other picture before it is put on the air.

preview monitor A large monitor that can be used to look at any camera picture or video effect before putting it on the program line.

producer The creator and originator of a television program, usually in charge of all above-the-line elements such as writing, art, music, securing actors, and financial considerations.

program buss The switcher bank that controls the actual picture being sent out on the air.

program time Time remaining in the overall program—until the program fades to black—indicating the time signals that must be given to the director.

props (properties) 1. Hand props that include all items actually to be handled and used in a television production. 2. Stage props (*see* Set Dressings).

proscenium arch In the theater, the arch that separates the stage from the auditorium.

pull focus (rack focus) Changing the focus of a camera from one extreme to the other—using a selective focus technique—in order to shift attention from one object to another (either in the foreground or background).

quadruplex (transverse) VTR (quad head) A videotape recording format that uses four rotating heads in a pattern transverse to the movement of the videotape.

quartz light A highly efficient lamp with a high-intensity tungsten-halogen filament in a quartz or silica housing.

rack focus *See* Pull Focus.

racking 1. Rotating the lens turret in order to place a different lens in front of the pickup tube. 2. On monochrome cameras, moving the pickup tube closer to or farther from the lens (*see* Tube Focus).

"ready" The standard command of preparation preceding a camera take or cut.

real-time editing Assembly of multiple-camera production using a switcher or SEG during the continuing action of an event or performance.

rear focus *See* Tube Focus.

rear screen (R.P., rear projection) A translucent screen set up in the studio; slides or film are projected from the rear and photographed from the front.

receiver The device that receives the radio broadcast signal (radio set) or television signal (TV set) and demodulates the carrier wave to reproduce the original studio electrical signals.

recording The process whereby the audio and/or video electronic signal is used to arrange iron oxide particles on the magnetic recording tape to store a record of the electronic signal for later retrieval.

reel-to-reel Audiotape or videotape recording format that uses open reels (a supply reel and a take-up reel) and manual threading, as opposed to closed *cassette* or *cartridge* systems.

reflected light Light bounced back from the surface of an object.

remote production (on-location production) A television production, usually directed from a portable control room, that takes place outside of a regular studio.

reportorial perspective Use of a camera with the talent talking directly to the audience through the camera.

resolution Sharpness and detail of a television picture.

RF (radio frequency) Modulation of a specific radio frequency carrier wave with a video and audio signal—necessary for broadcasting and most closed-circuit distribution.

rheostat A device that can control the amount of current or signal flowing to a specific control point or circuit—allowing a gradual increase or decrease in the amount of flow—such as the *pot* on the audio console, the *dimmer* handle on a lighting circuit, or the *fader arm* on a switcher buss.

ribbon microphone (velocity mike) A sensitive microphone whose transducing element consists of a ribbon suspended in a magnetic field.

riding gain (riding levels) Continually watching the VU meter and adjusting audio faders accordingly, in order to maintain proper volume levels throughout a program.

roll cue The exact words or actions that a talent will use at the precise point when a film or videotape insert is to be rolled a few seconds before it is actually put on the air.

rule-of-thirds Principle of composition that divides the television screen into thirds, horizontally and vertically, and places objects of interest at the points where the lines intersect.

run-down sheet (show format) Abbreviated scripting format that simply lists the various program segments in sequence.

run-through Usually, the first full facilities (start-and-stop) rehearsal.

saturation (chroma) The strength or intensity of a color—how far removed it is from a neutral or gray shade.

scanning The pattern of movement of the electron beam, in both the camera and the TV receiver, horizontally and from top to bottom.

scanning area The portion of a graphic card that actually can be seen by the camera pickup tube.

scanning beam The electron beam that is pulled back and forth, up and down, across the television tube to produce the scanning pattern.

scoop A rounded floodlight with a spherical diffusing reflector.

scrim A translucent filter, often made of fiberglass or fine screening, used in front of either a spotlight or floodlight to soften and diffuse the light quality.

segment timing sheet A list of all of the segments of a production with space for unit times and cumulative times (ideal and actual) for each segment.

segue An audio transition in which one sound is completely faded out and then a second source is immediately faded in (similar to a video cross-fade).

selective focus The technique of using a shallow depth of field to deliberately keep either foreground or background objects out of focus, in order to concentrate attention on a particular object that is in focus.

semiscripted outline A summarization of a program's content—with opening and closing material (and other crucial elements such as roll cues) written out in full while the remaining content is presented in outline form.

set dressings (stage props) Major items of furniture (desks, tables), large props (bicycles, tree stumps), and minor items (ashtrays, books), used to dress up a set.

set light (background light) General lighting of the set and background behind the talent.

set pieces Three-dimensional items, usually functional, that are integrated into the set—platforms, stairways, pillars, arches, lampposts, and so forth.

setting The major pieces that comprise the background and environment of a scene—set units, hanging units, and set pieces.

set units Staging units such as flats, two-folds, and other standing background pieces.

shading (video engineering) Operating the video controls of a CCU in order to maintain the best engineering quality control of the picture.

shaping The alteration of an audio signal by controlling volume, filtering out certain frequencies, emphasizing upper or lower pitches, creating an echo effect, and so forth.

short lens (wide-angle lens) A short focal-length lens with a wide viewing angle; it includes quite a bit in the picture, but tends to exaggerate distance.

shotgun microphone A highly directional microphone, used for picking up sounds from a great distance.

shot sheet A small sheet or card, attached to the rear of the camera, listing a summary of all shots the camera operator is to get during the production.

show format *See* Run-Down Sheet.

silhouette A lighting effect where the foreground figures are dark and the background is fully lit.

silicon chip A tiny electronic component containing microscopic electrical circuits that amplify and in other ways control the flow of electromagnetic information, the heart of every computer operation.

single Shot of just one person.

single-camera production Television production situation where a single electronic camera is used to record all of the action—similar to the traditional film-camera technique; one camera is repositioned for each shot, and the individual shots are then electronically edited together in the postproduction editing process.

slant-track recorder *See* Helical-Scan.

small-format television (video) Inexpensive, small, lightweight television gear (camera, microphone, and video recorder)—usually portable—that can be used for a variety of nonbroadcast (and nonprofessional) applications.

SMPTE time code A frame-location "address" system—developed by the Society of Motion Picture and Television Engineers—that can label and find any section of a videotape by hour, minute, second, and frame.

snoot A stovepipe-like attachment that can be put on the front of a spotlight to reduce the beam to a smaller clearly defined circle, without increasing the intensity of the spot.

SOF (sound-on-film) A designation used to denote a film soundtrack.

speaker (loudspeaker) An electronic device, actually a transducer, that converts an electronic audio signal back into audible sound waves.

special effects Fancy electronic video transitions and methods of combining video sources, such as wipes, keys, mattes, inserts, and so forth.

special effects generator (SEG) Part of a sophisticated switcher that can produce a variety of special electronic effects.

speed up A signal to the talent to read faster or get through the script outline faster.

split screen A special effect with the screen split into two or more sections, with a picture from a different camera filling each portion of the screen.

spotlight A lighting instrument that produces a highly directional, controlled source of light.

spread To open up or enlarge the beam of a spotlight by moving the bulb-reflector unit closer to the lens.

sprocket holes Small, square holes on the side of film, used to guide the film and keep it moving at a constant speed.

squeeze-zoom A digital-based electronic transition in which the picture is reduced in size and squeezed down to a pinpoint before disappearing from the screen.

stage manager (floor manager, floor director) The director's key assistant in charge of all production concerns on the studio floor.

staging effects Special optical and mechanical studio effects, such as smoke, wind, fog, rain, fire, and so forth.

"standby" General command of preparation.

start-and-stop rehearsal (stop-start, stop-and-go) Usually the first full facilities rehearsal with cameras operating—designed to be interrupted to work out problems as the production progresses.

still frame See Pause Mode.

stop-start (stop-and-go) rehearsal See Start-and-Stop Rehearsal.

stretch A signal to the talent to slow down, read slower, and stretch out the remaining script.

strike Removing specific set pieces or props; taking down and removing everything on the studio floor at the end of a production.

strip lights A series of broads (pan lights) or low-wattage bulbs mounted in a row of three to twelve lights in one housing, used as a specialized floodlight for lighting a cyclorama or other large background area.

studio The primary room devoted to television production, containing all of the paraphernalia for sets, lighting, cameras, microphones, and so forth—the space where all acting and performing takes place.

studio address (S.A., talkback) A public address loudspeaker system, allowing the control room to talk directly to the studio floor.

subjective perspective Use of a camera as an actual participant or actor in a dramatic sequence, viewing the scene from the standpoint of a person who is involved.

super (superimposition)   A picture resulting from the simultaneous display of two complete images on the screen.

super card   A graphics card with white lettering on a black background, used either to *super* or to *key* the printed information over a background picture.

sweep reversal   Reversing the scanning pattern of a camera (either horizontally or vertically) to attain either a mirror image or an upside-down image.

switcher   1. A video mixing panel, consisting of selection buttons and control levers (fader arms), that permits the selection and combining of incoming video signals to form the final program picture. 2. The person who operates the video switcher, usually the technical director.

symmetrical balance   Formal arrangement with the most important element centered in the picture and other equal objects placed equidistant from the center.

sync generator   The part of the video system that produces a synchronizing signal (sync pulse), which keeps all video pictures locked together.

sync pulse   A complex signal (added to the picture information) consisting of electronic control information that keeps all video components synchronized.

take   1. An instantaneous change from one video source to another (cut). 2. The final production of a program as recorded or distributed live.

talent   Any person who appears in front of a camera.

talkback system   *See* Studio Address.

tally lights   Small red indicator lights on each camera to let the talent and camera operator(s) know which camera is on the air.

target   The electronic elements that form the light-sensitive (photoemissive) front surface of the pickup tube, which is read by the scanning beam.

technical director (T.D.)   Engineer or production person who operates the switcher.

techniques   Those learned and acquired skills utilized in operating various pieces of equipment and in performing specific crew assignments.

telecine   1. Same as film chain. 2. The room where the film chain is located.

telephoto lens   A lens with a very long focal length, used for close-ups of objects from great distances.

teleprompter   A mechanical device that projects the moving script, via mirrors, directly in front of the camera lens. (The word *TelePrompTer* is a registered trademark of the Teleprompter Corporation.)

telescope hanger   A lighting mount consisting of a system of telescoping pipes, which enable the lighting instrument to be positioned at varying heights.

three-point lighting   The traditional arrangement of key, fill, and back lights.

tie lines   Permanent audio lines connecting various control rooms or patch bays and engineering locations.

tighten a shot (tighten up)   To increase the size of the object in a picture, either by zooming in or by dollying in.

tilt card   A tall, vertical graphic card designed to be tilted on the air.

tilting   Pivoting the camera vertically by pointing the camera mounting head up or down.

time-base corrector   Piece of electronic apparatus that can substantially upgrade the video signal of a video recorder by rebuilding the control track sync information.

title card   A graphics card containing basic information about the program title, used at the open (and close) of a program.

tonguing   Moving the tongue or boom arm of a camera crane laterally to the left or right.

transducer Any device (such as a microphone or camera) that receives energy in one form (sound waves or light energy) and converts it into another form of energy (electrical signals).

transfer edit The electronic re-recording (or dubbing) of video and audio information from an original videotape to a second tape for assembly in program sequence.

transmitter The broadcasting apparatus that modulates the audio and video signals onto a carrier frequency and, through an antenna, broadcasts the signals as electromagnetic waves.

transverse video recorder *See* Quadruplex.

trim To adjust a lighting instrument by aiming the housing and focusing (pinning or spreading) the beam.

tripod Three-legged camera mount, usually with casters to facilitate camera movement.

trucking Moving the entire camera mount laterally to the left or right.

tube focus (back focus, rear focus, rack focus) Changing focus, on monochrome cameras, by physically moving the pickup tube in relation to the lens.

turret *See* Lens Turret.

two-fold Two stage flats, hinged together to form a self-standing unit.

two-shot Camera shot that includes two people or a person and one other prominent object.

undercut To change one video source of a two-camera super or effect instantaneously while the effect is on the air.

unidirectional (cardioid) A microphone pickup pattern in which sounds are received best from one direction, in a heart-shaped or cardioid pattern.

upcut During either production or editing, the loss of a small amount of audio and/or video material at the beginning of a segment—usually occurring at the point of transition between program elements from two different sources.

variable-focal-length lens *See* Zoom Lens.

vertical sync pulse The portion of the synchronizing pulse that controls the vertical movement of the scanning beam between fields.

video 1. The visual portion of a television production. 2. An unmodulated electronic picture signal distributed over a closed-circuit system without converting to an RF signal, resulting in a higher quality picture. 3. *See* Small-Format Television.

video disc 1. A magnetic video recording format in which short segments can be recorded for instant playback, freeze frame, and slow-motion production applications. 2. A distribution medium in which lengthy programs are pressed onto discs for consumer retail.

video engineering *See* Shading.

video feedback Feeding a camera's signal into a floor monitor and then using the same camera to shoot the face of the monitor (*see* Feedback, definition 2).

video signal flow The theoretical schematic model that traces every step of the video path from the picture picked up by the camera to the home TV set.

videotape A plastic tape, coated with iron oxide, that can magnetically record various audio, video, and control track information.

videotape recorder (video recorder, VTR) A magnetic-electronic recording machine that records audio, video, and control signals on videotape.

vidicon A simple and inexpensive type of camera pickup tube used for many basic television purposes.

VU meter (volume unit meter) A display meter that shows the relative volume of program audio.

walk-through rehearsal An abbreviated rehearsal—conducted from the studio floor—to acquaint the talent and/or production crew with the major outline of the production.

wavelength Measurement of the length of an electromagnetic wave from one theoretical crest to the next; since the velocity of all electromagnetic waves is constant (186,000 miles per second), the longer the wavelength, the lower the frequency.

wide-angle lens *See* Short Lens.

wipe A camera transition whereby one image is gradually pushed off the screen—horizontally, vertically, or diagonally—as another picture replaces it.

wireless mike A microphone with a self-contained miniature FM transmitter built in; the microphone-transmitter can send its signal several hundred feet to the control room, eliminating the use of mike cables.

wow The audible result of putting a record on the air before the turntable has reached full speed.

wrap-up (wind up) A cue to the talent that there are about fifteen seconds remaining in this program segment or in the total program.

zoom in To change a zoom lens to a narrow angle (long focal length) position.

zoom lens A variable-focal-length lens that, through a complicated optical system, can be smoothly changed from one focal length to another.

zoom out (zoom back) To change a zoom lens to a wide angle (short focal length) position.

bibliography

The following list of additional sources is presented for the student who may want to pursue specific topics in more detail than has been possible in this text. The bibliography has been divided into seven sections.

General Background

Bermingham, Alan, et al. *The Small TV Studio: Equipment and Facilities.* New York: Hastings House, 1975.

Chester, Giraud; Garrison, Garnet R.; and Willis, Edgar E. *Television and Radio,* 4th ed. New York: Appleton-Century-Crofts, 1971.

Gross, Lynne S. *See/Hear: An Introduction to Broadcasting.* Dubuque, Iowa: Wm. C. Brown Company Publishers, 1979.

Head, Sydney W. *Broadcasting in America,* 3d ed. Boston: Houghton Mifflin Co., 1976.

Seidle, Ronald J. *Air Time.* Boston: Holbrook Press, 1977.

Sterling, Christopher H., and Kittross, John M. *Stay Tuned: A Concise History of American Broadcasting.* Belmont, Calif.: Wadsworth Publishing Co., 1978.

Audio, Technical

Alten, Stanley R. *Audio in Media.* Belmont, Calif.: Wadsworth Publishing Co., 1981.

Burroughs, Lou. *Microphones: Design and Application.* Plainview, N.Y.: Sagamore Publishing Co., 1973.

Jeans, James. *Science and Music.* New York: Dover Publications, 1966.

Lowery, H. *A Guide to Musical Acoustics.* New York: Dover Publications, 1966.

Nisbett, Alec. *The Use of Microphones.* New York: Hastings House, 1974.

Oringel, Robert. *Audio Control Handbook.* New York: Hastings House, 1972.

Woram, John M. *The Recording Studio Handbook.* Plainview, N.Y.: Sagamore Publishing Co., 1976.

Video, Technical

Bensinger, Charles. *The Video Guide, Vol. 1.* Santa Barbara: Video-Info Publications, 1977.

Fink, Donald, and Lutyens, David. *The Physics of Television.* Garden City: Anchor Books, Doubleday & Co., 1960.

Hewish, A., ed. *Seeing Beyond the Visible.* New York: American Elsevier Publishing Corp., 1967.

Howorth, D., and Wharton, W. *Principles of Television Reception.* New York: Pitman Publishing Corp., 1967.

Marsh, Ken. *Independent Video: A Complete Guide to the Physics, Operation, and Application of the New Television.* San Francisco: Straight Arrow Books, 1974.

Video Freex. *Spaghetti City Video Manual.* New York: Praeger Publications, 1973.

Production, General

Bensinger, Charles. *Peterson's Guide to Video Tape Recording.* Los Angeles: Peterson Publishing Co., 1973.

Costa, Sylvia Allen. *How to Prepare a Production Budget for Film and Video Tape.* Blue Ridge Summit, Pa.: Tab Books, 1973.

Gross, Lynne S. *Self Instruction in Radio Production.* Los Alamitos, Calif.: Hwong Publishing Co., 1977.

Jones, Gary William. *Electronic Film/Tape Post-Production Handbook.* Edmonton, Alberta, Canada: Jones Family Reunion, 1974.

Millerson, Gerald. *The Techniques of Television Production,* 9th ed. New York: Hastings House, 1972.

Millerson, Gerald. *TV Camera Operation.* New York: Hastings House, 1974.

Nisbett, Alec. *The Technique of the Sound Studio,* 3d ed. New York: Hastings House, 1972.

Wurtzel, Alan. *Television Production.* New York: McGraw-Hill, 1979.

Zettl, Herbert. *Television Production Handbook,* 3d ed. Belmont, Calif.: Wadsworth Publishing Co., 1976.

Directing and Aesthetics

Bretz, Rudy, and Stasheff, Edward. *Television Scripts for Staging and Study: With a Guide to Creative Camerawork.* New York: A. A. Wyn, 1953.

Davis, Desmond. *The Grammar of Television Production,* 3d ed. London: Barrie & Jenkins, 1974.

Lewis, Colby. *The TV Director/Interpreter.* New York: Hastings House, 1972.

Stasheff, Edward, and Bretz, Rudy. *The Television Program: Its Direction and Production,* 4th ed. New York: Hill & Wang, 1968.

Zettl, Herbert. *Sight-Sound-Motion: Applied Media Aesthetics.* Belmont, Calif.: Wadsworth Publishing Co., 1973.

Staging, Design, and Graphics

Bay, Howard. *Stage Design.* New York: Drama Book Specialists, 1974.

Bellman, Willard F. *Scenography and Stage Technology: An Introduction.* New York: Thomas Y. Crowell Co., 1977.

Clarke, Beverley. *Graphic Design in Educational Television.* New York: Watson-Guptill, 1974.

Hurrell, Ron. *Van Nostrand Reinhold Manual of Television Graphics.* New York: Van Nostrand Reinhold Co., 1974.

Millerson, Gerald. *Basic TV Staging.* New York: Hastings House, 1974.

Millerson, Gerald. *The Technique of Lighting for Television and Motion Pictures.* New York: Hastings House, 1974.

Parker, W. Oren, and Smith, Harvey K. *Scene Design and Stage Lighting,* 2d ed. New York: Holt, Rinehart & Winston, 1968.

Small Format Video

Frederickson, H. Allen. *Community Access Video.* Santa Cruz, Calif.: Johnny Videotape, 1972.

Murray, Michael. *The Videotape Book.* New York: Bantam Books, 1975.

Robinson, Richard. *The Video Primer.* New York: Links Books, 1974.

Shamberg, Michael, and Raindance Corporation. *Guerrilla Television.* New York: Holt, Rinehart & Winston, 1971.

index